D1714423

Biblical narrative in the
philosophy of Paul Ricoeur

Biblical narrative in the philosophy of Paul Ricoeur

A study in hermeneutics and theology

KEVIN J. VANHOOZER

Trinity Evangelical Divinity School

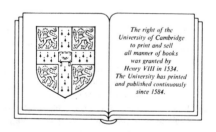

The right of the
University of Cambridge
to print and sell
all manner of books
was granted by
Henry VIII in 1534.
The University has printed
and published continuously
since 1584.

CAMBRIDGE UNIVERSITY PRESS

CAMBRIDGE

NEW YORK   PORT CHESTER

MELBOURNE   SYDNEY

B
2430
.R554
V37
1990

Published by the Press Syndicate of the University of Cambridge
The Pitt Building, Trumpington Street, Cambridge CB2 1RP
40 West 20th Street, New York, NY 10011, USA
10 Stamford Road, Oakleigh, Melbourne 3166, Australia

© Cambridge University Press 1990

First published 1990

Printed in Great Britain at
the University Press, Cambridge

British Library cataloguing in publication data
Vanhoozer, Kevin J. (Kevin Jon), *1957*–
Biblical narrative in the philosophy of Paul Ricoeur
1. Philosophy of religion. Ricoeur, Paul
I. Title
200.1

Library of Congress cataloguing in publication data
Vanhoozer, Kevin J.
Biblical narrative in the philosophy of Paul Ricoeur: a study in
hermeneutics and theology / by Kevin J. Vanhoozer.
p. cm.
Bibliography.
Includes index.
ISBN 0-521-34425-5
1. Ricoeur, Paul. 2. Narration in the Bible – History – 20th
century. 3. Bible – Philosophy – History – 20th century.
4. Hermeneutics – History – 20th century. I. Title.
B2430.R554V37 1990 89-7288 CIP
220.6'01 – dc20

ISBN 0 521 34425 5

WG

JESUIT - KRAUSS - McCORMICK - LIBRARY
1100 EAST 55th STREET
CHICAGO, ILLINOIS 60615

TO MY PARENTS

To believe only possibilities, is not faith, but mere Philosophy.

Sir Thomas Browne, *Religio Medici*

My soul has lost its potentiality. If I were to wish for anything, I should not wish for wealth and power, but for the passionate sense of the potential, for the eye, which ever young and ardent, sees the possible. Pleasure disappoints, possibility never. And what wine is so foaming, what so fragrant, what so intoxicating, as possibility!

Sören Kierkegaard, *Either-Or*

Nothing great has ever been accomplished in the world without passion.

G. W. F. Hegel, *Lectures on the Philosophy of History*

CONTENTS

PREFACE

The present work began its life in much different form as a doctoral dissertation at Cambridge University. The present text sets out on a career of its own, however, by focusing on the theme of a "passion for the possible" and aspiring towards greater clarity and readability than its predecessor. I am most grateful to Nicholas Lash, who first started me reading Ricoeur and who supervised my research with enthusiasm and critical care. I wish also to thank John Macquarrie, the external examiner of my thesis, for his comments. I am especially grateful to Stephen Sykes, my internal examiner, for encouraging me to pursue publication and for his many helpful remarks.

I would like to acknowledge two groups who together made possible a wonderful year of post-doctoral study in Cambridge, where I was able to begin the process of rewriting: first, the Fellows of Wolfson College, Cambridge, who elected me into a Junior Research Fellowship, and second, the Trustees of the Burney Studentship in the Philosophy of Religion, who gave considerable financial aid along with the Studentship for the academic year 1985 – 6.

I am indebted in other ways to Hans Frei, who was good enough to meet with me twice at short notice and who was most generous with some of his unpublished manuscripts. I owe a special debt of gratitude to Paul Ricoeur for agreeing to meet with yet another graduate student and making himself available for several extended discussions and, of course, for providing the works from which I have greatly profited over the past few years.

Parts of the book and many of its arguments were forced upon students in my seminar on Ricoeur's philosophy of religion. I am grateful both to those students and to those colleagues who have offered suggestions or simply moral support. I have also benefited from, at one time or another, conversations with Robert Gundry and Stuart Hackett.

ix

I owe a special acknowledgement to two long-standing (and often long-suffering!) friends for their influence on my thinking and their faithful support. I benefited from discussions with Dustin Anderson during the early stages of this work. Philip Clayton read the entire manuscript (some parts more than once) and made more comments and criticisms than I can here enumerate. Both have saved me from making costly mistakes and, for any errors that are left, I ask their pardon in advance.

To my parents, who have played a Kantian role as ''conditions of the possibility'' of my graduate studies, I owe a ''transcendental'' thanks. Their support of my career has been constant and is deeply appreciated. Dedicating this work to them is but a small token of my respect. Lastly, it is my pleasure to thank my wife Sylvie for her cheerful toleration of this project. While I labored over minutiae, she doubled the size of our family, learned to drive, and managed the household with efficient resourcefulness. Even my two daughters helped with the book after their own fashion: my intermittent descent from the rarefied stratosphere of the philosophy of language to prattle with Mary Dorothea and Emma Clare was always an eagerly anticipated mono-syllabic relief.

ABBREVIATIONS

References to Aristotle's works follow the standard pagination of
Bekker's edition of the Greek text. References to Kant's *Critique of Pure
Reason* give the A and B numbers to his first and second editions
respectively. The abbreviations to Ricoeur's works are of two kinds:
initials for books and shortened words for articles. When possible, I have
used the English translations of Ricoeur's works. All translations from
works cited in the bibliography in French are my own.

Works by Ricoeur

BOOKS

CFH	*The Contribution of French Historiography to the Theory of History*
CI	*The Conflict of Interpretations*
EBI	*Essays on Biblical Interpretation*
FM	*Fallible Man*
FN	*Freedom and Nature: The Voluntary and the Involuntary*
FP	*Freud and Philosophy: An Essay on Interpretation*
HHS	*Hermeneutics and the Human Sciences*
HT	*History and Truth*
H	*Husserl*
IT	*Interpretation Theory*
LIU	*Lectures on Ideology and Utopia*
PPR	*The Philosophy of Paul Ricoeur: An Anthology of his Work*
RHP	*The Reality of the Historical Past*
RM	*The Rule of Metaphor*
SE	*The Symbolism of Evil*
TN	*Time and Narrative* (3 vols.)

ARTICLES

"Proclamation"	"From Proclamation to Narrative"
"Récit"	"Le récit interprétatif: Exegèse et Théologie dans les récits de la Passion"
"Reply"	"Reply to Lewis S. Mudge"
"SchlHerm"	"Schleiermacher's Hermeneutics"
"TempsBib"	"Temps biblique"
"Temps"	"Le temps raconté"
"Unity"	"The Unity of the Voluntary and the Involuntary as a Limiting Idea"

Other works

BT	Heidegger, *Being and Time*
CD	Karl Barth, *Church Dogmatics*
CJ	Kant, *Critique of Judgment*
CPR	Kant, *Critique of Pure Reason*
CPrR	Kant, *Critique of Practical Reason*
JAAR	*Journal of the American Academy of Religion*
JR	*Journal of Religion*
NT	New Testament
OT	Old Testament
PT	*Philosophy Today*

INTRODUCTION

1

The passion for the
possible: preface to Paul Ricoeur

The aim of this book is to render Ricoeur's thought, particularly his
recent work on narrative, accessible to English-speaking students of
religion and theology, and to offer an appreciative yet critical interpretation of his hermeneutics and its application to the Gospels.

"Ricoeur deserves to be presented as the most theologically sophisticated of the major contemporary theorists of interpretation."[1] While
this is undoubtedly true, it is somewhat surprising that few booklength
studies have explored Ricoeur's "theological sophistication," and this
despite Ricoeur's many forays into matters biblical and theological.[2]
Indeed, many commentators pass over this aspect of Ricoeur in silence,
even though it is arguably fundamental to his whole enterprise.[3] The
theological tenor of his work is lost in studies which focus on his
interpretation theory to the exclusion of the larger context of his
hermeneutic philosophy, namely, his search for the meaning of human
being. Moreover, Ricoeur has been subjected to extended analysis by
philosophers, theorists of interpretation, literary critics and social
scientists, but seldom by theologians.[4] Theologians, however, have
been quick to use Ricoeur's approach and insights when convenient,[5]
and many Ricoeurrian terms and phrases are now part of the common
theological currency ("the conflict of interpretations," "the
hermeneutics of suspicion," "second naiveté," "the symbol gives rise
to thought"). The present work intends to bridge the gap between those
treatments of Ricoeur that focus on his philosophy and hermeneutics
to the exclusion of his theology on the one hand, and those that focus
on the theological significance of his hermeneutics without attending
to his larger philosophical project on the other.

Ricoeur's own interest and work in matters theological, together with
the widespread interest in the resources of his thought for theological
reflection, clearly justify the present study. What theological reviews

of Ricoeur's hermeneutics there are have thus far been mixed. While for the most·part many of Ricoeur's seminal insights concerning textual interpretation have been appropriated with little or no criticism by theologians as well as exegetes, one group of theologians (all, interestingly enough, connected with Yale University) has seen fit to reject Ricoeur's approach outright.[6] The issue is one of theological method and the battlefield is the Gospel narrative. Ricoeur's recently completed magnum opus, *Temps et récit* (English translation, *Time and Narrative*), provides additional fuel to this debate. Ricoeur's three-volume, 1,000-page study of narrative represents a major contribution to our understanding of narrative, has far-reaching implications for the currently fashionable "narrative theology" and reveals Ricoeur's own theology in a new light.

Exegetes too are divided on the merits of Ricoeur's hermeneutics for biblical interpretation. In his recent book on canonical criticism, James Barr speaks of Ricoeur's approach as one of the most viable options in the exegetical marketplace.[7] Brevard Childs expresses an opposing viewpoint, questioning what he sees as a cavalier disregard for historical questions in Ricoeur's treatment of the Bible as a deposit of free-floating metaphors.[8] But Barr insists that Ricoeur is "far more interested in historical study" than is Childs.[9] In short, there are not only divergent opinions regarding the *value* of Ricoeur's hermeneutic philosophy for theology, but there is a "conflict of interpretations" concerning its very *description*. Thus the goal of this book: description and evaluation.

Why should theologians and exegetes bother reading Ricoeur? His vocabulary is strange, his arguments dense and sinuous, and he is steeped in French and German phenomenology, a philosophical tradition whose conceptual apparatus is as opaque as its prose. This would be a perfunctory reading indeed. Ricoeur is grappling with fundamental questions of language, meaning and truth that exegetes and theologians ignore only at the risk of losing their interpretative integrity. Moreover, Ricoeur's hermeneutic philosophy commends itself to theologians by its prime "theological" virtue: charity. While the Christian faith affirms a single mediator between humanity and God, mediators between human beings are always welcome. The style of Ricoeur's philosophy is irenic: he rarely criticizes other positions, but tries to assimilate them when he can.[10] This accounts for the "grafting" of one position on to another, the "detours," the "long routes" – it takes longer to forge agreements than to disagree. Ricoeur marches to a conciliating drummer: as far as possible, be at peace with all other philosophical positions.

Ricoeur, then, is a mediating thinker. What does he mediate? To begin with, Ricoeur mediates thinkers in the history of philosophy. For instance, he reads Kant through Hegel and Hegel through Kant. This "mutual indwelling" reflects Ricoeur's hope that all thinkers are to some extent "in the truth."[11] Ricoeur also attempts to mediate Anglo-Saxon and Continental philosophy, two traditions which often talk past each other.[12] His personal career reflects this mediating ambition: he simultaneously held professorial chairs in Paris and Chicago for a number of years. Perhaps of most significance for theology, however, is Ricoeur's mediation of the methods and goals of different disciplines. His narrative theory makes an original contribution, for example, in mediating the truth claims of history and fiction, the two major forms of narrative. One of the most impressive features of Ricoeur's philosophy is precisely this ability imaginatively to mediate seemingly irreconcilable oppositions.[13] Ricoeur is a mediator, then, not because he "bears sin," but because he "bears meaning" from afar and makes it intelligible or near. Ricoeur is particularly gifted in making positions which at first blush seem mutually exclusive to appear compatible and even mutually dependent.[14] This "bringing near" (*meta-pherein* = "trans-fer") is also the essence of metaphor, a "seeing together," which associates seemingly disparate realms of meaning and puts them to creative use.[15] As we shall see in Part II, Ricoeur ultimately strives to bring the world of the Bible "near" to the denizen of the twentieth century by creating philosophical "approximations" of theological ideas. By so doing, Ricoeur hopes to enable those who are blind to grace to "see" again. It is only fitting, then, that Ricoeur's favorite form of language, the metaphor, should itself characterize the spirit of Ricoeur's hermeneutic philosophy. Ricoeur's mediation is metaphorical.

And yet the mediation is never total, never perfect. The dialogue between philosophers and between different disciplines has truth as its regulative ideal, but never as its possession. The final synthesis is always delayed. Hegel appears as the serpent in Ricoeur's garden, beckoning him to eat of the Tree of Absolute Knowledge, representing the greatest attempt and the greatest temptation of the philosopher. Ricoeur would never think of writing a "systematic theology," for the work of interpretation never ends: "I maintain that the unity of truth is a timeless task only because it is at first an eschatological hope."[16]

"A passion for the possible"

My exposition of Ricoeur's work is, like all narratives, both chrono-logical and thematic. The story I will tell interprets Ricoeur's developing thought under the rubric of "a passion for the possible." I hope to show that this phrase is appropriate in several ways as a description of Ricoeur's project.[17] First and foremost, "the passion for the possible" is Kierkegaard's definition, with which Ricoeur is in full agreement, of hope. It is no exaggeration to claim that this "passion for the possible" is the driving force behind Ricoeur's whole philosophical enterprise. Accordingly, we would not be far off the mark in labelling Ricoeur a "philosopher of hope."[18]

A *passion* for the possible. Philosophy for Ricoeur is reflection on human existence. Ricoeur is not interested in abstract reflection, as was Descartes, where the subject directly inspects itself, as it were. Rather, Ricoeur begins his philosophical reflection from pre-philosophical experience. Thinking does not give rise to existence, but existence precedes thinking. And existence is desire and effort, that is, desire and effort *to be*. According to Ricoeur, the *passion* to exist, the desire to be, is more basic in human beings than the dread and anguish of existence. This intense *passion* to be, which surges up whenever human existence is threatened, indicates to Ricoeur that humans are constituted by an original, positive impetus rather than by a negation of being or nothingness (as in Sartre). In search of appropriate metaphors to express this thought, we might say that the most "originary" fact of human life is not a primal scream but a primal "Yes." That there is anything at all – that there is *me* – is primarily a source of wonder and cause for gratitude. Ricoeur's is an existentialism of affirmation rather than negation.[19] This positive charge which Ricoeur attributes to existence distinguishes him from his contemporary and compatriot, Sartre. It is precisely because the ultimate meaning of human existence remains illusory that Sartre can define man as absurd – "a useless passion."[20] By contrast, Ricoeur in an early essay entitled "Christianity and the Meaning of History" identifies his passion to exist with faith in the meaningfulness of existence: "Ambiguity is the last word for existentialism; for Christianity it is real, it is lived, but it is the next to last word."[21] The "central intuition" of Ricoeur's philosophy is that human existence is *meaningful*.[22] There is a "surplus of meaning" over meaninglessness. And, in direct opposition to Sartre, Ricoeur describes his philosophy as "a style of 'yes' and not a style of 'no,' and perhaps even a style characterized by joy and not by anguish."[23]

This passionate will to live, which is stronger and more fundamental than anguish, is hope enacted. This *passion* for the possible is thus hope which stands under the sign of the "already."

A passion for the *possible*. Hope is not an empty passion but a passion for the possible. Ricoeur is not interested in just any kind of possibility, but in *human possibilities*. Beginning with his 1950 doctoral dissertation, published as *Freedom and Nature*, to his most recent *Time and Narrative*, Ricoeur has been engaged in a constant search to articulate and recover worthwhile human possibilities. Moreover, according to Ricoeur, human being *is* possibility: "it does not yet appear what we shall be" (1 John 3:2). Human existence is "forward-oriented," constantly projecting itself in front of itself towards a possible way of being. Possibility is thus intimately connected to the imagination which projects it, and to time, specifically the future.[24] Human being, then, is not limited to the here and now, that is, to present actuality. It is one of the most important tenets of Ricoeur's philosophical anthropology that there is a "surplus of being" to human existence, and this surplus of being is nothing other than *possibility*. We are not as we shall be. Thanks to this surplus of being – possibility – humanity can hope. If there were no possibilities, there would be nothing to hope for, for we would live under the tyranny of the "what is." In the kingdom of possibility, however, we glimpse a vision of what *might be*. Chapters 2 and 3 present Ricoeur's philosophical anthropology, his thinking about the "surplus" of human being. In these chapters I argue that the passion for the possible is related both to human temporality (Heidegger) and to the creative imagination (Kant), and that Ricoeur's thought is best understood as a continuation of the "unfinished" projects of Heidegger and Kant.

How does Ricoeur determine what is humanly possible? His early work views human possibilities in terms of the fundamental structures of human volition. Ricoeur attempts directly to describe the project-forming capacity of the will. But human consciousness is not open to such direct inspection. Thus Ricoeur sets off on the first and most important of his many detours: the final destination is still an under-standing of human being, but the route now passes by symbols, myths, metaphors and texts – all of which attest to the meaning of human existence. These linguistic works are expressions of our desire to be, our passion for existence. Human existence is only reached via these works which *mediate* it. If understanding human existence is the goal, then language and texts are the means. But what kind of language and texts refer to the possible, to *what might be*? Here philosophy encounters a problem. For traditionally, only language which refers to *what is* is held to be true. Other types of language were thought to refer only to the "imaginary," in the sense of "unreal." But Ricoeur insists that to speak of possibility is to refer to an integral aspect of being: to *what might be* or to *what is not yet*. As Aristotle remarks, "Being may be said in many ways." Ricoeur proposes that it is poetic or creative language which best expresses the surplus, the "more than actuality," of human being. Poetic language responds to this surplus of being with a *surplus of meaning*. And among the various forms of poetic language, Ricoeur esteems metaphor and narratives above the rest. Metaphors offer different ways of seeing the world; narratives present different ways of seeing human being in the world. Metaphors and narratives are thus the preeminent linguistic forms of the passion for the possible – the language of hope. Chapters 4 and 5 examine these forms of creative language, and their relation to possibility, in further detail. The passion for the *possible* is hope under the category of the "not-yet."

A passion for the possible. This fruitful phrase is susceptible to a final, more explicitly theological, interpretation. The Gospels tell the story of a "passion" for the possible. It was Martin Kähler who first suggested that the Gospels are "passion narratives with extended introductions."[25] "Passion" in this sense means more "submission to suffering"[26] than "will to live," and "possibility" corresponds to what I will call the "Christian" possibility, namely, "new life" or simply "freedom." The Gospels therefore display the possibility of freedom which Jesus somehow "makes possible" through his suffering on the cross. In the Gospel narratives, then, Ricoeur sees the possibility of human "freedom in the light of hope," to borrow the title from one of his essays. In his "Preface to Bultmann," Ricoeur distinguishes the work of the philosopher who describes the formal possibility of authentic existence from the theologian who announces the realization of this possibility.[27]

Taken together, then, the various meanings of a "passion for the possible" converge in the notion of *narrative hope*. It is as a philosopher cum theologian of narrative hope that I will discuss Ricoeur's reading and interpretation of the Gospels in chapters 6 to 10.[28] In so doing we shall try to determine whether the biblical narrative serves to inform and found Ricoeur's passion for the possible, in which case Ricoeur's philosophy could be construed as fundamentally "Christian," or whether the Gospels merely illustrate a philosophical principle, in which case we may wonder in what sense and to what degree Ricoeur regards the stories and histories of Jesus as indispensable for philosophy and theology alike.

Invention and discovery

Is this passion for the possible an unhealthy, pathological passion or a healthy one? Is it the glory or the irony of the human condition that we strive for what might be and are never content with what is? Regardless of its sincerity or intensity, whether or not the passion is a healthy one can only be determined by first interrogating the possible. Is the possibility of, say, goodness or freedom real or imaginary? What of the Christian possibility of new life, or John Wesley's doctrine of human perfectibility? Are these possibilities genuine or illusory – prescriptions for fulfillment or frustration? These questions about ethical possibilities (namely, what can we do?) are related to an epistemological query: are human possibilities invented or discovered? Do we create imaginary possibilities which can never be realized or do we discover real possibilities that can become actual? How can we tell the difference between statements about the true meaning and capacity of human being and instances of wishful thinking?

The distinction between the real and the imaginary, Ricoeur believes, is symptomatic of a deeper dualism, namely, the metaphysical cleavage between being and non-being.[29] In traditional metaphysics, that which exists is temporal or eternal *presence*. Imagination is thus conceived as the faculty which brings to mind *absent* or non-existent things.[30] Book X of Plato's *Republic* represents the *locus classicus* of this critique of the imagination. According to Plato, artistic imitation (*mimesis*) is two steps removed from truth (eternal being), for it is but a copy of an appearance. Jean-Paul Sartre represents the culmination of the Platonic tradition with regard to the imagination. Sartre says of his *L'Imaginaire* that it describes "the great function of consciousness, or 'imagination,' to create a world of unrealities and its noetic correlative, the imaginary."[31] If this dichotomy is left intact, then possibilities that are created, i.e., imagined, will *ipso facto* be illusory, i.e., unreal.

Ricoeur, however, claims that poetic language transcends this dichotomy. There is an alternative to the Platonic view of *mimesis* as copy, namely, Aristotle's view of *mimesis* as "creative imitation." While images reproduce an already given reality, fiction "imitates" only because it recreates reality on a higher level. The problem with the traditional view of metaphysics is that the image or picture was taken to be the paradigm of the imagination. Ricoeur, on the other hand, takes fiction to be paradigmatic of the creative imagination. In the case of fiction, there is no original model to copy. Fiction thus refers to reality in a "productive" way. In fiction, then, we have a blurring of the dichotomy between the real and the imaginary. Ricoeur claims "that fiction changes reality, in the sense that it both 'invents' and 'discovers' it."[32] Ricoeur wants nothing less than the rehabilitation of the concept of imagination: "In short, we must restore to the fine word *invent* its twofold sense of both discovery and creation."[33]

The power of narrative fiction to "invent" reality in the sense just described may perhaps be illustrated by another creative domain – painting. Whereas Ricoeur's narrative theory studies the verbal representation of the real, E. H. Gombrich's classic study, *Art and Illusion*, investigates the visual representation of the real. The similarities as well as the differences between verbal and visual representation are instructive. Ricoeur and Gombrich agree that *mimesis* is the creative imitation of reality, and this distinguishes artistic from scientific representation which is more concerned with making accurate copies. In the final part of his book, entitled appropriately enough "Invention and Discovery," Gombrich asks why visual representation – painting – has a history. On the traditional view, the history of art is the story of the gradual discovery of appearances. Painters learned to see more accurately by disregarding what they thought they knew about the world, by progressing towards unbiased perception. But, according to Gombrich, there is no such thing as the "innocent eye." All seeing is interpretation. According to Gombrich, the discovery of appearances was due to the invention of pictorial effects. It is only by certain *inventions* that painters came to *discover* the appearances. In Gombrich's terms, there is no "matching" before "making." Commenting on Constable's experimentation with different styles, Gombrich writes that "Only through trying out new effects never seen before in paint could he learn about nature. Making still comes before matching."[34]

Ricoeur and Gombrich are thus suggesting that visual and verbal representation alike both invent and discover. Of course, the materials with which each works are different. Painting represents a possible world in terms of "configurations" of space and light; narratives display a possible world by configuring time. Narratives shape a beginning, middle and end into a temporal whole. Whereas paintings "invent" space and light, narratives "invent" human time. Time, according to Ricoeur, is not only the "stuff" of narratives but also of human being. Narratives express the temporality, that inevitable reckoning with past, present and future and their interrelations, which characterizes human existence. Consequently, Ricoeur argues that narratives "invent" plots in order to discover and explore the human historical condition. Ricoeur's concern to restore both a moment of creation and discovery to poetic discourse, the language of possibility, represents one of his most ambitious attempts at mediation.

Mediating invention and discovery has far-reaching consequences not only for literary criticism and historiography, but also for theology. Donald MacKinnon treats one of these consequences for theology in his discussion of the question of invention and discovery – a discussion which he places under the heading of idealism and realism.[35] How does our thinking relate to what is the case? Do we "fashion" or "find" the real?[36] Is reality of our own making or is it there, silent, waiting to be discovered? Here too Ricoeur wishes to mediate: idealism and realism need not be construed as opposites, for, as we have seen, the imagination, through its inventions and creations, discovers the real. Unlike Ricoeur, however, MacKinnon is less interested in mediating these two positions than in taking sides in the debate. MacKinnon insists that only a robust realism guarantees the intellectual integrity of Christianity:

we are fudging if we allow ourselves to suppose that we do not recognize a distinction between the actual and the non-actual, between the eruption of Vesuvius and the murder of Caesar on the one side, and the birth of Venus from the foam, and the exploits of St. George with his dragon, on the other; and it is a matter of crucial importance for Christian belief that the resurrection of Jesus belongs with the former, and not with the latter.[37]

Faith for MacKinnon is a new dimension of experience, and "what has made this new dimension possible ... are events which it is claimed have actually happened."[38] The possibility of redemption which Jesus procured "cannot belong merely to the world of ideas; it must be the stuff of reality, including indeed an act in flesh and blood as costing and as ultimate as the cross."[39] MacKinnon clearly believes that theology discovers the Christian possibility, and his realism finds its natural ally in history rather than fiction.

But this sharp dichotomy between history and fiction is just as misguided in Ricoeur's opinion as that between the real and the imaginary. It is Ricoeur's thesis that both history and fiction "invent" *and* "discover." Indeed, it is a virtual constant in Ricoeur's philosophy that we come to discover the real only by first inventing. In this way Ricoeur tries to mediate the approaches of historical and literary critics to biblical interpretation, not to mention the well-worn distinction between the "Jesus of history" and the "Christ of faith." We shall see that this mediation entails a view of the truth of the Gospel narratives which is neither the truth of historical correspondence nor the truth of fictional coherence. But conditions and criteria of truth there must be if the Gospel narratives, together with the possibility of resurrection life which they display, are to avoid the charge of being not only a "conjuring trick with bones," but also a "conjuring trick with words."

One salutary effect of Ricoeur's tendency to mediate is his resistance to all forms of methodological reductionism. And Ricoeur's skills as a mediator are nowhere better displayed than in his narrative theory. Ricoeur refuses to follow the historical critics in their reduction of a text to its constituent traditions or to confine its meaning to the original situation and its reference to "what actually happened." At the same time, Ricoeur will not countenance a purely structuralist or "theology as story" approach which reduces a text's sense to its immanent relations and cuts it off from any extra-linguistic reference. Theology, like narrative, lives to a great extent out of the field-encompassing, inter-disciplinary conversation which is typical of Ricoeur's method. It is a strength of Ricoeur's approach that he seeks to keep the conversation between disciplines alive and balanced.

Though Ricoeur's mediating methodology is a fundamental strength of his position, this same mediating ambition also gives rise to a potential weakness in Ricoeur's program and its significance for theology. If we follow Ricoeur, we may gain a precious *via media* between a kerygmatic or biblical theology on the one hand, and a philosophical theology on the other. But if we follow Ricoeur's mediation of the imaginary and the real, we risk losing the distinction between truth and fantasy with regard to possibility. If reality is a text to be interpreted, we need somehow to distinguish a legitimate reading from an absurd one, a true possibility from an illusory one. In coming to understand God, human being and the world, we must distinguish "exegesis" from "eisegesis." What does it mean to say that human possibilities are both invented and discovered? Is Ricoeur in a position to arbitrate the discussion between those who affirm the realism of the event of history and those who affirm the idealism of the word event? If we follow Ricoeur, do we arrive at a theology of salvation history or a philosophy of existence? Can Ricoeur mediate this dichotomy without reducing one aspect to the other? As G. K. Chesterton observes in his *Orthodoxy*, "an inch is everything when

you are balancing.''[40] Our task, then, will be to see to what degree
Ricoeur is faithful to his mediating mission in making his case for
narrative hope.

Notes

1 Mary Gerhart, "Paul Ricoeur's Hermeneutical Theory as Resource
   for Theological Reflection," *Thomist* 39 (1975), 497.
2 Ricoeur addresses matters of theology and biblical hermeneutics throughout
   his works. Some of his earliest articles, written in the early 1950s, were
   originally published in the left-wing Christian journal *Esprit*. By and large,
   however, Ricoeur's most explicit treatments are scattered in dozens of
   journals and miscellaneous articles, not readily accessible and often untrans-
   lated from the French. It is perhaps for this reason that a thorough study of
   Ricoeur's theology has been so long in coming.
3 A case in point is John B. Thompson's otherwise excellent *Critical Hermeneutics:
   A Study in the Thought of Paul Ricoeur and Jürgen Habermas* (Cambridge University
   Press, 1981). Thompson's exposition of Ricoeur's thought entirely ignores
   the extent to which Christian faith and an attention to the Bible informs
   Ricoeur's thought. Ricoeur has received an honorary doctorate in theology
   from the University of Nijmegen. See Edward Schillebeeckx, "Le philosophe
   Paul Ricoeur, docteur en théologie," *Christianisme social* 76 (1968), 639–45.
4 The secondary literature on Ricoeur is large and growing rapidly. The standard introduction to Ricoeur's early work (pre-1970) remains Don Ihde,
   Hermeneutic Phenomenology: The Philosophy of Paul Ricoeur (Evanston, North-
   western University Press, 1971). Other general works on Ricoeur's hermen-
   eutics include Patrick L. Bourgeois, *Extension of Ricoeur's Hermeneutic* (The
   Hague, Martinus Nijhoff, 1975); David E. Klemm, *The Hermeneutical Theory
   of Paul Ricoeur* (London, Associated Universities Press, 1983); David M.
   Rasmussen, *Mythic-Symbolic Language and Philosophical Anthropology* (The
   Hague, Martinus Nijhoff, 1971); John W. Van den Hengel, *The Home of
   Meaning: The Hermeneutics of the Subject of Paul Ricoeur* (Washington, University
   Press of America, 1982). See also Charles E. Reagan (ed.), *Studies in the
   Philosophy of Paul Ricoeur* (Ohio University Press, 1979). From the perspective
   of literary criticism, see Mary Gerhart, *The Question of Belief in Literary
   Criticism: An Introduction to the Hermeneutical Theory of Paul Ricoeur* (Stuttgart,
   Akademischer Verlag Hans-Dieter Heinz, 1979). Walter James Lowe con-
   tributes a study of Ricoeur's work on the consciousness and the unconscious
   in his *Mystery and the Unconscious: A Study in the Thought of Paul Ricoeur*
   (Metuchen, NJ, Scarecrow Press, 1977). From the social sciences, see
   Thompson, *Critical Hermeneutics*. For a brief introduction to Ricoeur from the
   vantage point of biblical studies and theology, see Loretta Dornisch,
   "Symbolic Systems and the Interpretation of Scripture: An Introduction
   to the Work of Paul Ricoeur," *Semeia* 4 (1975), 1–19.

5 Some of the more obvious cases of this borrowing include Werner G. Jeanrond, *Text and Interpretation as Categories of Theological Thinking* (New York, Crossroad, 1988); Sallie McFague, *Metaphorical Theology: Models of God in Religious Language* (London, SCM, 1983); William M. Thompson, *The Jesus Debate: A Survey and Synthesis* (New York, Paulist, 1985); David Tracy, *Blessed Rage for Order* (New York, Seabury, 1975); David Tracy, *The Analogical Imagination* (London, SCM, 1981). Note that virtually all of these works use aspects of Ricoeur's interpretation theory without relating it to his earlier work in philosophical anthropology.

6 The debate between the "Yale school" (represented by Hans Frei, David Kelsey and George Lindbeck) and the "Chicago school" (represented by Ricoeur and David Tracy) is one of the more interesting developments in recent American theology, and is the special subject of chapter 7 below, "A literal Gospel?"

7 James Barr, *Holy Scripture: Canon, Authority, Criticism* (Oxford, Clarendon, 1983): "It seems to me that, if a new direction of interpretation has to be taken up, there is much greater promise in something like structuralism or in the type of hermeneutic analysis offered by Ricoeur" (103).

8 Brevard Childs, *Introduction to the Old Testament as Scripture* (London, SCM, 1979), 77.

9 Barr, *Holy Scripture*, 104n.25.

10 Ricoeur himself suggests that this tendency to assimilate other positions is the philosophical equivalent of the Pauline principle of "charity" (*HT*, 6–7).

11 Ricoeur eloquently makes this point in his "Philosophy and the Unity of Truth," in *HT*, 53–5.

12 For Ricoeur's own account of his mediating ambition, see the Appendix to *RM*, "From Existentialism to the Philosophy of Language."

13 This point is convincingly made by Mary Schaldenbrand, "Metaphoric Imagination: Kinship through Conflict," in Reagan (ed.), *Studies in the Philosophy of Paul Ricoeur*, 57–81.

14 Among the more important oppositions which Ricoeur mediates are freedom and nature, history and fiction, real and imaginary, phenomenology and hermeneutics, structuralism and hermeneutics, history and hermeneutics, religion and atheism, philosophy and theology, etc. Many of these will be discussed below.

15 Ricoeur puts it like this: "What is at stake in a metaphorical utterance ... is the appearance of kinship where ordinary vision does not perceive any relationship" (*IT*, 51).

16 *HT*, 55.

17 Ricoeur finds telling his own story difficult: "I am more struck by the discontinuities of my wanderings than by the cumulative character of my works" ("Reply," 41). Yet Ricoeur has hazarded suggestions regarding the cohesiveness of his thought: "I will risk the following hypothesis: it is the mediating imagination which constitutes the guiding line of an

underlying philosophical anthropology; thus it has ontological value. On the other hand, the text has a paradigmatic value for the epistemology of this ontology'' (''Preface,'' xvii). And, ''the one problem that has interested me from the beginning of my work as a philosopher is that of creativity'' (''History,'' 222). We shall see that ''passion for the possible'' provides a means of integrating these central concerns.

18 Ricoeur is interested in exploring the conditions of hope. What makes hope possible? We shall see that his answer involves time, the imagination and the notion of possibility itself. David Stewart suggests that Ricoeur's analysis of hope as a vital aspect of the human condition provides an important supplement to a theology of hope: ''But perhaps Ricoeur's major contribution to hope theology will be in providing a philosophical foundation by raising hope to the level of a philosophical category'' (''In Quest of Hope: Paul Ricoeur and Jürgen Moltmann,'' *Restoration Quarterly* 13 [1970], 31 – 52). The underlying influence on Ricoeur's philosophical anthropology is Gabriel Marcel. Whereas some existentialists began their analyses of human being from the experience of dread or anxiety, Marcel began his philosophy from experiences such as love, fidelity, joy and hope. This was the basis of Marcel's ''Christian existentialism.'' See, for example, Marcel's ''Sketch of a Phenomenology and Metaphysic of Hope,'' in *Homo Viator: Introduction to a Metaphysic of Hope* (London, Victor Gollancz, 1951), 29 – 67.

19 So Herbert Spiegelberg, *The Phenomenological Movement*, vol. II (The Hague, Martinus Nijhoff, 1960), 568; John Macquarrie, *Twentieth-Century Religious Thought*, 2nd edn. (London, SCM, 1981). Here is Macquarrie's concise summation of Ricoeur: ''He criticized the dualism and pessimism of Sartre and also the one-sidedness of those existentialists who have stressed anxiety as the basic human affect. Ricoeur claims that joy has an equal claim to be regarded as an 'ontological effect,' that is to say, a clue to the human condition, and that an affirmative relation to being can be maintained over against feelings of alienation'' (386).

20 Jean-Paul Sartre, ''Conclusion'' to *L'Etre et le néant* (Paris, Gallimard, 1943).

21 *HT*, 95.

22 T. M. van Leeuwen explores how this central intuition is worked out in Ricoeur's works in *Surplus of Meaning* (Amsterdam, Rodopi, 1981).

23 *HT*, 305.

24 This understanding of hope is similar to that of Thomas Aquinas. According to Aquinas, there is hope only where the subject intends something which is (a) good (b) in the future (c) attainable only with difficulty (d) possible. See his *Summa Theologiae*, vol. XXI, trans. and ed. John Patrick Reid (London, Blackfriars, 1965), Q. 40, Arts. 1 – 8.

25 Martin Kähler, *The So-Called Historical Jesus and the Historic, Biblical Christ* (Philadelphia, Fortress, 1964), 80n.11.

26 The English word ''passion'' is in fact a derivative of the Greek (*pascho* = ''to suffer'').

27 *CI*, 393.

28 The passion for the possible underlying Ricoeur's hermeneutic philosophy may be construed as a theological impetus. Stewart Sutherland, in his *God, Jesus and Belief: The Legacy of Theism* (Oxford, Basil Blackwell, 1984), has recently defined theology as "the articulation of the possible" (77). The legacy of theism according to Sutherland is that its language embodies and protects "the possibility of a view of human affairs *sub specie aeternitatis*" (88). The Gospel narratives are significant for they define the Christian possibility: "His [Jesus'] achievement is that he has given intelligible form to the claim that human goodness is a possibility" (185–6).

29 See the excellent study by Richard Kearney, *Poétique du possible: Phénoménologie de la figuration* (Paris, Beauchesne, 1984), 11–21.

30 See Ricoeur's "Imagination," 4–6 for a fuller discussion of this point.

31 Jean-Paul Sartre, *L'Imaginaire* (Paris, Gallimard, 1940), 11.

32 "Fiction," 127.

33 *RM*, 306.

34 E. H. Gombrich, *Art and Illusion: A Study in the Psychology of Pictorial Representation*, 5th edn (London, Phaidon, 1977), 271.

35 See Donald MacKinnon's "Idealism and Realism: An Old Controversy Renewed" and "The Conflict between Realism and Idealism: Remarks on the Significance for the Philosophy of Religion of a Classical Philosophical Controversy Recently Renewed," in his *Explorations in Theology* 5 (London, SCM, 1979), 138–65. MacKinnon elsewhere discusses the opposition of invention and discovery in terms of "constructivism" and "realism." What is discovered may not be correctly described, but the point is that it is not brought into being by the discoverers, as is an invention (*The Problem of Metaphysics* [Cambridge University Press, 1974], 74).

36 Interestingly enough, MacKinnon lists Kant among the "finders" (*Problem of Metaphysics*, 7).

37 Donald MacKinnon, *Borderlands of Theology* (London, Lutterworth Press, 1968), 77.

38 Donald MacKinnon, "Introduction" to *Newman's University Sermons* (London, SPCK, 1970), 17–18.

39 Ibid., 19.

40 G. K. Chesterton, *Orthodoxy* (New York, Dodd, Mead & Co., 1959), p. 184.

I

THE PASSION FOR THE POSSIBLE IN RICOEUR'S PHILOSOPHY AND HERMENEUTICS

Reading maketh a full man ...

Francis Bacon, *Essays*

Part I sets Ricoeur's narrative theory in the broader context of his hermeneutic philosophy. Ricoeur's philosophy seeks to understand human being (What is man?) and thereby to achieve self-understanding (Who am I?). But the meaning of human being is gained only through interpretation of texts (including meaningful action) which attest to human existence. Philosophy is henceforth "hermeneutic." *Lego ut intelligam* – "I read in order to understand." I attain self-understanding when I grasp the range of my possibilities. This self-understanding may be transformed when in reading I confront the "world of the text" and apply to myself the existential possibility, the way of living and being in the world, which a given narrative displays. The two major kinds of narratives, stories and histories, together constitute a veritable catalogue of human possibilities. Ricoeur's narrative theory thus stands at the crossroads of his philosophical anthropology and his hermeneutics.

I interpret Ricoeur's philosophical program as a continuation of the "unfinished" projects of Kant and Heidegger. Ricoeur's philosophy of narrative *hope* emphasizes the imaginative and temporal aspects of human being. From Heidegger Ricoeur borrows the notion of temporality of human being, future-oriented to not-yet possibilities (chapter 2). From Kant Ricoeur takes up and develops the notion of the creative imagination as the "power of the possible" (chapter 3). I suggest that Ricoeur's unique contribution is to give a linguistic and literary orientation to the work of these two important thinkers. Creative language, especially metaphors, constitutes hope's vocabulary and gives expression to the possible or to the ways things might be (chapter 4). Stories and histories – creative writing – shape human identity, for narrative unites the power of the creative imagination and the concern with human temporality in order to explore specifically human possibilities (chapter 5).

2

Human being, possibility, and time

Heidegger's philosophy represents one of the most sustained attacks on the notion of human being as substance or stable essence. On the traditional view, human nature is something fixed, like Oliver Twist: throughout its adventures, it remains essentially the same. Oliver does not act, in the strong sense of the term, but things merely happen to him. And more importantly, "Oliver does not need time in which to become what he already is."[1] In Heidegger's opinion, human being is more like the figure of David Copperfield: here there is a real development of character through time as David takes decisive courses of action. David, unlike Oliver, is conscious that whether or not he is the hero of his own life depends on him alone. Human being is for Heidegger most clearly understood when it is seen in light of its possibilities rather than its present possessions. Man – David rather than Oliver – is the "not fully defined animal" (Nietzsche). Ricoeur's philosophy of the will leads him to privilege possibility as well, for what the will wills is a possible way of living or acting projected by the imagination.

Heidegger, however, discerns temporal limits to human possibilities. Human projects are limited by the finitude of one's lifetime, that is, by mortality. Mortality is the internal limit to human willing as well as the most "proper" possibility of human being. From these premises, Heidegger argues that "authentic" existence is that way of living in the world which recognizes this finitude and faces it resolutely. Though he follows Heidegger's interpretation of human being in terms of temporality, Ricoeur rejects Heidegger's particular construal of authentic existence. Mortality need not be considered humanity's most proper possibility. Here narrative is a help insofar as it envisages other types of temporal orientations. Ricoeur offers a "narrative correction" of Heidegger's project which gives a more hopeful orientation to the notion of authentic existence and puts the whole analysis of existential possibilities on firmer hermeneutical foundations. By dissociating humanity's most proper possibility from mortality and orienting it rather to "eternity," Ricoeur restores a *passion* for the possible to an otherwise somber philosophy of existence.

Philosophy of the will

Ricoeur's focus on the will in his early philosophical anthropology is significant. First, it allows him to deal with questions of guilt, evil and freedom – the staple of theological discourse as well. Questions regarding the "bondage" and "regeneration" of the will have long been at the heart of theological concern. Secondly, concentrating on the will allows Ricoeur to stress the possibilities between which we must choose. The will is itself a passion for the possible. And the possible, in turn, leads Ricoeur to the imagination and ultimately to narrative, for it is the imagination which projects possible courses of action, which are always narrative in nature.

Ricoeur describes the will by uncovering the sundry possibilities that tantalize and dance before it. Ricoeur's preferred method for this description in his earlier works is the method of phenomenology. Unfortunately, the mere mention of "phenomenology" is enough to dissuade many readers from approaching Ricoeur, conjuring up as it does visions of complex hyphenated terms or a quasi-mystical intuition-ism which bypasses the clarity of the concept and argumentation. However, without the jargon the method is quite simple. In the broadest possible terms, phenomenology describes the (non-physical) experience of the waking subject. That is, phenomenology describes the acts (or "intentions") and the objects (or "intentional correlates") of conscious-ness. For example, "perceiving" is an act of consciousness and "appearance" is an object of consciousness. Phenomenology's task is to describe both the "perceiving" and the "appearance," without raising the question of whether the "something" which the subject perceives "exists." Ricoeur claims that the "great discovery of phenom-enology ... remains intentionality ... the priority of the consciousness *of something* over self-consciousness."[2] Perceiving, thinking and willing are distinct acts of consciousness because they are directed towards different objects, different kinds of intentional correlates.

The point of phenomenology is to describe the *meaning* of "lived experience" rather than its factuality. Husserl calls the meaning of a thing its "essence" (*eidos*). We come to know the essence of a thing by exploring its various possibilities. These possibilities are explored in the workshop of the imagination. Ricoeur notes of phenomenology that "its favourite technique is the method of imaginative variations. It is in varying the possible realizations of the same essential structure that the fundamental articulations can be made manifest."[3] Husserl's example of the meaning or "essence" of a table is helpful.[4] By "free imaginative variation" we can alter its form, its color, its material. By then looking to see what there is in common among the various examples, we determine its essence. Of course, a table is more than something we perceive. We can also imagine possible *uses* of a table: we can eat a meal on it; we can write letters or do a jigsaw puzzle on it; we can stand on it to fix the lightbulb, etc. These variations are not present, but they are imagined as possible. Phenomenological description is thus closely related to fiction and the realm of *as if*. As far as phenomenology is concerned, we may define the meaning or "essence" of something as *the imagined ensemble of its possibilities*.

Ricoeur's *Freedom and Nature* is a phenomenology of willing. Ricoeur is here seeking to attain the essence of human being, and this opening volume of his *Philosophy of the Will* is a description of the fundamental possibilities of human willing. In so examining these essential possibilities, Ricoeur is less concerned with *actual* human existence than with the most basic structures of human existence. One of Ricoeur's goals in this undertaking is to demonstrate that guilt and evil are not part of the fundamental structure of human being. In Ricoeur's words, *Freedom and Nature* sketches "the undifferentiated keyboard upon which the guilty as well as the innocent man might play."[5] In *Fallible Man* Ricoeur shows that human being is "fallible": evil is here admitted as a possibility. Fallibility is for Ricoeur the constitutional weakness of human being, its "disproportion" "between the intended meaning of freedom and the experience of finitude."[6] In *The Symbolism of Evil* Ricoeur finally modifies his phenomenological approach and examines *actual* human existence, which is no longer one of innocence but one of guilt and fault. The subject is not simply what *could* be willed, but what *has* been willed. The actual historical condition of human kind is reached not by phenomenology but by a "detour" into symbols and myths which express the concrete human condition.

"Project" and "possibility"

What, in a description of willing, should be considered the object of this act of consciousness? Ricoeur suggests that the "object" which corresponds to willing is the *project* – a "state of affairs to be done by me.''[7] My project is dependent on me and my power. With the notion of a project Ricoeur claims that

> a dimension of the possible is discovered which is: neither a logical possibility – that is, the contrary of which does not imply a contradiction; nor a physical eventuality – that is, something which is compatible with the order of the world; nor a biological virtuality – something which I can consider a tendency of life. This "possible" designates the *capacity of the realization of the project* inasmuch as it is within my power.[8]

The passion for the possible is clearly seen in the project-forming nature of the human will. Ricoeur states that "[t]he most important trait of a project is undoubtedly its reference to the future."[9] By making projects, we view the future as something which we may practically determine; this future state of affairs depends on me.

Ricoeur claims that philosophers have traditionally treated possibilities as future contingents – contingent, that is, on certain conditions. On this view, a possibility is what the order of things permits. But a ''project'' is a possibility that is within my power, that is, within the order of my existence rather than the order of things. Ricoeur is unwilling to dismiss human projects as unreal just because they have not yet been realized or because their conditions do not yet obtain: "It is by virtue of an unjustifiable reduction that we decide to equate 'world' with the whole of observable facts; I inhabit a world in which there is something 'to be done by me'; the 'to be done by me' belongs to the structure which is the 'world'."[10] In the case of human willing, the possible precedes the actual, for the forming of a project precedes its realization: "The presence of man in the world means that the possible precedes the actual and clears the way for it; a part of the actual is a voluntary realization of possibilities anticipated by a project."[11] Moreover, in determining to do something, I likewise determine myself: "In the same way that a project opens up possibilities in the world, it opens up new possibilities in myself and reveals me to myself as a possibility of acting. My power-to-be manifests itself in my power-to-do ..."[12] The ''possible'' is therefore an essential component in self-understanding. I achieve self-understanding when I grasp what possibilities are open to me.[13]

Are human possibilities invented or discovered? This question betrays the very prejudice that Ricoeur is concerned to overcome, namely, that the object of the will is a construction ''of thought.'' The idea of a ''project'' thus becomes a test case for Ricoeur's mediation of the dichotomy between the real and the imaginary. As Ricoeur explains it, the project is part of the subject's "world;" but "world" here is not physical nature, but a world in which human existence is rooted. The "project" is a dimension of the real which is more "original" or "fundamental" than the "object" of natural science. Ricoeur's phenomenology of willing takes us back to a notion of "world" which is prior even to the distinction between subject and object: "Will ... reveals this enrooting of human existence in a world which is the field of its *praxis* before being a view for its theoretical reason."[14] Our projects, in other words, are not susceptible to empirical observation, yet they play an essential role in life and in our understanding of ourselves.

The status of the project *vis-à-vis* the real is thus one problem in Ricoeur's account. Another issue is his distinction between the will's "fundamental structures" and its "actual condition," a distinction that will doubtless remind theologians of that between the creation and fall. Is the innocent nature of the fundamental structures of willing still intact, or are these fundamental structures somehow undermined in the guilty reality of everyday existence? We may hope for freedom, but can we will to be free? Is that still a possibility "after the fall"? Or is it only an "ideal" possibility, i.e., one that can only be *imagined* but never *real-ized*? The apostle Paul provides eloquent testimony to the existential dilemma provoked by forming projects which are beyond one's power: "I do not understand my own actions. For I do not do what I want, but I do the very thing I hate" (Rom. 7:15). In light of this situation, Ricoeur must face two related questions: what are the limits of the humanly possible, and what are the criteria for the genuinely possible?

Imagination as "power of the possible"

In an interesting departure from his focus on the will, Ricoeur claims that it is the imagination which is the "power of the possible."[15] In his essay "The Image of God and the Epic of Man," Ricoeur suggests that humans are in the image of God because they too enjoy the power of creativity. Thus the image of God, creativity, gives rise to the images of man, in the sense of the images that man makes. These images constitute "the sum total of the ways in which man projects his vision on things."[16] Has this image of God, our power of creativity, been damaged by a fall? It would appear so, for in Ricoeur's analysis of the human condition, the problem is not so much a rebellious will as a forgetful imagination. Such a fall is not fatal. "Redemption" now becomes a matter of renewing or expanding the imagination. Ricoeur accords a metaphysical function to the imagination: "The imagination has a prospective and explorative function in regard to the inherent possibilities of man. It is, par excellence, the instituting and the constituting of what is humanly possible."[17] Moreover, "[i]n imagining his possibilities, man acts as a prophet of his own existence."[18] Ricoeur even speaks of a "redemption through imagination," thereby according a soteric function to the imagination as well: "By changing his imagination, man alters his existence."[19] In other words, the mere projection of a possibility would seem to suffice for its actualization. Again we must ask Ricoeur about the status of these possibilities. With regard to visions of human existence, are there not vain imaginings as well? Is not the imagination sometimes a false prophet?

Ricoeur's analysis of the "project" forbids any facile equation between creation and the "imaginary" on the one hand, and discovery and the "real" on the other. For the project is an act of the will which can *create* what Ricoeur claims is a *real* possibility. But the status of unrealized possibilities is hotly disputed. Nicholas Rescher states: "By definition, only the *actual* will ever exist in the world, never the un-actualized possible."[20] Rescher argues that while hypothetical possibilities can be thought of, they do not exist as such – they are not independent of the mind which conceives them. Rescher would thus classify Ricoeur as a proponent of "possibility-idealism."[21] These possibilities are the products of intellectual construction.[22] Rescher sides with Aristotle in giving ontological primacy to the actual rather than the potential. Speaking of potentiality, Rescher asserts that "its 'can-dos' are ultimately grounded in its 'ises'."[23]

Ricoeur's treatment of possibility seems to bear a closer resemblance to that of Ernst Bloch, the philosopher whose *The Principle of Hope* inspired Moltmann's *Theology of Hope* as well as liberation theologies.[24] In Bloch's work too hope appears as a "passion for the possible." Bloch's anthropology of hope is complemented by his ontology of the not-yet: "The openness of man which is apparent in his hopes corresponds to the openness of the world process which is apparent in its possibilities."[25] Just as in Ricoeur the intentional object of willing is the project, so in Bloch the intentional object of hoping is "real possibility" (*Real-Möglichkeit*). Bloch's notion of possibility is diametrically opposed to that of Rescher. Whereas Rescher views possibility as mind dependent (possibility idealism), Bloch's Marxist-materialist emphasis keeps possibility anchored in matter (possibility realism). For Bloch, the world is "not yet": S is not yet P. Against Rescher, existing reality is full of the "not yet."[26]

"By changing his imagination, man alters his existence."[27] With this thought, Ricoeur seems successfully to evade the criticism that Marx levelled at Feuerbach: "The philosophers have only interpreted the world, in various ways; the point is to change it."[28] Bloch and Ricoeur agree that the imagination projects possibilities which themselves seem to have a causal influence on what becomes really possible. But Bloch admits that some projections are merely fantasies with no hope of ever coming to pass. What, then, distinguishes a real from an ideal possibility? Interestingly enough, both Rescher and Bloch suggest the same criterion: praxis. The validity of our mind-invoking conceptions (Rescher) and our projection of possibilities (Bloch) can only come through *pragmatic testing.* To paraphrase Marx's second thesis on Feuerbach, we might say: "Man must *prove the possible,* i.e. the reality and power, the this-sidedness of his imagining in practice. The dispute over the reality or non-reality of imagining that is isolated from practice is a purely scholastic question."[29]

Possibility and temporality

Perhaps the most ambitious philosophical anthropology which takes as its principal category the notion of human possibility and its limits is Martin Heidegger's *Being and Time.* Ricoeur follows Heidegger on many points, most notably the all-embracing neo-Kantian distinction between "world" and "existence" which was of such importance to Bultmann.[30] Ricoeur's narrative theory is ultimately intelligible only in light of Heidegger's magisterial work. We find in Heidegger a masterful, though not entirely perspicuous, analysis of the ways in which human being may be said to be "temporal." Human temporality is finite; mortality represents an inner limit to human possibility. Ricoeur not only takes up Heidegger's project of describing the temporality of human being, but transforms it. The ultimate orientation of human temporality, and hence the *meaning* of human existence, is a matter of some dispute, for Ricoeur complains that Heidegger's account leaves little room for hope.

Being and Time is hardly susceptible to capsule summaries, but four steps in Heidegger's analysis are of particular importance. First and foremost, he identifies possibility as an "existential," or in other words, a basic structural aspect, of human being. Heidegger calls human being "Dasein" or "being-there" ("da" = "there"; "sein" = "being"). Human being finds itself thrown into the world – "there" – flotsam in a sea of actuality. This is the "facticity" of human existence. Yet, as we have seen, human being has the capacity to form projects – to "be." This is the "possibility" of human existence. As a former of projects, I am a being "ahead" of myself. It is most important for Heidegger that human being is different than other types of existents. For unlike, say, a tennis ball, *human being is aware of its possibilities and so can choose between them.* Heidegger calls this awareness of one's possibilities "understanding" (*Verstehen*).[31] As Ricoeur rightly notes: "*Verstehen* for Heidegger has an ontological signification. It is the response of a being thrown into the world who finds his way about by projecting onto his ownmost possibilities."[32] The distinctive feature about human being is that humans are aware of their possibilities (i.e., they have self-awareness; they "understand"). Because human being is the kind of being which projects itself "ahead of itself" in possibilities, Heidegger can say that "Dasein is constantly 'more' than it factually is …"[33] John Macquarrie's paraphrase of this thought is worth citing: "Man is possibility. He is always more than he is; his being is never complete at any given moment. He therefore has no essence as an object has."[34] Heidegger links this priority of the possible with his criticism of the metaphysics of presence. The essence of man is not given, but must be chosen by each individual: "Higher than actuality stands possibility."[35] It is in this sense that possibility is an existential structure of human being.

The second important step in Heidegger's analysis is his claim that some possibilities are more "authentic" than others. To exist authentically for Heidegger means to exist, first, in a way which views the world in terms of possibilities to be chosen by me, and second, in a way which recognizes a responsibility to choose the possibilities most proper to human being – one's "ownmost" possibilities. Inauthentic existence, on the other hand, views the self as an object in a world of actualities and things in the world as givens. In inauthentic existence I am so preoccupied with the actual things of the world that I do not make projects or choose possibilities. In inauthentic existence I renounce my responsibility to "make" my world. Inauthentic and authentic existence are the two ways in which humans can be in the world.

Temporality is introduced into the discussion with the third step. At the end of part one of *Being and Time*, Heidegger sums up his description of the fundamental structure of human being under the rubric, "care."[36] "Care" is the shorthand term which Heidegger uses to distinguish human being from all other kinds of being. A human being, unlike a tree or tennis ball, *cares* about existence and its meaning. But what makes care possible? To exist as possibility means that human being is constantly going beyond the given. This being-ahead-of-myself is only possible because of temporality. To be is to be temporal. Of course, other things exist "in" time, but only humans possess the capacity to project themselves forward in time, to perceive the connectedness of time and to seek its coherence. Only humans reckon with their past and their future as well as their present, and only humans can deal with the relations between these three temporal modes. This inevitable reckoning with time and temporality is at the heart of what Heidegger means by "care." Beings that are self-aware and aware of their possibilities "care." In the second half of *Being and Time*, then, Heidegger reinterprets his existential analysis of human being in temporal terms.[37] "Understanding" now becomes a function of the future: the future is meaningful because it is the way Dasein exists (i.e., being ahead of itself by projecting possibilities). Indeed, the basic tense of existential time is the future, for, to the extent that we have possibilities, we stand before an open future.[38] Possibility is now seen to be a temporal existential, oriented primarily towards the future.

How are we to understand inauthentic and authentic existence, if human existence is temporal? With this question we come to the fourth step and encounter the limits that Heidegger places on human possibility. The second part of *Being and Time* concerns not only temporality, but the unity of human being, its being-a-whole. This wholeness stems from the "master possibility" which orients one's life. This master possibility is, according to Heidegger, nothing less than the possibility of my death. I can grasp my being in its totality only from the perspective of its end. My death is both an inevitable possibility and a possibility which I cannot share with anyone else. As my *own* (*eigen*) possibility, it is my *authentic* (*eigentlich*) possibility. For Heidegger, being-there is authentic when it faces its "ownmost" possibility – mortality. Inauthentic existence is, according to Heidegger, a fleeing from this ruling possibility. In inauthentic existence we do not take control of our own existence but "lose" ourselves among the concerns of the world: "The average everydayness of concern becomes blind to its possibilities, and tranquilizes itself with that which is merely 'actual.'"[38] Authentic existence, on the other hand, is an "anticipatory resoluteness" in the face of this approaching finality. We should not passively wait for death, but have the courage to exist in the awareness of our finitude. This courage, the ultimate locus of authenticity, is *freedom* – freedom to accept the nothingness of our existence. Those who can accept this possibility find themselves free in the face of death. The possibility of death drives out all "accidental" possibilities and "concentrates the will'' on the fate which it must either ignore or choose. If human being is fundamentally temporal, then mortality designates the internal closure of this primordial temporality, the immovable and irrevocable limit to future possibilities.

Heidegger's analysis of authentic existence leaves little room for hope. He devotes only a passing reference to hope in *Being and Time*, and its function there seems to be limited to lightening the burden of being.[40] Here is no passion for the possible, but a reluctant hearkening to conscience which calls one to assume responsibility for one's own existence and a sober willingness to choose and endure the possibility of one's own death. In place of a passion of the possible, Heidegger's analysis of human existence leaves us in the end with a *pathos* of the possible.

The narrative correction of Heidegger's project

Ricoeur, in an important statement of his position, distinguishes two types of hermeneutic phenomenology: Heidegger's (the ''short route'' to human being) and his own (the ''long route'').[41] For Heidegger, ''understanding'' has nothing to do with epistemology or method, but is a mode of human being. Ricoeur is unwilling to take this ''short route'' to human being for two reasons: it passes over questions of method and it wrongly assigns guilt to humanity's fundamental constitution. Heidegger, Ricoeur objects, moves to the description of human existence too quickly, without adequate methodological preparation. In proceeding directly to existential questions, Heidegger leaves himself without the means to arbitrate between conflicting interpretations of human being. To take but one example, while Ricoeur sees guilt as an ''accident'' of human existence, Heidegger sees it as an inherent ingredient in human being.

Whereas Heidegger claims to inspect human being ''directly,'' as it were, Ricoeur chooses the longer route which attains human existence ''by degrees'' via language and semantics. Ricoeur believes that humans come to self-understanding only through the mediation of *language*. But it is precisely this important stage over which Heidegger has jumped. Ricoeur, on the contrary, proceeds to human existence by an analysis of language which best expresses it. Ricoeur states that, in so doing,

we will continue to keep in contact with the disciplines which seek to practice interpretation in a methodical manner, and we will resist the temptation to separate *truth*, characteristic of understanding, from the *method* put into operation by disciplines which have sprung from exegesis.[42]

That human existence is to be attained only through the mediation of and meditation on language is expressed by Ricoeur's celebrated "wager": "I wager that I shall have a better understanding of man and of the bond between the being of man and the being of all beings if I follow the indication of symbolic thought."[43] Human existence is mediated by semantics, that is, by an interpretation of linguistic meaning. This is perhaps the defining characteristic of Ricoeur's philosophical hermeneutics. The advantage of this semantic approach is twofold: questions of truth are not separated from questions of meaning; language is the common ground on which a number of philosophical approaches meet. Furthermore, in making full use of exegetical methods and explanations, Ricoeur hopes to give an analytical precision to Heidegger's existential description which is otherwise absent.

Between language and self-understanding stands reflection. As Ricoeur is fond of saying, consciousness is not a given but a task. Against Descartes, Ricoeur holds that the subject does not grasp itself in an immediate intuition:

The first truth – *I think, I am* – remains as abstract and empty as it is unassailable. It must be "mediated" by representations, actions, works, institutions, and monuments which objectify it; it is in these objects, in the largest sense of the word, that the *ego* must both lose itself and find itself.[44]

Moreover, Ricoeur's work on Freud and psychoanalysis convinced him that consciousness is first of all *false* consciousness. The subject of reflection must lose itself in order to find itself: "All of psychoanalysis speaks to me of lost objects to be found again symbolically."[45] This then is Ricoeur's "long route" to human being: no analysis of human being without the work of interpretation.

One can chart Ricoeur's increasing interest in language and interpretation simply by reviewing his bibliography. *The Symbolism of Evil* (1960) was Ricoeur's first major work to focus on language. His early interest in symbols widened to a consideration of myths, and in the early 1970s Ricoeur was writing on textual interpretation in general. His special love was creative language, and in 1975 he authored a book on metaphor. The companion volume to metaphor was nothing less than his magnum opus: a three-volume, 1,000-page work on narrative. And it is with his work on narrative that Ricoeur is most able to offer a correction to Heidegger's project, for narrative is the form of creative language par excellence which deals with human time and the historicity of the human condition.

Narrative is the "long route" which Heidegger ignores. It is Ricoeur's conviction that Heidegger needs a linguistic and literary method for dealing with the notions of time and possibility. Heidegger was himself perhaps aware of this need; in his later years he turned increasingly to poetry for fear that his philosophical language had "fallen" into traditional metaphysical categories.[46] Though Heidegger's instincts may well have been correct in prompting his transition to the language of poetry, he provides only an embryonic account of this poetic language and its proper interpretation.[47] But this is precisely what Ricoeur contributes to an analysis of human temporality and possibility: a full-fledged theory of narrative interpretation.

Ricoeur's narrative correction of Heidegger is threefold. Ricoeur gives to Heidegger's analysis of human temporality (1) a *literary* application and *analytic* precision (2) a *social* dimension (3) a *hopeful* orientation.

(1) The rich connection between Heidegger's *Being and Time* and Ricoeur's *Temps et récit* is obscured by the English translation of Ricoeur's book, *Time and Narrative*. Ricoeur's thesis is that time comes to expression through *telling*. Ricoeur paraphrases Wittgenstein: the language game "telling" corresponds to the form of life "historicity."[48] Though *récit* is a noun meaning "recital," "telling" better conveys the narrative activity with which Ricoeur is concerned. Calling the book *Time and Telling* would be a permissible translation, and in this form the allusion to Heidegger is more obvious. Ricoeur's thesis is that *telling* mediates *being* and *time*. Being-in-time comes to language, that is, through the telling of stories and histories.[49] In stories and histories, therefore, human temporality not only receives a literary application, but an analytic precision thanks to the exegetical and explanatory methods proper to historical and literary criticism.

(2) The power of Ricoeur's narrative theory to add a social dimension to Heidegger's analysis of human being may be seen in Ricoeur's amendment of Heidegger's treatment of historicity (*Geschichtlichkeit*). The issue here is the extent to which historiography is possible on Heidegger's account. Ricoeur writes that "[w]hat is ultimately at stake is the possibility of grounding the possibility of history as a science in the existential structure of time."[50] If care is oriented towards the future, why should we look in the past? Heidegger's answer is that we scan the past looking for possibilities which might effectively be "repeated" in the future.[51] In section 74 of *Being and Time*, "The Basic Constitution of Historicity," Heidegger discusses this "repetition" in terms of a "heritage." As "thrown" into the world, we find ourselves

with a heritage. Whereas Heidegger concentrates on the individual, non-transferrable possibility of being-towards-death, Ricoeur argues that the major forms of this heritage are stories and histories. Heidegger errs according to Ricoeur in viewing Dasein's historical heritage as "radically monadic" rather than inherently *social*.[52] In Heidegger's analysis, Dasein's historicity is individualistic. Stories and histories, on the other hand, are not only handed down by community tradition, but they continue beyond the fate of individuals. Ricoeur states that a heritage is something transmitted from *another* to the self. As public rather than private time, historicity thus breaks free from the stranglehold of mortality which Heidegger considers to be the authentic form of human being-in-time.

(3) In freeing human historicity from its internal limit, mortality, Ricoeur also challenges the whole Heideggerian analysis of being-towards-death as the preeminent form of authentic existence. Ricoeur's correction of Heidegger on this point is of great importance for our study concerning narrative hope, the passion for the possible. We therefore need to examine Ricoeur's correction on this point with the utmost care.

Ricoeur locates the heart of the problem in Heidegger's distinction between "existential" and "existentiell" possibilities.[53] "Existentiell" refers to a *concrete manner of living in the world*, the actual choice of certain possibilities or, in other words, one's ethical involvement in the world. "Existential" refers to the analysis which describes the fundamental structure which distinguishes human being from any other kind of being. Ricoeur believes that Heidegger obscures this distinction between the "existential" and the "existentiell" with his attempt to distinguish inauthentic from authentic existence. Ricoeur writes that

the search for authenticity cannot be conducted without constant appeal to the *testimony* of the existentiell. Commentators, it seems to me, have not sufficiently stressed this core of the entire hermeneutical phenomenology of *Being and Time*.[54]

Ricoeur's dissection of this "knot" is both painstaking and persuasive, and full justice cannot here be done to it. But Ricoeur's basic point is that Heidegger has confused the existential and the existentiell – a confusion with a momentous result. In short, Heidegger has mistaken being-towards-death, which is only *one* way of being-a-whole, for an existential. That is, Heidegger has used anticipatory resoluteness in the face of death (an existentiell) as his paradigm for being-a-whole (an existential).

Because of this confusion between the existential and existentiell,

Ricoeur wonders "whether the whole analysis of temporality is not carried on by Heidegger's personal conception of authenticity."[55] Resolution in the face of death is an authentic choice, but it belongs to a quasi-stoic ethics. We might say that Ricoeur accepts Heidegger's phenomenology (his existentials), but not his hermeneutics (his existentiells) of authentic existence. As we have seen, both Ricoeur and Heidegger view human being as possibility (being-ahead-of-itself). But whereas Heidegger sees death as the most authentic form of this being-ahead, Ricoeur says other ethical conceptions are possible as well: "For my part, I hold an analysis such as that of Sartre to be just as legitimate, an analysis which characterizes death as the interruption of our ability-to-be rather than its most authentic possibility."[56] There are other existentiell conceptions of what it means to be ahead of oneself or to be a whole, such as those of Pascal and Kierkegaard.

Heidegger's explanation of temporality and possibility is thus colored by a Stoical conception of authentic existence. But there are other kinds of conceptions, for instance, the Christian. Ricoeur devotes the first part of his *Temps et récit* to an analysis of Augustine's thought on temporality. Augustine makes a fitting contrast to Heidegger: where Heidegger oriented temporality to death and finitude, Augustine orients temporality towards the eternal rest of the soul. After a brief juxtaposition of Heidegger and Augustine, Ricoeur sets forth his underlying agenda for his work on narrative: "The most serious question that this book can pose is to know to what point a philosophical reflection on narrativity and time can help us to think about eternity and death together."[57] Augustine, and the whole Christian tradition after him, represent another existentiell response to being-ahead-of-itself. The Christian tradition bases its existential analysis of human being on an existentiell attitude which is more a carefreeness (*insouciance*) with regard to death than an anticipatory resoluteness in the face of death, and thus inclines towards a view of philosophy which is "more a celebration of life rather than a preparation for death."[58] Being-towards-death, then, is not the only possible mode of authentic existence according to Ricoeur. And we shall see in subsequent chapters that it is narrative more than any other form of language, and the Gospels more than any other form of narrative, that yields alternative conceptions of human temporality. It is in this way that Ricoeur's "correction" of Heidegger makes way for narrative hope.

Notes

1 Barry Westburg, *The Confessional Fictions of Charles Dickens* (Northern Illinois University Press, 1977), 1. Dickens himself indicates that Oliver's character is like an unchanging substance: "I wished to shew the principle of Good surviving through every adverse circumstance, and triumphing at last" ("Preface" to the third edition of *Oliver Twist*).
2 "Interpretation," 189. The phenomenological method was first worked out by Edmund Husserl, who chose to examine the act of perceiving and its correlate, the appearance. Ricoeur first encountered Husserl's philosophy while a prisoner of war. Ricoeur later introduced Husserl to France, both translating Husserl's *Ideen I* and writing several articles on his thought, now collected in *H*.
3 *PPR*, 66.
4 Edmund Husserl, *Cartesian Meditations* (The Hague, Martinus Nijhoff, 1960), 69–70.
5 *FM*, xvi.
6 *HHS*, 33.
7 *PPR*, 68.
8 Ibid. (my emphasis). The nature of possibility is a most difficult topic which involves fundamental metaphysical issues. The discussion begins, as is so often the case, with Aristotle. The *locus classicus* on this subject is Aristotle's *Metaphysics*, Bk. IX. There Aristotle writes: "And a thing is capable of doing something if there is nothing impossible in having the actuality [*energia*] of that which it is said to have the capacity [*dunamin*]" (1047^a 24–5). We may call this, following Bruce Aune, the "possibility of ability" ("Possibility," in P. Edwards [ed.], *The Encyclopedia of Philosophy* [New York, Macmillan & Free Press, 1967] 6, 419–24). This kind of possibility is expressed by such sentences as "I could do x." In Aristotle's account, actuality is temporally, logically and ontologically prior to possibility: "For from the potential the actual is always produced by an actual thing ... there is always some first mover; and the mover already exists actually " (*Metaphysics* 1049^b 24–6). Just how potential being becomes actual being is a complex question, on which see Franz Brentano, *On the Several Senses of Being in Aristotle* (University of California Press, 1975), ch. 4 "Potential and Actual Being." Jaakko Hintikka has written extensively on the relation of time to possibility in Aristotle, and claims that the most important assumption in western thought about the relation of time and possibility is "that all *genuine possibilities*, or at least all possibilities of some central and important kind, *are actualized in time*" (*Time and Necessity: Studies in Aristotle's Theory of Modality* [Oxford, Clarendon, 1973], 94). This implies that the world is "as full as it can be," and Hintikka attributes this "principle of plenitude" to Aristotle.
9 *FN*, 48.
10 *PPR*, 68.
11 *FN*, 54.

12 *PPR*, 69.
13 Of course, Ricoeur acknowledges that the will is limited in its power because it is inextricably linked to a body which is subject to necessity and limitation. Thus the possible is what I *can* do and not merely what I wish to do: "The possibility I project and the possibility I discover are knitted together by action. The man who boards a train joins possibility opened by his project with the possibility offered by the railway company" (*FN*, 54). Self-understanding is thus the awareness of the possibilities available to me in a given situation.
14 *PPR*, 70–1.
15 *CI*, 408.
16 *HT*, 119.
17 Ibid., 126–7.
18 Ibid., 127.
19 Ibid.
20 Nicholas Rescher, "The Ontology of the Possible," in Milton K. Munitz (ed.), *Logic and Ontology* (New York University Press, 1973), 215.
21 Ibid., 219.
22 Cf. Nicholas Rescher's *Conceptual Idealism* (Oxford, Basil Blackwell, 1973): "Any careful analysis of possibility inevitably carries one back to the common theme that only the actual can objectively be real, and that the modally variant areas of the possible and necessary depend essentially upon an invocation of mentalistic capacities" (49). Rescher's brand of idealism raises the question of invention or discovery with regard to narrative as well insofar as narrative too is a product of intellectual construction. What is mind dependent on Rescher's account is not reality itself, but reality as-we-picture-it.
23 Rescher, *Conceptual Idealism*, 52.
24 Ernst Bloch, *The Principle of Hope* (Oxford, Basil Blackwell, 1985).
25 Jürgen Moltmann, "Ernst Bloch and Hope Without Faith," in *The Experiment Hope* (London, SCM, 1975), 33.
26 For Bloch, the ground of hope is an inner "restlessness of matter": "This concept of reality comprehends reality together with its possibilities and matter together with its future" (Moltmann, "Ernst Bloch and Hope," 33).
27 *HT*, 127.
28 Karl Marx, "Theses on Feuerbach," Thesis II, in David McLellan (ed.), *Karl Marx: Selected Writings* (Oxford University Press, 1977), 158.
29 The original from Marx reads: "Man must prove the truth, i.e. the reality and power, the this-sidedness of his thinking in practice. The dispute over the reality or non-reality of thinking that is isolated from practice is a purely scholastic question" (McLellan, *Karl Marx*, 155). Ricoeur insists that the outcome of his hermeneutics should be an ethical one, and he suggests that only in this way can a hermeneutics respond to the challenge of Marx's eleventh thesis (see Ricoeur's "Preface" to Domenico Jervolino, *Il cogito*

e l'ermeneutica. La questione del soggetto in Ricoeur [Naples, Generoso Procaccini Editore, 1984], 9).

30 Reality is twofold: on the one hand there are the objects of the world, the things that are actual. On the other hand there is the human kind of reality, existence, which is the radical possibility to be or to become. Only in existence is there possibility, and hence, freedom. We shall see that the world/existence dichotomy is repeated in Ricoeur on a linguistic level in the distinction between literal and figurative language. On the world/existence dichotomy in Bultmann see Robert C. Roberts, *Rudolf Bultmann's Theology: A Critical Interpretation* (Grand Rapids, Eerdmans, 1976), 9–81.

31 Heidegger makes clear in his crucial section 31 of *Being and Time*, "Being-there as Understanding." Michael Gelven calls this section "the key to *Being and Time*" (*A Commentary on Heidegger's "Being and Time"* [New York, Harper & Row, 1970], 84). Heidegger distinguishes possibility as an existential structure from logical possibility and from contingency: "As a modal category of presence-at-hand, possibility signifies what is *not yet* actual and what is *not at any time necessary*. It characterizes the *merely* possible. Onto-logically it is on a lower level than actuality and necessity. On the other hand, possibility as an *existentiale* is the most primordial and ultimate positive way in which Dasein is characterized ontologically" (*BT*, 183). For our purposes this section is particularly important because Heidegger's notion of understanding is the focal point of his philosophical anthropology as well as his theory of interpretation. Human existence *is* understanding (i.e., projecting possibilities) and interpretation is the explicit unfolding of this implicit understanding. We shall see that narrative theory is the means by which Ricoeur carries on and transforms Heidegger's project. Narrative theory is also at the crossroads of Ricoeur's philosophical anthropology and hermeneutics.

32 "Interpretation," 190. In Heidegger's more technical words: "*Understanding is the existential Being of Dasein's own potentiality-for-being: and it is so in such a way that this Being discloses in itself what its Being is capable of*" (*BT*, 184).

33 *BT*, 185.

34 John Macquarrie, *An Existentialist Theology* (London, SCM, 1960), 32.

35 *BT*, 62–3.

36 Heidegger unifies the existentials of human being in the concept 'care' (*Sorge*). See section 41 of *BT* "Dasein's Being as Care" which expounds the threefold structure of "care," namely, as "ahead of itself" (possibility), "already in the world" (facticity) and "alongside other entities" (fallenness).

37 Gelven provides a handy summary of the way in which temporality is the ontological ground of (i.e., that which makes possible) care: "It is possible for Dasein *to be ahead of itself* because of its ontological *future*; it is possible for Dasein *to already be* in a world because of its ontological *past*; and it is possible for Dasein to *be alongside* entities because of its ontological *present*" (*Commentary on "Being and Time,"* 188).

38 And yet the past is also existentially significant when the subject matter of history is seen to be the possible. Dasein's "historicality" is its awareness that it has a fate as well as a future, and fate means that I have inherited a certain number of possibilities from which I must choose. History's interest in the past is for the sake of those "historic" possibilities that Dasein may "repeat" in the present. Through such a "repetition," the "monumental" possibilities of the past may be made my own, as possibilities for my future. This threefold structure of care (past, present, future) Heidegger calls temporality. This is the basic being of humanity. It is because man is first temporal that he can be historical, for to be historical means to be aware that the past and future are as real as the present.

39 *BT*, 239.

40 Ibid., 395–6.

41 "Existence and Hermeneutics," *CI*, 3–24.

42 *CI*, 11. For all his similarities to Hans-Georg Gadamer, this is also the point where Ricoeur parts company with him. Ricoeur believes that Gadamer has so stressed the condition of "belonging-to" a tradition for understanding that a critique of that tradition is no longer possible. Gadamer mistakenly believes that all distanciation defeats understanding. According to Ricoeur, however, distanciation (especially the distance separating a text from its author and original situation) is an integral element in understanding. See Gadamer's *Truth and Method* (London, Sheed and Ward, 1975). For Ricoeur's evaluation of Gadamer, see his "The Task of Hermeneutics" and "Hermeneutics and the Critique of Ideology," *HHS*, chs. 1 and 2.

43 *SE*, 355.

44 *CI*, 327.

45 Ibid., 20. Cf. *FP*.

46 George Steiner, *Heidegger* (London, Fontana, 1978), 78.

47 We shall see in the following chapter that Ricoeur levels a similar charge against Kant.

48 *HHS*, 288.

49 To anticipate the next chapter on Kant, we could say that narratives are literary "schemas" which create figures for human being in time.

50 "NarTime," 181.

51 "As concerns Heidegger, the stroke of genius is to have ascribed to what he calls *Wiederholen* ('repetition' or 'recollection') the fundamental structure thanks to which historicality is brought back to its origin in the originary structure of temporality" ("NarTime," 182).

52 Ricoeur opposes private or mortal time to public time, which is "the time of language itself, which continues on after the individual's death" ("Creativity," 20).

53 This is essentially the same distinction as that employed by Bultmann between "ontological" and "ontic" possibilities (see chapter 6 below).

54 *TN* III, 65.
55 Ibid., 67.
56 Ibid.
57 *TN* I, 87.
58 *TN* III, 254–5.

3

Hope within the limits of Kant alone?

A single question has inspired Ricoeur's many writings over a period of forty years: What is man? The focus of this ambitious project is Ricoeur's *Philosophy of the Will*, as yet still lacking the third and final part. If the will is the central problem of this philosophical anthropology, its theme is freedom and its limit – nature. This way of stating Ricoeur's concern sends us back to Kant, and it is only fitting that we continue our exposition of Ricoeur in the light of the philosopher who first charted the routes that Ricoeur travels further.

It was Kant who suggested that the query, What is man?, comprises three other questions: What can I know? What ought I to do? What may I hope?[1] This last question also serves to define religion and to set the agenda for a philosophy of religion. Adequately to answer the question of what we may hope requires a response not from speculative reason but from the creative imagination, the "power of the possible." Ricoeur takes up and continues Kant's incipient theory of the imagination as well as his related theory of symbols in his search for the conditions of the possibility of human freedom. Ricoeur gives Kant's notion of the creative imagination a surer linguistic and literary footing by displaying it "at work" in narrative. Ricoeur's narrative theory constitutes a "delicate extension of Kant's philosophy of religion"[2] as well as his philosophy of the creative imagination.

What may I hope?

There is a remarkable similarity between Ricoeur's three-volume *Philosophy of the Will* and Kant's three *Critiques*. Both trilogies aim at understanding the relation between human freedom and nature by progressing through a speculative, a practical and, finally, an aesthetic or "poetic" stage.[3] Ricoeur accepts the Kantian paradigm of a humanity situated precariously between freedom and nature. Hope may be the passion for the possible, but not every possibility can be realized. Human being is limited in what it can accomplish by, among other things, the world – nature – and its own finitude, not to mention evil. Human capacity is no match for human desires. The intoxicating joy of infinite ambition is quickly sobered by the clear-eyed recognition of finite abilities.

However, neither Kant nor Ricoeur consider the dichotomy between freedom and nature to be either absolute or final. In the experience of evil, freedom discovers itself as bound, a captive freedom. Human freedom can thus be other than it is. Both Kant and Ricoeur are familiar with stories or myths that picture a future reconciliation of human freedom with nature or a future triumph of good over evil. Indeed, the Gospels are paradigmatic in this regard for Kant and Ricoeur alike. In these visions of a reconciled humanity, human will or capacity is equal to human desire. While such is manifestly not the case at present, may we hope for such a paradisiacal possibility? Or must we, with heavy resignation, accept what is – the current incomplete and broken state of affairs – as something necessary?

In a creative, or what Ricoeur calls a "post-Hegelian," reading of Kant, Ricoeur interprets the Kantian limits on human knowledge and action in such a way that, far from quenching the passion for the possible, they actually serve as its very condition. For Ricoeur, Kant "remains the philosopher who thought the limits of knowledge and of action and who linked the possibility of a philosophy of hope to this meditation about the theoretical and practical limitations of man."[4] To see how the idea of limit, which Ricoeur regards as the "soul of the Kantian philosophy,"[5] contributes to a philosophy of hope, Ricoeur proposes a "post-Hegelian" reading of Kant's first two *Critiques*. While Hegel represents for Ricoeur philosophy's totalizing ambition – the quest for comprehensive conceptual systematization – Kant represents philosophy's chastened admission that such totalization is beyond our grasp.[6]

Ricoeur contrasts Kant's *Critique of Pure Reason* with Hegel's system. Ricoeur admits that in Hegel's philosophy the speculative claim of religion has been emphatically recognized. But the price to be paid is "the total absorption of the 'figurative' in the 'conceptual'."[7] Reducing religious symbols to concepts is according to Ricoeur tantamount to short-circuiting hope, for the end of Hegel's philosophy is absolute knowledge – a closed system. There is nothing new in absolute knowledge, merely the philosophical repetition of antecedent mediations. The "end" of the Hegelian system is not something that can be expected and anticipated: it is the eternal present of thought. The Hegelian system "represents the contrary to a philosophy of hope. It is a philosophy of reminiscence ..."[8] If religious representations can be reduced to concepts, then they cannot portray a future state of affairs for which we may hope. In the Hegelian system, the discourse of religion is swallowed up in the discourse of philosophy; consequently, the question "What may I hope?" is swallowed up in the question "What can I know?".

The irreducibility of religious symbols to concepts, of hope to knowledge, forces Ricoeur to turn from the hubris of Hegel to the humility of Kant. The negative conclusion of the *Critique of Pure Reason* is that speculative theology, knowledge of God, is beyond the limits of human knowledge. But the idea of limit need not exercise a wholly negative function. On the contrary: "If we do not start with the first *Critique* and with its *Dialectic* we miss something essential to a philosophy of hope, i.e., the destruction of absolute knowledge. Between hope and absolute knowledge we have to choose."[9] The first step in a philosophy of hope therefore "consists in the act of renunciation by which pure speculative reason gives up its claim to fulfill the thought of the unconditioned along the lines of knowledge of empirical objects."[10] Ricoeur places the greatest importance on Kant's distinction between *Denken*, or thinking of the unconditioned, and *Erkennen*, or thinking of objects. Objects are conditioned by space and time, and hence they are within the limits of empirical knowledge. Hegel's cardinal error, his "transcendental illusion," was to try and think the unconditioned (namely, God, self, freedom) in an objectifying manner, thus making the unconditioned subject to the conditions of space and time. According to Ricoeur, such an error is possible only because there is a *legitimate thought of the unconditioned*. We shall see below that this legitimate thinking is a thinking "according to the symbol" which does not come to rest in a finished concept. In short, the limit does not close the philosophical discourse, but breaks it open by denying the claim of objective knowledge to close it off at the level of spatio-temporal objects. It is in this sense that we should take Kant's celebrated comment: "I have therefore found it necessary to deny *knowledge*, in order to make room for *faith*."[11] In similar fashion, we may say that Ricoeur denies "knowledge" of the unconditioned in order to make room for *imagination*.

The Kantian limits are not merely theoretical, but practical. In the *Critique of Practical Reason*, "reason" appears as a kind of "Dickensian" requirement that everything fit together in the end. In the moral context of Kant's second *Critique*, reason is the mandate to "complete" the will. That is, reason requires an appropriate or happy end to moral striving; the *summum bonum* is for Kant the conjunction of duty and happiness. This demand for the realization of the supreme good is the practical counterpart of Hegel's absolute knowledge. Reason is the horizon of both knowledge and action which demands completeness even though humanity is theoretically and practically limited. While Ricoeur accepts this impulse towards totalization as a practical requirement of philosophy, he parts with Kant in giving a scope to ethics which escapes the narrowness of morality. Ethics for Ricoeur is the movement from bondage to freedom's actualization whereby we fulfill our desire to be.[12] In order for morality to be meaningful, Kant postulates human freedom, as well as a world in which the strivings of human freedom will not be frustrated by the workings of nature. But though there is a demand for completion, there is only limited ethical achievement.

Here again a recognition of limits contrasts sharply with Hegel. For Hegel, philosophy "always comes too late" to say what the world ought to be like:

As *thought* of the world it appears at a time when actuality has completed its developmental process and is finished ... When philosophy paints its gray in gray, a form of life has become old, and this gray in gray cannot rejuvenate it, only understand it. The owl of Minerva begins its flight only when dusk is falling.[13]

For Hegel, philosophy cannot say what ought to be in the future, but only that what has come to be is the rational outworking of *Geist*. Philosophy can only recover an awareness of self and mind by tracing a development that has already taken place. According to Ricoeur, Hegel extrapolates from a limited experience of the fulfilled achievements of humanity to construct a system of total rationality. But in denying that there is still a sea of irrationality, a number of unfulfilled achievements which remain to be done, Ricoeur claims that Hegel destroys the very spring of action. The course of history for Hegel appears both rational and necessary. But Ricoeur will have none of it: "The Hegel I reject is the philosopher of retrospection."[14] Limits are therefore to be found in the practical realm as well. The lesson to be drawn from the *Critique of Practical Reason* is that the reconciliation of virtue and happiness is not at our disposal. Kant proffers the postulates of God, freedom and immortality not as objects of knowledge but as requirements of reason which alone guarantees the possibility of the *summum bonum*.

In Ricoeur's post-Hegelian reading of Kant's second *Critique*, then, ethics is given a larger scope than the one assigned to it by Kant, who restricted it to questions of law and morality. Ricoeur focuses on the *Dialectics*, where Kant considers the possibility of the complete fulfillment of the will. To this question is linked the not-yet given but demanded connection of virtue and happiness, the reconciliation of freedom and nature. But there is another limit to human practice, one which Kant develops in his *Religion Within the Limits of Reason Alone*: radical evil. Ricoeur observes that the experience of evil prevents us from claiming that practical reason has been fulfilled. Evil is real and irrational. As such, it presents an intolerable problem for a notion of ethics as the actualization of human freedom. Ricoeur concludes that "evil makes of freedom an impossible possibility ... not only our knowledge but our power has limits."[15] As a consequence, "[t]he postulate of freedom must henceforth pass through the night of understanding with the crisis of transcendental illusion, and through the night of powerlessness with the crisis of radical evil."[16]

The phenomenon of radical evil which Kant explores in *Religion Within the Limits of Reason Alone* is thus related to ethics as defined by Ricoeur, insofar as evil impedes the actualization of freedom.[17] But in interpreting ethics in this broader sense, Ricoeur claims to give to Kant's third question, What may I hope?, "a real autonomy in respect to the second question – What must we do?"[18] In Ricoeur's post-Hegelian re-reading of Kant, the *problem of the actualization of human freedom is the proper domain of human hope*. Interestingly enough, Michel Despland suggests that the problem which incited Kant to write *Religion Within the Limits of Reason Alone* was not only radical evil but the *temporality* of human being, that is, the historical failure of humanity to become good.[19]

While the Hegelian dialectic between freedom and its full actualization is the philosophical equivalent of a speculative theology centered on the eternal Now of absolute knowledge, the Kantian dialectic is non-conclusive and has, in Ricoeur's opinion, more affinity with a theology of hope. Hope opens up what absolute knowledge claims to close. In thus specifying the limits on human knowledge and human action, Kant's philosophy of limits makes a positive contribution to "a critique of hope within the limits of reason alone."[20] Insofar as Kant ties hope to the temporal overcoming of evil and the actualization of freedom, we may conclude that Ricoeur takes up Kant's philosophy of religion. Ricoeur transforms Kant's project by giving an even greater role to the function of the creative imagination in making hope possible. For Kant as well as Heidegger, then, human being projects possibilities "in front of" itself. In linking time and imagination together in his narrative theory, Ricoeur shows himself to be not only a post-Hegelian, but a post-Heideggerian Kantian as well.

The creative imagination

In limiting human understanding and human action, Ricoeur believes that Kant has "made room" for hope. But neither the speculative phase (knowledge) nor the practical phase (experience) provides grounds for hope, for the harmony of the realms of freedom and nature is unachieved. That such a reconciliation and realization of our hope is truly possible can be confirmed neither by speculation nor historical experience. There remains, however, a third option: the poetic. Both Kant's *Critique of Judgment* and Ricoeur's promised but postponed "Poetics of the Will" deal with the "poetic" reconciliation of freedom and nature. Kant claims that the *Critique of Judgment* brings his critical philosophy to a systematic conclusion by mediating the realms of freedom and nature in art.[21] Art – "poetic" creation – is a means of thinking the unconditioned in a way which is irreducible either to concepts of understanding or experiences of sensibility. Ricoeur is never more Kantian than when he follows Kant's lead in mediating oppositions with the creative imagination.

However, it is not immediately obvious how hope is served by the imagination. Indeed, philosophers have called attention to the notorious failure of the third *Critique* to provide a response to Kant's third question, "What may I hope?". Despland remarks that "[t]his neglect is one of the major unresolved tensions in the whole of Kantian thought."[22] It is not the least valuable of Ricoeur's services to Kant studies that through his taking up Kant's insight concerning poetic mediation he goes a considerable way in resolving this tension.

Art is a work of the creative imagination. This creative imagination is the means of thinking beyond the limits of human understanding and human action; it is also central to the philosophical enterprises of Ricoeur and Kant alike. In order adequately to grasp Kant's view of the creative imagination, we must begin by examining its role in the *Critique of Pure Reason*. I shall argue that Ricoeur gives to the "schematizing" imagination of the first *Critique* and to the "symbolizing" imagination of the third *Critique* a linguistic and literary intelligibility, thus bringing these important Kantian notions out of their philosophical obscurity and into the daylight of a theory of creative or "poetic" language and literature. Ricoeur takes up Kant's notion of the creative imagination and puts it to use both in a narrative theory and a philosophy of religion. We turn first to consider the Kantian ingredients in Ricoeur's narrative theory.

According to Kant's first *Critique*, the imagination has two fundamental tasks which make objective knowledge possible. The first function, that of the "reproductive" imagination, consists in reproducing images of absent objects.[23] Ricoeur observes that this popular conception of imagination "suffers from the disrepute in which the term 'image' is held following its misuse in the empiricist theory of knowledge."[24] On this view, the imaginary is equated with the unreal, that is, with absent being. As early as his *The Symbolism of Evil*, before his "turn" to a study of linguistics and the philosophy of language, Ricoeur decried the facile identification of "image" and "imagination." To understand the creative or "poetic" imagination, says Ricoeur,

it is necessary firmly to distinguish imagination from image, if by image is understood a function of absence, the annulment of the real in an imaginary unreal. This image-representation, conceived on the model of a portrait of the absent, is still too dependent on the thing that it makes unreal; it remains a process for *making present* to oneself the things of the world.[25]

Ricoeur presages his later interest in a *literary* imagination when, in the same work, he states that "[a] poetic image is much closer to a word than to a portrait."[26]

But in Kant there is a second form of imagination – the "productive" imagination. This function of the imagination is less familiar to us, but it serves as the cornerstone of Kant's theory of knowledge and as the stepping-stone to Ricoeur's notion of narrative. The central problem of the "Transcendental Analytic" in the *Critique of Pure Reason* deals with how concepts not derived from experience, namely, the categories, can be applied to experience. How, asks Kant, is such an application possible? He replies that there must obviously be "some third thing, which is homogeneous on the one hand with the category, and on the other hand with the appearance, and which thus makes the application of the former to the latter possible."[27] This "third thing" is the productive imagination, or more exactly, what Kant calls the "schema," which is a product of the imagination. Here then is the first instance of the mediating imagination in Kant: the productive imagination is responsible for mediating concepts and intuition, and thus serves as the cornerstone of the epistemology presented in the first *Critique*.

Kant's notion of "schematism" is admittedly a difficult one. Obviously there must be some "third thing" which mediates our concepts and our experience, but just what is it? How does imagination mediate our understanding and our experience? Kant himself confesses that schematism is an "art hidden in the depths of the human soul."[28] Ricoeur's narrative theory, however, has no better philosophical antecedent than Kant's doctrine of schematism. For in formulating the notion of schema, Kant became the first thinker explicitly to link the problem of *time* to that of the *imagination*.[29] And it is precisely this conjunction of time and imagination which is the principal ingredient in Ricoeur's narrative theory.

How then does the schema enable concepts to be applied to experience, and what might this possibly have to do with narrative? In Kant's philosophy, the only feature common to every object of experience is *time*. To be in time is a condition for the very possibility of being experienced. The schema shows what the concept means when applied to things in time (the phenomenal realm) only by placing it under a particular "determination" or "figure" of time.[30] Kant defines "schema" in the following, not altogether helpful, manner: "This representation of a universal procedure of imagination in providing an image for a concept, I entitle the schema of this concept."[31] The image provided for a concept is thus a *creative figure of time*. To the category "reality," for example, corresponds the figure "being in time." Substance, necessity and causality, are also categories which can be applied to experience only to the extent that the imagination can create figures of time for them: "permanence through time," "existence at all times" and "succession in time" respectively. In its schematizing capacity, the imagination is creative; it does not simply reproduce images of objects in the world, but creates figures of time which allow categories to be applied to the world.

Ricoeur's application of the Kantian creative imagination and its schematizing function to narrative theory is itself a creative and brilliant stroke.[32] At one blow narrative no longer appears to be an imitation of something in the world, the product of the reproductive imagination, but rather as a creative figure of time, the product of the creative imagination. Here we may recall Gombrich's comments on painters who invent effects by which better to explore space (perspective) and light. While other forms of the creative imagination, such as painting or poetry, exist, narrative is the most appropriate linguistic equivalent to the Kantian schematism. For narrative is a *creative shaping of time*.[33] Ricoeur defines the plot of a narrative as a *creative synthesis which makes a temporal whole out of a beginning, middle and end.* Narrative figures and configures human time in stories and histories. But if schematism frees narrative from being construed as a form of reproductive imagination which simply imitates things in the world, narrative gives something in return to schematism. Ricoeur makes schematism more intelligible by giving literary flesh and blood to Kant's bare skeletal schemata. That is, Ricoeur makes schematism more intelligible by showing it *in operation*, as it were, in narrative. Far from being hidden in the depths of the soul, then, Ricoeur displays the relation of imagination and time in the narrative operation, for the narrative imagination creates figures of time. In sum, Ricoeur's narrative theory continues Kant's project by giving a verbal or literary application to the schematizing imagination.

The literary imagination

While the idea of "limits" may be the "soul" of the Kantian philosophy, Kant's *Critique of Judgment* provides a basis which permits thinking to continue where theoretical knowledge is thwarted. Here the imagination produces symbols rather than schemata. The imagination also appears as "reflective judgment," a synoptic power which creates unity out of diversity. It is by these means that the creative imagination permits thought to continue beyond the limits of reason alone. It is because Kant did not have the linguistic and literary resources to articulate this power of the imagination that the question of hope had to be deferred to his later work, *Religion Within the Limits of Reason Alone.* And yet in the third *Critique* the necessary resources for expressing hope were present, even if Kant did not exploit them. For if the creative imagination provides the means to *think* what is beyond the bounds of objective knowledge, its product, figurative language, provides the means to *speak* what is beyond the bounds of descriptive language.[34] Ricoeur's succinct verdict on Kant is telling: "It is because Kant had no idea of a language which would not be *empirical* that he had to replace metaphysics by *empty* concepts."[35] We may say then that Ricoeur, in the spirit of Kant's third *Critique, has found it necessary to deny knowledge in order to make room for creative language, namely, for symbols, metaphors and narrative.*

Kant defines judgment as the "faculty of thinking the particular as contained under the universal"[36] or alternatively the "faculty of subsuming under rules."[37] If the universal (i.e., a law or concept) is given in advance, the judgment which subsumes the particular under it is "determinant." Such are the judgments of the understanding, which subsume appearances under concepts. There is no making here, only matching. But if, on the other hand, only the particular is given for which the universal must be *found*, Kant terms the judgment "reflective." The third *Critique* deals with this latter type of judgment.

Reflective judgment is best illustrated by Kant's theory of "genius" in section 49 of the third *Critique*. By "genius" Kant is referring to a mental faculty which we may regard as equivalent to the creative imagination. Kant opposes genius to the "spirit of imitation," thus recalling the earlier distinction between the "reproductive" and "productive" imagination. Far from copying a pre-existing model or pattern, Kant defines genius as "the talent which *gives* the rule to art."[38] Art gives pleasure according to Kant precisely because it manifests a rule-governedness:

> For [in every art] some purpose must be conceived; otherwise we could not ascribe the product to art at all; it would be a mere product of chance. But in order to accomplish a purpose, definite rules from which we cannot dispense ourselves are requisite.[39]

It is the peculiar power of the creative imagination that it does not begin with but rather *contributes* the rule to a work of art in the very process of creating it. In Ricoeur's own studies on imagination, Kant's influence can again be perceived. Ricoeur defines the imagination as a "rule-governed form of invention" and a "norm-governed productivity."[40] This "ruled creativity" is best seen, in Ricoeur's opinion, in the phenomenon of story-telling, where the same theme, for example the quest, gives rise to countless variations.[41]

Ricoeur's great discovery about narrative, its "configurative" dimension, was made standing on the shoulders of Kant. Narrative is not only an episodic sequence, but a configurational unity. Ricoeur maintains that it is "[b]y means of the plot [that] goals, causes and chance are brought together within the temporal unity of a whole and complete action."[42] In other words, Ricoeur views the plot as a form of reflective judgment. The plot makes a whole out of a diversity of incidents, characters and actions. The universal is not given in advance, but the rule or unity of this collection of particulars has to be *created*. That Kant's "reflective judgment" is a first cousin to Ricoeur's "plot" is evident from a remark by Ricoeur: "A text is a whole, a totality. The relation between whole and parts – as in a work of art or in an animal – requires a specific kind of 'judgment' for which Kant gives the theory in the third *Critique*."[43]

If the reflective judgment is a power of the creative imagination, the symbol is its product. Whereas the reproductive imagination has to do with images, and the schematizing imagination with concepts, genius or the creative imagination presents Ideas. The creative imagination presents aesthetic ideas, which Kant defines as "that representation of the imagination which occasions much thought, without however any definite thought, i.e. any *concept*, being capable of being adequate to it."[44] Here are the Kantian roots of Ricoeur's oft-cited phrase, "The symbol gives rise to thought." Symbolism supplies what Kant calls a "schematism of analogy": in symbolism we think about an idea (to which no experience corresponds) *as* we think of something to which an experience does correspond. Kant gives the example of a monarchical state which is symbolized by a living body if governed by democratic laws, or alternately by a mere machine if governed by a single autocratic will. The similarity is not between the despotic state and the machine, "but there is a similarity in the rules according to which we reflect upon these two things and their causality."[45] The similarity between an Idea and its symbol is not ontological, but a similarity in the way we are to think about both. Symbolism thus provides a rule for thought – think *as if* – but does not extend our objective knowledge.[46]

Despite the important role symbols play in the *Critique of Judgment* as means for thinking beyond the limits of reason, Kant takes only a few tentative steps towards a thoroughgoing theory of symbols. Kant admits that the matter has not been "sufficiently analyzed hitherto" and deserves a "deeper investigation," but "this is not the place to linger over it."[47] Kant's project is "unfinished," then, to the extent that his theory of symbols and the creative imagination is incomplete. But though Kant does not attempt anything so grandiose as a theory of language or literature, there are a few significant references to poetry in the third *Critique*, references which yield a foretaste of the way Ricoeur will take up Kant's ideas in order to formulate a *literary* imagination.

The poet, says Kant, ventures to make aesthetic and rational ideas, such as eternity or creation, "sensible." And even when the poet presents things of which there are examples in experience – e.g., love, death – he strives "to go beyond the limits of experience and to present them to sense with a completeness of which there is no example in nature."[48] There is even Kantian precedent for extending the notion of schematism into language. It is most significant that Kant deems poetry supreme among the arts:

It strengthens the mind by making it feel its faculty – free, spontaneous, and independent of natural determination – of considering and judging nature as a phenomenon in accordance with aspects which it does not present in experience either for sense or understanding, and therefore of using it on behalf of, and as a sort of schema for, the supersensible.[49]

With the idea of poetry as a schema of the supersensible, the schematizing and symbolizing functions of the imagination converge. It is but a short step from Kant's conception of poetry as a schema of the supersensible to Ricoeur's narrative theory. For narratives are both *verbal* figures and figures of *time*. Indeed, Ricoeur speaks of the "schematism" of the narrative function. By this, he means that narratives, as products of the poetic imagination, give verbal form to that which is beyond the reach of concepts. And as products of the schematizing imagination, narratives give verbal form to that which even the poets can hardly express: time. With his narrative theory, Ricoeur thus gives a surer linguistic orientation and literary application to Kant's symbolizing imagination.

Imagination and hope

If, as Sartre held, the imagination is a function of the unreal, then the projected synthesis of freedom and nature which gives meaning to human existence and moral striving is merely solipsistic and hopeless. This synthesis, what Sartre terms the "ultimate possibility" of man, is really an impossibility, and man is a "useless" passion for the possible.[50] In Sartre, the Kantian demand for practical completion is prematurely cut off. In Ricoeur's continuation of Kant's project, the situation is quite the reverse: here the demand and desire for the completion of the will is not frustrated but fulfilled – at least *poetically*.

We are now in a position to see the extent to which Kant's third *Critique* does in fact address the question of hope. The poetic imagination portrays a purposiveness in nature that is neither a category of the understanding nor a fact of experience, but rather a reflective judgment. We might say that the poetic imagination *contributes* the rule to nature. From now on, nature will be viewed *as if* there were purposiveness, *as if* there were a Creator. As Creation, nature may be viewed in such a way "that the conformity to law of its form at least harmonizes with the possibility of the purposes to be effected in it according to laws of freedom."[51] Kant is here proposing that we think of nature as Creation, and hence, of a nature that is made in such a way that it will not frustrate freedom's actualization. Of course, this harmony between freedom and nature is not an object of knowledge, but a thinking *as if*, a meaningful possibility. According to Kant, this supersensible ground for the reconciliation of nature and freedom is not an object of cognition, but of *feeling*. Feeling is the mental faculty most closely associated to the creative imagination. When we think of nature *as if* it were created, this is less theoretical cognition than moral feeling. As is well known, Kant's work on the productive imagination and its concomitant feeling inspired German Romanticism and eventually Heidegger.[52] Our basic orientation to reality is for Heidegger a matter of "mood." Feelings and moods, evoked by poetic language, orient us to the world and thus have an ontological bearing.

All this bears a close resemblance to Ricoeur's "Poetics of the Will." In his introduction to the whole project of a *Philosophy of the Will*, Ricoeur describes poetry as "the art of conjuring up the world as created."[53] We can consent to this "only human freedom," says Ricoeur, only if we judge the world ultimately suitable for freedom. But suffering and evil make our "yes" to the world a qualified one:

Admiration says, the world is good, it is the *possible* home of freedom; I can consent. Hope says: the world is not the *final* home of freedom; I consent as much as possible, but hope to be delivered of the terrible and at the end of time to enjoy a new body and a new nature granted to freedom.[54]

In *Fallible Man*, Ricoeur examines the freedom of human being as fallible but not fallen. Ricoeur is convinced that evil is not part of the fundamental constitution of human being. The poetic imagination can thus conjure up dreams of innocence, played out at the beginning time. The hope of freedom is linked to this reminiscence of innocence. In *Symbolism of Evil*, Ricoeur deals with the will as actually fallen. Here the imagination dreams of future deliverance, reserved for end-time. In short, the poetic imagination nourishes hope by holding out before the will a possible world in which we yearn to live. Indeed, the special function of poetic language as Ricoeur understands it is to disclose possibilities.[55] Ricoeur's increasing interest in language and texts has given a verbal orientation to his proposed "Poetics" as well. In his most recent work, it would appear that the "Poetics" has become nothing less than the project of developing a philosophy of the literary imagination:

Finally, the constantly postponed project of a "Poetics of the Will" is that of a general philosophy of the creative imagination, considered in turn on the level of semantic innovation and practical representation, on the individual level, and on the cultural and social level.[56]

Once more we see that Kant was there before. One function of reason for Kant was to provide concrete representations of completed human virtue, representations which serve as the goal of moral striving. Philip Rossi suggests that reason here functions as a "moral imagination" and provides access "to that which has, for moral purposes, firm title to be 'most real' – the realm of what ought to be."[57] In the first *Critique*, Kant speaks of the "moral world" that the world can be because of freedom. However, reason can only portray this world as possible:

> To this extent, therefore, it is a mere idea, though at the same time a practical idea, which can really have, as it also ought to have, an influence upon the sensible world, to bring that world, so far as may be possible, into conformity with the idea.[58]

This optimism regarding the influence of moral ideas on actual human history is tempered somewhat by Kant in his later *Religion Within the Limits of Reason Alone*, where he observes: "That 'the world lieth in evil' is a plaint as old as history, old even as the older art poetry."[59] Yet Kant still ventures to suggest that the archetype of the good principle, "which reason presents to us for our zealous emulation, can give us power."[60]

If human being in its moral perfection is the end of creation, Kant only finds this idea represented in a dramatic story: the story of Jesus or the triumph of the Good over the Evil principle in humanity. In answer to the question of what we may hope, Kant leaves us with the *symbol of an idea*. Ricoeur too considers these narratives which represent the regeneration of the will – the end of evil – as indispensable for hope. Moreover, they are neither "within" nor "beyond" the limits of reason alone. They would be beyond the limits if they claimed to contribute to our store of objective knowledge concerning the supersensible. They would be within the bounds of reason if they were reducible to moral allegories. However, the status of narratives concerning the end of evil is for Ricoeur "rather that of a 'schematism' of hope. They are neither 'within' nor 'without' a rational philosophy. They are on the boundary-line."[61]

Can we think the projects of Heidegger and Kant together? To what conception of human being and hope does such a conjunction give rise? The question for narrative in the context of Ricoeur's broader philosophy is simply this: what must the human condition be to account for the possibility of a creative imagination of hope?[62] We have seen that both Heidegger and Kant employ the notions imagination, time and possibility for their respective purposes. We have also seen that Ricoeur's narrative theory provides a surer linguistic and literary foundation for many of their ideas. Together, Heidegger and Kant constitute for Ricoeur a way to conceive human beings as finite while preserving the possibility of hope. By virtue of the imagination, we may go beyond both the present (Heidegger) and the limits of empirical knowledge and practice (Kant) towards the possible:

> Our existence is not literal, but figurative: it is the temporal surpassing of that which is actually given towards a possible horizon always to come. Let us be precise on this point. We are creative beings who figure the world *as* this or that. To "figure" the world ... is to see something here and now *as* something which is not yet.[63]

What Ricoeur takes from Heidegger and Kant is this notion of human existence as "figurative." It is to this conception of human existence, framed in the shadows of Heidegger and Kant, that narrative ultimately responds.

Notes

1 *CPR* A, 805/B, 833. Cf. Kant's letter to C. Fr. Stäudlin, cited in Kant's *Die Religion innerhalb der Grenzen der bloßen Vernunft* (Hamburg, Felix Meiner Verlag, 1978), xxxi.

2 This is Van den Hengel's phrase to describe what he calls Ricoeur's "hermeneutics of hope" (*Home of Meaning*, xix).

3 Kant's first *Critique* describes human understanding; Ricoeur's *Freedom and Nature* describes human volition. The middle volumes of each turn to the practical (practical reason and morality in Kant's second *Critique*; fallibility and fault in Ricoeur's *Fallible Man* and *Symbolism of Evil*). Kant's third *Critique* mediates the concepts of nature and freedom with a critique of aesthetic feeling; Ricoeur has given several indications that his yet unwritten third volume, the "Poetics of the Will," also concerns the ultimate reconciliation of freedom and nature. However, Ricoeur's hints suggest that he will give his "Poetics" a verbal orientation, thus mediating freedom and nature with a specifically literary art. Narrative admirably responds to the need for this kind of mediation, as we shall see (see chapter 5 below).

4 "Hope," 63–4.

5 *H*, 176.

6 In a revealing comment on a collection of his early essays, Ricoeur notes that he is at once obsessed with reconciling unresolved tensions and distrustful of premature solutions. Ricoeur here evidences a post-Hegelian Kantianism even before he coined the phrase. See his *HT*, 11.

7 "BibHerm," 141.

8 "Hope," 60.

9 Ibid., 64.

10 Ibid., 65.

11 *CPR* B, xxx.

12 Cf. Ricoeur's definition in "Foundation": "I will call ethics therefore this movement of actualization, this odyssey of freedom across the world of works, this proof-texting of the being-able-to-do-something (*pouvoir-faire*) in effective actions which bear witness to it. Ethics is the movement between naked and blind belief in a primordial 'I can,' and the real history where I attest to this 'I can'" (177).

13 G. W. F. Hegel, *The Philosophy of Right*, trans. T. M. Knox (Oxford University Press, 1942), Preface, *ad fin.*

14 *CI*, 414.

15 "Hope," 68.

16 Ibid.

17 Cf. Ricoeur's remark in *CI*: "Now, if I ask what is the specifically religious way of speaking about evil, I would not hesitate for a moment to answer: the language is that of hope" (436).

18 "BibHerm," 145.

19 Michel Despland, *Kant on History and Religion* (Montreal, McGill-Queen's University Press, 1973), 160. According to Despland, the second *Critique* raises the question of hope in an a-temporal way: "It speaks of joining happiness to virtue, not historical success to moral effort" (271).

20 "Hope," 68.

21 *CJ*, 34. Cf. Kant's note on the same page defending his characteristic tripartite divisions, a stylistic feature which Ricoeur also inherits.

22 Despland, *Kant on History and Religion*, 302 n. 30.

23 In Kant's words: "the faculty of representing in intuition an object that is not itself present" (*CPR* B, 151).

24 "Imagination," 4.

25 *SE*, 13.

26 Ibid.

27 *CPR* A, 138/B, 177.

28 Ibid., A, 141/B, 180.

29 "NarDisc," 61.

30 Kant writes: "We thus find that the schema of each category contains and makes capable of representation only a determination of time [*Zeitinbegriff*]" (*CPR* A, 145/B, 184).

31 *CPR* A, 140/B, 179–80.

32 Heidegger's *Kant and the Problem of Metaphysics* (Bloomington, Indiana University Press, 1962 [1927]) is another re-reading of Kant. According to Heidegger, the theme of the first *Critique* is the finitude of man. Heidegger believes that Kant discovered the temporality of human being but then, in the second edition, "recoiled from the ground which he himself had established" (221). Heidegger assigns an importance to Kant's chapter on schematism which far belies its modest size: "these eleven pages of the *Critique of Pure Reason* form the heart of the whole work" (94). Heidegger calls Kant's

"productive imagination" the "ontological imagination," "because it sets out in advance the to-be characteristics which we are able to discern in the things that appear to us" (135). For a more extended treatment of Heidegger's "retrieval" of Kant, see the stimulating study by Charles M. Sherover, *Heidegger, Kant and Time* (Bloomington, Indiana University Press, 1971). Sherover's "Postscript: Being, Possibility and Time" is especially important for our purposes. Sherover writes: "perhaps the central lesson of Heidegger's retrieve of Kant is the retrieve of the primordial problematic of the nature and Being of the Possible ..." (288). Sherover makes no attempt to relate imagination or schematism to narrative, but this is precisely the point of Ricoeur's work. Can Ricoeur's narrative theory better treat the "nature and Being of the Possible"?

33 As we shall see in chapter 5, Ricoeur construes many works of modern fiction as themselves "tales about time." The experiments with time so common in contemporary fiction can thus be seen as distant relations to Kant's schema.

34 Figurative language (metaphor) and figurative literature (narrative) are the subjects of chapters 4 and 5 respectively.

35 "BibHerm," 143.

36 *CJ*, 15.

37 *CPR* A, 132/B, 171.

38 *CJ*, 150.

39 Ibid., 153.

40 See his "BibImag," 49ff. Ricoeur acknowledges the influence of Kant: "This is how Kant conceived imagination in his *Critique of Judgment* by coordinating the free play of the imagination in a teleology that had no goal beyond itself" (49–50). That the imagination is rule-governed is important in another respect: it is precisely this rule-governedness that renders works of the creative imagination susceptible to explanation.

41 Ricoeur similarly appeals to Chomsky's work on "generative grammar" as an example of "ruled creativity." The sentence is the best illustration that language is an infinite use of finite means.

42 *TN* I, ix.

43 *HHS*, 211.

44 *CJ*, 157.

45 *CJ*, 198.

46 All "knowledge" about God is symbolical in Kant's view. See section 59 "Of Beauty as the Symbol of Morality" in *CJ*. Despland claims that Kant finds in symbolism "the general answer to the problem of what language we can apply to the supersensible" (*Kant on History and Religion*, 150). Indeed, Despland describes Kant's investigation of the supersensible as a philosophy of religion which tries to "think normatively about symbols" (155). In a similar vein, Philip Rossi calls Kant a "Christian philosopher" whose subject matter is Christian symbols ("Kant as a Christian Philosopher: Hope and the Symbols of Christian Faith," *PT* 25 [1981], 24–33).

47 *CJ*, 198.
48 Ibid., 158.
49 Ibid., 171.
50 Sartre, *L'Etre et le néant*, 139–41.
51 *CJ*, 12.
52 See Stephen Prickett's treatment of the "poetic" in German Romanticism and Heidegger in his *Words and the Word: Language, Poetics and Biblical Interpretation* (Cambridge University Press, 1986), ch. 2 "The peculiar language of heaven ..." Prickett notes that for the Romantics, poetic language and the feelings it evokes is what makes man human.
53 *FN*, 30.
54 Ibid., 480.
55 "Myth," 45.
56 *HHS*, 39.
57 Rossi, "Kant as Christian Philosopher," 27.
58 *CPR* A, 808/B, 836.
59 Kant, *Religion Within the Limits of Reason Alone* (New York, Harper Torchbooks, 1960), 15.
60 Ibid., 54. The extent to which the notion that ideas have power is a response to Marx's eleventh thesis on Feuerbach will be considered in later chapters.
61 "BibHerm," 145.
62 In Ricoeur's words: "So the question is whether it is possible to overcome what I called above a lateral and partial approach to the problem of creativity and to conceive a philosophical anthropology which would deepen into an ontology of finitude" (*HHS*, 39).
63 Kearney, *Poétique du possible*, 32.

4

Metaphor, poetry, and the possible

Human being, marked by the passion for the possible, constantly projects itself beyond the readily identifiable here and now. This capacity imaginatively to form future projects and orient oneself to them sets human existence apart from other types of life. No other beings "figure" the world as something it is not or is not yet. To be human is to create such figures.[1] Ricoeur therefore proposes to begin his philosophical anthropology with a study of human creativity. Now the most striking evidence of human creativity for Ricoeur is our use of language. It is thanks to language that we can "figure" out what we will do "tomorrow." And in poetry as nowhere else we see the myriad ways that a limited number of signs – the twenty-four letters of the Roman alphabet to be exact – have been arranged to speak to and about the depths of human being.[2] Language as spoken and written is truly the infinite use of finite means. Ricoeur's fundamental philosophical "wager" is that he will have a better understanding of human being by attending to creative language.[3] If to be human means to be constituted by a passion for the possible, then Ricoeur needs to examine the language of the possible. For if human existence is "figurative," what better place to explore it than language which is figurative? The present chapter therefore studies the significance of metaphor for Ricoeur's general philosophical project. What are the implications for meaning and truth of a philosophy, and theology, that focuses on metaphor?

Ricoeur's work on metaphor is part of his general project of rehabilitating the creative imagination. In the tradition of earlier German Romantic philosophers, Ricoeur believes that the creative imagination is a, if not the, quintessential "humanizing" capacity. Like Kant, he sees poetry as chief among the liberal arts or "humanities." Ricoeur carries the Romantic tradition further, however, by seeking intelligibility

56

for a poetic power that usually is associated more with intuition and mysticism.[4] His book on metaphor methodically explores the phenomenon of the creation of meaning. In keeping with his linguistic and literary orientation of the imagination (the moral of his revision of Kant), Ricoeur studies this phenomenon as it occurs in language. He locates it in creative language, especially metaphors and narratives. Ricoeur's work on metaphor represents a concentrated effort to deal with the verbal dimension of the creative imagination. In so doing, Ricoeur hopes to render the workings of the creative imagination more accessible. The question of creativity is habitually either too easy or too difficult: too easy, insofar as it invites imprecision and waffling; too difficult in that it is "an art hidden in the depths of the soul."

The significance of Ricoeur the philosopher's fascination with metaphor should not be lost. Though traditionally metaphor and other forms of poetic language have not been the object of much philosophical investigation, Ricoeur has succeeded in incorporating metaphor into both the style and substance of his thought. We have already mentioned that Ricoeur's style of philosophy is one of imaginative mediation: he is able to perceive interesting similarities and connections in what appears to be an irreconcilable opposition. But this is precisely the work of a good metaphor too. But metaphor also informs the substance of Ricoeur's work. With regard to epistemology, metaphor appears as a unique cognitive instrument for exploring the real. With regard to ontology, the language of metaphor gives Ricoeur access to the field of the possible, thus expanding the "real." To the extent that his philosophy of religion is informed by a passion for the possible, Ricoeur is less interested in a knowledge of "what is" than in imagining what "might be." Because of its capacity to express and create possibilities, metaphor is ideally suited to be the discourse of a theology that is oriented to eschatology.

Poetic, scientific and "ordinary" language

Bertrand Russell once commented, "The study of grammar, in my opinion, is capable of throwing far more light on philosophical questions than is commonly supposed by philosophers."[5] This remark could today represent the belief of a large number of philosophers in the Anglo-American tradition whose philosophical method is indeed characterized by a close analysis and description of language and its uses.[6] On the one hand, the grammatical form may mislead, obscuring a logical distinction; on the other hand, charting the uses of a term may elucidate a philosophical problem. Though Russell and the earlier Wittgenstein preferred the precision of formal or artificial languages to the ambiguity and impreciseness of informal or ordinary language, the later Wittgenstein began his philosophy from the richness of everyday uses of language.

Ricoeur too begins his philosophy from the fullness of language. Everything has been said before philosophy, but philosophy must "recover" it. As one who understands philosophy to be reflection on human existence, however, Ricoeur deals primarily with language of existential significance. That is, his concern with the meaning (i.e., the range of possibilities) of human being rather than with its mere description leads Ricoeur to focus on poetic language rather than "ordinary" language, for reasons that will soon become apparent. His project is, therefore, both like and unlike that of most philosophers of linguistic analysis.[7] For though it does call for sustained reflection, the field of poetic language is not as susceptible to exact conceptual clearing. In an early programmatic essay, "The Hermeneutics of Symbols and Philosophical Reflection," Ricoeur states his wish to join the rationality of philosophy to the "revealing power" of symbols.[8] Borrowing from Kant's *Critique of Judgment*, Ricoeur adopts as his personal and philosophical maxim the formula "The symbol gives rise to thought." Ricoeur's project of thinking about human being does not begin in the vacuum of pure subjectivity. Ricoeur assumes that knowledge about the self must proceed by way of hermeneutic reflection. We cannot "see" ourselves directly; rather, we must "read" ourselves by interpreting what we say and do. It is just here that the poet assumes an important role, for it is the poet above all who struggles and works with language to express the human condition. Faced with poetic symbols and myths, Ricoeur wagers that we are in contact not with an individual's expression of his private feelings, but with the great universal features of humanity. Reflection on existence therefore needs the sustenance of symbols and poetry. A slight alteration of a Kantian thought sums up Ricoeur's position on this matter: poetry without philosophy is blind; philosophy without poetry is empty.[9]

The basic feature of language according to Ricoeur is polysemy: the phenomenon of each word in ordinary language having more than one meaning. Take, for example, the word "arm." Its meaning varies according to its context: "The bomb is unarmed," "One cannot escape the long arm of the law," "God will deliver us by his strong right arm." In none of these three cases does "arm" refer primarily to the actual limb by virtue of which we grasp or do things. In ordinary language, then, unwanted possible meanings are screened out by the sentence or the overall context of discourse. Polysemy, the potential meanings of a word, is limited only by actual instances of speech.

Ricoeur views scientific and poetic language as two strategies applied to the problem of polysemy. Why is polysemy a problem? When unchecked, polysemy becomes ambiguity, and ambiguity, if acute enough, threatens communication and therefore one of the chief functions of language itself.[10] Scientific language attempts systematically to eliminate ambiguity. It does so by exaggerating the tendency of ordinary language to define or delimit the range of possible meanings. Ricoeur suggests that the ''mathematization'' of nature which is the legacy of the Galilean and Copernican revolutions leads to a similar exigency for exactitude in the language of science. This tendency reaches its extreme in the construction of artificial languages, such as those invented for computers, where the murkiness of ordinary language is banished in the clear light of mathematical and logical symbols. And, citing Russell and the early Wittgenstein as examples, Ricoeur notes that this urge for conceptual transparency has sometimes led to an attempt to banish ambiguity from all types of discourse – ethical, political, aesthetic and even religious.[11]

Although science is embarrassed by ambiguity, poetry exults in it, as does Ricoeur the philosopher. But what benefit does Ricoeur hope to gain by allowing ambiguity to intrude in his philosophy? Just this: by magnifying polysemy, by making words and sentences mean all that they can mean, Ricoeur hopes to bring back to language its capacity for meaningfulness. Though scientific language is clear and precise, it is not existentially *nourishing*. It has everything to do with the empirical world, and nothing to do with the existential. For Ricoeur, this omission of existence is the ''original philosophical sin.''[12] Such a philosophy does not *speak* to us. It does not give us new meanings. Poetic language is, on the other hand, creative of meaning. Polysemy for Ricoeur is a virtue, not a vice, of language. In their own ways, then, symbols, metaphors and poems *give* something vitally important to be thought. This, at least, is part of Ricoeur's *credo*. Ricoeur believes

that language, which bears symbols, is not so much spoken by man as spoken to men, that men are born into language, into the light of the logos ''who enlightens every man who comes into the world.'' It is this expectation, this confidence, this belief, that confers on the study of symbols its particular seriousness. To be truthful, I must say it is what animates all my research.[13]

In Ricoeur's view of the contemporary situation, polysemy seems more the solution than the problem. In a culture dominated by science and technology, the primary danger is the loss of meaningfulness. The world is there to be used, not valued. Objects are there to be mastered, not cherished. Ricoeur fears that such a view of the world is in danger of losing the human itself. It is only thanks to the poetic dimension of language that we can view the world as "meaningful" and not merely "manipulable." Ultimately, Ricoeur traces this technological orientation to the world and concomitant loss of meaningfulness back not to a scientific but a philosophical revolution: Descartes' elevation of the knowing subject into a position of epistemological superiority over the known object misleads by implying that the subject is somehow detached from the world. The knowing subject autonomously constitutes objects more than they constitute him. In this schema, the subject is the giver of meaning, primarily by naming and predicating. But the end result of Descartes' subject – object distinction is the alienation of human being from the world. As we shall see, Ricoeur turns to poetry in order to overcome the distance which separates the subject from the world. Poetic feeling, as the Romantics well knew, alone restores the longing-for and sense of belonging-to the world. In any case, because of science's focus on empirical objects and Descartes' separation of subject and object, Ricoeur believes that in our contemporary situation language is increasingly viewed as purely instrumental.[14] The only language that is allowed to be "meaningful" – literal language – is that which refers to empirical objects. Whereas scientific language encourages us to look at things in terms of how they might be used, poetic language impedes this "fanaticism of the manipulable."[15] Ricoeur is adamant about the redemptive or humanizing power of the poetic imagination:

What would the stirring spectacle of this perceived world, the matrix of our existence, be if the artist did not convey to us the joy of it ... By preserving color, sound, and the flavor of the word, the artist, without willing it explicitly, revives the most primitive truth of the world of our life which the scientist shrouds. By creating figures and myths, the artist interprets the world ... *Poetry is a criticism of life.*[16]

Ricoeur's perception of the wasteland of contemporary language provides the necessary backdrop to appreciate his theory of poetic language, of which metaphor is the prime instance. When philosophers refuse to take metaphor or poetic language seriously, they reinforce the prejudice that the only adequate relation between language and reality is the literal and that reality itself is limited to the actual and the manipulable. Literal or descriptive language alone ultimately diminishes human being because it is unable to articulate those fundamental values that orient our lives. In sum, scientific and literal language fail to serve humanity because they are unable to express the possible. Bereft of this access to the possible, humanity loses its passion and must resign itself either to the actual or to the necessary, to "what is" or "what must be" – not to "what might be."

Feeling

Poetry is of supreme value because it resists this reduction of the world to the actual. The poet, says Ricoeur, "is the one who saves the words and even expands the meaning of the words."[17] The relation between man and man and between man and world is not sufficiently expressed by descriptive language. The relation is not merely instrumental. Poetry struggles to express these more profound relations by restoring the capacity of language to speak about them. In Ricoeur's view, certain experiences and aspects of human existence can be expressed only if the poet rejuvenates or recreates language. Poetry fights against the "flattening" of language, and against the "flattening" of human experience.[18] There is in poetry, therefore, a tendency to stretch, cultivate, play with language for the sake of discovering new ways for expressing vital human experiences: "On the one hand, to give a voice to lost layers of experience and on the other hand, to liberate language from its relation to things and to reality."[19] The poet is the one who breaks the bond between language and things on one level in order to express significant truths about the human condition on another.

Two mistaken prejudices about poetry and the imagination are current among contemporary thinkers according to Ricoeur. First, the notion that "the poet nothing affirmeth," that is, the idea that because poetry does not describe the actual world it does not say anything about reality. It is Ricoeur's thesis that though poetry yields no *information* about the world, it does indeed reach and express another "layer" of reality.

Secondly, philosophers frequently deride poetry because it is said to express "feelings."[20] Ricoeur agrees, but then asks, what *is* a feeling? A feeling is much more than an "emotion."[21] It is a way of orienting oneself in the world. Feelings relate us to the world in quite a different manner than does knowledge. At the same time, Ricoeur insists that feelings are intentional acts that have intentional objects or referents. Whereas knowledge tends to make the subject feel "distant" from the

object, feelings "involve" us with things on another level. The mystery
of feeling for Ricoeur is that we have to do not only with subjective states
but with our profound connection to beings and Being. Through poetry,
things that we normally take for granted, say ocean waves, become
objects of concern. Ricoeur appeals precisely to this example in a
discussion of a German Romantic poet:

The "joyous undulation of the waves" in Hölderlin's poem is neither an
objective reality in the positivist sense nor a mood in the emotivist sense. Such
a contrast applies to a conception in which reality is first reduced to scientific
objectivity.[22]

Feelings insert us in the world in a non-objectifying manner. Thanks
to poetry, we no longer feel alienated from the world, but rather we feel
as though we somehow "belong" to it. At the limit, poetry is able to
create a bond of love between the reader and the world.

  Ricoeur is here echoing Heidegger's claim that our feelings or
"moods" have ontological bearing; they are the means by which we
"tune" ourselves to reality.[23] Ricoeur defines "mood" as "a specific
manner of being in the world and relating oneself to it."[24] Poetry is
therefore related to the world. It refers not to particular objects but to
the vision of the whole. It creates not objects but a general atmosphere.
Thanks to poetic feeling, one can view the things of the world not as
something foreign to my existence, but as things of value to my
existence. In Ricoeur's words: "Nothing is more ontological than
feeling. It is by means of feeling that we inhabit the world."[25] Here
then is a relation to the world that is no longer that of alienation and
manipulation. In cultivating feelings, then, poetry humanizes both the
world and our relation to it. Consequently, the philosopher in search
of the meaning of human being must attend to human feelings as well
as to poetic language. This is precisely what Ricoeur does.

Metaphorical sense: surplus of meaning

Thomas Hobbes is perhaps representative of many philosophers in his
dismissal of the cognitive value of metaphor. Hobbes discusses metaphor
in a section on abuses of speech, and locates it between self-deception
and lying. Metaphor is an abuse of speech because words are used "in
other senses than they are ordained for – and thereby deceive
others."[26] Aristotle's famous definition is characteristic of how
metaphor is viewed in traditional rhetoric: "Metaphor consists in giving
the thing a name that belongs to something else."[27] On this view,

metaphor is a deviant naming, where one word (the figurative) is substituted for another (the literal) on the basis of a presumed resemblance. What is important here is the assumption that the resemblance is discovered apart from the metaphor. The metaphor is simply an embellishment, and a dispensable one at that. This "substitution theory" of metaphor assumes first, that literal language is "normal" or proper, and second, that metaphor involves the exchange of words.[28] It is understood that metaphor may be "translated" back to its literal form. There is no creation but only a substitution of meaning. Metaphor may be said in another, better way. Accordingly, metaphor appears merely to be an ornament of language, icing on the cake of speech, a pretty device that yields no new information about reality. Metaphor adorns but does not teach. Its value is emotive rather than cognitive.

For Ricoeur, the substitution model fails to explain the "fundamental problem" of metaphor, namely, the creation of meaning. Ricoeur prefers the more recent "interaction theory" of metaphor to explain this phenomenon of semantic innovation.[29] On this view, metaphor is not a matter of substituting words but rather of a tension within the whole sentence, a tension that arises because of an "impertinent predication" that, taken literally, does not make sense ("Time is a beggar"). In his crucial third chapter of *The Rule of Metaphor*, Ricoeur moves decisively from a word oriented theory of metaphor as deviant naming to a sentence oriented theory of metaphor as deviant predication. From now on, Ricoeur will speak of metaphorical *statements*.[30] This is a most important move, for it allows Ricoeur to discuss metaphorical *discourse* rather than metaphor as a misplaced lexical entity. As an instance of discourse, metaphor is something said to someone about something. The statement has a metaphorical sense, a metaphorical reference, and is addressed to a hearer. Ricoeur's contribution to a theory of metaphor is to be found just here, in his analysis of metaphor as a form of discourse.[31]

Adam named the animals, but language makes sense of the world in ways that go beyond attaching labels to it. For Ricoeur, discourse is nothing less than "the creative process of giving form to both the human mind and the world ... this power of indefinitely extending the battlefront of the expressed at the expense of the unexpressed."[32] In this verbal battle, metaphor is the principal strategy of attack. How does metaphor work? How does it say new things? A metaphorical statement, if taken literally, is absurd. If the reader is to make sense of this absurd predication, he does so not so much by perceiving a resemblance as by creating it.[33] Ricoeur holds that the absurd literal meaning is merely the negative condition for a new "making sense." Against the substitution theory's claim that the metaphor is made on the basis of an already known resemblance ("Time is a beggar in this and this respect"), Ricoeur contends that this new-found similarity is actually the work of the creative imagination.

Metaphor operates by "confusing the established logical boundaries for the sake of detecting new similarities which previous categorization prevented our noticing."[34] Metaphor brings together two categories that previously were "far" and makes them "near" (who would have thought that time and beggars had something in common?). By bringing two previously "distant" ideas together, metaphor *creates a resemblance* between them. Ricoeur says that metaphors are intentional category mistakes: things that do not normally belong together are brought together, and from the resulting tension a new connection is discovered that our previous ways of classifying the world hid from us. In mediating this logical opposition, metaphor makes sense of what would otherwise be nonsense. Metaphor therefore "designates the general process by which we grasp kinship, break the distance between remote ideas, build similarities on dissimilarities."[35] The resemblance that metaphor initiates "is nothing else than this rapprochement which reveals a generic kinship between heterogeneous ideas."[36] Metaphor makes new connections thanks to the creative imagination, which spots similarities in differences.[37] In Ricoeur's account, therefore, metaphor is a unique cognitive instrument: first, metaphors are not susceptible of a literal paraphrase; and second, metaphors tell us something new about reality. We cannot have the creative insight apart from the metaphorical statement.[38] Moreover, we cannot dispense with the metaphor. The meaning of the metaphor is always richer than our attempts to paraphrase it. There is a "surplus" of meaning in the metaphor. Ricoeur thus rehabilitates metaphor and rescues it from its pedestrian fate as mere "window dressing" to discourse. Henceforth, says Ricoeur, "I will consider metaphor as the touchstone of the cognitive value of literary works …"[39]

To read some of its recent champions is to be struck by metaphor's new-found epistemological responsibilities. Ricoeur agrees with those philosophers of science who suggest that scientific discovery proceeds by metaphorical imagination. Max Black and Mary Hesse, among others, have compared scientific models to metaphors. Both scientist and poet are investigating their respective aspects of the real by constructing linguistic models. Mary Hesse states that rationality consists in the continuous adaptation of our language to our continuously expanding world, "and metaphor is one of the chief means by which this is accomplished."[40] Similarly, revolutions in science often involve a change of metaphors.[41] Human beings think metaphorically: unlike computers, we make imaginative connections. Thanks to metaphors, we are ever setting the familiar in the context of the unfamiliar in order to glimpse the world in new ways. It would not be too far off to say that for Ricoeur, *all human discovery is by way of metaphoric invention.* The creative imagination, seen particularly in its verbal form of metaphor, is the primary means by which we explore and colonize the world with our language.[42]

Aristotle says that "a good metaphor implies an intuitive perception of the similarity in dissimilars."[43] Metaphor involves both seeing and constructing: "It is at once the 'gift of genius' and the skill of the geometer."[44] To say "Time is a beggar" is simultaneously to invent and discover. But what, asks Ricoeur, is it to perceive similarity? Aristotle says that metaphor has the power to "set before the eyes." Metaphor is thus the point of intersection of "saying" and "seeing as," and as such, it is the foundation for Ricoeur's verbal orientation of the imagination. Interestingly enough, the "image" in Ricoeur's theory of the creative imagination comes not at the beginning but at the end of his metaphor theory. Metaphor is a strategy for seeing as, but the image is ruled by the verbal figure.[45] The reader's imagination must follow the semantic direction of the metaphor.[46] Only then can sense be won from apparent nonsense. Somehow, Time must be seen *as* a beggar. Ricoeur likens the metaphorical process to Kant's theory of schematism: to imagine is not to have a picture of something, but to generate images out of language. Metaphor does not reproduce, but rather produces, a likeness. Ricoeur works a Kantian variation on Aristotle's notion that metaphor "sets before the eyes."[47]

Just as Ricoeur reincorporates "image" in his understanding of metaphor as a cognitive instrument, so too "feeling" plays an important role. Both "seeing as" and "feeling" are necessary to achieve the semantic bearing of metaphor.[48] The new predication (i.e., the beggarly quality of time) is not only seen but felt. Like metaphor itself, feeling overcomes distance: "To *feel* ... is to make *ours* what has been put at a distance by thought in its objectifying phase."[49] As metaphor abolishes the logical distance, so feelings abolish the existential distance between the knowing subject and the known object. Thanks to *seeing* time as a beggar, we are now *related* to time in a new way. And just as metaphors abolish the literal meaning of a statement, so poetic feelings transcend "literal" emotions, that is, emotions that correspond to objects in the world (for instance, one hates spinach). The feelings to which metaphors give rise find no correlates among the empirical things of the world. This denial of "literal" feelings is only the negative condition for a more profound relation to the world. For the poetic feelings that Ricoeur has in mind, feelings such as "anxiety" or "joy," do not correspond to any particular objects in the world. Rather, they are ways of orienting oneself to life itself, and they are bound not to objects but to metaphors and poems. Metaphors, therefore, not only yield new insights into reality, but also suggest new ways of orienting oneself in the world.

Lacking in Ricoeur's otherwise brilliant philosophical rehabilitation of metaphor is any indication of how one may judge the difference between good and bad metaphors. Also, does the primary onus for making sense of what would otherwise be an absurd predication lie with the author of the metaphor or its reader? Though Ricoeur speaks of metaphor as an "intentional category mistake," he seems reluctant to say that an author first has an insight and then translates it into a metaphor. If this were how metaphors were made, one would have to conclude that there was some non-metaphorical access to this new vision of the world. But such independent access is precisely what Ricoeur denies by rejecting the substitution theory of metaphor and by insisting that metaphors perform a unique cognitive function. The question is simply this: if metaphors are our only access to a redescription of the real, how can we know whether or not to believe the metaphor? If what the metaphor affirms cannot be checked by non-metaphorical means, how can we tell the difference between a helpful and a misleading metaphor?

A recent work on the cognitive function of metaphor in religious and scientific understanding by Mary Gerhart and Allen Russell addresses this very problem.[50] *Metaphoric Process: The Creation of Scientific and Religious Understanding* builds on Ricoeur's theory of metaphor and argues that both religious and scientific understanding grow by a metaphoric process. The authors distinguish this process from constructing analogies. With Ricoeur, they insist that metaphor "invents ideas"[51] and causes us to look at the world in a new way. But they take us no farther than did Ricoeur when they attempt to explain how one gains the insight from which metaphor emerges. They speak vaguely of a "Eureka experience" or an "ontological flash."[52] Such metaphors do not reassure those who worry about the apparent subjectivity of metaphors that flow from private experience. Are we really to believe that a metaphor and the scientific or religious model it generates "fits" reality simply on the basis of an individual's ontological flash?

As we shall see in Part II, Ricoeur does believe that there are criteria for distinguishing between good and bad metaphors. The most important criterion is that of illumination: does a particular metaphor make my experience of the world more meaningful or intelligible? For Ricoeur, this type of query leads not to an empirical but rather "existential" verification. As Sallie McFague correctly observes, however, making my experience more meaningful does not necessarily mean describing what it is actually like. Theological metaphors and models, she contends, do not show us life as conventionally lived but life as it could, or should, be lived. In other words, existential verification acknowledges that the possibility opened up by the metaphor is an illuminating one. It still remains to be seen whether a given possibility, however illuminating or meaningful, is one that can be realized or made actual in life. Only such a possibility, I believe, deserves to be called "true."

Metaphorical truth: a surplus of being

There is more in the well-chosen metaphor than can be captured by speculative thought. This surplus or abundance of meaning is the glory of metaphorical discourse. But it is only when we raise the question of reference that we can fully appreciate the significance of Ricoeur's treating metaphor as a species of discourse. Viewed as an improperly applied name, as the substitution theory maintains, metaphor no more reaches the world than do other instances of deviant naming, such as "The present king of France is bald." Viewed as an instance of discourse, metaphor, like all kinds of discourse, has both a sense and a referent. What do metaphors refer to? No less a philosopher than Gottlob Frege, from whom Ricoeur borrows the distinction between sense and reference, disallowed any kind of reference other than the literal. Considering an example from epic poetry, Frege held that the proper name *Ulysses* had no reference.[53] In contrast to science, poetry has only sense and not reference. Ricoeur is quick to repudiate such a suggestion: "My whole aim is to do away with this restriction of reference to scientific statements."[54] As discourse, metaphor enjoys the "power to refer to a reality outside language."[55] With this idea, Ricoeur brings his work on metaphor "to its most important theme, namely, that metaphor is the rhetorical process by which discourse unleashes the power that certain fictions have to redescribe reality."[56]

Ricoeur's rehabilitation of the creative imagination, as well as his mediation of the dichotomy between the real and imaginary, ultimately depends on his ability to frame an intelligible concept of metaphorical reference.

Ricoeur notes that it is not only philosophers and scientists but linguists and literary critics who deny that metaphor and poetry refer. On the one hand, logical positivists claim that all non-descriptive language is merely emotive, expressing the poet's inner state but nothing about the world. This epistemological prejudice against the referential function of poetic language is reinforced by many literary critics, such as Northrop Frye, who distinguishes "literature" from other types of discourse because its movement is "centripetal" or towards itself rather than "centrifugal" or towards the world. In informative or descriptive discourse, says Frye, language "points to" or "stands for" something. In literary discourse, however, language represents nothing outside itself but simply links the verbal parts to the verbal whole. The poet constructs a *coherent* verbal structure that is fully self-contained; the scientist constructs a verbal structure that *corresponds* to the world.[57]

While Ricoeur agrees that metaphors and poems initially break the relation between language and thing, he claims that the language–world relation is restored on a higher level: "Just as the metaphorical statement captures its sense as metaphorical midst the ruins of the literal sense, it also achieves its reference upon the ruins of what might be called (in symmetrical fashion) its literal reference."[58] Abolishing this descriptive reference frees the metaphorical statement to refer to reality in another way: "metaphor is that strategy of discourse by which language divests itself of its function of direct description in order to reach the mythic level where its function of discovery is set free."[59] Freed from the constraints of description, metaphor is free to *redescribe* reality.[60] In this regard, metaphors function much like scientific models. Ricoeur appeals to the work of philosophers of science who view theoretical models as having a similar heuristic power of redescribing realities inaccessible to direct description. Metaphors and models are creative imitations of reality: "both poetic and scientific language aim at a reality more real than the appearances."[61] The creation of heuristic fictions is the road to discovering new aspects about the real: "It would seem that the enigma of metaphorical discourse is that it 'invents' in both senses of the word: what it creates, it discovers; and what it finds, it invents."[62]

But what is this deeper reality to which metaphor refers? One way to characterize it would be to say that it is "human" reality. Poets are not interested in describing the way nature works; rather, they establish another world, a world "that corresponds to other possibilities of existence, to possibilities that would be most deeply our own."[63] Poetry and metaphors explore (and, as we shall see, expand) the human condition. The "world" is more than the sum total of things and processes, causes and effects: "It is by virtue of an unjustifiable reduction that we decide to equate 'world' with the whole of observable facts."[64] Metaphors and poetry display different feelings, different ways of orienting oneself to the world. The poet is more interested in redescribing the world, in seeing and feeling the world *as*. It is because metaphors and poetry project different manners of orienting oneself to reality – different feelings – that Ricoeur can say that poetic language makes a *Welt* – a habitable world – out of an *Umwelt* – environment.[65]

But if metaphors can refer to reality, if reality can be redescribed, then what is reality? What is truth? Ricoeur does not shy away from these questions. Indeed, he acknowledges that what is ultimately at stake in his theory of metaphorical reference is nothing less than the meaning of "reality" and "truth." In sketching out his concept of metaphorical truth, Ricoeur appeals to the tension in the metaphorical statement between its absurd literal sense and its metaphoric meaning. He locates the main source of tension in the copula of the verb "to be": "The metaphorical 'is' at once signifies both 'is not' and 'is like'."[66] The heart of the metaphorical statement is the verb "to be." Metaphors do not describe what things literally *are*, but they redescribe what things are *like*. Ricoeur refers to the preamble to Majorcan fairy tales, "the wonderful 'It was and it was not,' which contains *in nuce* all that can be said about metaphorical truth."[67]

On the one hand, we must not ignore the "is not" of the metaphorical "is." To believe that Time is literally a beggar is ontologically naive and false. On the other hand, Ricoeur does not wish to exaggerate the "is not" and so lose the "is." Metaphor is not simply a subterfuge that needs to be demythologized. Ricoeur resists reducing the claim of the metaphorical "is" to a weak-kneed "as-if." In mediating these two extremes, Ricoeur believes he does better justice to the "tensional" character of the metaphorical "is" and to metaphorical truth itself. "Is there something like metaphor-faith beyond demythologization? A second *naïveté* beyond iconoclasm? ... Can one create metaphors without believing them and without believing that, in a certain way, 'that is'?"[68] In a metaphorical affirmation, "is like" involves both "is" and "is not." If metaphors truly refer and refer truly, then "tension must be introduced into metaphorically affirmed being."[69] *The ultimate*

implication of Ricoeur's theory of metaphorical reference is that what it is "to be"
is itself redescribed.

In Western thought, truth has traditionally been associated with
present being, "what is" or actuality. Truth was defined as the
correspondence of mind to what is (the actual) – as *adequatio intellectus*
et rei. Ricoeur believes that metaphorical truth demands a new notion
of being, one in which a "being-as" would correspond to the "seeing-
as" initiated by metaphor. In eleven dense pages (the same number as
Kant's section on schematism), Ricoeur undertakes in the conclusion
to *The Rule of Metaphor* an ontological clarification of "being-as." How
are we to think this "being as"? What does metaphorical discourse give
to thought? What does metaphor bring to language that would otherwise
be inaccessible? We shall see that Ricoeur links the expansion of our
language to a commensurate expansion of being. That is, the poetic
capacity of metaphor to create meaning is also a capacity of being. What
metaphors refer to is the creativity of being itself.

Metaphor first challenges our ordinary conceptions of reality; it
shatters and increases "our sense of reality by shattering and increasing
our language."[70] Metaphor refers to a world that is "deeper" than the
world of empirical objects where "being" is limited to the here and now,
to the actual. Similarly, metaphor enlarges the concept "truth" so that
it is not merely the truth of empirical verification. Most importantly,
metaphor enlarges our vision of the world by expanding the real to
include the "possible." Ricoeur turns once again to Aristotle as a source
of inspiration: according to Aristotle, "live" metaphors, ones in which
the tension is still present, "represent things as in a state of activity."[71]
Ricoeur's paraphrase is worth pondering: "*Lively* expression is that
which expresses existence as *alive*."[72] Ricoeur suggests that it was
perhaps because the Greeks did not simply equate *phusis* (Nature) with
some inert "given" that they were able to construct *creative* imitations
of nature.[73] In a similar way, metaphor does not refer to the real as if
it were an inert given. Rather, metaphor presents things "as in act,"
as *becoming*. This is the "*ontological* function of metaphorical discourse,
in which every dormant potentiality of existence appears *as* blossoming
forth, every latent capacity for action *as* actualized."[74] In other words,
corresponding to the polysemy of language is a polysemy of being: "the
reference of metaphorical utterance brings being as actuality and
potentiality into play."[75]

While literal language can speak only of the actual and so limits the
real to what is, metaphor speaks of the possible. With Aristotle, Ricoeur
considers possibility (potentiality, power) a bona fide mode of being.[76]

But in the closing pages of *The Rule of Metaphor* Aristotle's "signifying things in act" is given a peculiarly Heideggerian twist. Ricoeur suggests that seeing things *as* in act is to see them as naturally "blossoming forth." But this is to see things as having possibility and the power to become:

> Would the poet then be the one who perceives power as act and act as power? He who sees as whole and complete what is sketchy and in process, who perceives every form attained as a promise of newness?[77]

New meaning blossoms forth from metaphor just as new possibilities blossom forth from Being. Metaphor refers to the real as a dynamic becoming rather than a static being. We have already seen that Heidegger privileges possibility over actuality in his quest for the meaning of Being.[78] But for Heidegger the *place* where existence "blossoms forth" is *language*. Being shows itself in language in an "event" (*Ereignis*). Philosophers have always sought a means for speaking and thinking about Being. But though Heidegger and Ricoeur agree that Being includes the possible, Heidegger lacked the means to *say* it and to *think* it.[79] In his theory of metaphorical discourse, Ricoeur has found a means for expressing the real in terms of the possible.

It is precisely this redescription of the world as dynamic and in process that renders metaphorical discourse humanizing, even redemptive. As passions for the possible, humans are never more alive than when they are informed by "lively expressions" that depict a "lively" existence. Thanks to metaphor, we may entertain visions of what might be. For this reason alone we could infer that metaphorical discourse is perhaps the most appropriate language with which to express an eschatological vision of the world, for it is precisely the "more than actuality" which is the object of our hope.

And yet there is an important ambiguity in Ricoeur's treatment of metaphorical reference. By "reference" does Ricoeur mean to say that metaphors correspond to the way the world *actually* is? Do metaphors refer because they correspond to the way the world actually is – to the world's dynamic being-in-process? If so, then metaphor is performing a metaphysical task. On the other hand, if metaphors refer to Being as possibility, then we must face the question of verification. How do we know that a given possibility is really there? Yet a third option for understanding metaphorical reference suggests itself, namely, that metaphor "refers" to the world in the sense that its chief aim is to alter the way we look at the world. At times it seems that Ricoeur assigns each of these meanings to the phenomenon of metaphorical reference.

If metaphor does indeed perform a metaphysical function, exploring either actuality or possibility, then we are left with a final query: does Ricoeur's metaphor theory make philosophy poetry or does it raise poetry to the status of philosophy?

Ricoeur mediates this dichotomy in a final confrontation with Heidegger in the final chapter of *The Rule of Metaphor*, "Metaphor and Philosophical Discourse."[80] He here parts with Heidegger by saying that metaphors do not simply replace metaphysics. The later Heidegger notwithstanding, poetry does not replace the work of philosophy.[81] Ricoeur carefully distinguishes the respective roles and responsibilities of poetic and philosophical discourse. Poetry and philosophy are not autonomous language games, for they interact with one another, but they each enjoy a relative autonomy. Speculative discourse has its condition of possibility in the surplus of meaning – the "more" in poetic language that demands to be thought – and its necessity in itself, in establishing the first principles with which thought works. Poetry needs to be interpreted, and Ricoeur states that *interpretation is the work of concepts.* "Every interpretation aims at relocating the semantic outline sketched by metaphorical utterance inside an available horizon of understanding that can be mastered conceptually."[82] But because the concept can never exhaust the metaphor, the metaphor remains alive:

> Interpretation is then a mode of discourse that functions at the intersection of two domains, metaphorical and speculative ... On one side, interpretation seeks the clarity of the concept; on the other, it hopes to preserve the dynamism of meaning that the concept holds and pins down ... Metaphor is living by virtue of the fact that it introduces the spark of imagination into a "thinking more" at the conceptual level. The struggle to "think more," guided by the "vivifying principle," is the "soul" of interpretation.[83]

What the poet sees the philosopher thinks, and the goal of this process of interpretation is nothing short of a new discovery of the real. However, I have argued that even when the work of interpretation is done, we still have the problem of verification. Our earlier question of how to recognize a good metaphor now becomes one of deciding which possibilities referred to by metaphors are genuine and which are misleading. To what would a bad metaphor refer? Ricoeur does not address this issue.

Metaphor for Ricoeur can apparently do no wrong. One of Ricoeur's favorite Pauline phrases, "how much more," well expresses the richness of metaphor. Metaphor creates sense out of nonsense and so evidences a surplus of meaning. Metaphor refers to hitherto unseen possibilities in the world and to a world in process; a surplus of being – a "more than actuality" – is the correlate of metaphor's surplus of meaning. Finally, metaphor is inexhaustible with regard to philosophical paraphrase. No closed conceptual system can capture the liveliness of metaphor. Here then is a form of language well suited to articulate the passion for the possible. Metaphor, and creative language in general, corresponds on the semantic level to human being on the level of existence. The surplus of being in human existence – possibility – only comes to expression in metaphorical discourse. This correlation should come as no surprise, for we have argued that Ricoeur's attention to language and literature ultimately serves his interest in understanding the meaning of human being.

Metaphor and theology

Of late, theologians too have evidenced a passion for metaphor.[84] Eberhard Jüngel's essay, "Metaphorical Truth," in a book coauthored with Ricoeur, proceeds from the conviction that religious language must resist the hegemony of literal discourse and call into question the ultimacy of its referent, actuality.[85] The language of faith does not correspond to actuality.[86] Rather, Jüngel explores the capacity of metaphor as a form of religious language insofar as it expresses *more* than actuality, that is, possibility. We must not restrict the language of faith to speaking about what is or "actuality." Jüngel agrees with Ricoeur that the category "being" embraces both actuality and possibility. In another essay Jüngel cites the doctrine of justification by faith as an example of a reference to a state of affairs that is "more than actual."[87] As justified, man's being is constituted less by his works (actuality) than by the new possibility given by God. As justified, the believer is *more* than the sum total of his works or actuality. Jüngel's point is that faith is about the "more than actuality" – the possibilities – that come to speech only in non-literal language. To take metaphor seriously means for Jüngel that we demand "a realism capable of embracing the ontological force of possibility."[88] This is Ricoeur's intent too. The language of faith must speak of things beyond our actual situation, and therefore beyond the reach of literal or descriptive language. Such an argument restores the religious significance of poetic language to heights hitherto reached only in German Romanticism.

Many biblical scholars have followed Ricoeur's lead in stressing the metaphorical nature of the language of faith and the language of the New Testament, especially the parables.[89] On this view, theology begins from the fullness of metaphorical discourse. Here the emphasis is not on the surplus of being, the "more than actuality" that metaphor expresses, but rather the surplus of meaning. Speculative thought – in this case, theology – is forever bound to the metaphors. Ricoeur's own work is a case in point: his *The Symbolism of Evil* is a good example of how theology reflects on figurative speech without reducing it to concepts. For 400 pages Ricoeur thinks through symbols that speak of human fault and failure. If the theologian's currency is largely symbolic and metaphorical, then is the theologian more like the philosopher or the literary critic? Should the theologian create a system which organizes and explains the metaphors (and then discards them), or should the theologian keep the metaphor alive? Ricoeur believes the latter strategy better enables a fresh and more authentic hearing of the biblical word. It is because of the "lively" and unsettling nature of metaphorical redescription of the world in terms of possibility that the reader's present world is both challenged and charged with hope.

Janet M. Soskice's *Metaphor and Religious Language* construes the theological significance of metaphor in a way that raises questions about Ricoeur's work. Soskice attempts to put the surplus of meaning which is metaphor's cognitive contribution to work for the sake of a theological realism. Noting that Christian theology has been plagued in its attempts to speak metaphorically of God by an empiricist mentality, Soskice argues not for a return to literal theological language but for a better understanding of metaphor:

It is our hope that a defence of metaphor and of its use as a conceptual vehicle will support the Christian in his seemingly paradoxical conviction that, despite the utter inability to comprehend God, he is justified in speaking of God and that metaphor is the principal means by which he does so.[90]

Soskice's theory of metaphor challenges Ricoeur's theory of metaphor in two important respects. First, she suggests that Ricoeur comes "perilously close" to a "dual meaning" and "dual truth" thesis where the literal meaning of the metaphorical utterance is considered "false" and the metaphorical sense is considered "true." But this, says Soskice, is to ignore the actual context of metaphorical discourse. The speaker is not making two assertions in his metaphorical statement, but only one.[91] According to Soskice, plurality at the level of sense (the surplus of meaning) is compatible with a unity of referential intent. A truth may be expressed by a metaphor, but it need not follow that it expresses a kind of truth that is different than the kind of truth enjoyed by literal language. It therefore follows that "Ricoeur's suggestion that the tension of metaphor is ontological is somewhat ambiguous."[92]

Second, and more fundamentally, Soskice's work raises anew the question of the nature of the reference of metaphorical discourse and, by implication, casts doubt on the suitability of Ricoeur's metaphor theory for a theological realism. Soskice disagrees with Ricoeur's refusal to view metaphor as a form of descriptive language. She notes that Ricoeur and the theologians that are his disciples take the reference of theistic models, such as the parables, to be human experience rather than God. Ricoeur claims that the "kingdom of God" which is the object of the parables ultimately refers to a mode of human existence. She associates this position with idealism, where theological models are "fictive constructs without any pretension to depict a reality independent of the human condition."[93] Of course, there is nothing to prevent the theologian from abandoning realism if he chooses to do so and from saying that metaphorical discourse is only an account of existential significance. Soskice contends, however, that we can legitimately refer to God even though complete description is beyond our grasp. Metaphors depict reality, which is a realist project, but they do so not "literally" but "critically."[94] We may refer to God even though our descriptions are revisable and incomplete.[95] The theist's description is open to revision, thus allowing for the possibility of error – this is the risk of realism. We may legitimately refer to God and at the same time realize that we will never reach an exhaustive definition of God. The crucial point for the realist is that the referent of our discourse – God, the world, human being – does not change at the behest of our redescriptions of it.

Is Soskice's call for a critical realism of metaphor compatible with Ricoeur's insistence that metaphors both discover and invent, and that what is redescribed by the language of faith is the manner of human being in the world? At first blush, it would appear that we would be right to classify Ricoeur with the "idealists" because he holds that metaphorical discourse, like other forms of poetic language, functions more to generate an "emotional" model that orients us to the world and to our existence than to describe some aspect of reality.[96] But Ricoeur's position eventually eludes Soskice's categories, for as we have seen, in focusing on the feelings elicited by metaphor it is not only the human subject that is redescribed but the world itself. Feelings have both an "intention" towards the world and an "affection" toward the self. Soskice seems to assume that in order to refer to the real, religious language must refer to something other than human experience. For instance, she assumes that the parables "do purport to tell us of God," but she does so without herself entering into the conflict of interpretations about the parables.[97] However, there is a tradition of modern theology stemming from Schleiermacher and continuing through existential theology that maintains a close link between theology and anthropology. It may be that the real issue between Soskice and Ricoeur is not *whether* metaphors refer to the real, but rather, to *what* reality do metaphors refer.[98] For Ricoeur hopes that through an analysis of certain human feelings and of the metaphoric redescription of human ways of being in the world, we may come to know something not only of the human condition but of the world – and perhaps, at the limit, something of the very ways of God.

Soskice's challenge does not go away easily, however, for Ricoeur's "metaphorical faith" self-consciously remains within Kantian limits.[99] As I have suggested, Ricoeur's mediation of the "is" and "is not" of metaphor results in the ambiguous notion of "being as." The question remains whether Ricoeur's view of metaphor does not in the end slide down the "slippery slope" towards the "as if," into the arms not of Bultmann but Vaihinger. H. Vaihinger's *The Philosophy of "As If,"* a study of religious fictions inspired by Kant, suggests that the referent of poetic discourse is ideal, by which he means unreal (or better, not actual).[100] However, though they are only mental constructs, religious fictions are practically necessary:

It must be remembered that the object of the world of ideas as a whole is not the portrayal of reality – this would be an utterly impossible task – but rather to provide us with an *instrument for feeling our way about more easily in the world.*[101]

This comment is strikingly similar to Ricoeur's vision for poetic language and the moods it evokes. In his attempt to incorporate both invention and discovery in his theory of metaphor, does Ricoeur ever get beyond idealism? To put it another way, why should we want to see the world in a new way, with new possibilities blossoming forth, if this vision does not, in some way, correspond to the potentialities of the actual present?

Vaihinger observes that symbolic or poetic fictions (which include metaphors) are especially popular in theology. For example, the relation of God to the world, which is as unknowable for Schleiermacher the philosopher as it was for Kant, is conceived by Schleiermacher the theologian in terms of the metaphorical statement which addresses God as "Our Father who art in heaven." God is to be thought of "as if"

He were our "heavenly father." Schleiermacher similarly "transformed all dogmas from hypotheses to fictions."[102] Similarly, McFague suggests that the biblical ways of speaking about God, because they are metaphors or models, do not actually correspond to the nature of God. We are therefore free to invent new metaphors in order to express the relation of God to humanity in new ways. McFague believes that metaphors such as "mother" or "lover" more accurately convey this relation than the patriarchal models of father and king.

Interestingly enough, Vaihinger, like Ricoeur, locates the essence of the religious fiction in the "ambiguity of the copula." The metaphorical "is" constitutes "a very short abbreviation for an exceedingly complicated train of thought."[103] Indeed, the Reformation dispute over the meaning of Jesus' "This is my body" represents a striking illustration of the "ambiguity of the copula." Whereas Zwingli acknowledged the fictive "as if" aspect, Luther took the "is" more literally. For his part, Ricoeur wishes to preserve the tension in the polemical encounter of "This is my body" and "This is not my body."[104] "Seeing as" must not be reduced to "as if." Eschewing both a Lutheran and Reformed approach, Ricoeur would mediate the opposing notions of *finitum capax infinitum* and *finitum non capax infinitum*.[105] But this particular mediation is the very mystery of human existence as well, situated as it is between the finite and the infinite. We have a finite situation (*Da*) but we are also "open" (*sein*). To be human means that one is partly constituted by that which transcends the here and now of the actual.

Now it is precisely metaphor that best expresses this "transgression." Just as metaphors refer beyond the actual to the possible, so too human being is both actuality and potentiality. Man, like metaphor, is the "intermediate being," and it is feelings above all that express this "more than actuality" through poetic speech.[106] By going beyond the given, metaphor encourages us to look at the world as well as ourselves in terms of what might be.[107] We may therefore call the type of philosophy to which metaphorical discourse gives rise, for lack of a better metaphor, a "realism" of possibility. As such, metaphor is the indispensable expression of the passion for the possible.[108]

Notes

1 In his "The Image of God and the Epic of Man" (in *HT*) Ricoeur suggests that it is the power of human creativity, particularly as it is displayed through our corporate history, that most closely approximates the symbol of the *imago Dei*.

2 Discourse "is the creative process of giving form to both the human mind and the world, of forming (*Bildung*) man and reality at the same time" ("Creativity," 123).

3 This has been convincingly argued by Rasmussen, *Mythic-Symbolic Language and Philosophical Anthropology*. Ricoeur first turned to consider creative language in his *SE*. He was forced to study the symbols of evil because his analysis of the essential structural capacities of human being, gained through phenomenology, could not account for the actuality of human evil. In other words, self-knowledge cannot be gleaned by direct inspection, be it private introspection or the more sophisticated method of phenomenological observation. Self-understanding is not immediate, but mediate, and creative language provides the principal access.

4 As we saw in chapter 2, even Heidegger, especially in his later work, evidences a dependence on mysticism more befitting the poet than the philosopher.

5 Bertand Russell, *The Principles of Mathematics* (Cambridge University Press, 1903), 42.

6 See J. O. Urmson, *Philosophical Analysis: Its Development Between the Two World Wars* (Oxford University Press, 1956).

7 Ricoeur sees the contribution of ordinary language philosophy as twofold: first, it has shown that ordinary language cannot be reduced to a perfect formal language, like that of mathematics (Ricoeur has extended this insight to biblical language as well, which resists a wholesale reduction to a system of theology). Second, ordinary language constitutes a kind of conservatory of human experience. Ricoeur suggests that the phenomenological project of examining the meaning of human experience might fruitfully be wed to ordinary language philosophy ("From Existentialism to the Philosophy of Language," in *RM*, 321–2).

8 This two-part essay may be found in *CI*. Cf. his "Hermeneutic Method and Reflective Philosophy," in *FP*.

9 "An experience which is not *brought to language* remains blind, confused and incommunicable" ("Poétique," 37). Interestingly enough, Ricoeur devotes his last chapter in *RM* to a discussion of the complex relations between poetry and philosophical discourse. Ricoeur seeks to avoid two extremes: making the poem a mere ornament to the philosophy, and making the philosophy the poem's translation (*RM*, 310).

10 Ricoeur views language itself as an instrument of mediation. As communication or dialog, language mediates man and man. As instrument of reflection, language enables one to come to self-knowledge. And as reference, language mediates mind and world. Ricoeur assigns an impressive responsibility to this function of language: "That which language *changes* is simultaneously our vision of the world, our power to communicate and the understanding that we have of ourselves" ("Poétique," 40). Of course, a fourth mediation of language that Ricoeur discusses at length elsewhere is that between man and God (see Part II).

11 Ricoeur believes that theologians are sometimes guilty of eliminating necessary ambiguities. By interpreting the symbols and myths which speak of human evil, Ricoeur arrives at the conceptual enigma of a "captive freedom." But he believes that Augustine goes too far in positing a univocal concept – original sin – that displaces the equivocal symbols of human evil ("'Original Sin': A Study in Meaning," in *CI*).

12 The phrase comes from Emmanuel Mounier's "personalist" philosophy, but Ricoeur cites and apparently applauds it (*HT*, 156).

13 *FP*, 29–30.

14 Cf. Heidegger's distinction between *Zuhanden* and *Vorhanden*. Ricoeur is making a fundamentally Heideggerian point: scientific language can only depict the world of manipulable objects; it cannot depict the world of care, the world that matters most to *Dasein*. For an interesting confirmation of Ricoeur's thesis, see Oliver O'Donovan, *Begotten or Made?* (Oxford University Press, 1984), which argues that technology so governs our thinking that the creation of life itself is now viewed more as a product than a gift. This is precisely Ricoeur's worry.

15 "Power," 69.

16 *HT*, 174.

17 "Poetry," 9.

18 Ibid.

19 Ibid., 10.

20 Ricoeur reflected on the significance of feelings for philosophy even before his book on metaphor. See his *FM*, where he speaks of the possibility of a "philosophy of the heart" (124).

21 The structure of Ricoeur's *FM* corresponds to Kant's three *Critiques* and their themes: understanding, doing and the aesthetic judgment or imagination.

22 *RM*, 246.

23 *BT*, 172. Cf. John Macquarrie, "Feeling and Understanding," in *Studies in Christian Existentialism* (London, SCM, 1966), 31–42.

24 *IT*, 60.

25 "Power," 69.

26 Thomas Hobbes, *Leviathan* (New York, Liberal Arts Press, 1958), ch. 4, 39.

27 Aristotle, *Poetics*, 1457^b 7–8.

28 Janet Martin Soskice claims that this crude substitution view of metaphor is not so much that of the rhetoricians as of their empiricist critics, particularly seventeenth-century philosophers such as John Locke who chose the natural sciences or mathematics as their model of rationality (*Metaphor and Religious Language* [Oxford, Clarendon, 1985], 10–11).

29 True to its nature, metaphor is bringing even academic disciplines that were previously distant closer together. Both scientists and literary critics in this century have come to appreciate the unique cognitive contribution of metaphor, with theologians not far behind (see below). Among the literary critics, Ricoeur follows I. A. Richards, *The Philosophy of Rhetoric* (Oxford

University Press, 1936), chs. 5, 6 and Monroe Beardsley, *Aesthetics* (New York, Harcourt, Brace, and World, 1958), 115–47 and "The Metaphorical Twist," *Philosophy and Phenomenological Research* 22 (1962), 293–307. From the scientific realm, Ricoeur borrows appreciatively from Max Black, *Models and Metaphors* (Cornell University Press, 1962), 25–47 and Mary B. Hesse, "The Explanatory Function of Metaphor," appendix to *Models and Analogies in Science* (University of Notre Dame Press, 1966).

30 *RM*, 65.

31 The third chapter of *RM* is appropriately titled: "Metaphor and the Semantics of Discourse." In this chapter Ricoeur opposes semantics, the study of meaning, to semiotics, the science of signs. Viewed as a sign system, language refers only to itself. Viewed as discourse, language refers to extra-linguistic reality: "This trait, more than others perhaps, marks the fundamental difference between semantics and semiotics" (*RM*, 74). I. A. Richards is the hero here, for it was he who broke from the tradition of classifying different forms of figurative speech. Ricoeur says that Richards "attacks the cardinal distinction in classical rhetoric between proper meaning and figurative meaning, a distinction for which he blames the 'Proper Meaning Superstition'" (*RM*, 77).

32 "Creativity," 123.

33 It is just here that Ricoeur differs from the other interaction theorists. Richards, Black and Beardsley all say that the resemblance is based on latent connotations of the two things being compared. Ricoeur points out that this eventually reverts to a substitution theory. Rather, "one must adopt the point of view of the hearer or reader and treat the novelty of an emerging meaning as his work within the very act of hearing or reading. If we do not take this route, we do not really get rid of the theory of substitution" (*RM*, 98). In other words, it is only as discourse that Ricoeur believes we can explain the creation of meaning. The resemblance is not there waiting to be discovered, but it is invented. Metaphor is less a latent connection in a system of language and more a creation *ex nihilo*: "To say that a new metaphor is not taken from anywhere is to recognize it for what it is, namely, a creation of language that comes to be at that moment, a *semantic innovation* without status in the language as something already established with respect to either a designation or connotation" (*RM*, 98). Only a theory of discourse (i.e., a theory of the use of language and not merely the system of language) can explain how new meanings can emerge in language.

34 "Creativity," 131.

35 Ibid., 132.

36 "Metaphor," 147. Ricoeur tentatively suggests a more "venturesome hypothesis," namely, that this same metaphorical process that disturbs a certain logical or conceptual order "is the same as that from which all classification proceeds" (*RM*, 22). In other words, may not a metaphorical process be at the root of all thought and language?

37 As I mentioned in chapter 1, metaphor is a fitting figure for Ricoeur's own philosophical style, for Ricoeur also mediates oppositions by creative insight by spotting resemblances between philosophical notions that had not previously been seen. Cf. Mary Schaldenbrand, "Metaphoric Imagination: Kinship through Conflict," in Charles E. Reagan (ed.), *Studies in the Philosophy of Paul Ricoeur* (Ohio University Press, 1979), 57–81.

38 C. S. Lewis, "Bluspels and Flalansferes," in *Selected Literary Essays* (Cambridge University Press, 1969), 251–65.

39 *IT*, 45.

40 Hesse, *Models and Analogies in Science*, 259.

41 Thomas Kuhn's work on paradigm shifts in the history of science is apt. What Kuhn means by paradigm is not far removed from what Ricoeur and others mean by metaphor. See Kuhn's *The Structure of Scientific Revolutions* (University of Chicago Press, 1962). The shift from Newtonian physics to relativity could be construed as a shift in metaphors, and Einstein might well be regarded as a master poet, inventing new metaphors in order to discover more about the universe. Ricoeur acknowledges the specificity of science as opposed to poetry, however: (1) a scientific proposition is falsifiable (2) the scientist seeks community consensus (3) scientific discoveries must conform to the rest of acquired knowledge ("Poetry", 16).

42 Sallie McFague links metaphor to the human passion for the possible: "Metaphor is movement, human movement; without it, we would not be what we are – the only creatures in the universe to our knowledge who can *envision* a future and consciously work toward achieving it ... All our dreams, scientific revolutions, theories, and works of art are so many attempts to 'figure' the universe"(*Speaking in Parables* [Philadelphia, Fortress, 1975], 58, 64).

43 Aristotle, *Poetics* 1459^a 7–8.

44 *RM*, 195.

45 "Like the icon of the Byzantine cult, the verbal icon consists in this fusion of sense and the sensible" (*RM*, 209).

46 Ricoeur follows the suggestion of Marcus B. Hester that the imaginative "seeing" is guided by and bound to the verbal element (*The Meaning of Poetic Metaphor* [The Hague, Mouton, 1967], 160–9).

47 "It seems to me that this notion of imagery tied by meaning is in accord with Kant's idea that the schema is a method for constructing images ... The poet, in effect, is that artisan who sustains and shapes imagery using no means other than language" (*RM*, 211); "Thus, 'seeing as' quite precisely plays the role of the schema that unites the *empty* concept and the *blind* impression" (*RM*, 213).

48 In "The Metaphorical Process as Cognition, Imagination, and Feeling," an article which serves as an appendix of sorts to *RM*, Ricoeur shows how not only images but feelings are "bound" to poetic words.

49 "Metaphor," 156.

50 Mary Gerhart and Allen M. Russell, *Metaphoric Process: The Creation of Scientific and Religious Understanding* (Texas Christian University Press, 1984).

51 Ibid., 108.

52 Ibid., 113–20.

53 Gottlob Frege, "On Sense and Reference," in *Philosophical Writings of Gottlob Frege*, trans. Max Black and Peter Geach (Oxford, Basil Blackwell, 1952), 63.

54 *RM*, 221.

55 Ibid., 6. Reference to reality distinguishes semantics from semiotics: "Whereas the sign points back only to other signs immanent within a system, discourse is about things. Sign differs from sign, discourse refers to the world" (216).

56 Ibid., 7.

57 Ricoeur discusses Frye under the heading "The Case Against Reference," in *RM*, 221–8. Even in Frye, however, Ricoeur finds indications that poetry does indeed refer. Frye says that the unity of the poem is a unity of mood, and we have seen that Ricoeur treats feelings and moods as a way of orienting oneself to reality: "Under the name of mood, an extra-linguistic factor is introduced, which is the index of a manner of being" (*RM*, 229).

58 *RM*, 221.

59 Ibid., 247.

60 In *RM* Ricoeur speaks of metaphorical reference in terms of redescription. By the time of *TN*, however, he has abandoned all talk of reference and instead prefers the terminology of "refiguration." The change in terms indicates more than a semantic difference. "Redescription" tends to focus our attention on the thing being redescribed, and is thus more in line with what we could call a "realism of metaphor" that seeks to bring new aspects of the actual world to light. "Refiguration," on the other hand, tends to focus on the interpretive schema and the new way in which a person sees the world. The emphasis is not on the thing but rather on the way we look at it. Metaphor here appears as a strategy for changing minds rather than describing the world. By preferring refiguration over reference, Ricoeur seems to be leaning towards an idealism rather than realism of metaphor.

61 *IT*, 67.

62 *RM*, 239.

63 Ibid., 229. "Poetic discourse brings to language a pre-objective world in which we find ourselves already rooted, but in which we project our innermost possibilities" (*RM*, 142). Husserl and Heidegger call it a *Lebenswelt* or "life-world."

64 *PPR*, 68.

65 Ricoeur claims that poetic feelings are heuristic models for discovering the real too: "Only a feeling transformed into myth can open and discover a world ... poetic feeling itself also develops an experience of reality in which invention and discovery cease being opposed and where creation and revelation coincide" (*RM*, 245).

66 *RM*, 7.

67 Ibid., 224.

68 Ibid., 254.

69 Ibid., 247.

70 "Creativity," 133.

71 Aristotle, *Rhetoric* 1411^{b} 27–8 (cited in *RM*, 307).

72 *RM*, 43.

73 Ibid., 42.

74 Ibid., 43.

75 Ibid., 307.

76 In Aristotle, possibility and actuality are defined correlatively: potentiality is to actuality as the "power to be" is to "being." See Ricoeur's commentary on Aristotle's *Metaphysics* in *RM*, 307–9 (esp. the footnotes).

77 *RM*, 308.

78 See chapter 2.

79 Ricoeur remarks that Heidegger's break with the metaphysics of Presence left him virtually mute and gave rise to a kind of "despair of language" along the lines of Wittgenstein's "Whereof we cannot speak, we must needs be silent" (*RM*, 313). Ricoeur approves both Kant's and Heidegger's intuition concerning poetry's ability to speak of Being where philosophy could only be silent. I have tried to show that Ricoeur is trying to put their intuitions on the firmer basis of a full-fledged theory of creative language and literature.

80 This chapter is of the utmost interest to the theologian as well, insofar as theological discourse is related to and yet distinct from biblical modes of discourse, many of which are poetical in nature.

81 In Part II we shall ask whether Ricoeur views the relation of poetry and theology in a similar way.

82 *RM*, 302–3.

83 Ibid. Here is an admirable programme for theological method as well insofar as it desires to be "biblical."

84 See, for instance, Soskice, *Metaphor and Religious Language*; Tracy, *The Analogical Imagination*; Gerhart and Russell, *Metaphoric Process*; McFague, *Speaking in Parables*. Gerhart, TeSelle and Tracy all acknowledge their indebtedness to Ricoeur.

85 Paul Ricoeur and Eberhard Jüngel, *Metapher: Zur Hermeneutik religiöser Sprache* (*Evangelische Theologie* Sonderheft, 1974), 70–122.

86 See John Webster, *Eberhard Jüngel: An Introduction to his Theology* (Cambridge University Press, 1986), 43–7.

87 "Die Welt als Möglichkeit und Wirklichkeit," *Unterwegs zur Sache* (Munich, Kaiser, 1972).

88 Webster, *Eberhard Jüngel*, 46.

89 See, for instance, Ricoeur's "BibHerm" and McFague's *Speaking in Parables*. C. H. Dodd remarked that parables are a species of "extended metaphors." We will examine Ricoeur's interpretation of the parables in chapter 7.

90 Soskice, *Metaphor and Religious Language*, x. As has been noted by Nicholas
    Lash, many of the contributors to *The Myth of God Incarnate* suffer from an
    anemic imagination in their christological discussion, one of whose
    symptoms is a distrust of anything other than literal language. Lash finds
    an implicit assumption in many of the essays that literal discourse is
    ''objective'' and ''fact-asserting,'' while metaphorical discourse is ''sub-
    jective'' and ''expressive of attitudes'' (''Interpretation and Imagination,''
    in Michael Goulder (ed.), *The Debate Continued: Incarnation and Myth* [London,
    SCM, 1979], 19–26).

91 Soskice, *Metaphor and Religious Language*, 84–90. Soskice's account differs
    from Ricoeur's in arguing that meaning and reference can only be discussed
    in relation to a speaker's intentions and to the complete context of the
    utterance. Ricoeur, as we shall see, believes that written discourse is cut
    off from its original author and context.

92 Ibid., 89. Soskice also finds Ricoeur's use of the term ''redescription''
    troubling, implying as it does that what metaphor is about was accessible
    before the metaphor and is only being re-described. She suggests that,
    contrary to Ricoeur's basic intention, he does not explain how metaphors
    can say something genuinely new.

93 Ibid., 145. As we shall see, this complaint is particularly apt, for Ricoeur
    is squarely in this tradition. See below, chapter 6. Soskice's complaint is
    worth citing in full: ''We have no theoretical objection to an idealist-inspired
    theological programme which emphasizes that the truths of religion are of
    relational and personal nature ... What we object to are theories which claim
    to account for Christian religious language as genuinely cognitive in the way
    Christians have characteristically held it to be, but which at some critical
    point say that, because we cannot know God, the theist's claims must refer
    only to aspects of the human condition'' (178 n. 11).

94 ''It is because senses are important but not fully definitive that metaphor
    becomes extremely useful in the project of reality depiction, which is ... a
    realist project'' (132). It is the vagueness of metaphor ''which *allows* for the
    revisability necessary to any account that aims to adapt itself to the world''
    (133). Note that for Soskice the realist is not committed to any one particular
    description, but only to the *distinction* between the world and our descriptions.

95 This ''critical'' qualification of the realist's enterprise bears a marked
    similarity to Ricoeur's hermeneutic philosophy. In the absence of absolute
    knowledge, rationality proceeds by way of the conflict of interpretations.

96 Soskice cites McTaggart's comment that religion is ''an emotion resting
    on a conviction of a harmony between ourselves and the universe at large''
    (147).

97 Ibid., 106.

98 Walter Lowe's thought is worth pondering. Lowe suggests that while
    Ricoeur is trying to address the Heideggerian question of Being, in practice
    he focuses on human being-in-the-world: ''In other words, Ricoeur is

oriented less to ontology than to philosophical anthropology, less to the problem of truth than to the question of human meaningfulness" ("The Coherence of Paul Ricoeur," *JR* 61 [1981], 400).

99 Cf. chapter 2 above.

100 Vaihinger is quite explicit in tracing his theory of religious fictions back to Kant (cf. Part III of *The Philosophy of "As If": A System of the Theoretical, Practical and Religious Fictions of Mankind*, 2nd edn, tr. C. K. Ogden [New York, Barnes and Noble, 1935], 271–318).

101 Vaihinger, *Philosophy of "As if,"* 15. "Ideas" are fictions, and "ideals" are practical fictions that are justified in spite of their unreality. Ricoeur is uneasy with this easy distinction between "ideal" and "real." Kant is often considered an idealist, yet he wrote a "Refutation of Idealism." Plato believed that Ideas were "real" – was he a realist then or an idealist? Ricoeur would prefer to abandon the distinction altogether (a point made in personal conversation with the author).

102 *Philosophy of "As If,"* 28. Vaihinger says that Schleiermacher is simply working out insights first gained by Kant. As Kant saw so clearly, religion is the fiction that is practically necessary to ground morality: we must be moral *as if* we were free, *as if* Nature were suited to our freedom and *as if* God would assist and reward us.

103 Ibid., 264.

104 See David Klemm, " 'This is my Body': Hermeneutics and Eucharistic Language," *Anglican Theological Review* 64 (1982), 293–310.

105 Walter Lowe intriguingly suggests that this desire to preserve the tension between the finite and the infinite is the constant factor that permits us to speak of the "coherence" of Ricoeur's thought ("The Coherence of Paul Ricoeur," 384–402).

106 "Our working hypothesis concerning the paradox of the finite–infinite implies that we must speak of infinitude as much as of human infinitude" (*FM*, 7). The greatness and the misery of humanity is given to philosophy to think through in the form of symbols, myths, etc. And: "To put it in a formula, I doubt that the central concept of philosophical anthropology is finitude, it is rather the triad finitude–infinitude–intermediary" ("Autonomy," 21).

107 Ray Hart's *Unfinished Man and the Imagination: Toward an Ontology and a Rhetoric of Revelation* (London, Herder & Herder, 1968) is worth mentioning here. Hart contends that human being is unfinished, "on the way," goes forward only by imagining possibilities. Both Hart and Ricoeur eventually link this imagining of possibilities to the Christian doctrine of revelation.

108 We shall come back to metaphor in our chapters on narrative discourse and again when we consider the Gospels, for Ricoeur sees a certain metaphorical process at work in stories and histories as well.

5

Narrative: the "substance" of things hoped for

Ricoeur's is a hermeneutic philosophy. The goal of this philosophy is an understanding of human being, and interpretation is the means to the end. If philosophy is to reflect on human existence, it must proceed by way of a reflection on those forms of language (as well as human actions and history itself) that best express human existence. Metaphor and poetry are important in this regard because they express the possible ways in which human beings can orient themselves to the world. But human beings are, as we have seen, also related in complex ways to time. Part of being human means being aware of oneself as related to the past and future. This is what Ricoeur means by the "historicity" of human being. Ricoeur's new wager is that the form of language that best expresses human temporality is narrative.[1] Narratives represent concrete possibilities of *action*, possible ways of doing things, possible "worlds." By bridging his concern for language and hermeneutics with his concern for philosophical anthropology, narrative may well be viewed as the culmination of Ricoeur's intellectual journey. Not only does it bring these two major concerns together, but narrative is also the place where three of Ricoeur's central themes converge, namely, possibility, temporality and creative imagination. We give voice to hope's object, a desired but not-yet-actual form of human life, through narrative histories and fictions. By displaying a possible world or way of being in time and soliciting the reader to make it his own, narrative fulfills the aim of Ricoeur's long-awaited "Poetics of the Will."

History and fiction, the two modes of the narrative imagination, are ways in which human historicity is redescribed. History and fiction together thus constitute a narrative "schematism" for what is humanly possible. Narratives create and display the myriad ways that we can live. Moreover, the possibilities that narratives display are not only possibilities for the individual, but for whole societies or communities as well.

86

It is through stories and histories that we discover what we can do individually and corporately: thanks to narratives, our passion for the possible is not an empty one. In creating possible worlds, stories and histories thus make up the "substance" of things hoped for.

From metaphor to text

Initially it is difficult to see how Ricoeur makes his imaginative leap from metaphor to narrative, but a clue may be had in Ricoeur's comment that metaphor is a kind of "miniature text."[2] A brief review of Ricoeur's general interpretation theory may therefore be in order.[3] In his quest for the meaning of human being, Ricoeur feels obliged to take a detour through textual hermeneutics because the same language to which Ricoeur was trustfully listening in order to comprehend the human condition was elsewhere being viewed with suspicion. Not every philosopher, historian or literary critic "trusts" the texts he reads.[4] Nor, for that matter, do all agree on the meaning of texts. Given the very real and present conflict of interpretations, Ricoeur deemed it necessary to develop a full-fledged textual hermeneutics. In his interpretation theory, Ricoeur fights on two hermeneutical fronts: first, against the irrationalism of immediate understanding, represented by a Romanticist hermeneutics which would intuitively recover the author's intention; and second, against the rationalism of complete explanation, represented by structuralist approaches which ignore the author and the reader and focus on the "system" or immanent pattern of the text. *The central hermeneutical problem for Ricoeur is the mediation of explanation and understanding in the process of text interpretation.* How do we combine both method (i.e., explanatory techniques) and truth (existential understanding) in our interpretation theory?[5]

To begin with, a "text" for Ricoeur is "any discourse fixed by writing,"[6] and hermeneutics is "the art of discerning the discourse in the work."[7] Because it is "fixed," the text displays a certain structure. This structure is the text's "sense," and this sense – the "what" of discourse – is "immanent" to the text. Accordingly, one "makes sense" of the text by explaining the work's structure. One can explain the structure of the text without ever referring to anything outside the text; one simply points out the principles of its inner organization – its "architecture," as it were. On the other hand, the reference of the text – the "about what" of discourse – points away from the text to the world, or rather, to the "world of the text." Text interpretation thus consists of two parts: "To understand a text is to follow its movement

from sense to reference: from what it says, to what it talks about.''[8]
Interpretation is not over when the work is merely explained. One can
examine and explain the structure of Brahms's *Fourth Symphony*, for
instance, but this is not to interpret it. For Ricoeur, ''reading is like
the execution of a musical score; it marks the realization, the enactment,
of the semantic possibilities of the text.''[9]

These semantic possibilities must not only be uncovered but must
be seriously considered by the reader, for only when the message is
received can we say that something has been communicated:

> We can, as readers, remain in the suspense of the text, treating it as a worldless
> and authorless object; in this case, we explain the text in terms of its internal
> relations, its structure. On the other hand, we can lift the suspense and fulfill
> the text in speech, restoring it to living communication; in this case, we interpret
> the text.[10]

Interpretation includes a critical distance from the text (method) as well
as existential involvement (truth). To explain is to bring out the structure
of the text; to understand is to follow the semantic path laid out by the
text. And Ricoeur follows the maxim that ''to explain more is to understand better.'' The subjective moment of existential appropriation is
based on the objective moment of structural analysis. Understanding
and explanation are therefore two complementary elements in a single
interpretative process. Explanation mediates a naive preunderstanding
and an ''informed'' understanding that has been educated by a
structural analysis of the text.[11]

Ricoeur's goal of understanding human existence converges with
a textual hermeneutics in the notion of appropriation, for ''the interpretation of a text culminates in the self-interpretation of a subject who
thenceforth understands himself better.''[12] Ricoeur is fond of citing
Proust's idea that the reader ''reads'' himself when he reads a book.
But what exactly is appropriated by the reader? Ricoeur holds that in
between a structural explanation of the text's sense and the moment of
self-understanding stands the text's reference – the ''world'' of the text:
''It is by an understanding of the worlds, actual and possible, opened by
language that we may arrive at a better understanding of ourselves.''[13]

This notion of the ''world of the text'' is perhaps Ricoeur's most
important contribution to interpretation theory. Indeed, Ricoeur recasts
the whole hermeneutic enterprise in light of this notion:

> Hermeneutics can be defined no longer as an inquiry into the psychological
> intentions which are hidden beneath the text, but rather as the explication of
> the being-in-the-world displayed by the text. What is to be interpreted in the

text is a proposed world which I could inhabit and in which I could project my ownmost possibilities.[14]

Unlike the earlier Romantics, Ricoeur is unable to say that what is appropriated is the author's intention. But unlike modern structuralists, Ricoeur is unwilling to abandon his key idea that discourse is *about* something. The notion of the "world of the text" provides him with a solution to both problems. The reader, by following the semantic itineraries sketched out in the text, eventually comes to see the text's world, and himself, in light of that world. However, the world of the text, much like the referent of metaphor, should not be confused with the empirical world. Because of the distance between author and reader, no common situation is shared to which ostensive reference could be made. Like metaphor, texts refer productively – they create worlds. To be precise, texts offer to the reader a possible way of being-in-the-world, a new way of living in the world.[15]

Ricoeur thus finds a second-order reference, characteristic of metaphors, in all texts. Ricoeur privileges this second-order reference because it speaks of reality beyond the actuality of the everyday world. Freed from the burdens of ostensive reference and empirical description, texts can project *meaningful* worlds. As we have seen, humans are privileged of all the species because, thanks to poetic literature, they can view nature not as a hostile impersonal environment, but as their home: "Thanks to writing, man and only man has a world and not just a situation."[16] *The world of the text is the world of human values and existential possibilities*. Ricoeur writes: "For me, the world is the ensemble of references opened up by every kind of text, descriptive or poetic, that I have read, understood, and loved."[17] Who persons are, and what they may become, is a function of what they read and how they respond to it. Far from being an addendum to a hermeneutic philosophy then, reading is rather a world-forming and world-shattering prospect.

Both metaphor and narrative are forms of creative discourse. Ricoeur states that "*The Rule of Metaphor* and *Time and Narrative* form a pair: published one after the other, these works were conceived together."[18] Both metaphor and narrative manifest the same phenomenon of semantic innovation. While metaphor creates new resemblances between things not ordinarily linked, narrative creates a temporal unity out of a diversity of characters, events, goals and causes: "It is this synthesis of the heterogeneous that brings narrative close to metaphor."[19] In both metaphor and narrative, then, there is a production of meaning that is the work of the creative imagination. Narratives create sense and order where previously there was only nonsense and chaos. The parallel between metaphor and narrative extends even further. Beyond the level of sense or meaning, there is a connection between metaphor and narrative with regard to reference and truth. Like metaphor, narrative redescribes the world – in this case the temporal world of human action. Here we are challenged and invited to consider and adopt not simply different ways of seeing but of *doing*.

Time and narrative

Ricoeur's basic hypothesis in *Time and Narrative* is that the language game which Wittgenstein calls "telling of stories" corresponds to the form of life "historicity."[20] All the various kinds of telling, from fairy tales to chronicles, from science fiction to history, are "about" the temporal character of human being. Ricoeur's narrative study thus makes a startling twofold claim: first, on the level of sense, there is a structural similarity between all forms of narrative. All narratives, whether historical or fictional, "make sense" in a similar way. Second, on the level of reference, all narratives point to the same fundamental character of individual and corporate experience: "The world unfolded by every narrative work is always a temporal world."[21] With narrative, poetics approaches ethics, for what narrative redescribes is the world of human action. It follows for Ricoeur that narrative is bound up with the question of human identity (we are what we do) and with the very meaning of human existence (as beings-in-time). In suggesting that human identity and existence is itself narrative in shape, we see once again how Ricoeur's textual hermeneutics serves as handmaiden to a philosophical anthropology.[22]

Augustine's *Confessions* represents for Ricoeur the paradoxes to which every philosophical attempt to understand time gives rise. Ricoeur notes that time is not problematic when considered as a succession of abstract "nows" (clock time). We might call this "natural time," for this is the time of things (which have no memory and no expectation) and of those instruments that measure natural phenomena. But humans are related to time in a more complex fashion.[23] Humans are conscious of the difference between past, present, and future and the relations between them. Augustine poses the basic philosophical problem: how can time exist if the past is no longer here, the future is not yet and the present passes away? To Augustine's credit, he proposes a solution: the three tenses are functions of the soul. The past is present in the soul as memory; the future is present as anticipation; the present as attention.

But this, of course, gives rise to a new paradox, for Augustine is left with three kinds of "present."[24] These and other paradoxes are so persistent that Augustine laments: "What is time? I know when nobody asks me. But when asked to explain it, I no longer know."[25]

Faced with this philosophical conundrum, Ricoeur offers not a speculative but a "poetic" solution. Drawing upon the analysis of tragedy in Aristotle's *Poetics* for his inspiration, Ricoeur suggests that narrative activity – story-telling and history-writing – responds to our confusing experience of time by *organizing time into meaningful wholes.* Ricoeur borrows from Aristotle the two notions of *mythos* (plot) and *mimesis* (imitation). Tragedy, says Aristotle, is "an imitation of an action" (*praxis*), and the imitation of action is accomplished through the plot. The poet is a maker of plots and an imitator of actions. Poets do not merely reproduce the world, as detractors of the imagination claim.[26] Rather, as we have seen, poets invent and discover. Even Aristotle says that tragedy, far from being a reduplication of reality, "represents men better than they actually are."[27] Like all poetic work, narratives suspend reference to the ordinary world in order to redescribe the world in a more meaningful way. Indeed, Ricoeur suggests that the mimetic function of narrative is an instance of metaphoric reference applied to the sphere of human action.[28] The whole analysis of narrative is therefore qualified by the rubric "poetics," for *poiesis* pertains to a creating or a making. Mythos and mimesis are to be understood as creative operations, not as inert structures: "Imitating or representing is a mimetic activity inasmuch as it produces something, namely, the organization of events by emplotment."[29] Narrative is thus a form of creative language which responds to the paradoxes of our experience with time by constructing order out of temporal chaos.

In order to support his claim that narrative is a poetic strategy for transforming natural time (*chronos*) into meaningful or human time, Ricoeur must demonstrate the structural unity as well as the common referent of all narratives. It is just here that Ricoeur encounters a problem, namely, the "ugly ditch" that separates the two major modes of narrative discourse – history and fiction. Aristotle states it best:

The distinction between historian and poet ... consists really in this, that the one describes the thing that has been, and the other a kind of thing that might be. Hence poetry is something more philosophic and of graver import than history, since its statements are of the nature rather of universals, whereas those of history are singulars.[30]

The nature of this ditch is twofold: there is first the epistemological gap. Where Aristotle accorded superiority to poetry because it dealt with the essential, in modern times history has often been considered superior thanks to attempts to give it a scientific method. Moreover, from a positivistic and empiricist perspective, history also enjoys an ontological priority, for it studies the "real" or actual past whereas poetry deals with the "unreal" or imaginary possible. Stated either in its ancient or modern form, however, the gap between history and fiction presents Ricoeur with a "perplexing and exciting" dichotomy and so another opportunity for an imaginative mediation. His task in *Time and Narrative* is twofold: on the one hand, he needs to show how history is more like fiction in relying on the power of the imagination to construct plots; on the other, he needs to show how fiction is more like history in its reference to the real world of human action. We shall see that in Ricoeur's opinion history and fiction constitute two varieties of passions for the possible: histories remind us of what was possible, fictions of what might be possible.

History and the imagination

Historical contingency is an embarrassment for theologian and historian alike. For many modern historians, narratives simply recount a series of events ("and then, and then ...") and are consequently viewed as stumbling blocks to a properly "scientific" approach to historical method. Critics of narrative argue that to tell is not yet to explain. Karl Hempel, for instance, suggests that historical events may be explained by laws, as are natural events.[31] That histories just happen to be written as narratives is of no cognitive significance. As a result of this ambivalence, narrative is considered to be a second-class form of discourse, a mere ornament of historical discourse in much the same way that metaphor is regarded as an ornament of poetic discourse. Ricoeur challenges this denigration of narrative, as he did before with metaphor. Ricoeur's thesis is that narrative understanding is what gives history its unique status among the human sciences.[32] Narrative provides us with a means to think the contingent particular without negating its contingency – the very quality that renders it historical. Far from relegating narrative to the fringes of historical discourse, Ricoeur defines history as the study of past human actions by "emplotment." As a result, history is reunited with its original sister discipline: Clio is related to Calliope.[33]

In suggesting that history relies on a narrative understanding,

Ricoeur makes two important moves: first, he takes the Aristotelian model of plot as "organization of events" beyond tragedy; and second, he claims that the narrative form carries its own kind of cognitive significance. Whereas the chronicle follows the logic of *chronos*, narratives have a "logic" all their own, a logic related to the organizing activity of the plot. A plot, which is the soul of narrative, invents an ordered and intelligible whole out of a diversity of incidents and actions. "To make up a plot is already to make the intelligible spring from the accidental, the universal from the singular, the necessary or the probable from the episodic."[34] Wholeness is the key concept, emphasizing as it does a narrative order other than the chronological. For instance, out of the tumult of ideas, emotions, events, struggles, etc. that unraveled in late-eighteenth-century France, historians created the "single and complete action" now known as the "French revolution." Emplotment is thus a special kind of thinking, what we might call "poetic reason." By "poetic reason" I am referring to the kind of imaginative judgment that creates wholes out of parts, which Kant calls the "reflective" judgment and Ricoeur calls "configuration."[35] Narratives have two dimensions according to Ricoeur: the episodic dimension ("and then, and then ...") and the configurative dimension (the theme). It is thanks to the latter that a succession of events is transformed into a meaningful whole. "By means of the plot, goals, causes, and chance are brought together within the temporal unity of a whole and complete action."[36]

The plot is thus the necessary mediation between the individual events, incidents, accidents, characters, etc. on the one hand and the story taken as a whole on the other. It is thanks to the plot that a diversity of actions and events may be grasped together and so "thought." Like metaphor, narrative brings things together. But to what kind of thinking does the poetic reasoning of the plot give rise? Narrative understanding for Ricoeur is both temporal and teleological. The beginning, middle and end of a history refer not only to their chronological place, but to their place in the logic of the plot. The "end" is not simply the last thing to happen in a sequence, but the conclusion of a story. This conclusion "follows" neither chronologically nor logically from what has gone before, but rather teleologically. An historical event, therefore, is not only an occurrence, something that happens, but a narrative component that contributes to a plot. The same event, say the birth of a king, may be the beginning of one history or the end of another, depending on the logic of the plot.

We are now in a position to see how the historian has recourse to the imagination and to narrative understanding.[37] Thanks to the imagination and the work of emplotment, the historian sees diverse things and events grouped together in time in meaningful patterns. Thanks to the intelligibility proper to the plot, stories and histories may be "followed."[38] Following a story is not like following an argument. To "follow" a story or history is to see how each event and action displays a particular directedness, an orientation governed by the conclusion.[39] Each individual event is understood in light of its place in the temporal – teleological whole. The pieces of a historical puzzle are thus elements of a story. Ricoeur contends that history ceases to be history if it loses its basic narrative "competence," that is, its ability to "follow" stories. Historians who belittle narrative understanding fail to recognize the configurative aspect of plots that give stories a cognitive significance beyond the "and then, and then, and then." Ricoeur believes that a naive notion of narrative, considered as a disconnected series of events, is always to be found behind the critique of the narrative character of history. Thanks to its configurative dimension, however, narrative has its own kind of cognitive significance. To follow is to understand. Ricoeur allows for other types of historical explanation, but these explanatory techniques are always at the service of under-standing.[40] The proper function of an historical explanation is to help us to follow the story better. Again we see Ricoeur's unique hermeneutical arch, where explanation exists only for the sake of understanding and appropriation.

Historians, however, are not simply story-tellers. Unlike novelists, historians not only spin tales but do research. A historian must not tell just any story; rather, the historian is under the constraint of the past. The historian's plots are constrained by documents and other types of evidence that remain and demand to be accounted for. The novelist is under no such constraint. Whereas the novelist's story is self-explanatory, the historian must have recourse to explanatory procedures proper to historical inquiry:

> It is for this reason that historians are not simply narrators: they give reasons why they consider a particular factor *rather than some other* to be the sufficient cause of a given course of events ... they argue because they know that we can explain *in other ways*.[41]

Interestingly enough, historians determine the significance of various causes by imagining what would have happened if an event had not occurred.[42] Like the poet, the historian is involved in constructing an imaginary laboratory of the possible and the probable. Finally, there is the problem of objectivity in history, which means that one historian's results should complement another's, since both accounts are about the same world.[43] In sum, what sets the historian's epistemology apart from the other human sciences is its twofold allegiance to criticism (historical research) and imagination (narrative emplotment).[44] Story and history remain distinct, but the epistemological ditch is a good deal narrower.

The historian is motivated by his desire to do justice to the past. Ricoeur is fond of saying that the historian is a "debtor" to the past. This is what distinguishes the historian from the novelist: history alone claims to speak of events that have *actually* happened. This ambition creates the ontological gap between the respective references of fiction and history. But where conventional wisdom takes this reference to the real to be the distinguishing characteristic of history, Ricoeur is not so sure. What, he asks, does the term "real" signify when it is applied to the historical past?[45] Ricoeur believes we can continue to speak of the "reality" of the historical past, but at the same time he insists that history does not refer to the past in the same way that empirical descriptions refer to the present:

Not that the past is unreal, but past reality is, in the strict sense of the word, unverifiable. Insofar as it no longer exists, the discourse of history can seek to grasp it only *indirectly*. It is here that the relationship with fiction shows itself as crucial.[46]

The historian has only "traces" of the past, a past which is now absent. On the one hand, the trace functions as a limit-idea, reminding us that the past is not to be had, an inaccessible thing-in-itself. On the other hand, the trace functions as a guiding concept for historical research: *something* once happened: "It is the past *such as* it was that moves the historian to provide historical configurations and that is behind their endless rectifications, as they touch up the painting."[47] This obligation to do justice to the traces of the past and so correspond to what actually happened allows history to remain distinct from fiction.

However, because the past is no longer here, history refers to the past only indirectly. The historian's reconstruction is not a reproduction of the actual course of events. In trying to define the relation of history to the past, Ricoeur takes his point of departure from von Ranke's celebrated formula that historians describe the past *as* it actually happened (*wie es eigentlich gewesen*). However, Ricoeur differs from von Ranke and other historians by stressing the metaphorical nature of the *as* – *as* it actually happened. The historian does not describe but redescribes. History for Ricoeur, like metaphor, is also a matter of "seeing as." Histories are imaginative configurations: the historian invents figures that represent the past. Like the master of metaphor, the historian does not make copies but invents in order to discover. We may recall Ricoeur's analysis of metaphorical reference – a claim to say what things are *like*. The historian's narrative is a "model" of the past, but Ricoeur observes that "there is no original given with which to compare the model."[48] In other words, historical narratives are *creative* imitations.

Thanks to their metaphoric function by which histories create figures of the past, Ricoeur shows that the reference of history, no less than its manner of making sense, has an irreducibly fictive aspect. In so doing he has accomplished the first step in bridging the epistemological and ontological ditch between history and fiction. However, lest the distinction disappear, Ricoeur reminds us that what keeps a narrative historical is its accountability to traces that both call for and correct history's redescriptions of the past.

Fiction and the real

Ricoeur builds the bridge between history and fiction from both sides. History, both in its method and its truth claim, has recourse to the imagination and its operation of narrative emplotment more than has previously been thought. Fiction, for its part, is "about" the real, for it too is a representation (mimesis) of human actions. But note that the reference of fictional discourse is incomplete or suspended until it is received and applied by a reader. The purpose of fiction in configuring human action is to affect the reader in some way. Fiction is thus implicated not only in poetics but also in ethics and rhetoric insofar as it is "effective discourse" that is not only about human action but actually affects it.[49] In other words, works of fiction make a difference in the world. It is not for nothing that we say that stories may "move" us. Ricoeur notes that the phenomenon of catharsis as it appears in Aristotle's *Poetics* is the paradigm for "the movement from the work to the spectator."[50] The plot has the power to evoke feelings in the reader. The "affects" one experiences through reading are "effects" of fictional discourse.

Ricoeur laments the epistemological disrepute into which fictions, like metaphors and the imagination itself, have fallen. It is not that fictions refer to something that is absent, but that they refer to something unreal that is the true scandal for many philosophers. But Ricoeur seizes on this freedom from the burden of reference to "what is" to exploit what he considers to be the unique cognitive function of fictions. Fictions enjoy a special epistemological role: they discover through inventing. In the history of painting, the invention of oil paint in the fifteenth century allowed Flemish painters to rediscover the "luminosity" of the universe. Similarly, the new techniques of the impressionists enabled them to capture something of the fleetingness of reality. In fiction as in painting, mimesis "is no longer a reduplication of reality but a creative rendering of it."[51]

According to Ricoeur, fictions are not less real than the things they represent but more real, in the sense that they focus on what is essential. In Ricoeur's opinion, Plato got it wrong: far from diminishing reality, images and fictions actually "augment" it. By abbreviating, selecting and condensing, the painter enhances certain colors and shapes. The writer of fiction does the same for time and human actions. Fictions therefore "magnify" certain aspects of reality.[52] A short poem may better capture the "essence" of an event than a detailed journalistic description. We come to understand the "essence" of jealousy not by studying statistics or journal articles but by watching *Othello*. It is only because fictions are free from referring to the actual world, however, that they can "increase" reality. This paradoxical feature of fiction should not be overlooked:

The more imagination deviates from that which is called reality in ordinary language and vision, the more it approaches the heart of the reality which is no longer the world of manipulable objects, but the world into which we have been thrown by birth and within which we try to orient ourselves by projecting our innermost possibilities upon it, in order that we *dwell* there, in the strongest sense of that word.[53]

Ricoeur's understanding of fiction applies to more than narrative. Fictions share something in common with scientific models and political utopias: "All of them are cognitive in the sense that they make reality appear as it does. All of them have this organizing power because ... they generate *novel* grids for reading experience."[54] In so saying, Ricoeur believes he has rehabilitated the epistemic worth of fictions.

Narrative fictions, of course, are "about" human actions. While it is history's intention to refer to human actions in the past, the specificity of fiction is to project possible worlds of human action and so to express and occasion "fictive" experiences. The narrative voice in each work of fiction presents the world of the text to the reader, much like the voice that told Augustine "Tolle, lege" ("Take, read").[55] Each fictional work invites the reader to see the world from the vantage point of the story. Fiction asks us to suspend our attention to the actual world and attend to another world: "In this state of non-engagement we try new ideas, new values, new ways of being-in-the-world. Imagination is this free play of possibilities."[56] Indeed, Ricoeur relates fiction to our very capacity to act: "It is, in fact, in the anticipatory imagining of action that I 'try out' different possible courses of action and that I 'play' ... with practical possibilities."[57] In sum, we may describe fictional narratives as the imaginative work that metaphorically projects a world. By projecting worlds, fictions "remake" reality.

Fiction has the power to "remake" reality and, within the framework of narrative fiction in particular, to remake real praxis to the extent that the text intentionally aims at a horizon of new reality which we may call a world. It is this world of the text which intervenes in the world of action in order to give it a new configuration or, as we might say, in order to transfigure it.[58]

What must reality be if fiction can remake it? Ricoeur here treads cautiously: just as he criticizes the naive concept of the "reality" of the historical past, so too he rejects the naive notion of the "unreality" of fictions. Ricoeur complains that the tendency to reduce fiction to illusion "closes the way to any ontology of fiction."[59] On the other hand, he acknowledges that "[u]nder the shock of fiction, reality becomes problematic."[60] Ricoeur has entitled one of his articles "The function of fiction in shaping reality" – but what *is* reality if it can be so shaped? The answer is clear: *the world that fiction shapes is the world of the reader.* It is most significant that when he finally comes to discuss the truth of fiction Ricoeur shifts his terminology: henceforth he speaks of "refiguration" rather than reference. By "refiguration" Ricoeur means "the revelatory and transformative power exercised by narrative configurations when they are 'applied' to actual human acting and suffering."[61] The crucial notion here is "applied": the world of the text has ontological status only when it is read. Fiction is revealing insofar as it discloses important but hidden aspects of human existence, and transformative "in the sense that a life thus examined is a changed life, another life."[62] In so relating fiction to the world, Ricoeur holds that we have reached the point where invention and discovery are indistinguishable, that is, the point where the notion of "reference" no longer works. Fictions refigure the world by enabling us to see it, and ourselves, in new ways.

The world of the text only encounters the real world when the text is *read*.[63] Reading mediates the fictive world of the text and the actual world of the reader; it is the privileged place where the text's possible world intersects with the actual world. Whatever ontological status the world of the text enjoys remains in suspense until it is "taken up" and read. Fictions reach the real world through their effects, namely, the revelation and transformation of life and morals.[64] Ricoeur thus explores the truth of fiction not with a theory of reference but with a *theory of effects*. Fictions have revelatory and transforming power because of their contrast with actual experience. Freed from the everyday, fiction frees the reader for new evaluations of reality and himself. In other words, the relation of fiction to the real is one of *application* or appropriation rather than reference. Whereas in history we move from life to literature by narratives that "take the place of" the past, in fiction we move from literature to life by narratives that enter the world of the reader. In the end, it is not reality per se that is shaped, but the manner in which the reader perceives reality. Does this mean that fiction does not "remake" the world? On the contrary, fictions remake the only world that matters, the only world that I *care* about – *my* world. Ricoeur holds that by broadening our horizons, by proposing new possibilities, the reader's world is remade or refigured, for our "world" is nothing else than the scope of our possibilities. Thanks to this "fusion of horizons" between my world and the world of the text, my self-understanding is challenged. Application is inherent in the task of hermeneutics as Ricoeur conceives it, for the purpose of interpretation is to conquer the distance between text and interpreter so that the interpreter can appropriate the meaning for himself:

It is thus the growth of his own understanding of himself that he pursues through his understanding of the other. Every hermeneutics is thus, explicitly or implicitly, self-understanding by means of understanding others.[65]

Ontology and the travail of narrative: worlds without end?

Vanity, vanity, all is vanity. What does a man gain from all his labor and his toil here under the sun? Generations come and go, while the earth endures forever ... And who can tell what is good for a man in this life, this brief span of empty existence through which he passes like a shadow?[66]

Perhaps no other reflection on the mystery of time so eloquently expresses the meaninglessness of human existence as this passage from Ecclesiastes. Under the burden of an indifferent cosmic time ("under the sun"), all human striving appears vain – a "useless passion." The briefness of human life as opposed to the immensity of cosmic time makes life appear futile and insignificant. Indeed, this is the central paradox for a philosophical anthropology: on the cosmic scale the duration of our life is insignificant, "yet this brief lapse of time where we appear on the scene of the world is the very place from which proceeds every question of significance."[67] For Ricoeur, all philosophical reflections on time serve only to deepen this fundamental paradox.[68] The meaning of life is put into question because of the acute gap between "lived" time and "clock" time, between a time with a present and a time without a present, between a time "full" of the past and coming future, and a time of successive "instants." We experience this discontinuity between "lived" time and "cosmic" time as the misery of the human condition. No other species is "historical" in the same way as the human: only persons are conscious of past and future, memory and hope. Without such historical consciousness, there would be no human being, no passion for the possible.

Ricoeur proposes a solution to the Preacher's cry: if we are to "redeem the time," if we are to make time "human" by gaining a historical consciousness, we must have stories and histories. Ricoeur finds in narratives the resources to mediate between lived time and cosmic time and so articulate a "human" time. While Kant may have been the first thinker to link imagination and time in his theory of schematization, Ricoeur's originality lies in his claim that *specifically human being in time comes to expression through narrative schema*, at the crossroads of history and fiction. Thanks to their respective "configurations" of human actions in terms of temporal wholes, history and fiction together "refigure" (i.e., illumine and transform) time and so render it meaningful. Ricoeur observes that the term "history" (*histoire*, *Geschichte*) in most Indo-European languages has "the intriguing ambiguity of meaning both 'what actually happened' and the report of those happenings."[69] Telling history and being in history belong together: "We belong to history before telling stories or writing histories."[70] Ricoeur suggests that history and fiction have a common referential aim: our "belonging to" history. In short, if we are to discover the meaning of human existence, we need to understand the nature of our being in time. But the way humans exist in time comes to language only through narrative telling. History and fiction therefore work together towards expressing the meaning of human being "under the sun."

Ricoeur believes that history responds to the disproportion between lived time and cosmic time by inventing a third time – "historical time."[71] History invents certain instruments of thought that serve to connect these two estranged times. The first "invention" of history is the calendar. By relating days and events to the movement of the sun, the calendar integrates human actions into the cosmic order.[72] The calendar inscribes lived time in cosmic time. It is a creative mediation insofar as it "cosmologizes" lived time and "humanizes" cosmic time. The calendar is thus one strategy for rendering human being in time more meaningful. The second connector is the "trace" of the past. The trace, as an empirical object, belongs to the "still" of cosmic time, but its presence signifies a human world that is "no more."[73] The trace belongs to the order of things, but, insofar as it represents past human possibilities, it carries a "world." Because it belongs both to the empirical and existential order, the trace is perhaps the ultimate connector of cosmic time and lived time. Generations may come and go, but their striving is not wholly in vain, for *traces* of their desire and effort to exist are left "under the sun."[74]

Fiction responds to the dichotomy between lived and cosmic time by constructing imaginative "variations on a theme." Works of fiction, that is, are free to experiment with different ways in which we deal with this gap between lived time and cosmic time. Fiction can explore various orientations to time because it is not subject to the constraints of history (i.e., adherence to calendar time, conformity to documents and traces). Fictional narratives are thus Ricoeur's "privileged domain"[75] and in *Time and Narrative* Ricoeur focuses in particular on "tales about time."[76] Ricoeur reads Virginia Woolf's *Mrs. Dalloway* as a story about two extreme human responses to the burden of cosmic time, represented in the novel by Big Ben ("First a warning, musical; then the hour, irrevocable"). For Septimus, like the Preacher, there is no reconciliation between the time of the soul and the time of the world. Alienated and unable to effect a mediation with cosmic time, he eventually commits suicide. Mrs. Dalloway's response to cosmic time is opposite: the news of Septimus' death (i.e., the victory of cosmic time) serves as the impetus which leads her to reaffirm life despite cosmic time. In displaying different ways of being-towards-death, fiction has the power to show us modes of authentic existence that we have perhaps forgotten – or never known.[77]

In their own ways, both histories and fictions, by inventing a time between lived and cosmic time, aim at making human being in time more meaningful. Accordingly, narratives contribute to Ricoeur's general project of studying the meaning of human being. Indeed, because of the constitutive role stories and histories play in displaying possible values and ways of life, we might say that Ricoeur has laid the foundation for a peculiarly narrative humanism.[78] Though history is to be distinguished from fiction because of its interest in objective inquiry, Ricoeur believes a deeper interest governs historical research and reveals a fundamental bond between the references of history and fiction. This deeper interest of the historian is that of communication. The job of the historian is to remember and remind; accordingly, he selects from the past what he believes is memorable.

And what is most worthy of being kept in our memories are the *values* which ruled the individual actions, the life of institutions, and the social struggles of the past. Thanks to the objective work of the historian, these values are added to the common treasure of mankind.[79]

Insofar as these past values are different from present ones, the historian opens up the real towards the possible: "The 'true' stories of the past expose the potentialities of the present."[80] History's interest in communication demands that we be open to these possibilities, and this in turn involves a practical competence, namely, "letting ourselves be exposed to the efficacity of history."[81] Following Gadamer, Ricoeur observes that we are affected by history largely through reading. The possibilities that history opens must be imaginatively appropriated.

Fiction too is about possible ways of human being in the world. Because of its freedom from the constraints of history, however, fiction is able to take us to the "heart" of the real. Fiction can project those possibilities that might have taken place or should have taken place. But just as history in its representation of the past is "fictionalized," so Ricoeur believes that fiction undergoes a certain "historicization." Fiction represents actions "as if" they had taken place. Fictions, that is, are about a "quasi-past." Though this quasi-past is freed from the constraints that bind history (i.e. the calendar), there are interior constraints that are just as compelling. Ricoeur cites the incident of the *madeleine* from Proust's *A la recherche du temps perdu*. The narrator "recovers" lost time when, upon seeing the *madeleine*, he is able to discern something essential. Literature is nothing less than the attempt to articulate this impression, and in so doing, to recognize the real. The novelist is in debt to this vision of another world, of which the *madeleine* is a "trace," just as much a debt as the historian is in debt to the dead.

Together, history and fiction constitute a "schematism" of human action by creating figures for human being in time. At the intersection of their respective references, we see what is humanly possible. Both stories and histories uncover buried possibilities of the past: history reminds us of what has happened, and fiction reminds us of what could have happened. In reading histories and fictions, therefore, our own horizons are challenged and broadened. We are able to see the world and ourselves in a different light. History and fiction therefore appear in Ricoeur's thought as two kinds of passions for the possible that together contribute to what we are calling a narrative humanism. In order to apply these possibilities to oneself, however, and let them refigure one's own way of being in the world, the reader must "dispossess" himself of his prejudices. We all have horizons that are historically conditioned; but though these horizons are always situated, they may be expanded. In reading stories and histories, new possibilities of existence are displayed. An individual or society bereft of stories and histories and the possibilities they display will be to that degree diminished. If a people have no stories or histories, they can have no past nor future. For Ricoeur, the meaning of human being is a function of the possibilities open to it. To be human is to have a passion for the possible. Humanity is enhanced when exposed to memorable and essential possibilities of action and living in the world.

Again, Ricoeur argues that time becomes "human" time only as one inhabits a constellation of historical and fictional worlds. Thanks to narrative, we gain a historical consciousness, an awareness that there are possible worlds behind and before me. Human being is "historical" because it is always conscious of past, present and future. Historical consciousness means that expectations and memories are always criss-crossing and affecting the present. Most importantly for Ricoeur, we gain an awareness that the present is now a time "to do" something, "to act" – a "historical present."[82] On the one hand, this historical present is the result of the past; on the other, it is the potential inaugurating force of a history to-be-done. Historical consciousness is thus aware of being affected by the past but also of "making history." Charged with a memory and a hope, the present is henceforth the "time of initiative," the time when the passion for the possible is translated into action.[83] Ricoeur characterizes the historical present by the term "begin." The concept of beginning or doing implies that the world is not totally actualized; the world includes something "to be done by me."[84]

Finally, in giving us a historical consciousness, narrative bestows an identity as well. Indeed, Ricoeur suggests that personal identity is inherently narrative in nature. To understand who we are is to be able to follow our stories. Narrative also provides the all-important link between the continuity and discontinuity of the self. As historical, the self changes; yet it remains itself.[85] One implication of narrative identity is that we must be "readers" of our own lives. One way of

making sense of who we are is to identify with characters in other stories
and histories. To the extent that this is so, these narratives "refigure"
our lives. Ricoeur has from the beginning of his philosophical career
denied to Descartes the privilege of direct inspection of consciousness.
The human subject is neither self-transparent nor illusory: rather, the
subject is a being in time that leaves behind traces of its existence that
must be interpreted: "The subject thus appears constituted simultaneously as reader and writer of his own life."[86] The "self" of self-
knowledge is the "examined" life, "a life purified and clarified by the
cathartic effects of historical as well as fictional narratives carried by
our culture."[87] Narrative identity works on the social level as well.
Both individuals and communities are formed in their identity by certain
narratives which become *their* story or history. Ricoeur says that it is
largely by telling stories of certain foundation events that biblical Israel
became a historical community. Israel received the same stories it
produced.

   Coming to self-understanding is thus the counterpart of reading for
Ricoeur. Narrative consequently marks the most appropriate meeting
ground for a philosophical anthropology that is also hermeneutical: "To
rework language is to rediscover what we are."[88] The act of reading,
however, is initially more a matter of imagination than of will. Even
though narrative is about human action, the possible worlds are
addressed first of all to our imagination. Without the prior imaginative
appropriation of a possibility, the will would have no projects to realize.
Henceforth, Ricoeur's *Philosophy of the Will* comes second, after a
philosophy of the imagination. But both will and imagination are
constitutive of narrative identity. Reading is an invitation to inhabit
another world. At some point, this invitation must either be accepted
or rejected by a decision. My identity will be constituted by my decision
to inhabit this world rather than another. But in which world will I
declare "Here I stand"? The vision of the world displayed by narratives
is never ethically neutral, and neither is the reader: "It only remains
that it belongs to the reader, henceforth as *agent*, initiator of *action*, to
choose between the multiple propositions of ethical rightness bodied
forth in reading."[89]

Ideology and utopia: critique of poetic reason

"It is by an understanding of the worlds, actual and possible, opened
by language that we may arrive at a better understanding of ourselves."[90] This is well and good, but the Preacher's complaint that

"of the reading of books there is no end" leads to a similar confusion of worlds without end. In which one or several worlds projected by narrative texts should I live? This question becomes even more troublesome when one begins to suspect that the narrative form sometimes projects false worlds and false possibilities. Is the narrative form, whether employed in fictions or histories, itself an artifice, an artificial order imposed on an orderless human experience? Hans Kellner suggests that for Ricoeur narrative serves primarily to create a sense of time that would allow humanity to feel as though it "belongs" to history and the world.[91] Narrative refers to human temporality by a process that Hayden White likens to allegorical reference. What goes on on the surface level of the plot does not matter, it is the spiritual (in this case temporal) meaning that counts.[92] Kellner suggests that in Ricoeur's theory, historical narrative can be seen as "an allegorical creation for a human purpose."[93] In evoking this sense of belonging and a sense of human time, narrativity may indeed console us – but is it true? Kellner observes the irony of the situation: "Ultimately, allegory questions its own authority by inescapably drawing attention to the *will* exerted in its creation; this will to represent is revealed as a human need, the product of desire or 'Care'."[94]

Language, in other words, may distort as well as reveal. Texts may project evil or false visions of the world (e.g., fascist myths). The "function of fiction in remaking reality" is potentially dangerous if the possibilities projected are dehumanizing, or at least misleading, if they are not capable of being realized. Karl Marx would agree with Ricoeur that we remake our praxis in terms of fiction, but he dubs these fictions "ideologies" and defines them by their distance from the real (praxis). According to Marx, to control the "social imaginary" is to control what people believe to be possible in practice. For Marx and others who are suspicious of ideologies, narrative's power to display communal possibilities and construct social reality may console us, but only at the price of distracting us from concrete problems in the "real" world. Marx, whom Ricoeur considers to be one of the three modern masters of suspicion, represents those who believe the narrative form as such to be an opiate of the people. Ricoeur addresses problems concerning the social imaginary in his *Lectures on Ideology and Utopia*. Ricoeur tries to overcome the dichotomy between the real and the imaginary on the communal level of the imagination as well, a dichotomy represented by Karl Mannheim's treatment of ideology and utopia as two deviant attitudes toward reality.[95]

Unlike many critical social theorists, Ricoeur begins his analysis of

i. e. possible worlds are not necessarily something good

ideology and utopia by stressing the positive functions. Ideologies serve
"to identify a society and to preserve that identity."[96] Ideologies only
go wrong when the dominant power uses ideas and narratives to
legitimize an authority that exceeds what the society is willing to
accord it. Ricoeur links utopias with the productive imagination and
other fictions. By expressing a vision that goes beyond the actual, they
effect a "metaphorization of the real, a creation of new meaning."[97]
Narrative utopias project a new way of living. Utopia sketches a vision
of the future that gives society its goals. "This is a very positive function
and on it depends everything new that is created ... Utopia is the thrust
of the possible."[98] Utopia means "nowhere" (not yet in time): it is
from this "nonplace" "that we can take a fresh look at reality, in relation
to which nothing can henceforth be taken for granted. The field of the
possible now extends out beyond the real."[99] Utopia is a passion for
what is socially possible. Utopia only goes wrong when its proponents
are dreamers who have no idea how to *initiate* their vision in concrete
practice. Ricoeur believes that a healthy society needs both ideology and
utopia in order to have an identity and a destiny: "In short, *ideology* as
a symbolic confirmation of the past and *utopia* as a symbolic opening
towards the future are complementary."[100]

Of the two forms of social imagination, utopia is the one that projects
possible worlds and thus raises the question of the reality of these
possibilities. How can we know whether our projections – our hopes
– are genuine or illusory? For instance, is the way of being projected
by the Gospels "utopian" in the positive or the pejorative sense of the
term, and what criteria can help us decide this question? That the issue
of criteria must be posed follows from the plurality of conflicting
utopias presently tantalizing the social imagination. As "imaginative
variations" on the themes of family, society, government and religion,
each utopian vision seeks to impassionate society. Decisions must be
made; courses of action must be chosen. Our wagers will be costly.

Creative language, especially narrative, is intimately bound up with
utopias. Utopia is a form of poetic vision which, like metaphor, shatters
the present order of things. Ernst Bloch, in his *The Principle of Hope*,
suggests that the poet is the one who sees potentialism coming to fruition.
Indeed, by creatively anticipating a future, the artist or poet actually
contributes to the hastening of that future toward the present. Ricoeur
too has remarked that "The poet is the prophet of his own
existence."[101] Bloch, as a Marxist philosopher and materialist who
nevertheless believes in a "principle of hope," makes an interesting
counterfoil to Ricoeur's philosophy of narrative hope. Bloch believes

that whether what is anticipated in art becomes actual or not depends not on poetry but on society, on what people decide to do.

As a philosopher of hope, Bloch claims that the utopian imagination has an objective correlate: "Real Possibility." Bloch considers possibility to be "the Benjamin among the great concepts."[102] Most philosophers study only the formally or conceptually possible; they ask what are the necessary conditions for such and such possibility, but they do not realize that the conditions themselves may evolve. In his analysis of possibility, Bloch discovers a hitherto unknown continent: the objectively real possible. This category refers to possibilities whose conditions have not yet "ripened."[103] Man is the real possibility of everything which has become of him in his history and "above all, which can still become of him if his progress is not blocked."[104] The same is true for matter, which for Bloch is in process, an open "being-in-possibility" which contains the seeds of its own transcendence.[105] To this process metaphysics, Bloch's Marxist materialism adds the thought that human beings need to *work* with matter in history in order to bring about the possible. Here then is a passion for the possible that, unlike Ricoeur's, is wholly independent of the language of faith.

In order to evaluate the utopian imagination which is common to Bloch and to Ricoeur, we need a new critique, a "critique of poetic reason." This critique would inquire into the realizability of the possible worlds projected by the poetic vision which form the content of utopias and the "substance" of things hoped for. Is the vision of a "reconciled humanity" a real possibility? Comparing Bloch's ontology of the "not yet" with Ricoeur's philosophy of the creative imagination raises two interesting questions – especially for the theologian. First, how do we know that we are (or will be) genuinely capable of appropriating a possible world, that is, of realizing a given utopia? Stated more generally, how can we discern illusory possibilities from ones that are capable of being actualized? As one of Bloch's critics remarks, the criterion of real possibility cannot simply be "the continued appearance of an ideal in utopian imagination."[106] Though Bloch and Ricoeur can marshall impressive evidence for the reality of the utopian imagination, none of this proves "that such intentionality has a correlate in real possibility."[107] Bloch admits that the conditions of the possible are not yet completely sufficient, but he maintains that they may become so. However, they need not do so, and Bloch cites the scholastic principle *a posse ad esse non valet consequentia* ("There is no necessary development from potential to being").[108] This leads to the second issue: how are these conditions of the possible sufficiently realized? For Bloch, this depends on a process metaphysics and a Marxist ethic: matter is "open," but humans must work to achieve certain possibilities. Bloch's is a secularized eschatology that looks only to open material possibilities. This is a far cry from a theological position such as that of Gabriel Marcel, which holds that hope does not continue but contradicts the processes immanent to this world. The passion for the possible is directed more towards an intervention from without than a working from within.

A critique of poetic reason is directed more towards utopia than ideology. But where Marx contrasts things as they appear in ideas and things as they really are (praxis), Ricoeur is much less willing to see a dichotomy. Imagining, for Ricoeur, narrative or otherwise, involves both invention and discovery. Given the conflict of utopias, however, we must have some means of saying that the way of life a narrative displays is more than a product of the "magic of thought."[109] How can we say "these ideas are valid in this situation, these are not"? Mannheim assumes we need a standpoint of absolute knowledge.[110] For Ricoeur, however, the answer lies in our preserving a historical consciousness and a hermeneutical discourse. "We must confront who we may be by who we are."[111] That is, the prospects for the future must be read in light of possibilities past and present. Without a sense of the past and present, we will lack concrete paths to utopia. Without utopias, however, we will forever be slaves to the past and present.[112] Because we do not have absolute knowledge, we must ultimately make a wager: "We wager on a certain set of values and then try to be consistent with them; verification is therefore a question of our whole life. No one can escape this."[113] Similarly, faith lives out of the tension between ideology and utopia:

As the Remembrance of some epoch-making events – the Exodus and the Resurrection – it shares something with the positive concept of ideology. As the Expectation of the Kingdom to come it shares something with the positive concept of utopia ... The root of faith is somewhere near that point where Expectation springs forth out of memory.[114]

In the end, whether the hopeful vision is that of a prophet and evangelist, on the one hand, or madman and demagogue, on the other, will only be proved in practice – a practice informed, of course, by a hope in narrative redescriptions of human life.

Notes

1 Thanks to this link to temporality, Ricoeur raises narrative theory to an entirely new level, carrying it beyond historiography and literary criticism to philosophy and, as we shall see in Part II, theology. Significantly, Ricoeur's interest in narrative also stems from his belief in the essentially narrative character of biblical faith: "the act of telling has a religious dimension which is probably not at all foreign to narrative's power to structure time" ("History," 214).

2 See *HHS*, ch. 6 "Metaphor and the Central Problem of Hermeneutics."

3 Cf. *HHS*, Part II "Studies in the Theory of Interpretation" and the whole of *IT*.

4 In one way or another, Freud, Marx and Nietzsche – the three "masters of suspicion" – have stressed how language can distort rather than reveal the world.

5 Ricoeur is here mediating two hermeneutical traditions: "If there is a feature which distinguishes me not only from the hermeneutics of Schleiermacher and Dilthey, but also from that of Heidegger and even Gadamer ... it is indeed my concern to avoid the pitfall of an opposition between an 'understanding' which would be reserved for the 'human sciences' and an 'explanation' which would be common to the latter and to the nomological sciences, primarily the physical sciences" (*HHS*, 36).

6 *HHS*, 145.

7 Ibid., 138. Writing does more than preserve discourse. Writing entails a veritable upheaval of the language–world relation, which results in what Ricoeur terms the "threefold semantic autonomy" of the text. This means, first, that the meaning of the text is no longer equated with the author's intention. Because the author is no longer there to clarify his intentions, "the text's career escapes the finite horizon lived by its author" (*IT*, 30). Second, the text is also cut off from its original context and its original audience. Free from its original *Sitz im Leben*, the text is open to an unlimited series of reading by other audiences. Third, the autonomy of the text from its original situation means it is no longer able to refer ostensively. What the text and the reader share is not a situation, but what Ricoeur calls a "world."

8 *IT*, 87–8.

9 *HHS*, 159.

10 Ibid., 152.

11 "Understanding precedes, accompanies, closes and thus *envelops* explanation. In return, explanation *develops* understanding analytically" (*PPR*, 165).

12 *HHS*, 158. See also his essay on "Appropriation" in *HHS*.

13 "Myth," 45.

14 *HHS*, 112.

15 That this terminology is reminiscent of Heidegger is no coincidence. Ricoeur has recreated on the textual level the whole process of Heideggerian interpretation, i.e., understanding by projecting possibilities.

16 *IT*, 36.

17 Ibid., 37.

18 *TN* I, ix.

19 Ibid.

20 Wittgenstein lists "telling of stories" next to "solving problems" in his *Philosophical Investigations*.

21 *TN* I, 3.

22 Cf. Stephen Crites, "The Narrative Quality of Experience," *JAAR* 39 (1971), 291–311.

23 Heidegger makes a similar point: humans are not simply "within" time, but they "reckon" with time and "care" about it. Cf. chapter 2 above.

24 To account for the experience of "short" or "long" times, Augustine suggests that the soul itself is "stretched." Time is measured not by the movement of the stars but by the "movement" of the soul. See Ricoeur's extended analysis of Book XI of the *Confessions* in *TN* I, 5–30.

25 Augustine, *Confessions*, Book XI.

26 Ricoeur writes: "If we continue to translate mimesis by 'imitation,' we have to understand something completely contrary to a copy of some preexisting reality and speak instead of a creative imitation" (*TN* I, 45). Plato entertained a very low view of the epistemic worth of artistic representation, as a copy of the world, which is itself only a copy of the Forms. Art and literature are thus two steps removed from Truth. See his *Republic*, Book X.

27 *Poetics* 1448^a 16–17 (translation modified).

28 *TN* I, xi. Elsewhere, Ricoeur says that mimesis "is a kind of metaphor of reality" and suggests that the conjunction of mythos and mimesis is the paradigm for the kind of reference common to all fictions ("Fiction," 8).

29 *TN* I, 34.

30 Aristotle, *Poetics* 1451^b 1–7. Aristotle's remark contains the seed for another ditch – one that has been particularly difficult for theologians to navigate: "the accidental truths of history can never become the universal proofs of reason" (G. E. Lessing, "On the Proof of the Spirit and of Power," in Henry Chadwick (ed.), *Lessing's Theological Writings* [London, Black, 1956], 53).

31 Karl Hempel, "The Function of General Laws in History," in Patrick Gardiner (ed.), *Theories of History* (New York, Free Press, 1959), 344–56.

32 "My thesis rests on the assertion of an indirect connection of derivation by which historical knowledge proceeds from our narrative understanding without losing anything of its scientific ambition" (*TN* I, 92).

33 Clio is the muse of history, Calliope of epic poetry. T. P. Wiseman speaks of the "rouge of rhetoric" that typically adorned ancient historiography. Not only were ancient historians trained in rhetoric, but history and the

poetic epic shared a common aim: moral education through the example of heroic deeds, or in Aristotle's words, showing people better than they actually are (*Clio's Cosmetics: Three Studies in Greco-Roman Literature* [Leicester University Press, 1979]).

34 *TN* I, 41. Specifically, narratives express "poetic" universals (*TN* I, 40). These universals are not Platonic ideas, but are rather related to practical wisdom, to what one would probably do or say in such-and-such a situation. Of course, what is considered a probable course of action may differ from one culture to another.

35 In the third *Critique* Kant treats aesthetic and teleological judgments, both of which pertain to the invention or discovery of organic wholes. Ricoeur acknowledges the affinity of his notion of "emplotment" and Kant's reflective judgment: "I cannot overemphasize the kinship between this 'grasping together,' proper to the configurational act, and what Kant has to say about the operation of judging" (*TN* I, 66). And: "Emplotment, to my mind, is one of the most striking expressions of the power of schematization that Kant ascribes to the 'productive imagination'" ("NarHerm," 155). It is this synthesizing work of the plot that allows Ricoeur to consider narrative a form of semantic innovation along with metaphor. Cf. Louis O. Mink, "The Autonomy of Historical Understanding," *History and Theory* 5 (1966), 24–47 and "History and Fiction as Modes of Comprehension," *New Literary History* 1 (1970), 541–58.

36 *TN* I, ix.

37 See also Mary Gerhart, "Imagination and History in Ricoeur's Interpretation Theory," *PT* 23 (1979), 51–6.

38 Ricoeur borrowed the notion of "followability" from W. B. Gaillie's *Philosophy and the Historical Understanding* (London, Chatto and Windus, 1964). Ricoeur cannot follow Gaillie's claim that "History is a species of the genus story" (66) because this eliminates methods of explanation peculiar to history.

39 Gaillie explains followability as a "teleologically guided form of attention" (*Philosophy and Historical Understanding*, 38).

40 Ricoeur also interacts with Hayden White's *Metahistory: The Historical Imagination in Nineteenth Century Europe* (Baltimore, Johns Hopkins University Press, 1973) and his "The Text as Literary Artifact," in Robert H. Canary and H. Kozicki (eds.), *The Writing of History: Literary Form and Historical Understanding* (University of Wisconsin Press, 1978). White pushes the fictive quality of history to an extreme, suggesting that the same series of events can be emplotted in different ways. Historical explanation for White consists in identifying the kind of plot the historian uses (i.e., Tragedy, Comedy, etc.). Ricoeur prevents history from becoming poetry by insisting that history is accountable to traces from the past in a way that poetry is not.

41 *TN* I, 186.

42 Cf. Ricoeur's analysis of Max Weber's notion of "singular causal impu-
tation." He cites Weber as an example of a historian who determines the
causal significance of an event by imagining what would have happened
if the event had not taken place, and quotes Weber as follows: "In order
to penetrate the real causal interrelationships, *we construct unreal ones*" (cited
in *TN* I, 183). Ricoeur characterizes Weber's historical method as explanation by "quasi-plots."

43 "The credo of objectivity is nothing other than this twofold conviction that
the facts related by different histories can be linked together and that the
results of these histories can complete one another" (*TN* I, 176).

44 Ricoeur's demonstration of the indirect tie between historical research and
narrative competence is too detailed and complex to treat here. See *TN* I,
ch. 6 "Historical Intentionality," 175–225.

45 This question is the primary subject of *RHP* and of *TN* III, 142–56.

46 "Interpretation," 181.

47 *RHP*, 4.

48 Ibid., 32.

49 That texts affect the world should come as no surprise, for we have seen
that Ricoeur treats narrative as a form of discourse, and discourse concerns
language *as used*. As we have seen, Ricoeur refuses to reduce hermeneutics
to a study of the text as such. To guard against approaches that reduce the
text to a closed system of immanent relations, he speaks of a triple mimesis:
a "prefiguration" of action "before" the text, a "configuration" of action
by the plot "in" the text and a "refiguration" of action "after" the text
when the reader views his world in light of the plot. The plot, or mimesis$_2$,
leads us "from one side of the text to the other, transfiguring the one side
into the other through its power of configuration" (*TN* I, 53).

50 *TN* I, 50. Cf. "Metaphor" where Ricoeur suggests that catharsis is the
integrating point of the metaphorical process that conjoins cognition,
imagination and feeling.

51 "Function," 138.

52 "Every icon is a graphic figure which recreates reality at a higher level of
realism" ("Imagination," 10). "That fiction changes reality, in the sense
that it both 'invents' and 'discovers' it, could not be acknowledged as long
as the concept of image was merely identified with that of picture. Images
could not increase reality since they had no referents other than those of their
originals" ("Function," 127).

53 "Function," 139.

54 "Fiction," 10.

55 *TN* II, 99.

56 "Function," 134.

57 "Imagination," 12.

58 "Interpretation," 185.

59 "Function," 135.

60 Ibid., 139.

61 "Temps," 437. In replacing the language of reference with that of application, Ricoeur sides with the hermeneutic tradition of H. G. Gadamer (e.g., the "fusion of horizons") over against an epistemology.

62 *TN* III, 158. We shall have reason to examine this "truth-function" of fiction in greater detail in Part II.

63 Ricoeur is aware of the significance of the move from reference to refiguration, and links it to his conclusion that fiction is related to the real only in reading: "This recourse to the mediation of reading marks the most perceptible difference between the present work and *The Rule of Metaphor*" (*TN* III, 230).

64 "The effects of fiction, revelation and transformation, are essentially the effects of reading" (*TN* III, 101).

65 *CI*, 17.

66 Eccl. 1:2,3; 6:12.

67 "Temps," 440. Ricoeur has reformulated the "basic antinomy" of human being: the disproportion between finitude and infinity which is humanity's common lot is now given a specifically temporal orientation.

68 Roughly the first half of *TN* III is devoted to displaying the aporias of temporality. The second half of the book treats narrative's "poetic" response to these paradoxes.

69 "Fiction," 3.

70 *HHS*, 294. As we have seen, Ricoeur corrects Heidegger by insisting that "telling" mediates "being" and "time." See above, chapter 2.

71 Here again we see Ricoeur's favorite strategy of mediating an opposition with some "third term." Indeed, Ricoeur calls historical time a "third time" (*TN* III, 99).

72 See the discussion in *TN* III, 105–9.

73 By "traces," Ricoeur has in mind not only archeological evidence of the past but also documentary evidence (archives).

74 The Preacher's remark that generations come and go points to a third connector: the idea of the succession of generations. This is the biblical notion that the blessings and curses of the fathers will be visited upon their children. Here we have to do with biological more than cosmic time, namely, the fact that the dead are replaced by the living every thirty years. But because different generations live at the same moment, memories and traditions may be passed on. Ricoeur therefore considers historical succession to be a connector as well (*TN* III, 109–16).

75 "Temps," 447.

76 We shall consider the extent to which the Gospels may be considered "tales about time" in chapter 8 below.

77 Narrative is not limited to displaying 'withintimeness," but can respond to each of Heidegger's levels of temporality. Narrative approximates

historicality or being-a-whole thanks to its configurative dimension which makes wholes out of a beginning, middle and end.

78 Cf. David Stewart's "Existential Humanism" in Charles E. Reagan (ed.), *Studies in the Philosophy of Paul Ricoeur* (Ohio University, 1979), 21–32.

79 "Fiction," 16.

80 Ibid.

81 "HistHerm," 690.

82 John E. Smith suggests that we need to rehabilitate the *kairos* aspect of time, by which he means "right" or "opportune" time, time that marks an opportunity – "a time to …" Smith calls this "qualitative" time, but he means essentially the same thing as does Ricoeur by "human" time. *Kairos* points to the significance of historical events "and to the idea that there are constellations of events pregnant with a possibility or possibilities not to be met with at other times and under different circumstances" ("Time and Qualitative Time," *The Review of Metaphysics* 40 [1986], 5).

83 *TN* III, 207. For Heidegger, oriented as he was to the future, the present was an inauthentic mode of care. By tying the fate of the "historical present" to the notion of initiative, Ricoeur restores an authenticity to the present. See the extended discussion on the "historical present" in *TN* III, 230–40.

84 For an interesting confirmation of Ricoeur's point, see Richard Taylor's comment: "Time, I shall contend, has little significant reality except in the context of beings who not only think and feel, but who *create*" ("Time and Life's Meaning," *The Review of Metaphysics* 40 [1987], 676). Like Ricoeur, Taylor finds the uniqueness of human beings in their creativity: meaningful existence is only possible if something happens that is not the result of natural processes. The non-human world is meaningless because "there is never anything new, no purpose, no goal; in a word, nothing is ever created" (679). And like Ricoeur, Taylor believes that historical time is also the product of human creation (681).

85 Identity in the sense of sameness (*idem*) does not work for human being, for it does not account for what is most specific about human being, namely, historicity. Identity in the sense of "oneself" (*ipse*) can escape the dilemma of sameness or otherness insofar as it is construed as narrative. Narrative, as we have seen, accounts both for change (episode) and coherence (configuration). See the first conclusion in *TN* III, 244–9.

86 *TN* III, 246.

87 Ibid.

88 "Myth," 28. "What would we know of love and hate, of moral feelings and, in general, of all that we can call the *self*, if these had not been brought to language and articulated by literature?" (*HHS*, 143).

89 *TN* III, 249.

90 "Myth," 45.

91 Hans Kellner, "Narrativity in History," *History and Theory* 26 (1987), 15–18.

92 Hayden White, "The Question of Narrative in Contemporary Historical Theory," *History and Theory* 23 (1984), 26–30.

93 Kellner, "Narrativity," 29.

94 Ibid., 27.

95 Karl Mannheim, *Ideology and Utopia: An Introduction to the Sociology of Knowledge* (New York, Harcourt & Brace, 1936). Ricoeur discusses Mannheim in ch. 16 of *LIU*.

96 "History," 220.

97 "Myth," 24. "Utopia introduces imaginative variations on the topics of society, power, government, family, religion. The kind of neutralization that constitutes imagination as fiction is at work in utopia" (*LIU*, 16).

98 "History," 221.

99 "Imagination," 19.

100 "Myth," 30.

101 *HT*, 127.

102 *The Principle of Hope* (Oxford, Basil Blackwell, 1985), 242.

103 Ibid., 235. The idea of "ripening" suggests the notion of *kairos* – the "right" time. Interestingly enough, Ricoeur notes that Mannheim discovers a particular sense of time in each utopia. For a chiliastic utopia like that of Thomas Münzer, the present is the time of crisis (see *LIU*, 277).

104 *The Principle of Hope*, 235.

105 Bloch derives "being-in-possibility" from Aristotle's *dunamei on* (*Principle of Hope*, 205–10).

106 Wayne Hudson, *The Marxist Philosophy of Ernst Bloch* (London, Macmillan, 1982), 136.

107 Ibid., 108.

108 Bloch, *The Principle of Hope*, 226.

109 *LIU* (lecture 17).

110 "IdeologyCrit," 151.

111 *LIU*, xxxiii.

112 Ricoeur sees liberation theology as a positive example of utopian discourse because it links its future vision to symbols of *past* liberations such as the Exodus and to a political transformation of *present* reality ("Myth," 30).

113 *LIU* (lecture 18).

114 "Ideology," 28.

II

THE PASSION FOR THE POSSIBLE AND BIBLICAL NARRATIVE: STORIES OR HISTORIES OF JESUS?

> No one Evangelist would have sufficed
> To tell us of the pains of Jesus Christ,
> Nor does each tell it as the others do;
> Nevertheless, what each has said is true ...

> Chaucer, *The Canterbury Tales*

Part II sets Ricoeur's narrative theory in the context of contemporary theology. Exegetes and theologians replace poets and historians as Ricoeur's principal conversation partners. Self-understanding and a determination of what is humanly possible are here related to reading the Gospels, for Ricoeur is a philosopher who hearkens to the Christian word. I wager that Ricoeur's narrative theory provides new resources for theology's task of combining a particular historical fate (Jesus' passion) with a universal rational framework (the possibility of freedom). Similarly, Ricoeur's mediation of history and fiction transforms the troublesome dichotomy between the Jesus of history and the Christ of faith. Ricoeur suggests that the indispensability of Jesus for the "Christian possibility" of freedom or "new life" is related to the necessity for the Gospel to be a narrative. But in enlisting the poet as well as the historian to serve the believer, does Ricoeur make Jesus a mere illustration of the Christian possibility rather than its inaugurator?

I interpret Ricoeur's philosophy of narrative hope as a "thinking what was left unthought" in existentialist theology. Ricoeur agrees with the correlation of the self-understanding of faith and the kerygmatic word typical of Bultmannian theology, but he gives a surer linguistic and literary foundation to this moment of existential understanding (chapter 6). Ricoeur's theory of biblical narrative comes into sharp opposition with that of Hans Frei and the Yale school, an encounter that raises questions about the nature of theological method. Frei and Ricoeur represent two opposing strategies on the matter of how a theologian ought to use the Gospel narratives in order to formulate a christology (chapter 7). For Ricoeur, the narrative form as well as the subject matter eminently qualifies the Gospels as "tales about time." As such, they uniquely refigure human being by projecting a mode of being-in-the-world oriented towards "eternity" more than mortality. The Gospels thus function as schemas for authentic human existence (chapter 8). With regard to plot, the Gospel narratives tell about a "passion" for the possible. Jesus' story or history is somehow a condition for the possibility of freedom, a possibility that Ricoeur takes to define the content of religion. In some way, the Gospels are able to manifest the possibility of freedom and transform the reader's self-understanding. Ricoeur explores the conditions for this possibility. By finding philosophical "approximations" of theological ideas such as resurrection and justification by faith, Ricoeur works as an apologist not for the factuality so much as the intelligibility of the Christian story (chapter 9).

6

A newer hermeneutic: postscript
to Bultmann

Insofar as the Gospel narratives present Jesus as the paradigm for true humanity, they answer Kant's (and Ricoeur's) query: What is man? Traditional christologies, however, go one step further, identifying Jesus "as someone who on behalf of God *brings* definitive and decisive salvation to man."[1] Does Jesus of Nazareth *illustrate* or *inaugurate* this reconciled humanity for which we hope? Are the passion narratives representations of a universally available way of life or accounts of a contingent salvific event? Are the Gospels history, fiction, both or some *tertium quid*? The nature of the Gospel narratives is a question of considerable theological significance and even more theological debate. Various construals of the Gospels, from Antioch to Alexandria, Rome to Wartburg and New Haven to Chicago, have left in their wake a virtual chorus of christologies. Why listen to the Gospels? Is it because, as Kant held, they represent the ideal victory of the Good and so encourage our moral striving? Or is it because, as Mackinnon insists, Jesus' redemptive work "cannot belong merely to the world of ideas; it must be the stuff of reality, including indeed an act in flesh and blood as costing and as ultimate as the cross"?[2]

Up to this point we have chosen to "bracket out" Ricoeur's works on biblical and theological themes, preferring to depict his hermeneutics as ancillary to his project of philosophical anthropology. We must now expand our inquiry and ask whether and to what extent Ricoeur's philosophical anthropology is fundamentally "Christian," or whether and to what extent Christianity is only a specific exemplification of his broader philosophy. How does Ricoeur's hermeneutic philosophy incorporate religious as well as poetic language, theology as well as anthropology? These questions lead me to confront Ricoeur with the work of Rudolf Bultmann, a thinker with whom he has much in common. Indeed, Ricoeur's hermeneutic philosophy serves both as

119

foundation for and correction of a theology that remains largely existentialist in orientation – a theology in which faith is equated with self-understanding and authentic existence. My thesis is that Ricoeur, unlike Bultmann, takes the ''long route'' to existential theology.[3] We can only decide whether Ricoeur is able to avoid Franz Buri's charge – that Bultmann's theology ultimately reduces to an anthropology – by examining Ricoeur's stance towards the possibility displayed in the Gospel narratives. Can Ricoeur mediate – where Bultmann could not – the dichotomy between a ''possibility in principle'' and a ''possibility in fact''? On this mediation depends the status of the pale Galilean: will he be a mere cipher in an equally pale philosophy of existence, or will he constitute the indispensable condition of the Christian possibility? I shall suggest that what saves Ricoeur from several Bultmannian pitfalls is his refusal to abandon the narrative form of the Gospel in his christological reflection.

Religious versus poetic language

All narratives project ''worlds'' and possible ways for humans to live in the world. What distinguishes specifically religious narratives from their poetic counterparts? Both Ricoeur and Bultmann, desirous of being ''called'' by Scripture, contrast religious language with ordinary or ''objectifying'' language. Bultmann betrays a neo-Kantian dualism by distinguishing between the mode of being of objects (the realm of Nature) and the mode of being of human persons (realm of Freedom).[4] The language of faith is precisely this language which explores human possibilities. On that Ricoeur and Bultmann are agreed.[5] Religious language is for Ricoeur a species of poetic language. What is ''poetical'' about religion is its ''capacity to create a new way of life and to open my eyes to new aspects of reality, new possibilities.''[6] Ricoeur goes so far as to assign to poetic language a revelatory function:

I believe that the fundamental theme of Revelation is this awakening and this call, into the heart of existence, of the imagination of the possible. The possibilities are opened before man which fundamentally constitute what is revealed. The revealed as such is an opening to existence, a possibility of existence.[7]

Typically, however, Ricoeur is careful not to confuse the two types of discourse.[8] Ricoeur distinguishes religious discourse from poetic discourse in three ways.[9]

(1) Whereas poetry imaginatively explores various human possibilities under the rule of play, religious language adds the dimension of commitment. Unlike poetry, that is, religious language calls for a decision. Moreover, religious language involves belonging to a specific community with a particular social and ethical stance.[10]

(2) Religious language is a modification or intensification of poetic language; not just any human possibilities are displayed, but only "limit possibilities." Religious language is "odd" because it speaks not of commitments *tout court*, but of total commitments or ultimate concerns, which Ricoeur calls "limit-experiences." These limit-experiences may be positive (e.g., wonder, joy, love) or negative (e.g., guilt, anxiety, mortality), but in either case they refer to a dimension that, though part of our experience, is not of our own making and is beyond our control.[11] These extreme experiences – the dread of a sickness unto death, the ecstasy of a new-found love – may lead to a radically new perspective on the "real" world. Religious language discloses a religious (= "limit") dimension in the heart of ordinary experience, a previously unknown depth in our everyday living: everyday activities such as eating and drinking may be done "to the glory of God" (1 Cor. 10:31). Like Schleiermacher's feeling of absolute dependence or Rudolf Otto's "numinous," the religious dimension conveys a sense of the "Wholly Other."[12]

Given the extreme nature of these experiences, it is not surprising that the language required to express them is "odd."[13] Religious language is like poetic language in that it serves as a model for redescribing human experience, but religious language differs in that its model involves a "qualifier." In the case of the parables, for instance, the symbol of the Kingdom of God radically "qualifies" the action of the story. The parables depict extraordinary kinds of behavior in ordinary situations of life:

The parables tell stories that could have happened or without a doubt have happened, but it is this realm of situations, characters, and plots that precisely heightens the eccentricity of the modes of behavior to which the Kingdom of heaven is compared.[14]

The possibility displayed in the parables is always "extravagant," often shocking. Ricoeur notes the unusual behavior of the landlord in the "Parable of the Wicked Husbandmen" who after losing his servants sends his son. The action of the host in the "Parable of the Great Feast" who looks for guests in the streets is also odd. What we have to do with in the parables is a way of being that challenges our ordinary way of doing things. However, religious language does not yield a complete "model" for life. Rather, the Kingdom of God qualifier serves as a continual scandal for action in that it refuses to be captured in a specific program or agenda: "the characteristic qualifier of religious language dislocates our project of making a whole of our lives – a project which St. Paul identifies with the act of 'self-glorification,' or, in short, 'salvation by works'."[15] Religious language, in other words, puts limits on the possibility of making our life a whole. Such a project is beyond our practical limits. "What I am saying is that the properly religious moment of all discourse ... is the 'still more' that it insinuates everywhere, intensifying every project in the same manner."[16] In sum, religious language pushes language to the limit in the attempt to express the height, breadth and depth of human experience. For Ricoeur, the ultimate referent of religious discourse is human reality in its wholeness: "This is where the unshakeable truth of the existential interpretation of the NT lies. Religious language discloses the religious dimension of *common* human experience."[17]

(3) "It is the naming of God by the biblical texts that specifies the religious at the interior of the poetic."[18] Two points are of significance. First, Ricoeur distinguishes religious from theological language. Religious language refers to the first-order or "originary" expressions of faith, not their subsequent conceptual clarification. Interestingly enough, Ricoeur's discussions of religious language are always discussions of biblical language. Furthermore, there is a a plurality of biblical forms of speech that name God. Thus Ricoeur is sensitive to the various kinds of discourse that comprise "religious language."[19] Second, "God" is named at the intersection of the various biblical genres. "The word 'God' says more than the word 'Being,' because it presupposes the entire context of narratives, prophecies, laws, wisdom writings, psalms, and so on."[20] "God" is what ties the various biblical discourses together. God is the referent of religious discourse, tying the various forms together but also rendering each incomplete.

Does religious language (at least the parables) have as its ultimate reference the reality of human wholeness (2) or does it name God (3)? Are these two separate criteria for religious language or does Ricoeur conflate them? Is religious language about anthropology or theology? It would be ironic indeed if Ricoeur, who so painstakingly attends to the differences between various forms of biblical discourse, ultimately fails to distinguish between God and man.

Philosophy and theology

Ricoeur shares with Bultmann the existentialist's passion for human possibilities.[21] The question remains whether or not he also shares the "structural inconsistency" that many commentators find in Bultmann's thought. As Schubert Ogden points out, critics from both the right and the left have noted the inherently contradictory nature of Bultmann's demythologizing project, wavering as it does between an existential interpretation of the NT and a preservation of its kerygmatic core.[22] Bultmann reads the NT as presenting a possibility that is both universally available and at the same time indissolubly tied to the Christ event. John Macquarrie therefore speaks of a limit to Bultmann's demythologizing: though the overall momentum of his interpretation of the NT is anthropologically directed, at one point he reverses direction and speaks of "God's act in Christ." Fritz Buri complains that Bultmann in so doing is guilty of "falling back into mythology," that is, of failing to interpret all of the Gospel as referring to human existence.[23]

Ogden locates the heart of Bultmann's inconsistency in the distinction between a "possibility in principle" and a "possibility in fact." "In principle" every person could realize the possibility of "authentic" existence. However, due to the effects of the fall, we have lost this possibility. Consequently, authentic existence only becomes a real possibility, a possibility in fact, thanks to God's act in Christ. In Johnson's words: "The universal possibility is thus made conditional for its becoming a 'possibility in fact' upon the historical particularity of the Christ event."[24] In defense of Bultmann, Macquarrie cites the example of Jean Valjean from *Les Misérables*. Valjean, as a human being, has the innate capacity to love; but through a series of unfortunate circumstances he has lost this capacity. The possibility is therefore ontological (that is, within the structural range of fundamental human possibilities or existence) but not ontic (that is, within the range of one's concrete possibilities or experience).[25] Some such unsteady distinction between the two kinds of possibility constitutes Bultmann's attempt to hold philosophy (the conceptual analysis of fundamental human possibilities) and theology (the announcement of a new or recovered possibility) together. Given Ricoeur's focus on human possibility, to what extent does he avoid a similar structural inconsistency with regard to his reading of the Gospels? How does Ricoeur relate the universal possibilities uncovered by his philosophical anthropology to that contingent and unique possibility associated with Jesus Christ? In short, how does Ricoeur relate philosophy and theology?

While Ricoeur is willing to call himself a "believing philosopher," he never refers to himself as a theologian. The reason seems to be Ricoeur's low regard for the theologian's hermeneutical skills. Theologians repeat Hegel's error, namely, reducing religious symbolism to a conceptual system. Ricoeur prefers to stay close to the original expressions of faith in all their literary diversity: "I like to say that the philosopher, when he reflects on religion, should have for his partner the exegete rather than the theologian."[26] In seeking to conceptualize religious discourse theologians actually hide its true intent in a false gnosis or pseudorationality. Religious myths are falsely taken to be explanations rather than explorations of the human condition. Ricoeur sees this tendency in two fundamental doctrines: original sin (involving as it does the inconsistent pairing of a judicial category of debt and a biological category of inheritance)[27] and the penal substitution theory of the atonement (involving as it does the inconsistent pairing of a physical evil that somehow compensates for and cancels out a moral evil).[28]

Despite Ricoeur's reservations about theology, he is no stranger to thinking about religion or the biblical kerygma. However, Ricoeur chooses to discuss the relation between theology and philosophy in terms of hope and reason rather than faith and reason.[29] Taking hope as our touchstone, we will consider three ways in which Ricoeur seeks to relate philosophy and religion while keeping them distinct: Ricoeur needs to establish such a distinction if he is to avoid the charge of reducing theology to philosophical anthropology.

First, then, hope is an impulse in philosophy as well as theology that keeps each humble and allows both reason and revelation to contribute something to the discussion. Second, the hope for the possibility of freedom is something that both a philosophical anthropology and religion share. Third, Ricoeur seeks to distance himself from Kant's "moral" religion by identifying the properly "religious" dimension in the quest for freedom with the economy of the "gift." The key question pertains to the *enabling* of human freedom. What will become increasingly apparent is how philosophy does not conflict with but "approximates" religion and hope itself. That is, Ricoeur tries to articulate philosophical equivalents for religious ideas without stepping over the line into theology. Ricoeur's approximation allows him to go beyond autonomy and heteronomy, that is, the old dichotomy of reason and revelation. The crucial question will be whether Ricoeur's hermeneutic philosophy can "approximate" religion without reducing theology to philosophy.

(1) Ricoeur refuses to link religion to an authoritative revelation that commands obedience, for this would entail the unacceptable sacrifice of reason. On the other hand, philosophy should not be conceived as proceeding from an autonomous thinking subject, for this would entail the unacceptable sacrifice of revelation. Ricoeur mediates the totalizing claims of reason and revelation by viewing each in light of hope. We may envisage the whole not as an item of theoretical knowledge or present experience but as possibility. The claims of both philosophy and religion must thus be cast in an interrogative mood: "For me the philosophical task is not to close the circle, to centralize or totalize knowledge, but to keep open the irreducible plurality of discourse."[30] This respect for other forms of discourse is Ricoeur's philosophical trademark, and it is conjoined to his hope that the various forms of discourse are somehow "in" the truth.[31] The humility inherent in Kant's philosophy of limits therefore permits Ricoeur to accommodate both reason and revelation.

(2) In his article "Philosopher après Kierkegaard," Ricoeur observes that after Kierkegaard philosophy is less concerned with grand systems than with the concrete problems of individuals. Kierkegaard instituted a new genre of critique, a critique of existential possibilities.[32] Religion too after Kierkegaard evidences a preoccupation with existential possibilities rather than absolute moral laws. That Ricoeur believes religion to be more than morality writ large may be seen by considering his criticism of Kant's "ethical vision."[33] While Kant's ethics are the product of autonomous reason, expressed in the rational duty owed the categorical imperative, religion is about the enabling of freedom, or what Kant calls the "practical possibility" of freedom. By "freedom" Kant means the capacity to initiate actions commensurate with rational moral agency. In Kant's critical philosophy freedom is not merely a postulate but an object of hope: I hope that I will be able to act as a morally rational agent. The theme of the practical possibility of freedom virtually dominates *Religion Within the Limits of Reason Alone*, where the issue is precisely the restoration of the moral capacity of human beings. The Christ symbol for Kant helps us in the process of self-liberation by providing an encouraging example. In Kant, says Ricoeur, religion adds nothing to ethics except the hope of being able to be morally free and fully autonomous.

In Ricoeur's opinion, Kant short-circuits the question of hope; religion is not primarily about our ability to fulfill the law's demand. Kant errs in considering only part of the Christian symbolism, the symbolics of sin and redemption, to which he gives a moralistic interpretation. For Ricoeur, both ethics and religion are constituted more by *desire* than by *demand*. Ricoeur understands ethics in a more fundamental sense, as referring to our most basic desire to be and our effort to exist. Philosophy "after Kierkegaard" is about that desire. Similarly, Ricoeur takes religion and the kerygma of salvation to be more about this fundamental desire, this passion for the possibility of a regenerated freedom, than an oppressive demand. Accordingly, Ricoeur speaks of the "false transcendence of the imperative" in Kant.[34] The point of intersection for both ethics and religion is the will, though in Ricoeur's opinion the will is constituted less by demand or a law than by desire. It is this completed desire that Ricoeur has in mind when he speaks of the "poetics" of the will. Such a poetics energizes the will by representing the world as Creation, a representation best seen in poetry that conveys a sense of nature's purposefulness.[35]

Both philosophical anthropology and theology are thus concerned with the "completion" of the will, the realization of the possibility of human freedom, albeit in different manners. The philosopher studies the conditions for this possibility; the theologian announces its realization. Philosophy is concerned with the desire to be and the effort to exist which characterize all human being; theology is concerned with the Christ event which represents the fulfillment of this desire and this effort. The respective concerns of philosophical anthropology and theology are mediated by the philosophy of religion, whose central question according to Ricoeur is this:

How is the will affected in its most intimate desire by the representation of this [Christological] model, this archetype of a humanity agreeable to God, which the believer calls the Son of God?[36]

For the philosopher, Christ is a symbol of the completion of our desire to be free. For the theologian, this does not suffice, for he is interested in the relation between the Christ symbol and the Jesus of history. The ultimate question for Ricoeur is whether his hermeneutics will be of service to the theologian as well as the philosopher.

(3) Freedom is the real theme of Kant's philosophy of religion. "God" makes an appearance, but only as a function of practical reason, a postulate of autonomous human thinking about morality. What Kant lacks is a notion of the radical dependence of human being on a Power other than itself. Ricoeur calls this radical sense of dependence the religious or "hyper-ethical" sense par excellence.[37] Religion is about the power which precedes and carries us along. In the religious perspective, existence is a *gift*. Ricoeur uses the notion of gift to express the

hyper-ethical aspect of religion. Kant had no notion of gift but explained his theory of religion in terms of an absolute demand. But for Ricoeur whatever ability we have to be at all – including the enabling of our freedom – is a gift. The gift generates an obligation, not of law but of love. Moreover, this "economy of gift" generates a whole-person response, not simply a response of an obedient will.[38]

Here, then, are three ways in which Ricoeur believes philosophy to be distinct from, though related to, religion. However, Ricoeur contends that philosophy can "approximate" the religious dimension together with its economy of gift. It is as a philosopher rather than a theologian that Ricoeur first discovers that human being is not autonomous. We are dependent on poetic words that illumine and transform our existence by offering new possibilities for human life. The poetic word for Ricoeur escapes the problem of autonomy and heteronomy that has plagued the discussion of reason and revelation for centuries. In the occurrence of the poetic word something is said over which I am not the master: it is a "revelation" that calls for thought. Moreover, "[t]his situation of nonmastery is the origin of both obedience and freedom."[39] Human autonomy is twice defeated: with regard to knowledge, human thinking is preceded by and carried along by a creative or kerygmatic word; with regard to living, human acting is preceded by poetic "revelation" and carried along by a creative power. The religious symbol that epitomizes the sense of radical dependence on a Power other than ourselves is for Ricoeur *Creation*. "Creation" is the symbol for our discovery that we are recipients of meaning, existence and other gifts that are not of our own making. It is therefore this symbol of Creation which best effects Ricoeur's second Copernican revolution: the overthrow of the self's pretensions to be the source of its own existence and meaning. We would know nothing of Creation, of course, without a poetic word that opens our eyes to this "gift" dimension of human experience. The poetic word therefore mediates between revelation and reason by opposing the pretentious claims of each: the phenomenon of the poetic word simultaneously shows revelation to be more a non-violent appeal than an "unreasonable" claim and reason to be dependent on a word that precedes it rather than autonomous.

Philosophy approximates theology but does not take its place. Approximation means that philosophy says something similar to the theologian about the kerygma of salvation and freedom but in a different language (the desire to be) and within the limits of reason. "This setting in proximity ... is both a work of listening and an autonomous enterprise, a thinking 'in the light of ...' and a free thinking."[40] What finally separates the two forms of discourse? We might say that philosophy sets the stage for religion but does not occupy it. As Ricoeur puts it, philosophical anthropology "makes space" for theological notions. Through his analysis of human existence, Ricoeur discovers themes also announced by the Christian kerygma: fallibility and fault approximate sin; the disclosure of possible worlds approximates revelation; the desire to be approximates hope; the sense of the meaningfulness of existence approximates creation.[41] Ricoeur does not see this approximation as a kind of backdoor apologetics, however: "If God speaks by the prophets, the philosopher does not have to justify His word, but rather to set off the horizon of significance where it may be heard. Such work has nothing to do with apologetics."[42] Ricoeur probably overstates his disclaimer here, for while philosophy does not argue for the factuality of the central claims of Christianity, it does argue for their meaningfulness. To defend the meaningfulness of Christianity rather than its truth may certainly be seen as a kind of defense of the faith.

Philosophy therefore "makes space" for religion by analyzing the conditions for the possibility of freedom. As to the actual announcement of the actualization of these conditions, the philosopher defers to the theologian. The "desire to be" that constitutes human being leaves a record of its "effort to exist" in histories. Accordingly, any claim that freedom has been realized will be in the form of testimony to an event of absolute importance. What finally separates philosophy and theology is that philosophy operates with a principle of reflection but theology deals with historical testimony to the "economy" of gift that defines the religious dimension of life.

To define theology by reference to testimony is to say that theologians are concerned with "absolute" events. Christ may be a symbol of our desire to be free for the philosopher, but the theologian asks how the symbol is rooted in the historical witness of the apostles. Whereas philosophy is concerned with analyzing human existence by exploring the human will and its possibilities, theology "deals with relations of intelligibility in the domain of witness. It is a logic of the Christological interpretation of salvation events."[43] This is precisely why Bultmann is unwilling to give up talk about the act of God in Christ: it is the single thread that keeps his reading of the NT from slipping into a philosophy of human existence *tout court*. Testimony belongs in the "economy of gift" according to Ricoeur because the initiative belongs to the absolute and the historical event. We witness to something that has happened. This is what Kant was unable to grasp. Ricoeur says that Kant misunderstands testimony: the avowal of the absolute cannot take place within Kantian limits. Consequently, Kant must treat the Christ event as an idea or symbol of the absolute, not an experience of it. But for Ricoeur the whole point about testimony is that its historicity matters as much as its meaning: "Testimony, each time singular, confers the sanction of reality on ideas, ideals, and modes of being that the symbol depicts and discovers for us only as our most personal possibilities."[44] The ahistorical character of reflection makes philosophy distinct from theology insofar as the latter is related to historical witness: "This invincible break is that of reason and faith, of philosophy and religion."[45]

Ricoeur's hermeneutic philosophy is not incompatible with testimony, however.[46] Philosophy for Ricoeur is reflection about human existence, and human existence may be explored by studying the desire to be as well as the effort to exist. Coming to self-knowledge means understanding both our desire and our effort to be fully human. Our desires reveal our ambitions and hopes; our efforts reveal our power and capacities. Although Ricoeur does not do so, we may say that stories best reveal our desire to be while histories best reveal our actual effort to exist. If to be human means to evidence a passion for the possible, both stories and histories are needed to express our imagined and our real possibilities. As Ricoeur displays the problem of philosophy and theology, the real dividing line seems to be the relation of the Christian possibility to history. It is precisely this relation and its subsequent neglect in Bultmann's thought that renders his theology suspect.

Ironically, the very success of Ricoeur's philosophical approximation of religious themes threatens the relative autonomy of theology with regard to philosophy.[47] All philosophy is a listening to a revelatory word: "It was in fact Karl Barth who first taught me that the subject is not a centralizing master but rather a disciple or auditor of a language larger than itself."[48] On the other hand, it is not only the Christian word that has the capacity to reveal Being or to conjure up the world as Creation. Ricoeur says he has never been persuaded by the "simplistic opposition of Jerusalem and Athens."[49] Though the ever-present rationality of scientific positivism has divorced itself from the sacred, Ricoeur sees other forms of connection between the rational and the sacred. Indeed, his own philosophy of religion is one of the major strategies of such an approximation.

Does Ricoeur reduce the Christian kerygma to philosophy? If other texts reveal ultimate possibilities, does not the Gospel forfeit its uniqueness and its indispensability? That Ricoeur is aware of this danger may be seen in his criticism of Karl Jaspers' philosophy of religion. For Jaspers, all of human existence is full of "ciphers" or traces of "transcendence." Accordingly, the particularism of the Christ event is unacceptable. Ricoeur puts the dilemma well: "One must choose between the 'encipherment' *of all things, and the Christian Incarnation.*"[50] In choosing the former option, Jaspers surbordinates everything to his philosophy. Ricoeur claims that Jaspers confuses two problems: speculation about being and the problem of salvation. If these two problems are kept apart, philosophy and religion can remain distinct: "Two modes of comprehension confront each other, one based on absolute events, the other based on a universal understanding or a human experience indefinitely open to history."[51] The problem with this solution to the problem of the relation of philosophy and religion is that Ricoeur himself, as we have seen, prefers to define the religious dimension in terms of *Creation* rather than salvation. Just how this affects Ricoeur's construal of the significance of the Christ event remains to be seen.

Masters of narrative suspicion

Bultmann regards the Gospels as forms of objectifying language – mythological narratives – that hide the true meaning of the kerygma. It is this unfortunate narrative packaging that renders the kerygma mythological, imposing as it does an unacceptable supernaturalistic and judicial framework which actually hinders a correct appreciation of the kerygma.[52] His solution is the celebrated method of demythologizing, which Bultmann takes to be a positive means to recover the real meaning of the Gospels. The goal of demythologizing is to express the kerygma of the NT in non-objectifying – that is, existential – terms. As Bultmann puts it:

To believe in the cross of Christ does not mean to concern ourselves with a mythical process wrought outside of us and our world, with an objective event turned by God to our advantage, but rather to make the cross of Christ our own.[53]

The Gospel narratives are misleading for Bultmann if they point to heaven or toward earth: neither the supernatural Son of God nor the historical Jesus is of theological significance, only the Christ who is the occasion for a preaching that challenges us to give up all for God. The kerygma has no content; it is a demand that has meaning only in the act of response. For Bultmann, the narrative form is an obstacle to the existential appropriation of the kerygmatic demand. Demythologizing therefore involves stripping the Gospels of their literary features; hence we may equally speak of Bultmann's "denarrativization."

Ricoeur, as we shall see, is largely sympathetic to Bultmann's effort to render the NT existentially relevant, except that for Ricoeur demythologizing must not abandon the narrative form of the kerygma. At the same time, there is a sense in which Ricoeur too "suspects" the biblical narrative. Two centuries of historical criticism have shown that the origin of the NT documents is not what it appears to be, nor are the texts simply accounts of "what actually happened." Ricoeur can accept this "surface" criticism of biblical narrative because there is another level which remains inviolate. Indeed, Ricoeur bases his entire approach to biblical narrative on the assumption that it is only through criticism that the true message of the texts may be heard.

Before turning to his evaluation of biblical narrative, however, it would be helpful to see the extent to which Ricoeur accepts the general critique of religion levelled by modern atheists. Freud, Marx and Nietszche may be deemed masters of narrative suspicion to the extent that they distrust the surface meaning of biblical narrative, and, indeed, of all religion. Ricoeur agrees with these masters of suspicion that religion needs to submit to critical investigation.[54] But what is religion? Ricoeur is clear: "I thus understand religion as a primitive structure of life which must always be overcome by faith and which is grounded in the fear of punishment and the desire for protection."[55] Ricoeur is interested in articulating a "postreligious" faith. Atheism itself contributes to this project insofar as it successfully attacks the god of punishment and protection. What Ricoeur objects to is the use of religion to support an ethical vision of the world. What Ricoeur applauds in the masters of suspicion is their iconoclasm: "to smash the idols is also to let symbols speak."[56]

The principal idol that must go is that of God the Father.[57] What better image of the God of morality than the Father, whose role is to punish and provide? Ricoeur's interpretation of the father figure in the NT leads in a different direction. The Passion of the Son is also the death of the Father, not a murder but a *dying for*. The Passion story redescribes the paternal image in the direction of kindness and compassion rather than authority and control. To the degree that the Son is also the Father, the Passion provides a "schema" of divine fatherhood. Death and dying are therefore inscribed into the figure of God the Father. For Hegel the death of God meant the death of God as "Wholly Other," the end of a separated transcendence. "God is dead" expresses true religion: not of an Authority above us but of a Spirit among us. Ricoeur concludes:

"Once overcome as an idol, the image of the father can be recovered as symbol."[58] God as father means that God in love goes out of himself for the sake of humanity. Ricoeur's mediation of religion and atheism results in a faith in and love of Creation: that God is absolute love rather than absolute authority is for Ricoeur the religious meaning of the atheist critique of classical theism. Here too philosophy approximates religion: Ricoeur says that the symbol of God as loving Father has its counterpart in a poetics of the will, for both help us to see the world as Creation.[59]

Atheism is an "external" critique of religion. Demythologizing, on the other hand, represents an "internal" critique. This too is a necessary step if we are to attain a postreligious faith. For Ricoeur, then, demythologizing is a necessary means for correctly interpreting the NT kerygma. While the kerygma itself is not the product of culture or human experience, it can only become "visible" by becoming part of culture. There is a false scandal, the scandal of a cultural vehicle which is no longer our own, that needs to be demythologized.[60] Indeed, it is only when this first scandal is set aside that the true scandal, the scandal of the cross, becomes apparent. Ricoeur seems to view demythologizing as similar to the process of interpreting metaphor: the absurd literal sense must be abolished in order to unleash the redescriptive power of the metaphor.[61] The literal sense of the myth is the supernatural (the three-decker universe) and judicial (the penal substitution theory) framework. Demythologizing applies to the explanatory function of myth; the proper function of myth is exploratory. Ricoeur applauds Bultmann's work to the extent that it seeks to dissolve the false scandal in order to reveal the true one. Ricoeur also agrees with Bultmann that the process of demythologizing begins in the NT itself. In John's Gospel the future is seen as already present; the Kingdom is here. In other words, the Fourth Gospel itself demythologizes the notion of a future kingdom by viewing it in terms of, say, our present experience of transcendence.[62]

Ricoeur ultimately parts company with Bultmann over the nature of demythologizing, however. While he is proficient in dismantling the objectivizing language of *myth*, Bultmann fails to think through the language of *faith*. This is the major thrust of Ricoeur's "Preface to Bultmann":

What is not yet sufficiently thought through in Bultmann is the specifically non-mythological core of biblical and theological statements and hence, by contrast, the mythological statements themselves.[63]

Elsewhere Ricoeur complains that Bultmann does not realize "that there is a symbolic as well as a pseudosymbolic or literal dimension to myth, and that demythologization is only valid in relation to this second dimension."[64] In other words, Ricoeur complains that Bultmann's demythologizing throws the narrative form out with the mythical. By contrast, Ricoeur insists that even after demythologizing the Gospels, the narrative still remains to be thought.

On demythologizing Bultmann

How did Jesus' preaching develop into preaching about Jesus? To pose Bultmann's celebrated query – how the proclaimer became the proclaimed – is to ask why the kerygma had to take on a peculiarly *narrative* form. Ricoeur observes that in the earliest church the proclamation "contained but the seed of a narrative, contracted to an almost pointlike event," as seen in such ancient formulations as those in 1 Cor. 15: 3–8, Christ died ... was buried ... was raised ... and appeared to Cephas and others.[65] Ricoeur claims that the narrative form is of theological significance: the presupposition of all Christian preaching "is the continuity and identity of the earthly Jesus and the Christ."[66] Even Bultmann affirms that the *Dass* of the cross is the historical minimum required by the *Was* of Easter faith. If the kerygma does not include Jesus' past in Christ's present, "it runs the risk of interpreting the latter in the gnostic sense or in that of Hellenistic myth."[67] Bultmann raises scientific and theological problems, however, concerning Jesus' past: form and redaction criticism have shown that the attempt to write a "life of Jesus" is vain, and even if it were possible the result would be that our (historical) works would preempt the decision of faith.

For Ricoeur, however, the Christian witness or testimony is expressed in narrative, in stories and histories. Furthermore, this narrative expression is no mere ornamentation of the kerygma but an essential aspect of the Christian preaching. As Ricoeur has repeatedly observed, not just any theology can be attached to the narrative form. What narrative contributes is an emphasis on the founding events of the OT covenant and the NT church as the trace of God's act: "God's mark is in history before being in speech."[68] Ricoeur agrees with Gerhard von Rad's point that Israel confessed God through stories which centered on a few kernel events.[69] Israel's identity, her desire and effort to be, was thus interpreted in light of certain foundation events that functioned as traces of God's acts and presence.

Bultmann's misdirected "denarrativization" leads him to overlook the special theological contribution of this literary form. Bereft of its narrative context, "act of God" for Bultmann derives its entire meaning from the surrender of the will that is the event of faith. Ricoeur complains that Bultmann cannot properly "think" the meaning of "act of God" because it is directly linked to a personal encounter. Accordingly, in his "Preface to Bultmann," Ricoeur proceeds to think more adequately "what remains unthought" in Bultmann. In particular, Ricoeur is concerned to demythologize Bultmann, or rather, the "myth" of intuitive or immediate understanding.

As a form of discourse, the kerygma is both *event* and *meaning*. With Bultmann, Ricoeur interprets narrative meaning in a non-objectivizing way, namely, as projecting a possible mode of living or being-in-the-world. Narratives may exercise a poetic function that enables them to carry a surplus of meaning that is not susceptible to exhaustive paraphrase. But against Bultmann, Ricoeur insists that in narrative discourse, form and content are inseparable. The corollary to this is that understanding requires explanation.[70] For Ricoeur the order is important: "The moment of exegesis is not that of existential decision but that of 'meaning' ..."[71] Existential appropriation, the moment of existential decision, is the final step in the process of interpretation. Ricoeur's verdict on Bultmann's demythologizing is clear:

A theory of interpretation which at the outset runs straight to the moment of decision moves too fast. It leaps over the moment of meaning, which is the objective stage ...[72]

Bultmann is "demythologized" when his theology of existential appropriation receives a surer hermeneutic foundation. What evokes the existential decision is not a bare address but the world-of-the-text which is the reference of the biblical narrative. Understanding is not a "mystical" event, but the result of interpretive work. Only by interpreting the narrative do we have access to the possibility to which the text refers. Significantly, Ricoeur concludes his "Preface to Bultmann" with the coy reflection that his criticisms should not be construed as a rejection of Bultmann's thought but rather as "a foundation supporting it."[73] Ricoeur's narrative theory, in other words, gives a surer hermeneutical foundation to a theology that remains fundamentally existential.[74]

Narrative theory is no theological panacea, however: it does not allow Ricoeur to pursue the Jesus of history as distinct from the kerygma about Christ. However, Ricoeur appeals to the recent critical consensus that acknowledges the partial authenticity of the tradition concerning Jesus' sayings and actions. What may be reconstructed about the life of Jesus is not itself a narrative, but certain "occasions" for narration.[75] By showing the relation of these occasions, Ricoeur hopes to demonstrate that the narrative form of the kerygma is no literary accident.

The first occasion is Jesus' announcement concerning the nearness of the Kingdom of God.[76] Jesus associated his own person and ministry with the nearness of the kingdom. Moreover, he forbade speculation as to the interval remaining before the kingdom's coming by giving "nearness" a non-chronological meaning. The rediscovery of Jesus' teaching concerning the kingdom therefore functions as a critical control on the structure of Christian hope and its apocalyptic interpretations.[77] The second occasion for the Gospel narratives pertains to the controversy which Jesus' teaching and table fellowship with the dregs of society provoked. Jesus' fellowship with sinners offended the religious establishment more than any other of his actions. Ricoeur views the connection between Jesus' teaching about the kingdom and the style of his life as giving rise to a certain "configuration" which possesses exemplary value, a configuration that serves as a paradigm for discipleship. These two "occasions" thus provide the basic rudiments of a plot as well as the style in which the events will be recounted.

Jesus' announcement and pattern of life thus lead to controversy, and ultimately, the cross. This third occasion calls for not just any narrative, but a passion narrative. Jesus is no conventional "hero": he wins no battles; he slays no dragons: "In contrast to official history, which celebrates the great deeds of rulers and masters, this will be a story of suffering."[78] A "passion" narrative is about weakness, suffering and self-giving. Unlike other heroes, Jesus does nothing to make his existence secure and his life meaningful – he trusts God for that. The kerygma has to be a narrative because it is about a way of being-in-the-world that leads to a history of suffering. Internal to the proclamation itself, then, is a requirement of a narrative form. It is because the proclaimer's announcement and way of life issues in a history of suffering that the proclaimer becomes the proclaimed. Ironically, Ricoeur finds the answer to Bultmann's riddle about NT theology in the narrative form that Bultmann so cavalierly dismissed.

On sense and self: beyond the new hermeneutic?

Ricoeur provides an existentially oriented theology with a surer hermeneutical foundation. This much is clear. We have seen that Ricoeur's non-objectivizing approach to the Gospels permits him to preserve its narrative form without falling back into mythology. He thus preserves the original language of faith in a way that Bultmann could not. Though Bultmann moves to the level of existential decision too fast, Ricoeur agrees that a transformed self-understanding is the eventual correlate of the language of faith. In Bultmann's words:

Faith is not choosing to understand one's self in one of several possible ways that are universally available to man but is man's response to God's word which encounters him in the proclamation of Jesus Christ.[79]

It remains to be seen whether and to what extent Ricoeur allows the language of faith to speak of historical events or whether it only displays existential possibilities. Can Ricoeur's attention to narrative, together with its function of aiming at God's trace in certain events, save him from reducing salvation to an event not of history but of human subjectivity, a reduction that again threatens the distinction between theology and philosophical anthropology? What, for instance, is the nature of this ''act of God'' of which Bultmann speaks?[80] Is it an event of history, an event of language, an event of self-understanding? Granted that for Ricoeur language is not only event but also meaning, does Ricoeur ever get beyond the meaning to the event?

Here Ricoeur's conversation partners are the theologians of the ''new hermeneutic'' – Ernst Fuchs and Gerhard Ebeling – who share an interest in self-understanding but go beyond Bultmann by initiating a new quest for the historical Jesus. The new hermeneutic seeks to combine an interest in the historical Jesus with the theme of faith as self-understanding by claiming that what comes to speech in the kerygma is Jesus' own self-understanding. To understand Jesus is to share in his self-understanding and thus to have a new understanding of oneself. Fuchs learned from Heidegger that language is *constitutive* of self-understanding, not a secondary expression of it. Jesus' own self-understanding enters language above all in his parables. Fuchs declares: ''I understand Jesus' proclamation as a 'language event' ... It is his parables which are typical of Jesus ... in the parables Jesus' under-standing of his situation 'enters language' in a special way.''[81] The parables therefore mediate the possibility of sharing Jesus' self-understanding. The key notion here for Fuchs is that of *Einverständnis*, which has been rendered variously by the English "empathy" or "penetrative understanding."[82]

On the one hand Ricoeur credits Ernst Fuchs and Gerhard Ebeling with helping him to coordinate "sense" and "self" by emphasizing the linguisticality of human being and experience.[83] Jesus' self-understanding only encounters the reader through his speech. The term "language event" serves to emphasize the climactic moment of existential appropriation by the reader. The text presents the reader with a possibility that allows him to see his life and the world in a new manner. All this Ricoeur can affirm. On the other hand, Ricoeur sounds a cautionary note about the "one-sided emphasis" of Fuchs and Ebeling on the "idealism of the word event."[84] This warning against "word event" theology comes in a passage where Ricoeur is discussing biblical narrative, and he goes on to say that in order to rectify the post-Bultmannian theologians of the new hermeneutic, we need to "reaffirm the realism of the event of history."[85]

As we have seen, Ricoeur does not restrict this correlation of a text's "sense" and self-understanding to biblical hermeneutics. Indeed, he makes this correlation the cornerstone of his hermeneutic philosophy – "reading maketh a full man." Ricoeur holds that textual interpretation results in self-understanding to the extent that the reader appropriates the text's subject matter – a possible way of living or orienting oneself to life: "interpretation is the process by which disclosures of new modes of being ... give to the subject a new capacity for knowing himself."[86]

Can Ricoeur's narrative theory provide an "objective" correction to the subjective language event of the new hermeneutic? On one level Ricoeur avoids the "idealism of the word event" by linking faith not to the *event* of language but to its *meaning* or "work." As do their predecessors Heidegger and Bultmann, theologians of the new hermeneutic move to the level of existence too fast. Norman Perrin pronounces the new hermeneutic a failure on the level of literary criticism because the "poetic" function of language is left unexplained. Perrin notes that the basic insight of the new hermeneutic – that language discloses being – "should have led to a consideration of the nature, function, and power of *metaphor*."[87] But this is precisely what Ricoeur does in his analysis of the parables. For Ricoeur, the parables apply a metaphoric process to a narrative form to occasion an existential event.[88] As we have seen, we only attain the world of the text through an analysis of the text as work. But if Ricoeur takes the "long route" of exegeting and explaining texts, the final destination is still "subjectivity," still word event. Indeed, it is fair to regard Ricoeur's work on the parables as an intriguing new chapter in the history of the notion "language event." Thanks to his analysis of metaphor, Ricoeur can explain the ability of language to disclose worlds and transform self-understanding where the practitioners of the new hermeneutic could only wonder. However, it is not clear at this juncture how Ricoeur preserves his ties to the "realism of the event of history."

Ricoeur shares another point in common with theologians of the new hermeneutic: a fascination with Jesus' parables. Indeed, Ricoeur analyzes the parables more than any other form of religious language and devotes most of his "Biblical Hermeneutics" to a study of the parables. Ricoeur believes the key to understanding parables is to view them as metaphorical narratives. Though the ostensive or literal reference of the parables is to "ordinary" life in first-century Palestine, Ricoeur believes that there are clues indicating that the parables should be taken metaphorically. The parable, he says, is a heuristic fiction that redescribes human experience.[89] The parables are ordinary stories with extraordinary conclusions: a host looks for guests in the streets after the well-to-do decline his invitation; a father provides a feast for his prodigal son. Ricoeur believes that this element of "extravagance" in the parables bursts a literal reading: the parables are not about what happens in first-century Palestine but rather about "limit" or religious human experience, for instance, an invitation without limit, a forgiveness without limit, to refer to the two aforementioned parables.[90]

Interpretation according to Ricoeur still aims at transforming our self-understanding, but this existential moment only follows the discipline of hermeneutics and the work of interpretation. Self-understanding is for Ricoeur therefore not simply a mystical language event or *Einverständnis*, but a "narrative event." Does this attention to the narrative form allow Ricoeur to avoid the "idealism of the word event"? On the one hand, Ricoeur gives "objectivity" a place insofar as the text's structure and sense must be explained through exegetical techniques. On the other hand, a narrative event that is mediated by the sense of the text remains a language event, that is, an event of language that engages and transforms self-understanding. There is little trace of the "realism" of historical events in Ricoeur's actual interpretation of the parables.[91]

We only attain the self via the sense, or, as Ricoeur puts it, existence via semantics. What does this mean? It means that the goal of Ricoeur's hermeneutics, of the Bible or anything else, is self-understanding.[92] The parables are no exception; they too metaphorically refer to possible ways of understanding oneself and of orienting oneself to life.[93] What is ultimately at stake in interpreting the parables, as with any texts, is self-understanding. Here again we see Ricoeur's fundamental allegiance to philosophical anthropology, to a way of thinking about human being that is closely tied to Heidegger. For it was Heidegger who discovered that human being is the kind of being who understands – hence the vital importance of self-understanding for a philosophical anthropology. What we understand in a text is a possible way of being-in-the-world. Indeed, Heidegger defines ''understanding'' (*Verstehen*) as a projection of our possibilities. Insofar as this is the work of narratives too, we could say that Ricoeur repeats the whole process of Heideggerian understanding on the narrative level.

What kind of being is disclosed in the narrative event? Though Ricoeur speaks of the ''desire for ontology'' in his philosophical hermeneutics, it should be understood that the kind of being he is after is human being, ''understanding'' being, being with a passion for and grasp of the possible.[94] As we have seen, the extra-linguistic reference of biblical narrative is to a possible mode of self-understanding. What is ultimately at stake when I read Scripture is *me* and my subjectivity. What becomes of ''objectivity'' and the ''realism of the event of history''? Is it swallowed up in the quest for self-understanding? Ricoeur claims that he is moving decisively beyond any kind of Romanticism or subjectivist hermeneutics. The reader does not project his own understanding onto the text; indeed, reading may call for the reader to abandon his previous self-understanding. Ricoeur tries to escape the charge of subjectivity by making the text the objective mediation of possible worlds: ''It is the text with its universal power of world disclosure, which gives a self to the ego.''[95] The world of the text is the objective mediation of sense and self: ''It is by an understanding of the worlds, actual and possible, opened by language that we may arrive at a better understanding of ourselves.''[96] To call the ''world'' of the text ''objective'' is somewhat misleading, however, for there are as many worlds as there are interpretations. Moreover, the ''world'' of the text itself refers to a mode of subjectivity, a way of being-in-the-world. The approach is still subject-oriented, even though the subject is no longer Descartes' autonomous knower but a being who only recognizes itself ''in front of'' the text. But is a possible way of being-in-the-world ''objective'' simply because it does not have its origin in the reader's consciousness? Is it somehow a truer possibility than what the subject might dream up for himself? And where did this possible world and way of living in it come from if not from some subject?

Ricoeur seeks to "decenter" the human subject by penetrating to a level of being that precedes the very subject – object distinction, the level of *Lebenswelt* or being-in-the-world. The subject does not create its own meaning, but receives it from narratives that display possible ways for the subject to be. We are not our own masters but rather vassals of poetic texts which alone can transform our self-understanding. The kind of "ontology" that language reveals is an ontology of the subject. It is true that Ricoeur does not reach the subject immediately or intuitively as did the Romantics. Certainly Ricoeur succeeds in dismantling the pretensions of the Cartesian cogito. But the subject is Ricoeur's final destination of his hermeneutic philosophy. It therefore appears that Ricoeur has merely transposed subjectivity into a new key by demonstrating how the self comes to itself only through an interpretation of texts. Ricoeur practices a reflective philosophy: everything has been said at some level before philosophy, but philosophy must self-consciously recover it. Ricoeur speaks of the "reflective" subject who by interpreting his life while interpreting texts discovers "that he is placed in being before he places and possesses himself."[97] Indeed, Ricoeur's deepest hope is for a "second Copernican revolution" that would rid us of the illusion that we can autonomously posit ourselves and turn our attention to "transcendence" as the true source of our being and meaning.[98] Perhaps this is Ricoeur's most startling philosophical approximation to theology: the idea that "whoever seeks to gain his life will lose it, but whoever loses his life will find it" (Luke 17:33). The subjectivity which interests Ricoeur is that of the chastened subject, the subject who receives selfhood as a gift.[99]

In sum, we may say that Ricoeur moves beyond the new hermeneutic on the level of method.[100] In analyzing the metaphorical process that occasions the narrative event, Ricoeur responds to Perrin's criticism of their literary failure. In Ricoeur, it is the world of the text rather than a bare word of address that transforms the selfhood of the reader. Accordingly, the process of world-disclosure and existential appropriation may be explained and analyzed rather than simply wondered at and accepted as an instance of empathy. This emphasis on the "world" of the text also allows Ricoeur to incorporate a social aspect in what was previously a very individualistic self-understanding. Thanks to the narrative form, we see that a being in the world is also a being-with-others. We may therefore speak of Ricoeur's "narrative correction" of Bultmann's existential theology.

Although Ricoeur improves the new hermeneutic by giving it a sounder literary method, we need to ask how far he is successful in heeding his own warning about the idealism of word events. Do we ever get beyond the reader's subjectivity, even if it is subjectivity in a new key? Ricoeur continues to associate interpretation and faith with self-understanding. Ricoeur seems to restrict what "extra-linguistic" reference there is to a mode of self-understanding or possible way of being-in-the-world. To put it bluntly, the reference of the biblical narrative seems to be the selfhood of the reader rather than the "realism of the event of history." Must we not conclude that Ricoeur, like Bultmann and the new hermeneutic, considers the historical Jesus important solely because of his self-understanding? The Gospels do confront us with a possible way of understanding the world and living in it. But it is one thing to project a possibility and another to perform it. Is it not the case that faith (self-understanding) without works (performance) is dead? The desire to be must be "proven" by the effort to be; the fictional possibility must be attested by its historical actualization. If the reference of biblical narrative is only to possible ways of self-understanding, what becomes of the "realism" of the event of history, the mediation of philosophy and theology and the mediation between the historical Jesus and the Christ of faith? These questions remain to be thought; our conclusion to the present chapter is that Ricoeur, serving as he does as a foundation to Bultmann and post-Bultmannian theology, must face them.

Notes

1 Edward Schillebeeckx, *Jesus: An Experiment in Christology* (London, Collins, 1979), 740–1 (my emphasis).

2 MacKinnon, "Introduction" to *Newman's University Sermons*, 18.

3 Ricoeur seeks to avoid both a rationalism that believes science is everything and an existentialism that holds all thinking to be objectifying. Ricoeur insists that "beyond science, there is still thought. The question of human existence does not mean the death of language and logic ..." ("Kierkegaard," 316).

4 For an extended treatment of the influence of Marburg neo-Kantianism on Bultmann, see Roger A. Johnson, *The Origins of Demythologizing: Philosophy and Historiography in the Theology of Rudolf Bultmann* (Leiden, Brill, 1974).

5 See Ricoeur's essay "The Language of Faith," in *PPR*, 223–38.

6 "Poetry," 13. "I do assume provisionally the assimilation of biblical texts to poetic texts" ("Naming," 216).

7 *PPR*, 237.

8 Mediation is not assimilation. Ricoeur as a philosopher is committed to relating different types of discourse to one another but also to guarding their specificity: "For me the philosophical task is not to close the circle, to

centralize or totalize knowledge, but to keep open the irreducible plurality of discourse. It is essential to show how the different discourses may inter-relate or intersect but one must resist the temptation to make them identical, the same" ("Myth," 27).

9 Cf. David Pellauer, "Paul Ricoeur on the Specificity of Religious Language," *JR* 61 (1981), 264–84.

10 See "Poetry," 14.

11 Cf. a remark by David Tracy: "Employed in our common discourse, 'religion' usually means a perspective which expresses a dominating interest in certain universal and elemental features of human existence as those features bear on the human desire for liberation and authentic existence" (*Blessed Rage for Order*, 93). With regard to these experiences being beyond our control, Tracy observes that we do not "work ourselves into a state of love," but we "fall" or "are" in love, in touch with a reality whose power we cannot deny (105–6).

12 See Friederich Schleiermacher, *On Religion* (New York, Harper & Brothers, 1958); and Rudolf Otto, *The Idea of the Holy* (Oxford University Press, 1958).

13 Ricoeur's analysis is indebted to Ian Ramsey's *Religious Language* (New York, Macmillan, 1957). Ricoeur points out that Ramsey was dealing with theological language rather than the biblical forms of discourse, but apart from that Ricoeur agrees that religious language involves an odd discernment, a total commitment, and a universal significance ("BibHerm," 124). Ricoeur's preferred term, "limit," has the advantage of referring both to Kant (limits to thought) and Karl Jaspers (limit of existence). Ricoeur also sees a convergence between limit-language and the language of paradox: in both cases, the essential is said only by means of a "broken" discourse ("Kierkegaard," 309).

14 "BibHerm," 115.

15 Ibid., 125.

16 Ibid., 126.

17 Ibid., 127–8.

18 "Naming," 219.

19 Ricoeur deals with the plurality of biblical forms of discourse in "Toward a Hermeneutic of the Idea of Revelation," in *EBI*, 73–117; "PhilHerm"; "PhilRel" and "Naming."

20 "Naming," 222.

21 Ricoeur's concern for concrete existence matches that of his mentor, Gabriel Marcel, who referred to his own philosophy as a "Christian existentialism."

22 Schubert Ogden, *Christ Without Myth: A Study Based on the Theology of Rudolf Bultmann* (New York, Harper & Brothers, 1961), 96. Cf. Johnson, *The Origins of Demythologizing*, 15–18.

23 Cited in Ogden, *Christ Without Myth*, 107.

24 Johnson, *The Origins of Demythologizing*, 16.

25 Bultmann speaks of philosophers who confuse theoretical possibilities with

actual ones in his seminal essay, "The New Testament and Mythology"
in Hans Werner Bartsch (ed.), *Kerygma and Myth: A Theological Debate*, 2nd
edn, vol. I (London, SPCK, 1964), 29.

26 *CI*, 482.

27 See Ricoeur's " 'Original Sin': A Study in Meaning," in *CI*, 269–86.

28 Does Christ's death on the cross adhere to the logic of equivalence that
stipulates an exact correspondence between the crime and its punishment?
Ricoeur believes that the Pauline doctrine of justification relies not on a logic
of equivalence but on a logic of superabundance. "For the wages of sin is
death, but the free gift of God is eternal life in Christ Jesus our Lord" (Rom.
6:23). Here is no tit-for-tat logic of exact retribution but, as Kierkegaard
calls it, an absurd logic. Theologians, says Ricoeur, who take the imagery
literally miss Paul's point altogether: the economy of the gift far surpasses
the economy of the law. The true logic employed by Paul in Romans
5:12–19 is not the logic of equivalence but of superabundance.

29 This accords with Ricoeur's agreement with Kant's defining religion by the
question, What may I hope?

30 "Myth," 27.

31 "If there is an ultimate unity, it resides elsewhere, in a sort of eschatological
hope. But this is my 'secret', if you wish, my personal wager ..." ("Myth,"
27).

32 "Kierkegaard," 308–16.

33 Ricoeur contrasts the "ethical vision" of life, where all experience is
understood as a product of human activity, with the "religious dimension,"
where human activity is seen as derivative and secondary ("Guilt, Ethics,
and Religion," in *CI*, 431–9).

34 *CI*, 336. Ricoeur discusses his opposition to Kant's ethics and philosophy
of religion in several articles, including "The Demythologization of
Accusation," "Freedom in the Light of Hope," "Guilt, Ethics, and
Religion" and "Beyond Autonomy and Heteronomy." This anti-legalistic
bent in Ricoeur should not surprise us given his dislike of "original sin"
and "penal substitution."

35 See chapter 3 above on Kant's third *Critique* and the capacity of art to mediate
the realms of nature and freedom.

36 *CI*, 345.

37 "Autonomy," 15.

38 Ricoeur claims that the Torah itself is a gift when seen as part of the story
of the Exodus liberation. The gift of the Law is linked to God's liberating
act: "I am the Lord your God, who brought you out of the land of Egypt,
out of the house of bondage" (Exod. 20:2).

39 *CI*, 450. Ricoeur asks us whether or not it is an accident that the words for
"hearing" and "obedience" are etymologically related in so many
languages.

40 *CI*, 411.

41 Van den Hengel sees Ricoeur's philosophy of the subject as an ambitious philosophical approximation of the theological doctrine of "justification of faith" – so much so that Van Hengel calls Ricoeur a "philosopher of justification" (*Home of Meaning*, 258).

42 *EBI*, 97.

43 *CI*, 343.

44 *EBI*, 122.

45 Ibid., 153.

46 Indeed, Ricoeur takes great pains to show that his philosophy is not the result of autonomous reflection, but rather of interpretation. Philosophy proceeds from the fullness of language, and testimony figures among the types of language upon which philosophy reflects. The fundamental claim of hermeneutic philosophy is that language precedes reflective thought.

47 Cf. Harold Wells, who doubts whether Ricoeur himself is clear on the relation of philosophy and theology. Wells comments that Ricoeur often makes theological statements when ostensibly speaking in a philosophical key (Wells, "Theology and Christian Philosophy: Their Relation in the Thought of Paul Ricoeur," *Studies in Religion* 5 (1975/76), 54).

48 "Myth," 27.

49 Ibid., 35.

50 "Jaspers," 624.

51 Ibid., 641.

52 In his *History of the Synoptic Traditions* (Oxford, Blackwell, 1963) Bultmann claims that the literary composition of the Gospel adds nothing that was not already present in the oral tradition except "ornamentation" (69–70).

53 Bultmann, "New Testament and Mythology," 36.

54 See especially his "Religion, Atheism, and Faith," "The Critique of Religion," "The Demythization of Accusation" and "Interpretation of the Myth of Punishment."

55 *CI*, 441.

56 "Critique," 209.

57 See Ricoeur's "Fatherhood: From Phantasm to Symbol," *CI*, 468–97. It is in this article that Ricoeur remarks on the importance of attending to literary forms.

58 *CI*, 467.

59 Ibid.

60 See "Critique," 211.

61 Ricoeur's stance on the "literal" sense of the Gospel narratives leads, as we shall see in the following chapter, to a confrontation with the theology of Hans Frei.

62 "From now on, demythologization proceeds from the very nature of Christian hope and from the relation that the *future of God* maintains with the present" (*CI*, 392).

63 *CI*, 394.

64 "Myth," 42.

65 "Proclamation," 501. But cf. Richard Hays, *The Faith of Jesus Christ: An Investigation of the Narrative Substructure of Paul's Theology in Galatians 3:1–4:11* (SBL Dissertation Series no. 56. Chico, CA, Scholars Press, 1983) who argues that there is a narrative "substructure" that governs Paul's theology. Appealing to Ricoeur's narrative theory, Hays suggests that Paul's epistles constitute the configurative or thematic dimension of the Jesus narrative.

66 "Proclamation," 501.

67 Ibid., 502.

68 *EBI*, 79.

69 Von Rad believes the most ancient kernel of this narrative confession is found in Deut. 26:5–10 (*Theology of the Old Testament* [New York, Harper & Row, 1962], vol. I, 121–2).

70 Cf. chapter 5 above. Ricoeur regards Bultmann as heir to the Diltheyan opposition of explanation and understanding that characterizes much neo-Kantian and Heideggerian thought: "Doubtless it is necessary today to award less importance to *Verstehen* ("Understanding"), which is too exclusively centered on existential decision, and to consider the problem of language and of interpretation in all its breadth" (*CI*, 306).

71 *CI*, 397.

72 Ibid.

73 Ibid., 401.

74 Cf. Walter J. Lowe's remark that Ricoeur's success in bridging the worlds of Continental and Anglo-American philosophy stems from his "twofold commitment to existential question and rigorous method" ("Introduction" to Ricoeur, *FM*, xiii).

75 It is somewhat puzzling that Ricoeur refers to Whitehead in speaking of "occasions" for narration. Why call attention to process philosophy when the ordinary sense of the term would have sufficed? On Ricoeur's possible affinities with process thought, see chapter 8 below.

76 Ricoeur depends here on Norman Perrin's *Rediscovering the Teaching of Jesus* (London, SCM, 1967) and *Jesus and the Language of the Kingdom* (London, SCM, 1976).

77 The three occasions perform separate theological functions according to Ricoeur. This is further evidence that Bultmann is mistaken when he suggests that the search for the historical Jesus is not only vain but dangerous.

78 "Proclamation," 510.

79 Rudolf Bultmann, *New Testament Theology*, vol. II (New York, Charles Scribner's Sons, 1955), 239. Cf. his *Faith and Understanding* (London, SCM, 1969).

80 Bultmann apparently equates "God's act" and "God's word," and what is definitive about "word" is not its content but *that* it is spoken. The "act of God" which matters for Bultmann is the divine address which calls for

faith (see Bultmann's "The Concept of the Word of God in the NT," in his *Faith and Understanding*, esp. 300–2).

81 Ernst Fuchs, *Studies of the Historical Jesus* (London, SCM, 1964), 220.

82 See Ernst Fuchs, "The Hermeneutical Problem," in J. M. Robinson (ed.), *The Future of Our Religious Past: Essays in Honor of Rudolf Bultmann* (London, SCM, 1971), 267–76, esp. 270.

83 *RM*, 320. Fuchs considers "freedom for the word" to be one of the fundamental structures of human existence; this is why theological anthropology is so closely tied to a doctrine of language and hermeneutics ("The Hermeneutical Problem," 276–7).

84 *EBI*, 80. In a similar passage, Ricoeur puts it like this: "God is named in 'the thing' recounted. This is counter to a certain emphasis among theologies of the Word that only note word events. To the extent that the narrative genre is primary, God's imprint is in history before being in speech" ("Naming," 220). Ricoeur's concern may be occasioned by passages in Fuchs such as the following: "The struggle between 'fact' and 'word' must be resolved in favour of the word" ("What is a 'Language-event'?" in Fuchs, *Studies of the Historical Jesus*, 211).

85 *EBI*, 80.

86 *IT*, 94.

87 Perrin, *Jesus and the Language of the Kingdom*, 123.

88 Ricoeur's "BibHerm" discusses each of these stages in turn.

89 Cf. "BibHerm," 32–5, 96–106. See also ch. 4, esp. pp. 67–73 above.

90 "The referent, we could say, of the parable ... is human experience, conceived as the experience of the whole man and of all men ..." ("BibHerm," 34).

91 We shall see in the next chapter that thanks to "intertextuality," Ricoeur extends the metaphorical process that characterizes the parables to the Gospels as a whole.

92 In relating existence to semantics and self-understanding to language, Ricoeur believes that he has fulfilled the "deepest wish of hermeneutics": "The purpose of all interpretation is to conquer a remoteness, a distance between the past cultural epoch to which the text belongs and the interpreter himself. By overcoming this distance, by making himself contemporary with the text, the exegete can appropriate its meaning to himself ... It is thus the growth of his own understanding of himself that he pursues through his understanding of the other. Every hermeneutics is thus, explicitly or implicitly, self-understanding by means of understanding others" (*CI*, 16–17).

93 Cf. Dan Via on the parables and ontological possibility: "A parable as a whole dramatizes an ontological possibility – that which is there and possible in principle for man as man – and the two basic ontological (human) possibilities which the parables present are the gain or loss of existence, becoming authentic or inauthentic ... But each parable also depicts how

existence is ontically – actually and concretely – gained or lost, and the aesthetic form presses the two – the ontological and the ontic – into a unity. We could say then that each parable dramatizes how the basic human possibilities of gaining or losing existence may actually occur'' (Dan Via, *The Parables: Their Literary and Existential Dimension* [Philadelphia, Fortress, 1967], 41).

94 *CI*, 6–7.
95 *IT*, 94–5.
96 "Myth," 45.
97 *CI*, 11.
98 See *FN*, 29–33.
99 Van den Hengel, *The Home of Meaning*, 258. For Van den Hengel, this approximation lies at the very heart of Ricoeur's work, for we ourselves are not the "home" of life's meaning. Being and meaning are both gifts of the Creator.
100 In his analysis of the parables, Ricoeur says that he is trying to show how a structural analysis may enrich an existential hermeneutic ("BibHerm," 64).

7

A literal Gospel?

Given the conclusions of the preceding chapter, it is striking that a number of writers, as well as Ricoeur himself, have suggested that he belongs on the theological spectrum nearer to Barth than to Bultmann.[1] One group of interpreters, however, all connected as colleagues or students with Hans Frei of Yale University, heartily dissents from this suggestion. Indeed, one could say that the Barth – Bultmann debate over theological method and hermeneutics is being rehearsed again between Hans Frei and Paul Ricoeur, but this time the field of hermeneutical battle is biblical narrative. It was Hans Frei who first suggested that Barth's theological method is best understood in terms of his reading of the Gospel narratives.[2] Frei claims that Barth preserves the literal sense of the Gospel narratives whereas Bultmann construes the narratives as expressions of faith's self-understanding couched in myth. Frei has put forward some severe criticisms of Ricoeur's biblical hermeneutics. That Ricoeur and Frei represent the two most prominent theological approaches to biblical narrative warrants a detailed study of their agreements and disagreements.

The solution to this paradoxical state of affairs – Ricoeur's claim that he is Barthian and the Yale Barthians' denial of this claim – turns on the extent to which Ricoeur's reading of the biblical narrative is determined by a philosophical or a theological hermeneutics. With Barth, Ricoeur agrees that the Word is prior to both faith and understanding. But, as we have seen, this is a principle of Ricoeur's general interpretation theory, and not only of his biblical hermeneutics. Just as Ricoeur's philosophy approximates theology, so we shall see that his philosophical hermeneutics has features that are normally associated with a theological hermeneutics. Indeed, this approximation is so close that it is sometimes difficult to distinguish which is which. Like Wittgenstein's duck-rabbit figure, Ricoeur's hermeneutics takes on two distinct shapes: at times his theological hermeneutics seems to be merely a regional instance of his general hermeneutics; at other times his general hermeneutics seems to take on theological characteristics (i.e., speaking of poetic "revelation"). Has Ricoeur secularized sacred hermeneutics, or has he sacralized secular hermeneutics? The ambiguity in Ricoeur's construal of the relation between philosophy and theology thus returns on the level of their respective hermeneutics. Can a philosophical hermeneutics informed by Christian notions such as revelation preserve its philosophical autonomy and integrity? Conversely, can a theological hermeneutics that depends on general theories of meaning and truth keep its theological autonomy and integrity?

One avenue to resolving this perplexing issue is the pathway of the possible. The status of the possible is still the red thread, only now we will follow Barth's weaving rather than Bultmann's. In discussing the starting point of theology, Barth was passionate about its "impossible possibility."[3] In Barth's opinion, this "impossible possibility", the entry of the divine into the realm of the human, is the necessary precondition for theological discourse. There must be a prior action, a self-revelation of God, before humans can know him. Barth furthermore claims that this revelation is the revelation of the wholly free God. God is not generally available, either in nature or in human experience, but only as he breaks into these. For Ricoeur, however, the possibilities revealed by poetic and religious language appear to be human possibilities, waiting only for imaginative and ethical appropriation. These two kinds of passions for the possibility of faith shape Frei's and Ricoeur's (1) conception of the task of theology and theological method, (2) interpretation of biblical narrative and (3) Christology. It is to these implications that we now turn.

Philosophical or theological hermeneutics?

There is considerable evidence that Ricoeur feels close to Barth in his hermeneutical intent. Have we not seen that Ricoeur believes that the philosopher begins not empty-handed, but with the word? Ricoeur credits Barth with this insight: "It was in fact Karl Barth who first taught me that the subject is not a centralizing master but rather a disciple or auditor of a language larger than itself."[4] In light of such an admission, must we not reverse our decision about Ricoeur's philosophy serving as a foundation to Bultmann?[5] Is it not arguable that Ricoeur has taken the whole philosophical enterprise captive to the word? Indeed, often Ricoeur talks as if he, like Barth, started from faith and moved to understanding:

> To confess that one is a listener is from the very beginning to break with the project dear to many, and even perhaps all, philosophers: to begin discourse without any presuppositions ... But if what I presuppose precedes everything I can choose to think about, how do I avoid the famous circle of believing in order to understand and understanding in order to believe.[6]

Mark Wallace has argued that the theological hermeneutics of Barth and Ricoeur converge in three important respects: first, both view theological hermeneutics as sustained exegetical inquiry into the subject matter of the biblical world; second, each believes or trusts this world in order better to understand it; third, each manifests an anti-historicist bias in stressing the content or world of the text rather than its original *Sitz im Leben*.[7] Wallace goes on to note that the major difference in the two approaches concerns their divergent construals of the "biblical world" in the text and their judgments concerning how the "strange new world" of the Bible is related to that of the reader.

Despite these points of convergence, I contend that if we find that Ricoeur's method of understanding as he approaches the biblical text is no different than his general approach to poetic texts, we will have to conclude that his biblical hermeneutics is only a regional instance of his general hermeneutics, as Frei claims. If this is so, then the resemblances to Barth, while hardly superficial, are nevertheless outweighed by an overall contrast. Furthermore, if the subject matter of poetic texts is always an existential possibility, then we may question whether Ricoeur is in fact open to the particular subject matter of the Gospels or whether he does not in fact impose a single foundational strategy for approaching poetic texts, including biblical ones. If this is indeed the case we may also have to infer that in the end Ricoeur is not being guided by the subject matter of the text, but by a theory of textual understanding. As we shall see, this is precisely the Yale school's worry.

Hans Frei, David Kelsey and George Lindbeck believe that Ricoeur is far removed from Barthian hermeneutics. They view Ricoeur as operating not according to the formula "faith seeking understanding", but rather to a "faith seeking foundational intelligibility" paradigm. That is, they see Ricoeur as recasting Christian faith into modern conceptualities in order to make it meaningful to contemporary persons. Such a capitulation to present-day thought forms is just what Barth reacted so violently against in his *Epistle to the Romans*, in his Anselm book and throughout his *Church Dogmatics*. What are the distinctives of this guilty conceptuality? In his discussion of Bultmann's and Tillich's use of Scripture, David Kelsey makes the following observation:

> If and when Paul Ricoeur's philosophical analyses of personal existence and evil are appropriated by a systematic theologian, it will involve the judgment, very like Tillich's, that religious symbols are what are important in scripture.[8]

For Kelsey, an existentially oriented philosophical anthropology dominates Ricoeur's use of Scripture.[9] Similarly George Lindbeck, deep in another footnote, speaks of Ricoeur's "experiential-expressivist" hermeneutics.[10] Lindbeck intends to say with this cumbersome phrase that Christian language and literature are for Ricoeur only one of a number of diverse expressions of a common core experience. Doctrines, on this position, therefore pertain to attitudes or "existential orientations."[11]

Hans Frei has offered what to this point has been the most searching critique of Ricoeur's theological hermeneutics and theory of narrative interpretation. Indeed, Frei's debate with Ricoeur may be seen as the culmination of Frei's sustained attack on philosophical hermeneutics. In *The Eclipse of Biblical Narrative* Frei argued that the literal sense of the biblical narrative began to be distinguished from the questions of historical reference or religious truth – questions that eventually rose to the forefront of theological discussion. Eventually, says Frei, the literal sense of biblical narrative was eclipsed altogether by the historical or ideal subject matter. The "meaning" of biblical narrative was conceived either in terms of historical reference or in terms of its "ideal" reference. Frei associates Ricoeur with the latter error.

The Yale theologians view Ricoeur as a modern representative of a tendency deriving from eighteenth-century hermeneutics in England and Germany that Frei calls "mediating theology." It was at this time that the breakup of the harmony between historical fact, literal meaning and religious truth occurred. Frei believes that modern theology has still not recovered from this putting asunder of what was joined together in biblical narrative. Mediating theology accepts the dissociation of historical factuality, literal meaning and religious truth but then attempts to hold onto both the religious truth of "Christ" and the historical actuality of "Jesus." For Frei the crucial issue is whether or not a theologian affirms that salvation depends not only on what Jesus said and did, but that he existed as God incarnate. Frei calls this belief that God in Jesus Christ directly intervened in the finite realm the "positivity" of Christian faith.[12] Increasingly, theologians who continued to affirm the historical positivity of revelation did so by stressing not so much the events of Jesus' life as what they indicated about the quality of Jesus' life. For these theologians, the stories of Jesus' miracles were not to be taken literally, but rather as figurative expressions of the uniqueness of Jesus' being. The theologically important moment resides not in the actuality of the event, but in its qualitative content. Frei observes that those theologians who affirm the religious content of biblical narrative rather than its historical factuality tend to focus on the quality of Jesus' teaching and life. Interestingly enough, Frei finds that the notion of the Kingdom of God became increasingly significant for the mediating theologians, being at once the content of Jesus' teaching and the orienting principle of his life. In this light, Ricoeur's emphasis on the parables of Jesus and the concomitant centrality of the Kingdom of God takes on new significance.

To repeat, mediating theologians view the external events of Jesus' life as manifestations of his qualitative being. After all, the external events were narrated in culturally conditioned, obsolete thought-forms that need not be taken as religiously authoritative. What counts is the religious truth content, not the narrative form. Frei notes that there was a good deal of confusion over whether saving knowledge and faith depended on the historical occasion of the cross and resurrection.[13] The tendency of mediating theologians was to acknowledge the historically conditioned nature of the literal sense, but then to go on and insist that the real meaning of the texts lay elsewhere.

The climax of Frei's story of mediating theology serves also as introduction to his critique of Ricoeur. According to Frei, narrative interpretation was lost in the late eighteenth century.[14] Instead of the biblical story providing the framework within which the rest of the world makes sense, the mediating theologians made sense of the biblical story by first putting it in a general moral, religious or philosophical framework. Mediating theologians held on to a historical faith, says Frei, "only as an indispensable solution to a universally experienced moral lack or dilemma."[15] Without an antecedent framework, the biblical narrative would be meaningless to modern readers. In other words, the mediating theologians required a conceptual framework within which to read the biblical narratives if they were going to be meaningful – and this quite apart from the question of their truth. This is for Frei "the great reversal" that took place across the theological spectrum in the late eighteenth century: "interpretation was a matter of fitting the biblical story into another world with another story rather than incorporating that world into the biblical story."[16] Frei notes that the contexts of meaningfulness to which mediating theologians appeal has changed drastically since the eighteenth century, but the overall logic and strategy of the mediating theologians has remained unchanged:

Whatever their differences, John Locke ... Friedrich Schleiermacher, Albrecht Ritschl, Wilhelm Herrmann, Emil Brunner, Rudolf Bultmann, Karl Rahner, Gerhard Ebeling, Wolfhart Pannenberg, and Jürgen Moltmann all agree on these principles. Most of them have disavowed that they were out to "prove" the truth of Christianity ... But they have all been agreed that one way or another the religious *meaningfulness* (as distinct from demonstration of the truth) of the claim could, indeed must, be perspicuous through its relation to other accounts of general human experience.[17]

The most significant change in hermeneutics during the nineteenth century according to Frei was the focus on the question of meaningfulness rather than on the rules and principles for interpreting texts. Schleiermacher is for Frei the paradigm of this new "hermeneutics of understanding" that seeks the meaning of texts in the "consciousness" expressed therein. Language (grammar) for Schleiermacher expresses thought (psyche). There is unity in the Gospel narrative not because of its verbal structure but because of its author, whose spirit must be grasped, and because of its "inner form" of coherence that Schleiermacher assigns to the consciousness of Jesus.[18] Indeed, it is Jesus' consciousness as it affected the disciples that accounts for the unity of the entire NT canon. For Schleiermacher, Jesus' consciousness "as manifested in a connected pattern"[19] is the "ideal" referent of the Gospels. Frei complains that this general hermeneutic simply does not do justice to certain kinds of narratives. Why should theology privilege a hermeneutics of consciousness? Frei points out that the philosophical assumption underlying Schleiermacher's theory of understanding – that a non-objectifiable human subject expresses itself in objectifiable speech – is not necessarily the only model for human being. Frei prefers a model for human being that focuses on intentional agency, and suggests that such a model is more appropriate for certain kinds of narrative texts, among which he includes the Gospels.

Frei's *Eclipse of the Biblical Narrative* constitutes a massive protest against the whole enterprise of philosophical hermeneutics, where one model of intelligibility is accepted a priori and all texts, regardless of their specific features, are subsumed under its categories of meaningfulness. Jeffrey Stout has called Frei's work an instance of "Anselmian ad hoc apologetics carried out by historiographical means."[20] He goes on to call Frei the leading Anselmian theologian of his generation.

Anselm, as Barth has shown, represents a form of theology that seeks to describe Christian faith on its own terms. Barth argues that Anselm's theological method seeks to explain the logic of biblical language rather than transposing it into a philosophical conceptuality, such as Aristotelianism or Platonism. Theology need not argue its case before a philosophical court; rather, its task is to achieve clarity and understanding of its own beliefs – *credo ut intelligam.* Frei is best understood, therefore, as a theologian who seeks to approach the Gospel narratives in an Anselmian way, letting them make sense in their own way. Indeed, Frei's defense of the ''literal sense'' of biblical narrative is simply his way of staking out this Anselmian enterprise. It is no accident that Karl Barth appears in Frei's *Eclipse of Biblical Narrative* as a model for a narrative reading of the Bible that preserves the literal sense ''without falling into the trap of instantly making history the test of the *meaning* of the realistic forms of the stories.''[21] True to his Anselmian methodology, Barth makes no a priori demands concerning the kind of meaning the Gospel narratives may have. The text alone determines that. Indeed, we might state the only general hermeneutical rule to which Barth adheres as follows: to the texts themselves.[22]

According to Frei, Ricoeur's project is far from being Anselmian. Ricoeur does not propound ad hoc rules for reading (the old sense of hermeneutics) but a full-fledged, systematic theory of understanding. With Schleiermacher, Ricoeur assumes a subject – object pattern that correlates ''(reader's) understanding'' and ''(textual) meaning.''[23] Frei has delivered several unpublished lectures and written ''The 'Literal Reading' of Biblical Narrative in the Christian Tradition'' attacking Ricoeur's philosophical hermeneutics. It is Ricoeur's very success in articulating a systematic theory of understanding that makes him so dangerous according to Frei. There have been other mediating theologians, but Ricoeur, by giving them a surer hermeneutic foundation, is their patron saint. Ricoeur's belief that the literal sense of poetic texts must be abolished in order to free the second-order, non-ostensive (or in Frei's terms, ''ideal'') reference does indeed fit Frei's description, as does the general convergence between philosophical anthropology and textual hermeneutics that I have argued is at the heart of Ricoeur's project. In Frei's opinion, Ricoeur's theological hermeneutics is by and large merely an extension or subset of a general philosophical hermeneutics.

Is this right? What are we to make of Ricoeur's profession of Barth and his allegiance to the priority of the word? As we have seen, the priority of the word is a characteristic of Ricoeur's general hermeneutics.

Are there any special procedures that one must follow with regard to biblical texts in particular? How does Ricoeur treat biblical texts as opposed to other kinds of texts? What is the relation of philosophical and theological hermeneutics in Ricoeur? The relation is, as Ricoeur himself admits, an ambiguous one: on the one hand, theological hermeneutics would appear to be a particular case of philosophical hermeneutics, insofar as it employs the same categories as the latter (i.e., discourse, text, explanation, appropriation, etc.). On the other hand, theological hermeneutics displays some unique traits which question the claim to universality of philosophical hermeneutics and, perhaps, overthrow it. Indeed, Ricoeur suggests that by interpreting biblical texts we shall see that theological hermeneutics ultimately encompasses philosophical hermeneutics: ''Nothing is more able to reveal the 'excentric' character of theology than the attempt to 'apply' to it the general categories of hermeneutics.''[24] How does Ricoeur reach this startling conclusion?

At the level of the text as written discourse, there is nothing special about the Bible. With regard to the problems of speech and writing and its various literary forms, the Bible is just like any other text. Similarly, with regard to reference, Ricoeur is clear that poetic texts, whether sacred or secular, project worlds, constellations of human possibilities. The world of the text is the central category for philosophical and theological hermeneutics alike: ''the 'issue' of the text, the 'new being' of the text, is *the* object of hermeneutics.''[25] Theological hermeneutics is not interested in structural analysis nor historical criticism, but rather in the world of the text that ''forms and transforms the self of the reader according to its intention.''[26] The world of the Bible opens up the reality of the possible, and to the extent that a possibility illumines my existence, we may say that it is ''revealed.''

Theological hermeneutics is therefore a particular case of a general hermeneutic and at the same time a unique case. On the one hand, theological hermeneutics is simply a regional instance of Ricoeur's world-proposing philosophical hermeneutics. On the other, the world opened up by the biblical texts is unique – no other text opens up a new covenant, a new birth and the Kingdom of God. However, we must not forget that the principles of understanding seem to be the same for non-biblical texts. Other texts function in a ''revelatory'' fashion; other texts open up the reality of the possible. Ricoeur has not shown us that theological hermeneutics is significantly different from his philosophical hermeneutics, only that his philosophical hermeneutics receives its most fruitful fulfillment when applied to the biblical texts.

In the end, it is not the kind of hermeneutics so much as the "issue" of the biblical text that sets the Bible apart from other poetic texts. "Theological hermeneutics" is simply the enterprise of unfolding all the implications of the world of the biblical text, not a special method for understanding Scripture. Accordingly, we may question both Ricoeur's distinction between philosophical and theological hermeneutics as well as the priority he claims to assign to the latter.

Unlike Frei and Barth, therefore, Ricoeur reads the biblical narrative within a general theory of textual discourse and human understanding. Against Ricoeur, Frei feels that it is incumbent upon the theologian to resist any general theory of meaning that purports to universal applicability. In the religious community, religious texts should govern theories of meaning and understanding, not vice versa. Whereas Ricoeur is trying to establish a universal theory of interpretation within which the Bible is to be understood, Frei is simply trying to read the Gospels on their own terms. For Frei, the movement is from particular to general; for Ricoeur, the opposite is the case. How do these opposing strategies actually affect the reading each makes of the Gospels?

Stories of Jesus: parabolic narrative

Frei criticizes Ricoeur's philosophical hermeneutics not only because it seeks to construct a general theory of textual understanding within which the Bible is only a regional instance, but more specifically because of the problems it raises when applied to the Gospels. Frei perceives these problems most clearly in the work of David Tracy, "a theologian whose NT hermeneutics is a close reading and precise regional application of Ricoeur's general hermeneutics."[27] William M. Thompson, in his book surveying contemporary options in Christology, correctly treats Ricoeur and Tracy together under the heading of "literary-critical" contributions:

While Tracy has contributed the most impressive "systematic" view of the biblical Christology, he has relied greatly upon Ricoeur's own seminal work in interpretation theory. It is often hard to know where Ricoeur ends and Tracy begins.[28]

Perhaps the best way to construe their relation is to say that Tracy is a thorough theological performance of Ricoeur's philosophical hermeneutics.[29]

The debate between the "Chicago school" and the "Yale school" has proven to be one of the most interesting theological exchanges in

North America in the 1980s, as the well-attended sessions of the narrative interpretation group in the American Academy of Religion amply attest.[30] Because Frei aims his criticisms at the theological implications of Ricoeur's hermeneutics, it is appropriate to examine Tracy's application of Ricoeur's interpretation theory to Christology. In so doing, we shall see that the real issues concern not merely the interpretation of narrative but the task of theology, the nature of theological method and the judgment as to what Christianity is all about.

In a programmatic article that set the agenda for his subsequent work, Tracy describes the task of theology in five theses.[31] First, "*The two principal sources for theology are the Christian fact and contemporary experience.*"[32] Such a thesis constitutes nothing less than a manifesto for mediating theology. Second, the task of theology involves a "critical correlation" of the Christian fact (Scripture and tradition) and contemporary human experience. Third, the principal method for investigating contemporary experience is a phenomenology of its religious dimension (here Tracy borrows Ricoeur's idea of the limit experience). Fourth, the principal method for investigating the Christian fact is a hermeneutics of the classic Christian text. Hermeneutics inquires into the mode of being referred to by the text. Fifth, to determine the truth status of the critical correlation, the theologian should employ a transcendental or metaphysical mode of reflection. The task here is to show that the "limit" of general human experience (revealed by the phenomenology of the religious dimension) is the same as the referent of the Christian text, namely, its "theistic specification of a religious way of being in the world."[33] Christian faith can thus be shown to represent that fundamental trust in existence that an examination of general human experience also discovers. From this brief analysis we can already see that Frei's fears are ultimately justified: Tracy fits the Christian text into a general conceptual framework of meaningfulness provided by a phenomenology of religious experience. Such an enterprise is a variation on natural theology to which both Barth and Frei respond "Nein!"

Tracy thoroughly develops these five theses in his *Blessed Rage for Order* and *The Analogical Imagination*. Before turning to these works, one more ingredient in Tracy's thinking must be noted: plurality. Tracy is keenly aware of the pluralist setting as he pursues the theological task.[34] His challenge is twofold: how to do justice and learn from the variety of religious and theological positions and at the same time remain loyal to his particular tradition. Tracy's solution is to recognize the fundamental trust in existence which Christians and non-Christians share ("secularity's faith") and then proceed to argue that "a proper understanding of explicitly Christian faith can render intellectually coherent and symbolically powerful that common secular faith which we share."[35]

It is just here that Tracy's appropriation of Ricoeur's narrative theory proves useful, for Tracy views systematic theology as a hermeneutical enterprise and the Christian theologian as an interpreter of poetic texts. The whole argument of Tracy's *magnum opus*, *The Analogical Imagination* stands or falls on the analogy between secular and religious classics and the way each reveals truth. Tracy devotes no less than five chapters totalling 240 pages to a sustained discussion of the phenomenon of the classic, the religious classic, the Christian classic and problems of interpretation pertaining to each.

Tracy defines classics as works that "so disclose a compelling truth about our lives that we cannot deny them some kind of normative status."[36] Moreover, the truth of the classic has a certain timelessness which calls for fresh interpretations for new situations. A classic work of art or literature is "true" if it engenders what Tracy terms the "realized experience of the essential."[37] What Tracy appears to be referring to here is a truth about our lives that, once we have confronted it, enjoys the immediate and complete authority of the undeniably self-evident. Face to face with a classic, we have to admit that it is *we* who are being described. We recognize an important truth about ourselves in the classic. Tracy appeals to the analogy with art: "In the actual experience of art ... we recognize the truth of the work's disclosure of a world of reality transforming, if only for a moment, ourselves: our lives, our sense for possibilities and actuality, our destiny."[38] Accordingly, "the issue of both the meaning and truth of religion is related to the analogous issue of the meaning and truth of art."[39] Both religion and art express the truth of the human experience in their respective classics.

In arguing that "[t]he claims to truth in both art and religion ... stand or fall together,"[40] Tracy acknowledges that his interpretation of the biblical narrative is only an instance of a general procedure. What are the results for theology and christology of applying this theory of interpretation to the Christian Scriptures? In Tracy's opinion the Bible is the Christian religious classic that presents, as do other classics, *permanent and essential possibilities for human existence*. Moreover, as with art, the truth of the Bible does not depend upon the events recorded therein actually having happened. Classic paintings and stories can reveal the truth of the human condition even if their reference is fictional rather than factual. Indeed, does not the power of Jesus' parables work in precisely this fashion?

Ricoeur's comment about the referent of parables being "common human experience" takes on added significance in light of Tracy's theory of the religious classic. Tracy's Ricoeurrian analysis of the Gospel narratives permits him to see not only the parables but the story of Jesus itself as a symbolic expression of a universal truth. The stories of Jesus function as "parables" of this universal truth. Just what this truth is will be the subject of the penultimate section of this chapter. The point to be made here is that Tracy's subsuming the Gospel narratives under the hermeneutic category "classic" has implications for theology as well as hermeneutics. If the Gospels disclose a universal truth about general human experience, what is the special significance of Jesus Christ?

With this question we come to Frei's fundamental criticism of Ricoeur's hermeneutics as exemplified by David Tracy. As we have seen, Ricoeur believes the special function of poetic literature is to reveal new human possibilities. Ricoeur and Tracy follow Bultmann's lead in claiming that the NT offers the reader a new possibility for self-understanding. There is a price to pay for this hermeneutic strategy, however. Frei charges Ricoeur and Tracy with failing to preserve a "literal" reading of the Gospels and thereby failing to preserve the indispensability of the person and actions of Jesus for Christian theology. How is this so? First, if the Gospels are really about general human experience and human possibilities, then the hermeneutical position of Ricoeur and Tracy will view Jesus as subject "chiefly in the form of consciousness, that is, of his selfhood as 'understanding'."[41] What happens to Jesus in the story is simply a foil that allows him to enact a self-understanding. The events that happen to Jesus are "carnal shadows" of a true secondary world of human possibilities. Frei objects that this reading fails to do justice to the Gospels as stories about a person in a world of actions, characters and events. At the limit, such a reading loses the peculiarly "theological" element of the Gospels, namely, the historical witness to God's act in Christ.

Could not Jesus still play an indispensable role as bearer of this self-understanding? Frei thinks not, for what the Gospel narratives represent in this hermeneutical scheme is not in the first place personal selves who are the subject of their predicates, but rather " 'the mode-of-being-in-the-world' which these selves exemplify and which is 're-presented' by being 'disclosed' to 'understanding'."[42] Tracy seems to say as much. For him, the principal referent of the Gospel narratives "is the disclosure of a certain limit-mode-of-being-in-the-world."[43] Frei suggests that on this account, the character of Jesus "is simply a temporary personal thickening" of a certain set of attitudes.[44] "Jesus" functions no longer as the name for the principal character in a story about him, but rather as a label for a particular mode of consciousness, a possibility of self-understanding. Frei judges this reading of the Gospel narratives to be "far closer to traditional allegorical than literal reading."[45] What happens to the personal subject "Jesus" is not what is of primary importance. Accordingly, Frei wonders whether a hermeneutics of understanding such as Ricoeur's can preserve the centrality of the story of Jesus: "At best the link between meaning-reference and ascription to a personal subject within the story is tenuous in this view. At worst it is eliminated."[46]

Frei notes the tendency in Ricoeur to subsume the teaching of Jesus concerning the Kingdom of God under a more general reference. In his "Biblical Hermeneutics," Ricoeur writes that "the ultimate referent of the parables ... is not the Kingdom of God, but human reality in its wholeness."[47] By postulating a secondary world of human possibilities and understanding "above" or "in front of" the world of the story, Ricoeur and Tracy are guilty of eclipsing the biblical narrative by dissociating its literal meaning from its ideal referent. No matter what seems to be happening in the story, "human reality in its wholeness" will be the true subject matter each time.

In fairness to Ricoeur and Tracy, Frei notes that they try to give unique significance to Jesus while at the same time they make general religious experience the referent of the Gospel narratives: "It is an uneasy alliance of conflicting hermeneutical aims."[48] Moreover, Frei concludes that when applied to the Gospels, this hermeneutical theory does not stretch but breaks a literal reading. In the climate of a consciousness-oriented anthropology and hermeneutics, the descriptive and ascriptive character of literal reading is lost, and with it the irreducible personal (literal!) subject Jesus Christ.

Stories of Jesus: realistic narrative

How does Frei propose that we read the Gospels? Frei follows Barth (and Anselm) in viewing theology as conceptual redescription. The task of theology is not to fit the meaning of the Bible into some other conceptuality, but rather to render the world of the Bible intelligible on its own terms. In his *Eclipse of the Biblical Narrative*, Frei had argued that the Gospels are neither straightforward histories nor myths. Unlike histories, the meaning of the Gospel narratives is not the historical reference outside the story; unlike myths, the meaning of the Gospel narratives is what the stories actually say rather than what they supposedly symbolize. In the hermeneutics of D. F. Strauss and other "mythophiles," the content of the biblical narrative was thought to be separable from its mythical form. But Frei points out that the Gospel narratives do not include obviously mythical elements; they are rather history-like or "realistic." This should give the mythophile pause:

It is at least possible that in regard to realistic narrative literature, the function of general hermeneutics should be formal rather than material; it should be confined to identifying a piece of literature as belonging to that particular genre rather than some other, rather than claim to interpret its meaning or subject matter.[49]

The same tendency to separate the meaning of the text from its subject matter is noticeable in those who insist that the meaning of the biblical narrative is the historical events to which it refers and which may be investigated independently of the stories.

Frei proposes that we view the Gospel narratives as history-like or realistic narratives. Realistic narratives are to be distinguished from myths, allegories or parables because their form and meaning are inseparable. In realistic narratives "meaning is in large part a function of the interaction of character and circumstances."[50] A realistic narrative depicts a world of people, actions and circumstances that is familiar to the reader. The meaning consists precisely in the interactions between these three factors. Accordingly, we cannot have the meaning without the story form. We could not have the point of the story without the narration itself. In Frei's words:

this meaning through instantiation is not *illustrated* (as though it were an intellectually presubsisting or preconceived archetype or ideal essence) but *constituted* through the mutual, specific determination of agents, speech, social context, and circumstances that form the indispensable narrative web.[51]

A reading of realistic narrative that respects this close identification of narrative form and meaning will not dissociate the subject matter or reference from the story itself. Frei considers both histories and novels realistic narratives because each deals with specific human identities and specific human actions.

Frei offers an interpretation of the Gospels viewed as realistic narratives in his *The Identity of Jesus Christ*.[52] Frei's effort is perhaps best viewed as an Anselmian exercise in narrative interpretaton. That is, Frei makes every effort to let the text speak for itself rather than casting it into an alien conceptual framework such as existentialism. The task of understanding is that of making intelligible what is given, not of placing the given in a foreign context. As we noted earlier, it is no accident that Frei appeals to Barth as a model of the kind of reading he has in mind. Barth too followed Anselm's program of letting the object of knowledge dictate the manner in which it is known and described. George Lindbeck calls this approach an "intratextual" one. The intratextual approach tries to make sense of a text or a religious tradition from the inside. The task of the theologian is to describe the world of the text, not the world "behind," "above" or "in front of the text."

This Anselmian, intratextual approach to texts is therefore one that seeks to respect the "literal" sense. But what is the literal sense? Strictly speaking, "literal" refers to the sense of the letter, to what the text says. Accordingly, for Frei the literal sense of the story is the story itself and the literal reference of the story is to the story's world – the world made up of the characters, circumstances and actions that figure in the story. To locate the meaning or reference in a world other than the world of the story is to depart from a literal reading. Respecting the literal sense demands that one take the text on its own terms rather than trying to fit it into a different context of meaning or truth. A respect for the literal sense and an Anselmian or "intratextual" approach go together. In Lindbeck's words:

Intratextual theology redescribes reality within the scriptural framework rather than translating Scripture into extrascriptural categories. It is the text, so to speak, which absorbs the world, rather than the world the text.[53]

Frei considers the Gospels realistic or history-like because they depict a world in which a central character acts, interacts with other agents and suffers. Whether or not the Gospels report history, "they literally mean what they say."[54] That is, there is no gap between the story and what it is about. There is no separable subject matter apart from the story itself. As an Anselmian, Frei's task is to explicate the meaning of the story. This is not simply a literary exercise, however, for interpreting this narrative entails theological consequences. The most important theological consequence is that the Gospel narratives render the identity of Jesus Christ. Realistic narrative is for Frei the ideal literary form to render personal identity. What is lost in Ricoeur's account of biblical narrative is precisely what Frei values, namely, the literal specificity of persons and events – the defining feature of realistic narratives. In Frei's view, Ricoeur's reading of the Gospels is akin to a mythological, even Gnostic, reading because the literal specificity of the person "Jesus" is sacrificed on the altar of metaphorical reference: "Myths are stories in which character and action are not irreducibly themselves."[55] Unlike the parabolic reading of Tracy and Ricoeur, Frei focuses on the specific individual "Jesus" and his actions. The Gospels are about the identity of Jesus, not his temporality, nor his existential significance, nor the ethical ideal he symbolizes.

For Frei, the Gospels realistically narrate the identity of Jesus. Jesus' identity is his "specific uniqueness as a person,"[56] a uniqueness which is the product of what he says and does as well as what happens to him. Frei's project is to describe the "intention-action" pattern that distinguishes the life of Jesus. Jesus' intentions and his actions do not merely illustrate his identity, but constitute it. The identity of Jesus is ineluctably bound up with what happens in the Gospels. The difference between the Gospel story and all others "is simply the unsubstitutable person about whom the story is told – his unsubstitutable deeds, words, and sufferings – that makes the real difference."[57] Moreover, it is this emphasis on the "unsubstitutable person" of Jesus that finally distinguishes realistic narrative from myth. With obvious satisfaction, Frei observes: "The Gospel story is a demythologization of the savior myth because the savior figure in the Gospel story is fully identified with Jesus of Nazareth."[58] The Church substitutes no other name: the NT is the story of "Jesus' singular obedience in passion and death."[59]

It is the passion narratives that most fully reveal Jesus' identity according to Frei. Here Jesus' intent to do the will of the Father, which has characterized his whole life, receives its climactic enactment. The story of Jesus is about his obedience to God. Frei notes that whereas the actions of Jesus decrease as the passion narrative unfolds, those of God increase, until in the resurrection "the initiative of God is finally and decisively climaxed and he alone is and can be active."[60] Jesus' person is thus the place of God's activity. The last, and decisive, event that determines Jesus' identity is the resurrection. Jesus is the risen one. To read the narrative of the post-resurrection appearances correctly, Frei claims, is to see that Jesus is the one who now lives. In other words, "knowing his identity is identical with having him present or being in his presence."[61] And again, "To know *who* he is in connection with what took place is to know *that* he is."[62]

Frei's work is twice Anselmian. Not only does he follow Anselm's method of letting the object direct the manner in which it is investigated, but he has done this for the second person of the Trinity in as striking (and controversial) a fashion as Anselm did with the first. Where Anselm asks us to consider the identity of God, the "being-than-which-nothing-greater-can-be-conceived," Frei asks us to consider the identity of the risen Jesus, the "one-who-cannot-be-thought-of-except-as-now-present." Frei is well aware of the startling nature of his conclusion.

The Gospel narratives are unique: they break out of their fictional description to a factual claim. In this one case, "we are forced to consent to the factuality of what we represent to ourselves as imaginary."[63] We are not thinking about the Jesus of the Gospels, says Frei, if we are not thinking of him as now present. His presence here and now is part and parcel with his identity. Jesus is the one who now lives. The intratextual rendering of Jesus' identity makes his extratextual non-existence inconceivable.

Frei is a conscientious Anselmian: he believes that faith must seek its own kind of intelligibility. He has striven for a reading that does not impose a foreign conceptuality on the Gospels. But Frei, like Barth before him, is acutely aware of the ease with which the Anselmian can slip into extratextual categories.[64] Indeed, Frei now regrets his elevation of the category "presence" in his explanation of Jesus' identity. Frei believes that he was too taken by a model of revelation as personal encounter. The theologian may use phrases like "the presence of Jesus," but only informally; elevating such phrases into technical theological concepts is to fall into extratextuality.[65] More important for our purposes, however, is Frei's recent change of heart concerning his own use of the category "realistic narrative." Is not an approach to the Gospels which subsumes them under the category "realistic narrative" itself an instance of a reading that forces an extratextual category onto the biblical narrative?[66] To make the Gospels a type of the category "realistic narrative" is to operate with what one might call an "analogy of being" on the level of narrative. One first determines how realistic narrative in general works, and then proceeds to an interpretation of the Gospels. But neither Frei nor Barth wishes to proceed to the things of God by first analyzing the world or language of the creature. Such was the error of natural theology. We might say that Frei objects to Ricoeur's development of a "natural theology of narrative."

Frei is presently seeking an intratextual approach to biblical narrative that eschews any contact with general theories of meaning and interpretation.[67] The first truth about the literal sense in Frei's opinion is that it "is a case-specific reading which may or may not find reduced analogues elsewhere."[68] The second point Frei now makes is that the literal sense "belongs first and foremost into the context of a socio-linguistic community ... rather than into a literary ambience."[69] Here Frei seems to adopt a maxim akin to Wittgenstein's "Look not to the meaning but to the use." Frei believes that defining the literal sense as the use the Gospels have in the believing community will allow him to pursue his Anselmian program of description more consistently. Now the theological task resembles the social anthropological description of a community. The theologian should be more concerned with the specific set of texts (the Gospels) and the most specific context (the Church), rather than with a general class of texts (realistic narrative) and the most general context (human experience).

Are the Gospels literally true?

Ricoeur and Frei make sense of the biblical narrative in different manners. Frei attempts to describe the literal sense; Ricoeur seeks to go beyond it. In this section we will be concerned primarily with the question of the reference or truth of the Gospels. Whereas for Barth and Frei the story world is all there is, for Ricoeur and Tracy the story world is metaphorically related to a secondary world, the "world-of-the-text." We have seen that this world of the text pertains not to its literal meaning, but rather to the human possibilities or modes of being-in-the-world displayed therein. For Ricoeur, the world of the story (the sense) is the means for attaining to a secondary world (the reference) which is not realistic. For Frei, on the other hand, *verbum* and *res*, sense and reference, are inseparable. The story does not refer beyond itself for its "true" meaning. My working hypothesis is that Ricoeur and Frei provide valuable insights into the question of narrative reference but ultimately do not provide an adequate explanation of the nature of the Gospel's referent.

Recall Tracy's statement that the truth claims of art and religion stand or fall together.[70] Tracy is in wholehearted agreement with Ricoeur's rehabilitation of the imagination as an organ of truth. A religious tradition discloses "in its symbols and in its reflections on those symbols (i.e., its theologies) some fundamental vision of the meaning of the individual and communal existence providing disclosive and transformative possibilities for the whole society."[71] In short, the Christian classic discloses a possible way of viewing existence as meaningful. This disclosure of the meaningfulness of existence is important for Tracy because the contemporary situation raises this very question. What sets the religious classic apart from other classics is that its disclosure concerns the *whole* of reality and derives from the "power of the whole" by a "gracious mystery."[72]

What truth does the Christian classic disclose? Tracy believes that the Gospels disclose the truth that the world is "always-already" graced and loved by God. This is the point of the stories about Jesus:

The always-already reality of a graced world is made present again decisively, paradigmatically, classically *as event* in Jesus Christ. The event, as re-presentative of the reality always already present to us as human beings, is present again as the decisive *that* it happens.[73]

Tracy correlates the truth of the Christian classic with the general truth that life is fundamentally trustworthy. In other words, the general trust in the meaningfulness of life (secularity's "faith") is the secular approximation or equivalent of specifically Christian faith. In the event of Jesus Christ, the believer senses that the meaning of the whole – of ourselves, of God, of the world – is decisively manifested as an event that is not of our own making and yet at the same time confirms our deepest longings for "wholeness" in the whole. The emphasis on "wholeness" is intended, I believe, to connote both the coherence of the believer's experience of the world and its healthiness when viewed in light of the Christ event. The Gospels convey the truth that all things shall be well. At the same time, the Gospels confirm our experience of evil and suffering in the world: before resurrection joy there is crucifixion dread. For Tracy this more nuanced view of the wholeness of the whole constitutes a firmer disclosure of the truth of lived existence, just as the tortured paintings of Van Gogh ring truer to contemporary experience than the untroubled, ethereal world disclosed in the art of Raphael.[74]

The central phenomenon of truth disclosure shared by art and religion merits special consideration, for it is also a connecting link between Ricoeur's philosophical hermeneutics and Tracy's theology. Tracy believes his account of the religious classic is an instance of Ricoeur's "hermeneutics of retrieval," in which the interpreter applies explanatory techniques to a text in order to pass from a surface interpretation to a depth interpretation, from a first to a second naiveté. "The sense of a text is not behind the text, but in front of it. It is not something hidden, but something disclosed."[75] The text discloses a possible world, not the surface or realistic world of the text, but a world of existential possibilities. Ricoeur writes: "Here showing is at the same time creating a new mode of being."[76] As he puts it, "It is the text, with its universal power of world disclosure, which gives a self to the ego."[77] My thesis is that Ricoeur and Tracy are theologians of manifestation, and that their emphasis on manifestation dramatically affects the kind of referent they perceive in the Gospels. Why do Ricoeur and Tracy choose to see truth in terms of manifestation?

Ricoeur relies on Heidegger's suggestion that Being "shows itself" in the work of art.[78] This accords well with Ricoeur's emphasis that the knowing subject is not the master of meaning and truth. The subject is at the mercy, as it were, of the classic text or work of art: if Being does not show itself here, then where? This emphasis on manifestation reflects Ricoeur's Copernican reversal: the subject is the hearer rather than the speaker of language.

Second, manifestation is the most appropriate expression of the material truth of the Christian classic namely, that the world is always-already graced. This is a most important claim and demands careful scrutiny. Tracy believes that the theologian can express the significance of the Christ event in two ways: proclamation and manifestation. Proclamation stresses the otherness or transcendence of God: the kerygma is both a word of judgment and of grace. In preaching God's coming as an eschatological event, it stresses the distanciation that separates God and man, the not-yet aspect of the Christ event. Manifestation, on the other hand, stresses the immanence of God: Being appears as something I belong to. In manifestation, God is disclosed as present even in ordinary things. Religious classics express "the ambiguous and complex actuality of a lived existence of participation and nonparticipation in a reality greater than the self."[79]

Tracy notes that today the power of manifestation is experienced mediately. People today no longer consult Delphic oracles. For most theologians, a first naiveté is no longer a live option. The sacred is not experienced directly, but mediately, and Tracy suggests that the "most familiar form of mediation in contemporary Christian theologies is a mediation of religious reality via philosophical reflection."[80] The route from secular to sacred

starts from some sense of wonder at existence, formulates that sense as a question of the whole through disciplined reflection to a renewed, religious sense of fundamental trust in the whole now reassured and reinforced by the mediation of philosophical reflection.[81]

This description could function equally well as an account of Ricoeur's intellectual pilgrimage. His is a philosophy that listens to the word, hoping to be called (by Being) again. It is a philosophy of affirmation and fundamental trust. The goodness of Being which Ricoeur pre-supposes finds its decisive manifestation in the event of Jesus Christ. But the point is that without reflection on art or classic texts, this truth of the trustworthiness of existence could not be had.

If the fundamental question of the age is in Tracy's view that of the meaningfulness of existence, then the manifestation of grace in Jesus Christ answers the need of the day. The world disclosed by the Gospel

narratives is one that is always-already loved by God: this is the meaning
of the "Christian fact." Accordingly, theologians of manifestation
"develop theologies designed to articulate the primal sense of the
ultimate meaning of the event of manifestation: all is grace."[82] The
focus on Jesus *intensifies* our hesitant trust in a meaningful reality. Jesus
is the answer to our fundamental question, Is life trustworthy, for the
reality disclosed by the event of Jesus Christ is grace: "grace prevails
for the Christian as the central clue to the nature of all reality."[83] The
Being that shows itself in the event of Jesus Christ is the God who loves,
and the reality of this God who loves is also the central clue to the
meaning of the human self both loved and loving:

In Christian systematics, there is no theology which is not also an anthropology
... The Christian doctrines of God and the human rise and fall together. The
key to both, and the key to their inter-relationships, may be found in the harsh,
demanding reality of radical agapic love.[84]

The Gospel narratives disclose a world that is always-already graced
and a mode of human being that corresponds to this world. This
manifestation of the love of God in Jesus Christ admirably answers our
need for an experience of belonging-to. Manifestation focuses on God's
immanence and our participation in his world. But is this not the poetic
dimension, the rumor of Creation, that Ricoeur strives to recover in
his broader hermeneutics? What poems do to a limited degree, the
Gospels do more intensely. Both poetry and Gospel conjure up the world
as Creation, that is, as the object of God's special favor.

Several serious implications follow from viewing the truth of the
Gospel narratives under the heading of manifestation. We shall mention
several of these, noting Frei's concerns at the same time. First and
foremost is the consequence that the truth disclosed by the Gospels refers
to an always-already state of affairs. The story of Jesus discloses a way
of being in the world that is always-already open to human beings by
virtue of the always-already graced nature of the world. To Jesus' query,
"Who do you say that I am?" Tracy might reply, "You are the Christ,
the symbolic representation of an agapic mode of being-in-the-world."
Frei rightly complains that "Jesus" is here turned into an allegory of
"universal meaningfulness."[85] The Gospels manifest universal truths
about humanity. The contrast between manifestation and proclamation,
in which the Gospels say something new, particular and unique, could
not be sharper: do the Gospels disclose a universal truth, or do they
announce something new and unprecedented?

I believe that Ricoeur and Tracy, though they try to incorporate both proclamation and manifestation in their theologies, ultimately privilege the manifestation pole. The very link between the truth claims of art and religion should attest to that. Moreover, their construal of the problem of our time in terms of the widespread feeling of alienation from the world and from ourselves calls for an answer stressing belonging-to and divine immanence. Ricoeur claims that poetic language in general functions to instill a sense of belonging rather than of alienation. There is a moment of critical distanciation, but this is surrounded by experiences of belonging (i.e., understanding as appropriation). Consequently, Ricoeur's whole hermeneutical arch is slightly off-balance, tilted slightly but decisively towards the manifestation model. Similarly, Tracy's idea of the analogical imagination presupposes the priority of the manifestation pole. Tracy is concerned to encourage conversation not simply between various Christian traditions, but also between different faiths. His working assumption is that all religious traditions, and secularity itself, have faith in the ultimate goodness of being. Each religion expresses its faith differently, but there are profound analogies between them if one only uses one's imagination to perceive them. The same universal truth about the graced or gifted nature of reality is variously expressed. Tracy believes that if each believer would only plumb the particularity of his or her own tradition, he would experience similar manifestations of the whole by the power of the whole. Tracy's analogical imagination is actually an instance of metaphoric redescription: religious traditions that were previously thought to be distant are in Tracy brought near.

Tracy's willingness to find analogical similarities between Christianity and other religions confirms Frei's suspicion that the biblical narratives, together with Christianity in general, are being subsumed in a framework of intelligibility and truth that is not their proper home. The same "power of the whole" manifests itself in different ways. While Jesus may be the indispensable symbol for the Christian religion, could not one gain access to this same power of the whole through other religious classics as well?

Tracy associates the manifestation model with religions of a mystical-priestly-aesthetic bent and proclamation with religions of a prophetic-ethical-historical emphasis. One traditional way of classifying these two approaches is by the rubrics "sacrament" and "word." Similarly, Ricoeur in his "Manifestation et proclamation" distinguishes between religions with a preverbal and verbal emphasis. Ricoeur notes that in manifestation religions the sacred cannot be put into words: the sacred manifests itself as do the Ideas of Kant: both rely on the schematizing imagination to produce the appropriate images. The sacred creates a symbolic universe where nature and rites are linked in a logic of correspondences (e.g., harvest rituals in autumn). Proclamation religions, of which the OT is paradigmatic for Ricoeur, focus on the word and its logic of meaning rather than the world and its logic of correspondences. The problem in our modern culture is that the cosmos is mute, the sacred unavailable. Ricoeur believes that humanity is not possible without the sacred, without a sense of transcendence. What then must we do to regain humanity?

Ricoeur attempts a mediation between the sacred and proclamation. Interestingly enough, Tracy suggests that Roman Catholicism is traditionally sacramental, more oriented to the visual than to the verbal, but then decides that Ricoeur's emphasis on the word is "classically Reformed."[86] I believe that Tracy has missed the really interesting point about Ricoeur's philosophical hermeneutics in seeing him as a Reformed theologian of the Word. He is a theologian of the Word, to be sure, but the Word he hearkens to is more a word of manifestation than of proclamation. That is, for Ricoeur *the poetic word functions sacramentally*. The sacramental function of the poetic/religious text consists above all in its power to disclose a graced world over and above the natural world.

Ricoeur's treatment of Jesus' parables attests to his assigning a manifestation function to religious language. The parables, thanks to their extravagance, disclose the religious or sacred dimension of human life for Ricoeur. The parables manifest the extraordinary in the ordinary. The sacred is disclosed in the secular. Of course, this is not the sacred of the cosmic symbols, but the sacred of human limit-experiences. Ricoeur believes that we are on the verge of a renaissance of the sacred, because the word itself has numinous qualities: the word is powerful because it can disclose new worlds.[87] The word not only announces new being but displays it.

We have insisted all along that the world of the text is not the story world, but a secondary world that displays/manifests significant human possibilities and ways of orienting oneself in life. It is one thing to proclaim "God so loves the world," and another thing to manifest it. Without a manifestation, can one respond to Mircea Eliade's pointed query: Does the Christian any longer really *feel* the world as God's creation?[88] Ricoeur believes that poetic and religious language can respond to this challenge. William Thompson correctly sees that biblical narrative, as read by Ricoeur and Tracy, more properly belongs to manifestation than to proclamation:

As manifestation refers to the release of our sense of participation in the Divine, so narratives unfold the course of that participation within our temporal experience. If you will, the world which the NT narratives open up before us is the world of a human, temporal existence permeated by a divine presence.[89]

Thompson also correctly identifies Ricoeur's emphasis on the metaphorical nature of the Gospel narratives as being the key that opens up the secondary world of the text: "Ricoeur's great contribution, I think, is in suggesting how the metaphor is the semantic device which discloses a new world of human possibility and existence."[90] The Gospels metaphorically refer to the divine (the extraordinary) in human existence (the ordinary).

We are now in a better position to recognize the fundamental difference which separates Ricoeur and Frei. For Ricoeur, the Gospels manifest a secondary world, a way of being-in-the-world or in the divine presence – a way of being-in-Creation. Frei's reading focuses on the particularity and specificity of the identity of Jesus Christ.[91] For Ricoeur, the referent of the Gospels is the Kingdom of God as it qualifies human experience: the "truth claims of the biblical stories are claims about the innovative capacities and persistent characteristics of our species."[92] For Frei, the referent of the Gospels is Jesus Christ. Frei himself observes that Ricoeur's allegiance to a model of truth as disclosure predisposes him to prefer "the metaphorical and disclosive character of the parables over the realistic, literally descriptive character of the passion and resurrection narratives."[93] For Ricoeur, the Gospels are parables about the Kingdom; for Frei, they are passion narratives with long introductions.

Frei rightly raises the problem of allegorizing. We have seen that Ricoeur's move from sense to reference is not a smooth and easy one. The connection between sense and reference, the literal and symbolic meaning, is mysterious, perhaps ineffable: "By living in the first meaning I am drawn beyond it beyond itself."[94] But just how is the secondary world disclosed by living in the literal sense? Is such residence infallible? What are the controls on the theologian's imagination when we move from the story world to the world of existential possibilities? The move from sense to reference by way of metaphorical process seems to follow a logic of creation rather than discovery.[95] Furthermore, the problematic nature of the relation between sense and reference raises not only hermeneutical but theological problems. Most importantly, asks Frei, what can Ricoeur make of the notion of "God's act"? Must not the literal reference to God's actions metaphorically refer to the secondary world of general human experience and possibilities as well?

Ronald Thiemann, acknowledging Frei's influence, takes up this last point in criticism of Ricoeur and Tracy. Thiemann believes that Ricoeur and Tracy have not approximated but lost the Christian doctrines of revelation and prevenient grace, that is, the idea that theology is a response to a prior act of God: "Our thought and speech about God are not simply the free creations of human imagination but are developed in obedient response to God's prior initiative."[96] At first glance, this would seem an odd criticism of a position that stakes its claim on the always-already nature of God's grace. However, Thiemann believes that this defence of divine prevenience by an argument which asserts the universality of a religious dimension in human experience falls short. The problem, says Thiemann, "is whether *any* coherent argument can be made which establishes God's prior reality."[97] The challenge for Ricoeur and Tracy is to resist reducing God's actual priority to his always-already relation, or in other words, to avoid reducing theology to anthropology. Like Frei, Thiemann prefers a non-foundational account of the priority of God's grace, that is, an account that does not rely on general theories about the religious dimension of human experience. Thiemann's emphasis on the divine initiative leads him towards a notion of the *contingent* prevenience of God's grace. It is not always-already there, a datum in human experience that we may generally assume; rather, if it is there it is only on the basis of a concrete act of God.

As is typical of students of the Yale school, Thiemann aims his sharpest criticisms at theological liberals who seek to correlate religion and general human experience. He singles out Schleiermacher as typical of the tendency to blur the distinction between God and humanity. For Schleiermacher, human consciousness, in particular the feeling of absolute dependence, is the locus of revelation. However, "Schleiermacher never clearly indicates how one distinguishes between an experience of the self's relationship to itself and the self's relationship to God."[98] Thiemann views Tracy and Ricoeur as following in the same tradition. If revelation is a function of poetic language, then the distinction between humanity and God or anthropology and theology is in peril, and with it the chance of affirming the priority of God's act. If revelation is not an act prior to its subjective reception, then how can we ever know what is the product of revelation and what is simply the product of our own vain imaginings?

In sum, the Yale school resists the attempt to interpret the Gospels by means of general theories of meaning and truth. Any such "foundational" theory risks compromising the specificity of the Gospels and their truth claims. Frei, Lindbeck and Thiemann are agreed that the task of theology is a non-foundational one. That is, theology should be less concerned with general frameworks of meaning and truth and more concerned with describing the specific object of Christian faith. Anselm's "faith seeking understanding" is still the watchword; theology is "primarily a descriptive activity, a second-order mode of reflection which displays the logic inherent in Christian belief and practice."[99] For Thiemann, this means discovering and describing the inner logic of the Gospel narratives. The grounds for Christian hope are the promises of God. The logic of the Gospels is the logic of divine promise and divine agency. The promise is a particularly felicitous category for Thiemann, conceiving of God and humanity as related but underlining the aspect of divine initiative.[100] Believing the divine promise, we rely for our salvation on God's making good his promises rather than on our own efforts. The Gospel is the narrative of God making good his promise. Jesus received promises given to Israel, and Jesus promises to be with us.[101] But the Gospel can be God's promise only if he has raised Jesus from the dead: "The Gospel's claim to truth thus demands acceptance of a deeply paradoxical claim that lies at the heart of the narrative's meaning."[102] Thiemann insists that it is the content of the Gospel narrative itself that allows the reader to move from sense to reference, from the narrated promise within the text to the narrated promise addressed to the reader.[103]

Thiemann and Frei are agreed that theology cannot demonstrate the truth of the Gospel's reference to the living Christ. "Theology can only show that the sense of the biblical text implies that referential claim."[104] To interpret the meaning of the Gospel as God's narrated promise (Thiemann) or as a description of the identity of Jesus Christ (Frei) is to believe that Jesus now lives. This leap from the meaning of a story to an extratextual truth claim remains a puzzle, but Frei and Thiemann believe that this is precisely what a literal reading of the text requires the theologian to hold. Frei appeals once again to the analogy with Anselm's argument for the existence of God: in the Gospels we are to make a referential truth inference from a formal coherence description. We can only make sense of the story if we acknowledge its extratextual truth claim. Theology's task is to describe and affirm even where explanation is not possible. The Gospels literally mean that Jesus Christ really lives. How this is so remains a mystery, but it is the central mystery of Christian theology.

We must now turn to a consideration of Frei's notion of "literal" truth. Frei has long been the champion of the literal truth of the Gospels, though he has recently moved away from the category "realistic narrative" for fear that he was succumbing to a general theory which covered a certain class of narratives. In his latest defense of the literal sense of the Gospel and the descriptive task of theology, Frei instead describes the use of the text in the believing community. Indeed, he now wishes to define "literal" in terms of the activity of reading rather than by some property of the text itself.[105] In focusing on the "proper" context for faithful reading (the Church), Frei hopes to remove himself as far as possible from "theoretical" discussions about meaning. Not theory, but actual practice, now determines the "literal" sense. If theory is admitted, it will be of more modest ilk, confined to "describing how and in what specific kinds of context a certain kind of reading functions."[106] The literal reading of the Gospels belongs in the specific context of the specific religion of which it is a part.[107] The task of the theologian is like that of the social anthropologist or ethnographer: specific description rather than general explanation.[108]

Two critical questions must be posed to Frei. First, in turning from realistic narrative to cultural-linguistic description, has not Frei simply exchanged theories? Does not the claim that meaning and truth are context-dependent notions betray a general theory as much (if not more) than the earlier allegiance to the category realistic narrative? Is not Wittgenstein's adage "Look not to the meaning but to the use" itself a manifesto for a general theory of meaning?[109] Second, does this turn to cultural-linguistic description do justice to the literal sense of the Gospel narratives, particularly to their truth claims? If the believing community's rules determine what counts as a "literal reading" of the Gospels, who is to determine which communities are the believing ones? Why not Alexandria rather than Antioch? Frei appeals to the "wide, though of course not unanimous, traditional consensus among Christians in the West"[110] on the primacy of the literal reading. At the same time, however, Frei notes that there was "no a priori reason why the 'plain' reading could not have been 'spiritual' in contrast to 'literal,' and certainly the temptation was strong."[111] In the end, Frei's strongest argument seems to be that, as a matter of fact, the believing community decided to read the Gospels literally. But surely the centrality of the ascriptive subject Jesus Christ is a function more of the literal sense of the text than of the historical decision (accident?) of the believing community to read the Gospels literally? If this is so, then we must conclude that Frei's earlier insistence that the Gospels are realistic narratives better preserves the indispensability of the unsubstitutable subject Jesus Christ.

In the final analysis, we must judge that both Ricoeur's and Frei's analyses of the referent of the Gospels are inadequate. Neither Ricoeur nor Frei himself has done justice to the Gospels' "literal" truth, though Frei has come much closer. With regard to Ricoeur, I believe that Frei is right in seeing a certain allegorizing tendency. Narratives allegorically refer to human temporality, and the Gospels refer to a mode of being-in-time before God, or something of the like.[112] The referent and truth of the Gospels consists in their disclosure of certain human possibilities that are open to us and need to be imaginatively appropriated.

The situation with Frei is more complicated. I applaud his desire to uncover the inner logic of the Gospel narratives. Only by so doing can we make the move from sense to reference, meaning to truth, other than arbitrarily. Frei reads the Gospels as history-like narratives. He insists that the literal sense of such texts is not to be equated with historical reference. But it is just here that we encounter a certain tension in Frei, for the literal *reading* of these texts has traditionally affirmed a *historical* reference. Indeed, Frei admits as much. For precritical readers of Scripture, "the true historical reference of a story was a direct and natural concomitant of its making literal sense."[113] For post-Enlightenment readers, however, the fact that a biblical story made sense at a literal level was seen as evidence for its historical factuality. Biblical critics saw this as an opportunity to examine the biblical referent and question its truth. Biblical critics and exegetes began to fit the Bible into their categories of reality rather than vice versa. The "common world" of biblical narrative and biblical critic turned out to be the world of Ernst Troeltsch, a world of criticism where one's present experience defines what is or is not historically possible. It is for this reason that Frei, in defending the literal sense, seems to have cut ties with the question of historical reference, even though the latter was originally an ingredient in precritical literal reading. For Frei, perhaps, just to raise the question of historical reference is to bring down a whole host of anti-supernaturalist historiographical assumptions that effectively eclipse the literal sense.

Though he makes a gallant effort to preserve the literal sense of the Gospels, Frei's stratagem of dissociating the literal sense from the historical referent threatens to eclipse not the biblical narrative, but biblical claims to truth. In order to do justice to the literal sense of the Gospel narratives, Frei will have to deal head-on with the question of their reference to history, however oblique it may be. Indeed, the inner logic that Frei seeks in the text sometimes seems to force him in this direction. For instance, though he is describing the structure of the

Gospels rather than their historical factuality, Frei says at some point the reader must decide whether to move from a literary to a faith judgment, from a judgment about their meaning to a judgment about their truth: "He would have to affirm that the NT authors were right in insisting that it is more nearly correct to think of Jesus as factually raised, bodily if you will, than not to think of him in this manner."[114] Statements such as this indicate that questions concerning the nature of the Gospels' reference, as well as the relation of fact and fiction, remain to be thought.

Garrett Green suggests that Frei's upholding the literal sense requires one to abandon the fact – fiction dichotomy. He quotes Frei as saying that we are actually fortunate in having accounts of Jesus that are "more nearly fictional than historical in narration."[115] Fictional description merges with factual claim: "The narration is at once intensely serious and historical in intent and fictional in form ..."[116] Green compares Frei's use of fictions not to Vaihinger's model of "as-if" but rather to Wittgenstein's model of "seeing as." The problem with Vaihinger's "as-if" is that he judges fictions to be false. However, recent philosophy and philosophy of science now see fictions as invaluable heuristic devices without which we would never gain the "facts." Believers do not act "as if" the world were God's creation; rather, they see the world *as* God's creation. Green writes: "Our challenge is to become 'literalists of the second naiveté' – readers whose critical awareness of the fictionlike quality of the text does not prevent them from affirming the truth of the story it tells."[117] Interestingly enough, with the enshrinement of "as" as the "key to the logic of religious belief,"[118] we have come full circle. We have returned to a general theory about fictions, and to Ricoeur's notion of metaphorical truth – the very notion of which Frei was so suspicious![119]

What neither Frei nor Ricoeur provides is a poetics of the Gospel narratives, that is, an account of the rules of composition – sense-making and reference-making – that pertain to a given literary form. Frei comes closer to catching their *sui generis* character, but founders on the question of reference. Such an enterprise, though obviously beyond the scope of the present chapter, is nevertheless what is called for in order properly to treat the question of the reference and truth of the Gospels. I think Frei is correct in observing that the Gospels may not be histories in the modern sense of the term. To force the Gospels to meet the requirements of modern historiography would be to impose a foreign criterion of intelligibility and truth. But, against Frei, it should be noted that he too imposes a foreign interpretive framework on the

Gospels – the category "realistic narrative" finds its proper home in fiction of the nineteenth century. The conventions governing the composition of realistic novels simply were not open to the biblical writers.[120] How then do the Gospels produce their meaning and intend their reference? I can here offer only an outline of an approach.[121]

Both Frei and Ricoeur associate the Gospels with forms of literature that at best resemble the Gospels only at certain points. Meir Sternberg observes that "the gravest danger to the literary approaches lurks in their importation of models that do not fit the Bible."[122] This was precisely Frei's worry about Ricoeur's and about his own use of the category "realistic" narrative. Sternberg, much like Frei's literary hero Erich Auerbach, is primarily concerned to make sense of the Bible on its own terms, that is, literally. Whereas Frei tends to read the Gospels as realistic novels, Ricoeur regards the Gospels as a species of "poetic" language. Prickett argues that such an understanding of the poetic function, stemming from Heidegger and German Romanticism, has little to do with the actual work of literary criticism. According to Prickett, the greatest weakness of the whole "Heideggerian" school of poetics in biblical criticism is "its distance from, and, in many cases, its lack of understanding of, actual poetry."[123] What are the literary features peculiar to biblical narrative?

Chief among the unique features of biblical narrative is perhaps its claim to divine authorship or inspiration. It is this claim that explains the omniscience of the narrator. Inspiration figures as a "rule" for reading the Bible like a grammatical "rule": "To make sense of the Bible in terms of its own conventions, one need not believe in either, but one must postulate both."[124] To postulate inspiration is to elevate the narrator to the status of an omniscient narrator. The Bible knows nothing of the dichotomy between the constrained historian and the licensed maker of fictions; the biblical narrator does both. Accordingly, approaching the Bible either as inferior history or superior fiction is inappropriate.

Sternberg chides Frei for dismissing the whole problem of the inspired narrator. Frei simply abandons the whole issue of the text's inspiration and historicity instead of "retaining them as institutional premises (features, coordinates) of the discourse ..."[125] Frei distinguishes history-likeness from historicity, but Sternberg claims that he ignores the history-telling feature of the narrative, its insistent claim to historical truth.[126] History-likeness by itself has no bearing on the issue of meaning and reference; it all depends on whether it appears in a historiographical or fictional context. And it is precisely here that the

Bible's "inspirational model of narrative" functions to resolve such indeterminacies of truth claim: "With God postulated as double author, the biblical narrator can enjoy the privileges of art without renouncing his historical titles."[127] The idea that omniscient narrators must be confined to fiction "is a much later arrival on the scene of narrative, deriving from an earthbound view both of the world and the rules for its representation."[128]

Both Frei and Ricoeur must face the challenge of taking the Bible literally, that is, in the sense of the letter rather than the tradition of its use. As I have suggested, this challenge involves discovering the rules that govern the particular sense-making and claims to truth at work in the Gospels – a "poetics" of Gospel narrative. Only then will Frei and Ricoeur be able to follow Anselm's agenda and let the text under consideration control the way it will be read or thought.[129]

Narrative theology

Narrative figures prominently in Frei's theology and Ricoeur's biblical hermeneutics. Can we therefore speak of them as "narrative theologians"? Do not Frei and Ricoeur speak about God in the setting of stories and accord a special cognitive (and theological) function to narrative? Strictly speaking, neither Frei nor Ricoeur is a "narrative theologian."[130] Gary Comstock wrongly calls Frei a "pure narrativist," that is, a person who "insists that stories are primary in the order of human knowing and acting."[131] Frei is not a narrativist if by this we mean someone who builds an epistemology or an ontology of human being on a narrative substructure. Rather, Frei is an Anselmian theologian who is seeking to understand the Christian faith, particularly its central narrative expression, on its own terms. That these terms happen to be narrative does not make Frei a narrative theologian, for he does not reason from them to a universal "narrative quality of experience."[132] The contours of Frei's theology are more a function of his Anselmian method than of the specific kind of data with which the method happens to be concerned (i.e., certain history-like stories). Narrative theologians, on the other hand, have in common a desire to make narratives central to the whole theological enterprise. Most narrative theologians insist on the importance of narratives for gaining a sense of personal and communal Christian identity. On this view, becoming a Christian is more a matter of changing stories than doctrines or beliefs.

The situation with Ricoeur is more complex. Unlike Frei, Ricoeur is willing to acknowledge the special cognitive function of narrative. Narrative is an essential component in Ricoeur's hermeneutics and philosophical anthropology: without narrative we could not render human temporality intelligible. Stories therefore carry epistemological and ontological freight; like symbols, they call for thought. The special status of narrative for theology consists in the unique contributions towards making human being-in-time intelligible and reorienting human temporality.[133] Of course, even with Ricoeur narrative is only one ingredient in his larger project of correlating philosophical hermeneutics and philosophical anthropology, for other forms of language and literature play similarly indispensable roles.

Ricoeur's willingness to listen to all forms of language and literature prevents him from embracing narrative as the chief or sole linguistic access to knowledge and being. His readiness to hearken to all forms of creative language and literature, and to treat them philosophically, gives Ricoeur greater depth than many of the narrative theologians. Indeed, even on the question of ''biblical time'' Ricoeur does not limit himself to a consideration of the biblical narratives, but investigates the Bible's other literary forms as well. Ricoeur might be more properly characterized as a ''theologian of biblical discourse.'' Ricoeur gains theological insights not simply from reading the biblical narratives, but by exploring how these narratives interrelate with other non-narrative portions of Scripture.

Having said this, I must confess that I cannot help thinking that Ricoeur does give a privileged position to narrative. Ricoeur is working towards a philosophy of narrative – something entirely absent in most so-called ''narrative theologies.'' On the one hand, narrative is only one of the Bible's many literary forms. But, on the other hand, Ricoeur uses stories not as a substitute for reflective thought, but as indispensable means for studying (and healing?) the human condition. We must not forget to view it in the context of his larger philosophical enterprise: narrative stands at the crossroads of philosophical hermeneutics and philosophical anthropology. The more Ricoeur orients his thinking about human being towards questions of temporality, the more narrative will occupy a central place in his thought and in his theology (i.e., his thinking about humanity before God). That Christian theology is attached to the narrative form is a fact of the highest significance. Conversely, that modern authors are increasingly turning away from the narrative form is a matter of the gravest concern. For Ricoeur, the abandoning of the narrative form by modern authors is symptomatic of a loss of faith – faith in the ability to make sense of our lives, faith in the "wholeness" of history, faith that the "ending" will have "sense."[134] For these thinkers who believe the world to be ultimately incoherent and unfollowable, narrative is the opiate of the people. In the face of narrative agnosticism, Ricoeur suggests that the fight for the "rebirth" of narrative in the postmodern world is a specific Christian task.[135]

This placing of Ricoeur and Frei with regard to narrative theology allows us better to see the true extent of their differences with regard to the Gospels, and consequently the way in which Ricoeur is and is not a follower of Karl Barth. Though Ricoeur sounds Barthian in his insistence that philosophy begins by listening to a prior word, his belief that poetic language "reveals" worlds betrays Barth's deepest intent. As manifestations of a second-order world of human possibilities that are always-already available, narratives are verbal sacraments of this other world – "Creation." Narratives have an innate capacity to disclose the world as "graced." What must be noted is that this revelatory, world-displaying capacity is a *natural* prerogative of narratives and indeed, of all poetic language. By attributing to the poetic word the sacramental function of manifesting transcendence, Ricoeur erases the very distinction between nature and grace that was so important to Barth. For Barth, God alone is the revealer, and neither nature nor a particular kind of narrative constrains God's freedom to reveal. For Ricoeur, however, revelation is not so much an "impossible possibility" as a natural possibility shared by sacred and secular narratives alike. Consequently, Ricoeur has a harder time distinguishing the significance of biblical narrative from other stories and histories.

Ricoeur differs from Barth in the following respects: (1) For Ricoeur the NT narratives disclose the religious dimension in human experience. For Barth, on the other hand, no form of human language has the innate capacity to accomplish such a feat. (2) For Ricoeur, poetic narratives manifest a world of human possibilities. The world disclosed by the Gospel narratives "is the world of a human, temporal existence permeated by a divine presence."[136] For Frei and Barth, the NT announces a new possibility that is ineluctably tied to an unsubstitutable story and an indispensable person. (3) For Ricoeur, the NT narratives manifest the way that the world is always-already graced by God's presence; the Christian possibility is always-already available, and may in fact be analogously disclosed by classic narratives of other religions or even non-religious texts. For Frei and Barth, the NT narratives proclaim what God has done in Christ; the NT narratives proclaim the new and impossible possibility of God making himself known as Jesus Christ and acting to save humanity.

The Yale school insists with Barth that we can only speak of God thanks to God's prior act of revelation. To say as Ricoeur does that narratives manifest the possibility of living in the divine presence is to make God an aspect of human experience. In the opinion of the Yale theologians, Ricoeur has repeated the error of the *analogia entis* on a literary level, and this in two ways. First, Ricoeur ties revelation to the narrative form itself. The referent of poetic narratives is a function of revelation or manifestation. Second, Ricoeur interprets biblical narratives as disclosing a world always-already filled with the divine presence. Just as nature reveals the Creator, so narratives reveal the religious dimension of human experience and point to the world as Creation.

Ricoeur therefore makes space for faith and revelation in his general theory of narrative by sacralizing secular hermeneutics. Theological realities become ingredients in a general theory of narrative. Frei's differences with Ricoeur over biblical narrative parallel Barth's problems with the *analogia entis* and with natural or philosophical theology in general. If there is one lesson that Barth was concerned to drive home, it was that man cannot find a way to God so God must find a way for us. Revelation for Barth is not an aspect of human experience or a function of poetic texts; rather, it is the miracle of God taking words and texts captive to his Word. If "religion" is understood in Barth's sense as referring to man's attempt to reach God, then Barth would have no problem with calling Ricoeur a philosopher of "religion" – but he would not be a Barthian.

Notes

1 See, for instance, Mark Wallace, "Hermeneutics in the Thought of Karl Barth and Paul Ricoeur," *Union Seminary Quarterly Review* 41 (1986), 1 – 15; Ricoeur, *CI*, 390, 343 – 4.

2 Hans Frei, *The Eclipse of Biblical Narrative* (Yale University Press, 1974), viii.

3 See Eberhard Jüngel, *Karl Barth: A Theological Legacy* (Grand Rapids, Eerdmans, 1986), ch. 1.

4 "Myth," 27.

5 Cf. chapter 6 above, esp. the section on "Philosophy and theology."

6 "Naming," 215. Ricoeur never loses sight of the distinction between philosophy and theology, however. Theology operates with the logic of witness. Its task is to make this witness intelligible: "In saying this, I am remaining basically Anselmian and Barthian. Theology is *intellectus fidei*"

(*CI*, 343–44). Ricoeur's task – the philosophy of religion – consists in making space for this witness.

7   Wallace, "Hermeneutics in the Thought of Karl Barth and Paul Ricoeur."

8   David Kelsey, *The Uses of Scripture in Recent Theology* (Philadelphia, Fortress, 1975), 87 n. 55.

9   Kelsey is thinking primarily of Ricoeur's *The Symbolism of Evil* here, but there is no indication that he would wish to reverse this judgment in light of Ricoeur's more recent works.

10 George Lindbeck, *The Nature of Doctrine: Religion and Theology in a Postliberal Age* (Philadelphia, Westminster, 1984). David Tracy is right in complaining about the misleading label "experiential-expressivist" (see his "Lindbeck's New Program for Theology: A Reflection," in *The Thomist* 49 [1985], 460–72). The name, and Lindbeck's subsequent exposition of the position, indicates that what is important about religion is to be found in the prereflective depths of the self which are subsequently "expressed" through religious language and symbols. Tracy correctly points out that for Ricoeur the relation between language and experience is dialectical: language precedes the subject and gives meaning to it. However, Lindbeck's point may still stand: for these thinkers, religious language and doctrine concern possible ways of being-in-the-world that are directed and oriented to the subject.

11 Lindbeck, *The Nature of Doctrine*, 16.

12 Frei, *Eclipse*, 58.

13 Frei comments that one device alone saved the earlier mediating theologians from a deistic belief in the general availability of revelation: an "affirmation of the specific historical event of original, inherited, and naturally inexpungeable guilt, the fatal moral, metaphysical, and noetic flaw which could be wiped out only by a similarly factual saving occurrence" (*Eclipse*, 61–2). Ricoeur in Frei's eyes is a mediating theologian who has abandoned even this small foothold; Ricoeur, as we have seen, treats the Adam story as symbolic of a general existential condition. Frei writes: "In other words, the mediating theologians rejected the Calvinists', Puritans', and Supernaturalists' version of the notion of sin in which its meaningfulness was strictly dependent on its making specific ostensive, referential sense as history, told by the particular story of Adam and his progeny" (*Eclipse*, 126).

14 Frei, *Eclipse*, ch. 7 "Apologetics, Criticism and the Loss of Narrative Interpretation," esp. pp. 124–36.

15 Ibid., 125.

16 Ibid., 130.

17 Ibid., 128. Note the conspicuous absence of Karl Barth from this list. It should be noted that Frei considers mediating theologians apologists of the *intelligibility* of Christianity, not necessarily its truth. And though Ricoeur disavows any apologetic ambitions, his whole project of approximating philosophy to theology may be seen as a large-scale apologetic effort to show the intelligibility of Christian faith.

18 Ibid., 311. Frei argues that this is the reason that Schleiermacher prefers the Gospel of John. While the Synoptics record a series of incidental events that are related only because they pertain to Jesus, the Fourth Gospel "provides a genuine bond which is nothing other than the unbroken consciousness of Jesus woven into a continuous series of self-manifestations."

19 Ibid., 313. In the next section we shall see that this substitution of consciousness for the narrative structure constitutes the main stumbling block for Frei in Ricoeur's theory of narrative interpretation.

20 Jeffrey Stout, "Hans Frei and Anselmian Theology," paper read at the annual meeting of the American Academy of Religion (Nov. 1987), 10.

21 Frei, *Eclipse*, viii.

22 See *CD* I, 2, 466 for Barth's statement that we only learn our general hermeneutics from the Bible. There is no such thing as a special biblical hermeneutics.

23 See Hans Frei, "The 'Literal Reading' of Biblical Narrative in the Christian Tradition: Does it Stretch or Will it Break?" in Frank McConnell (ed.), *The Bible and Narrative Tradition* (Oxford University Press, 1986), 52. Though Ricoeur disavows the Romantic side of Schleiermacher's quest to recover the spirit of the original author, Frei believes that consciousness is still the goal of Ricoeur's interpretation theory. Ricoeur himself admits that he intends to remain faithful to the original intention of Schleiermacher's hermeneutics, though, as we have seen, what is appropriated in the act of understanding is not the author's psyche but a "world" (see *IT*, 92–3). Noting Ricoeur's insistence that language refers to a real, though not necessarily to the "literal" or ostensive, world, Frei perceptively comments: "But obviously, it is actually *we*, the language users, who refer linguistically, so that the reality referent of language is at the same time a mode of human consciousness or of our 'being-in-the-world'" ("Literal Reading," 45). Frei notes that for Ricoeur biblical texts take understanding to its limit and so disclose transcendence as that which limits our being-in-the-world.

24 "PhilHerm," 17.

25 Ibid., 26.

26 Ibid.

27 Frei, "Literal Reading," 47. This connection between Ricoeur and Tracy is well attested. For several years the two were colleagues at the University of Chicago, and Tracy's books are replete with references to Ricoeur and, more importantly, assume the major contours of Ricoeur's philosophical hermeneutics.

28 Thompson, *The Jesus Debate*, 115.

29 I see the following points as areas where Tracy borrows generously or simply takes over from Ricoeur: the manner of analyzing human experience (reflective hermeneutics), the concept of "limit experience" as definition of religious experience, the paradigm of understanding – explanation – understanding which characterizes Ricoeur's theory of discourse, the

split-reference that characterizes poetic and religious language, the possibility-disclosing function of fiction.

30 The "Chicago school" includes a NT scholar (Norman Perrin), a philosopher of religion (Ricoeur) and a theologian (Tracy). The "Yale school" is made up, appropriately enough, of three theologians (Frei, Lindbeck, Kelsey). By referring to "schools" I mean only to highlight an informal connection.

31 David Tracy, "The Task of Fundamental Theology," *JR* 54 (1974), 13–34. In a later work, Tracy distinguishes the task of "fundamental" from "systematic" theology. The former is concerned to show the adequacy of theology's cognitive truth claims (i.e., it seeks to "make space" for theology), the latter seeks to interpret the meaning of the classic text and tradition of a religious community (see *The Analogical Imagination*, 54–82).

32 Tracy, "The Task of Fundamental Theology," 14.

33 Ibid., 31.

34 The first chapter in *Blessed Rage for Order* is entitled "The Pluralist Context of Contemporary Theology," the subtitle of *The Analogical Imagination* refers to the "culture of pluralism," and his recent book explaining the hermeneutical turn in post-modern thinking is called *Plurality and Ambiguity: Hermeneutics, Religion, Hope* (San Francisco, Harper & Row, 1987).

35 Tracy, *Blessed Rage for Order*, 9. Cf. Tracy's comment in *The Analogical Imagination*: "The major question this book addresses is a perplexing one. In a culture of pluralism must each religious tradition finally either dissolve into some lowest common denominator or accept a marginal existence as one interesting but purely private option?" (ix).

36 Tracy, *The Analogical Imagination*, 108.

37 Ibid., 115.

38 Ibid., 110. Tracy is also relying on Hans-Georg Gadamer's analysis of "the question of trust as it emerges in the experience of art," to use the title of the first part of his *Truth and Method*.

39 Tracy, *The Analogical Imagination*, x.

40 Ibid., 185 n. 37.

41 Frei, "Literal Reading", 46. Note that Frei is here repeating a complaint he first levelled against Schleiermacher. Frei reads Ricoeur as a Romantic, albeit a Romantic with more rigorous exegetical techniques.

42 Ibid., 47.

43 Tracy, *Blessed Rage for Order*, 221.

44 Frei, "'Literal Reading,'" 48.

45 Ibid. Frei says that in Tracy's interpretation "Jesus" becomes an allegory of universal meaningfulness (75 n. 16).

46 Ibid.

47 "BibHerm," 127.

48 Frei, "'Literal Reading,'" 50.

49 Frei, *Eclipse*, 273.

50 Ibid., 280.
51 Ibid.
52 Hans Frei, *The Identity of Jesus Christ: The Hermeneutical Bases of Dogmatic Theology* (Philadelphia, Fortress, 1974).
53 Lindbeck, *The Nature of Doctrine*, 118. This way of putting the matter owes much to Frei, as Lindbeck acknowledges (see 12, 137 n. 7., 138 n. 35).
54 Frei, *Identity of Jesus Christ*, xiv.
55 Ibid., 139.
56 Ibid., 37.
57 Ibid., 59.
58 Ibid.
59 Ibid., 60.
60 Ibid., 121.
61 Ibid., vii.
62 Ibid., 145.
63 Ibid., 15.
64 In Barth's case, the challenge was to articulate the biblical idea of revelation rather than impose an existentialist framework onto the discussion. Barth abandoned his first efforts at dogmatics because he felt there were too many vestiges of his early liberal training that remained.
65 Frei, *Identity of Jesus Christ*, vii–viii. Interestingly enough, Frei does not evidence the same scruples when it comes to his understanding of personal identity in terms of the "intention-action" paradigm.
66 Frei, "'Literal Reading,'" 66.
67 The debate about narrative between theologians is being paralleled in secular literary criticism. In their "Against Theory," Steven Knapp and Walter Benn Michaels propose a new anti-foundationalist manifesto: "By 'theory' we mean a special project in literary criticism: the attempt to govern interpretations of particular texts by appealing to an account of interpretation in general" (*Against Theory: Literary Studies and the New Pragmatism*, ed. W. J. T. Mitchell [University of Chicago, 1985], 11). Their basic point is that readers do not need to formulate a general theory of meaning but rather simply to focus on what the author intends to say. There is thus an interesting parallel between their defense of authorial intent and Frei's defense of the literal sense.
68 Frei, "'Literal Reading,'" 67.
69 Ibid.
70 Tracy observes that other theologians before him have provided explicit treatments of the similarities between the experience of religion and the experience of the work of art. These thinkers include Schleiermacher and Tillich (*The Analogical Imagination*, 188 n. 66).
71 Tracy, *The Analogical Imagination*, 12. In an intriguing footnote (85 n. 31), Tracy suggests that fundamental theology is concerned with the "true" in the sense of metaphysics, systematic theology with the "beautiful" as

disclosing the true (i.e., poetics and rhetoric), practical theology with the "good" as transformatively true (i.e., ethics and politics). I will concentrate on truth as disclosure here. In chapter 9 I shall examine Ricoeur's other claim, that the truth of poetic narrative is transformative.

72 Ibid., 163. It is precisely the "whole" that "limits" human experience and language. Both Ricoeur and Tracy agree that the religious dimension of religious experience is precisely this "limit" character of language and experience.

73 Ibid., 234.

74 Ibid., 166.

75 *IT*, 87.

76 Ibid., 88.

77 Ibid., 95.

78 Heidegger addresses the problem of the relation of truth and Being throughout his work, most notably in section 44 of *Being and Time* "Dasein, Disclosedness, and Truth" and his essay "The Origin of the Work of Art," where he discusses the truth of art in terms of *aletheia* or unconcealment (Martin Heidegger, *Basic Writings*, ed. David F. Krell [London, Harper & Row, 1977], 149–87).

79 Tracy, *The Analogical Imagination*, 200.

80 Ibid., 377.

81 Ibid. This is also a good statement of the program for what Frei calls mediating theology.

82 Tracy, *The Analogical Imagination*, 386.

83 Ibid., 430.

84 Ibid., 435.

85 Frei "'Literal Reading,'" 48 (cf. 75 n. 16).

86 Tracy, *The Analogical Imagination*, 221 n. 26.

87 Ricoeur, "Manifestation," 74.

88 Cf. Tracy, *The Analogical Imagination*, 215, Eliade on word as manifesting logos rather than as proclamatory power of address.

89 Thompson, *The Jesus Debate*, 127. I shall examine the Gospels as "tales about human time" in the next chapter.

90 Ibid., 137–8.

91 Gary Comstock, "Truth or Meaning: Ricoeur versus Frei on Biblical Narrative," *JR* 66 (1986), 117–40.

92 Ibid., 135.

93 Frei, "'Literal Reading,'" 62.

94 *CI*, 290.

95 We shall see below that for Frei the link between sense and reference is that of a discovered inner necessity. Deftly using a number of deconstructionist arguments, Frei insinuates that Ricoeur's "world of the text" is either inaccessible, illusory, or simultaneously present and absent (see the detailed criticism in "'Literal Reading,'" 53–9).

96 Ronald F. Thiemann, *Revelation and Theology: The Gospel as Narrated Promise* (University of Notre Dame Press, 1985), 2.

97 Ibid., 4.

98 Ibid., 31.

99 Ibid., 72.

100 Ibid., 109.

101 Noting that the Gospel of Matthew ends with Jesus' promise to be with his disciples, Thiemann says that the Gospel narratives function as reports of fulfilled promises and proclamations of new promises: "God as identified in Matthew's narrative is alone the gracious initiator, actor, and fulfiller of his own promises" (*Revelation and Theology*, 137).

102 Thiemann, "Radiance and Obscurity in Biblical Narrative," in Garrett Green (ed.), *Scriptural Authority and Narrative Interpretation* (Philadelphia, Fortress, 1987), 38.

103 See Thiemann's important discussion on the relation of text and context in *Revelation and Theology*, 146 – 8.

104 Ibid., 147.

105 Note the title of Frei's article "The 'Literal Reading' of Biblical Narrative in the Christian Tradition."

106 Frei, " 'Literal Reading,' " 62. "To understand a religion or a culture to which one is not native does not demand a general doctrine of the core of humanity, selfhood, and the grounds of inter-subjective experience" (71).

107 Ibid., 67.

108 Cf. George Lindbeck's proposal for a cultural-linguistic theory of religious language and doctrine in his *The Nature of Doctrine*.

109 The parallel in secular literary criticism is again instructive. W.J.T. Mitchell argues that the thesis of Knapp and Michaels in their "Against Theory" is no less theoretical than its antithesis (*Against Theory*, 8).

110 Frei, " 'Literal Reading,' " 36.

111 Ibid., 41.

112 I examine Ricoeur's treatment of the Gospels as "tales about time" more thoroughly in the following chapter.

113 Frei, *Eclipse*, 2.

114 Frei, *Identity of Jesus Christ*, 150.

115 Ibid., 144.

116 Ibid., 145.

117 Garrett Green, "Fictional Narrative and Scriptural Truth" in his *Scriptural Authority and Narrative Interpretation*, 91.

118 Ibid., 88.

119 In fairness to Green, it should be added that his account is intended as second-order. In other words, from the viewpoint of religious studies believers hear the Bible *as* the Word of God; from the standpoint of theology (the insiders), however, the Bible *is* the Word of God ("Fictional Narrative and Scriptural Truth," 92 – 3).

120 Cf. Stephen Prickett, *Words and the Word: Language, Poetics and Biblical Interpretation* (Cambridge University Press, 1986), 77–8. C. S. Lewis' remark on the Fourth Gospel is relevant: "Either this is reportage – though it may no doubt contain errors – pretty close up to the facts; nearly as close as Boswell. Or else, some unknown writer in the second century, without known predecessors or successors, suddenly anticipated the whole technique of modern, novelistic, realistic narrative" (*Fern-Seed and Elephants, and Other Essays on Christianity* [London, Collins, 1975], 107–8).

121 I am building largely on the work of Meir Sternberg, *The Poetics of Biblical Narrative: Ideological Literature and the Drama of Reading* (Indiana University Press, 1987). Many of Sternberg's points are worth noting. Though he is chiefly interested in the OT narratives, I believe many of his insights may justifiably be applied to the NT, though this remains to be done.

122 Ibid., 56.

123 Prickett, *Words and the Word*, 81.

124 Sternberg, *The Poetics of Biblical Narrative*, 81.

125 Ibid., 82.

126 Sternberg describes the difference between fiction and history not in terms of the presence or absence of truth value, but in terms of their commitment to truth value. A historian committed to telling the truth may still be wrong, but it is the commitment to "what actually happened" that renders the discourse historical (see the extended discussion on fiction and history in *The Poetics of Biblical Narrative*, 23–35).

127 Sternberg, *The Poetics of Biblical Narrative*, 82.

128 Ibid.

129 In chapter 9 I conduct a modest Anselmian exercise, that is, an attempt to discover the inner logic of the narrative of Luke-Acts.

130 On narrative theology, see George W. Stroup, "A Bibliographical Critique," *Theology Today* 32 (1975), 133–43, and *The Promise of Narrative Theology* (Atlanta, John Knox, 1981); Gabriel Fackre, "Narrative Theology: an Overview," *Interpretation* 37 (1983), 340–52; Nathan A. Scott, "The Rediscovery of Story in Recent Theology and the Refusal of Story in Recent Literature," in Robert Detweiler (ed.), *Art/Literature/Religion: Life on the Borders* (Chico, CA, Scholars Press, 1983), 139–55; Michael Goldberg, *Theology and Narrative* (Nashville, Abingdon, 1982).

131 Comstock, "Truth or Meaning," 120.

132 Cf. the classic expression of this viewpoint by Stephen Crites, "The Narrative Quality of Experience," *JAAR* 39 (1971), 291–311. Crites's thesis is clear: "I want to argue that the formal quality of experience through time is inherently narrative" (291).

133 We shall discuss the ways the Gospel narratives "play" with time in the following chapter.

134 Cf. Scott's "The Rediscovery of Story in Recent Theology and the Refusal of Story in Recent Literature." Frank Kermode believes that the "sense" that narratives confer on the jumble of events and circumstances that make up human history is an illusion, a means of consolation in the face of what would otherwise be horrific chaos.

135 A point Ricoeur made in his seventh Sarum lecture at Oxford University, "The Contemporary Discussion About 'Narrative Theology,'" 18 February 1980.

136 Thompson, *The Jesus Debate*, 127.

8

The Gospels as "tales about time"

There is no metaphysical problem more demanding in the range of expertise required for its effective treatment than that of time.[1]

The theological concept of eternity must be set free from the Babylonian captivity of an abstract opposition to the concept of time.[2]

Ricoeur conceives the human predicament in terms of a struggle between our experience of an inexorable cosmic time (*chronos*) and our experiences of meaningfulness (*kairos*).[3] Sometimes we feel as though life is merely a meaningless sequence of "now" moments, unconnected, lacking coherence, and all too fleeting. The time of nature seems all too indifferent to the short flicker of time associated with an individual's life. But other times we sense that moments can be laden with meaning, that our time is rich, that the various changes are not random but rather part of a master plan. In his early work, Ricoeur defined hope as the belief that meaning is hidden in human history. The Christian is the one "who lives in the ambiguity of secular history but with the invaluable treasure of a sacred history whose 'meaning' he perceives."[4] In this chapter we will examine the resources of narrative to articulate a concept of human time, a time in which we not only exist but can live meaningfully. It is Ricoeur's thesis that narrative is the appropriate strategy for responding to the apparent meaninglessness of cosmic time. The world in which we are to dwell must be a meaningful temporal world; otherwise, we are no better than beasts who have no consciousness of past, present or future and therefore have neither personal identity nor passion for the possible.

The notion of eternity plays a vital and constitutive role in Ricoeur's attempts to correlate narrative and human time. Here too Ricoeur is Kantian in his instincts. Meaningful human experience (in Kant's case, moral experience) becomes possible only by taming the intimidating and awful reality of cosmic time with a different temporal orientation (in Kant's case, the postulate of immortality). Why should we try to love, respect and nurture persons who are destined to return to the dust? How can we achieve a form of self-understanding that allows us to differentiate ourselves from finite objects in the realm of nature? It is just here that narrative is helpful. Narrative allows us to shape human experience in meaningful patterns rather than sheer chronological sequences. Narratives give shape to time and make it human. Is it possible that some temporal shapes can approximate eternity? This too is Ricoeur's wager. Perhaps the most authentic form of human temporality would not be Heidegger's being-towards-death, but Augustine's orientation towards eternity. In his *Time and Narrative* Ricoeur states: "The gravest question which this book can pose is of knowing at what point a philosophical reflection on narrativity and time can help in thinking eternity and death together."[5]

It is something of a surprise that Ricoeur has not written a full-fledged study of the Gospels as "tales about time." While he looks to the Gospels for their answers to the contemporary situation of meaninglessness, he does not focus on their proper subject matter – End-time. However, he does treat the parables as tales about time, and by extension, the Gospels. Moreover, in a discussion on the narrative character of biblical faith, Ricoeur notes that "the act of telling has a religious dimension which is probably not at all foreign to narrative's power to structure time."[6] At points, therefore, we shall have to extrapolate from his narrative theory in order to deal with the mode of human temporality refigured in the Gospels. What kind of human historicity is therein portrayed? We are now embarking on a quest not of the historical Jesus, but of the historicity of Jesus, that is, of Jesus' way of being-in-time. We shall see that Jesus displays a Christian way of being-in-time that is oriented more towards eternity than death. This should come as no surprise. We have known for some time that Jesus was an eschatological preacher, a preacher of end-time. The suggestion we wish to pursue here is whether his life-stories could not profitably be read as "tales about time" too.

A consideration of time and eternity is especially relevant to the project of christology as well. To suggest that the temporal can bear eternal meaning is another way of saying that a particular event can have universal significance. Theologians since Kierkegaard have tried, with varying degrees of success, to explain intelligibly the Incarnation as the movement into time of the eternal. Might Ricoeur's theory of narrativity provide resources for rethinking one of the most intractable problems of christology, namely, the relation of time and eternity? While theologies ancient and modern have been plagued by dualistic assumptions regarding time and eternity, the Gospel story knows no such absolute dichotomy.[7] Here then is a rigorous test for Ricoeur's thesis that narrative articulates temporality, as well as an opportunity for seeing how Ricoeur's theory of narrative might contribute to theological method.

History, fiction and human time

As we have seen, it is Ricoeur's thesis that both historical and fictional narratives are necessary if one is to understand the nature of human being-in-time. Among those narratives that present human temporality, the Gospels figure prominently insofar as one believes that they provide a clue to the true meaning of humanity. Does Ricoeur need to take a stand on whether the Gospels are history or fiction, or some third thing, for the figure of Jesus Christ to manifest an authentic form of being-in-time as a genuine human possibility? Does Ricoeur's theory of narrative predispose him to take the Gospels either as stories or histories or as some intermediary genre? The suggestion I would like to examine is whether there is not a tacit bias in Ricoeur's general narrative theory that prompts him to favor fictional narrative in his quest for the meaning of human being. I shall conclude that Ricoeur judges fictional narratives more apt to approximate experiences of eternity, for time is taken to its ''limit'' in fiction alone.

One important clue for determining whether Ricoeur displays a bias towards fictional narratives is perhaps his preference for the term ''refiguration'' rather than ''reference.'' On the one hand, Ricoeur is clear that the referent of narrative discourse is the order of human action.[8] However, the traditional understanding of historical reference as correspondence to what happened in the past is ill-suited to a mediation of the truth claims of history and fiction. Fiction cannot compete in the truth game if the real is defined in terms of correspondence to what was or to what actually happened. Accordingly, in the third volume of *Time and Narrative* Ricoeur discards the terminology of reference when discussing the respective truth claims of history and fiction for the terminology of ''refiguration.''[9] Narratives are still about human action, but not in the way of reference. That is, instead of corresponding to, describing or ''imitating'' human action (the pedestrian sense of mimesis), histories and fictions redescribe or remake it. Histories and fictions become interpretive grids through which we view human action. The move from reference to refiguration is a move from considering human action as it is to human action as it could be, a move from actuality to possibility. That Ricoeur prefers to refigure rather than refer to human action should come as no surprise. After all, Ricoeur's narrative theory derives from a fusion of Kant and Heidegger.

Narrative is the work of the creative imagination that produces schemata, or figures of time. And human being is only a particular kind of being-in-time. In applying the logic of schematas to understanding human being, Ricoeur gives a Heideggerian twist to Kant. Similarly, in insisting that human being-in-time may be studied only through the mediation of language and literature, Ricoeur gives a Kantian twist to Heidegger.

In sum, narrative refiguration "humanizes" our temporal experience. History relates human time to the time of the cosmos thanks to its device of the calendar and the phenomenon of the trace. But of the two narrative forms, fiction enjoys a greater freedom with respect to its capacity for refiguration. Fiction is not constrained by calendar time nor by documents and traces. Because fiction works by means of imaginative variations, it is the most appropriate phenomenological tool for exploring and experimenting with the human experience of being in time. Fiction, like phenomenology itself, is more concerned with meaning than with fact. Indeed, the "bracketing out" of the question of existence characterizes both fiction and phenomenology. It is precisely this freedom from historical constraints that permits fiction to deal with the essential rather than the contingent. Aristotle's dictum about poetry applies equally well to fiction: fiction is more philosophical than history because it deals with the universal rather than the particular. Fiction is therefore the more suitable narrative form for exploring possible ways of human being-in-time. In expanding our vision beyond the actual, fiction is to history as metaphor is to literal discourse.

Fictional narrative is thus Ricoeur's "privileged domain."[10] Fiction has more resources at its disposal for the important task of rendering temporal experience more meaningful or "human." Moreover, certain fictions actually have as their theme our experience of time. These "tales about time" focus on the gap between cosmic time and lived time and construct variations. This enables the reader to undergo "fictive experiences" of time, that is, to try out in the imagination different ways of envisaging the relation of one's lifetime to cosmic time, to death, or to eternity. These fictive experiences of time are no idle matter, no trivial amusement that bestows only momentary diversion. Rather, in displaying meaningful ways of being-in-time, these fictions suggest ways to be human in an impersonal cosmos. Such fictions are proposing worlds in which one's experience of time can be meaningful. Ricoeur offers an extended discussion of three of these "tales about time" to illustrate his point; I propose to examine one of these – Virginia Woolf's novel *Mrs. Dalloway*.[11]

Mrs. Dalloway is for Ricoeur a tale about time, or more precisely, it is a tale about two extreme human responses to cosmic time. Big Ben represents chronological time; there is frequent mention of its striking the hour: "First a warning, musical; then the hour, irrevocable. The leaden circles dissolved in the air."[12] Ricoeur suggests that Big Ben symbolizes "monumental" time, the irrevocability of the past of which Nietzsche was in such horror. According to Ricoeur, *Mrs. Dalloway* is about the different ways in which the characters react to monumental time. For Septimus, Big Ben's chimes sound the chord of death and futility. Eventually, the spectre of monumental time that marches on and over mortal time eventually pushes Septimus to commit suicide. This is one extreme response to the felt disproportion between an impersonal, even monstrous, cosmic time, and one's personal sense of lived time.

The character of Mrs. Dalloway represents another extreme response to monumental time. Whereas Septimus had to escape from monumental time, Mrs. Dalloway resolutely faces it. Significantly, Mrs. Dalloway (who for most of the book leads a rather ordinary existence) affirms life only upon hearing of the suicide of Septimus. The death of Septimus is for Mrs. Dalloway the occasion for her perception of the eternal in the transitory. Ricoeur explains this incident in Heideggerian terms:

What maintains her fragile equilibrium between mortal time and the time of resolution face to face with death – if one dares apply to her this major existential category from *Sein und Zeit* – is her love for life, of perishable beauty, of changing light, her passion for "the falling drop."[13]

Mrs. Dalloway is not oppressed by cosmic time because she can experience the moment as meaningful, even beautiful. For Mrs. Dalloway, the "falling drop" is no mere natural event, but an instant replete with joy, beauty and glory. Indeed, Mrs. Dalloway's affirmation of life is very much like Ricoeur's "originary affirmation" that he believes to be the primary impetus of human existence. What I wish to note here is that Virginia Woolf's fictional story becomes the means for the reader to undergo a fictive experience of time that bears a striking similarity to what Ricoeur and Tracy call "limit experiences." Here what is taken to the limit is the very experience of time. In entering Mrs. Dalloway's world, the reader too is invited to see the eternal in the transitory.

Septimus and Mrs. Dalloway therefore represent two ways in which human being-in-time may be fictionalized. Septimus embodies the experience of time's meaninglessness taken to its limit – suicide. Mrs.

Dalloway embodies the experience of time's meaningfulness taken to its limit – the eternal in the momentary. Face to face with cosmic time, one may either flee from it or attempt to humanize it. Mrs. Dalloway seeks to "redeem" the time by making each moment "aesthetic."[14] Faced with a time that is apparently meaningless, she discovers a "purposiveness without purpose," to use Kant's phrase that characterizes the aesthetic judgment. It is not that Mrs. Dalloway denies monumental time, but rather that she responds to it differently. Ricoeur acknowledges that mortality is a universal characteristic of the human condition (an existential), but one may respond to monumental time or mortality in different ways.

Heidegger errs in identifying the *existential* of being-towards-death with one *existentiell* response: a stoical resolution to face death and to let the certainty of death color every living moment. Ricoeur argues that there is not only one authentic existentiell response to death. The suicide of Septimus

marks the incarnation of the existential being-towards-death in a singular existentiell experience, an experience closer to the invitation to despair that Gabriel Marcel sees ineluctably secreted by the spectacle of the world than, for example, to the resolutory anticipation that Heidegger holds to be the most authentic testimony in favor of the originary character of being-towards-death.[15]

Mrs. Dalloway's response is much different. Ricoeur therefore concludes that the same existential, being-towards-death, leaves open a vast array of existentiell responses. The quasi-stoical resolution in the face of death affirmed by Heidegger in *Being and Time* is only one option among many: "It falls precisely to the imaginative variations displayed by tales about time to reopen the field of existentiell modalities susceptible of authenticating being-towards-death."[16] Is not Christian hope a possible existentiell response to mortal time that is just as authentic, if not more so, as a stoic resignation? Ricoeur observes: "It is in this interval between the existential and the existentiell that a mediation on eternity and death can be inserted."[17] Fiction is Ricoeur's preferred instrument for such a mediation. For fiction better displays temporal "limit experiences" than does history. In short, fiction is free from the constraints of chronology and able to explore ways of being-in-time other than linear. Whereas chronology is preoccupied with time as length, fiction is able to plumb time's depths. It is in the depths of temporal experience that Ricoeur seeks eternity.

Because they occasion fictive experiences of eternity, fictional narratives seem to warrant the privileged status Ricoeur accords them. Fictional narratives respond to the deepest needs of humanity. How is this so? It is fiction above all that allows us to make time human. By "humanizing" time fiction allows us to affirm the world rather than merely bear, or worse, negate it. By allowing us to dwell in the world and feel as though we belong, fictional narrative most fully realizes Ricoeur's ambition for poetic language to conjure up the world as Creation, a place where we feel we belong. This is the goal of the humanist vision for art and literature. Ricoeur's narrative theory is squarely in this tradition to the extent that it seeks to represent our experience of time not as alienating but as "human." In domesticating the apparent hostility of cosmic time to human being, fictional narrative contributes to the poetic project of making the earth a world where we can dwell. Ricoeur's theory of narrative interpretation thereby accomplishes a Kantian mediation: Art (fictional narrative) reconciles the opposing domains of Nature (cosmic time) and Freedom (human time).

Biblical time

Ricoeur understands human existence in terms of the relation between one's essential being and the way one is in time. What characterizes my particular way of being in this vast cosmos? My distinct style is my historicity, that peculiar manner of being-in-time that is mine, and perhaps that of others as well. If, as Ricoeur believes, the role of narratives is to refigure the relation of my essential being to time, what does the Bible contribute to an understanding of human existence? It is important to note that Ricoeur answers this question within his philosophical framework that correlates time and narrativity. As Ricoeur conceives it, the contemporary crisis in our western culture that elevates Techne is a loss of the *humanum*. In an age dominated by scientific technology the apt metaphor for humanity could be Chronological Man. Chronological Man's historicity is that of rectolinear time, where the only coherence in experience is that of "before and after" – hardly the categories that enable us to exist meaningfully. The loss of stories in our scientific culture has resulted in a loss of human possibilities that is nothing less than a diminishing of humanity itself.

Though Ricoeur does not explicitly call the Gospels "tales about time," it is clear that their value in Ricoeur's eyes stems from their ability to refigure and transfigure human historicity. Ricoeur believes that the biblical narratives display a unique manner of being-in-time that challenges our ordinary temporal experience. The Bible discloses a way of being-in-time that reveals and transforms my humanity: my values, my hopes and my actions. Thanks to the "limit-nature" of biblical narrative, a religious dimension is uncovered in everyday experience. In biblical narrative, particularly the parables, we see the extraordinary in the ordinary, the beauty of the "falling drop," the shimmers of the divine glory just beneath the surface of mundane reality. Experience need not remain in the shallow waters, but can be taken to its limit, transported by a vision of a saved new world. Biblical narrative thus reinvigorates our passion for the possible.

Ricoeur begins his reflection on the temporal aspect of biblical narrative with a consideration of the parables. By itself, this connection does not break any new ground. Ernst Fuchs had earlier presented the parables as a product of Jesus' understanding of time.[18] But Ricoeur explores the parable's narrative resources for refiguring human time in a way that Fuchs does not. As we have seen, Ricoeur views the plot as the connecting link between the parables and their referent, the Kingdom of God: the Kingdom is like what happens in the parable. The refiguration of human temporal experience takes place through the parabolic plot. Ricoeur suggests that the parables "draw attention to the 'miraculous' dimension of *time* ..."[19] The paradigm in this regard is the most condensed of the parables: "The kingdom of heaven is like treasure hidden in a field, which a man found and covered up; then in his joy he goes and sells all that he has and buys that field" (Matt. 13:44). These three critical moments in the plot – finding, selling, buying – represent much more than elements of a commercial transaction. The "finding" connotes for Ricoeur all kinds of encounters which render life more like receiving a gift than acquiring something by violence or works. Ricoeur claims that the parable points to a fundamental way of being-in-time, which he calls "Event."[20] As a result of this unexpected gift-event, the man who found the treasure has a future, a new world of previously unforeseen possibilities. He now has a life that he could never have won for himself. This wonderful Event (finding) provokes a Reversal of the former situation (selling) and prompts a Decision (buying). The Kingdom of God, says Ricoeur, is like *that*:

This succession is full of sense: the Kingdom of God is compared to the chain of these three acts: letting the Event blossom, looking in another direction, and doing with all one's strength in accordance with the new vision.[21]

The language of Event recalls us once more to Heidegger, who also saw Being in terms of an Event. Being is not some timeless cosmic substratum, but rather a dynamic happening in time. Ricoeur believes

that Heidegger's notion of *Ereignis* is the closest modern counterpart to
Aristotle's insight that Being involves both actuality and possibility.
Heidegger's problem was to find the linguistic means to speak of Being.
If Being is really a becoming, propositions and concepts are inadequate
to the task. Heidegger proposed poetry as the solution to this problem. It
is in poetry that Being as actuality and possibility first comes to speech:
"*All art*, as the letting happen of the advent of the truth of beings, is as
such, *in essence, poetry*."[22] Poetry is the form of language, in other words,
in which the Event of Being comes to speech and is first apprehended.
Ricoeur sees the biblical parables as fulfilling a similar function: it is
thanks to the Event recounted in the story that the reader encounters the
parable itself as an Event in his life. That is, just as the man in the parable
found a treasure in the field, so the reader finds a treasure (the Kingdom
of God) in the parables: in both cases, something is found that can only
be called Gift and which subsequently reorients one's whole life.[23]

Ricoeur sees a number of "parables of advent" that focus on the gift
and the surprise of the Kingdom of God (i.e., the parable of the sower,
a story of extraordinary growth). To "find" a pearl, a treasure, a lost
son, is to experience that moment as an unexpected gift. Something
comes to us which is not at our disposal. But this is precisely what
Ricoeur believes happens when we read any poetic text; something is
given that is not of the reader's own making. Poetic texts disclose
marvelous new worlds replete with hitherto unsuspected possibilities
for our lives. In the case of the parables, they disrupt our ordinary world
with its chronological time. Thanks to the Event recounted by the
parables, and to the Event which comes to speech in parable, an
otherwise empty instant is filled to overflowing with meaningfulness.
The parables are therefore poetic events:

The poetic power of the Parable is the power of the Event … And it is in the
heart of our imagination that we let the Event happen … To listen to the Parables
of Jesus, it seems to me, is to let one's imagination be opened to the new
possibilities disclosed by the extravagance of these short dramas.[24]

Parables are in Ricoeur's view the privileged place where Being and
Time together come to expression in a "poetic" event. It is difficult to
say whether this "event" is literary or theological, for Ricoeur seems
to conflate these two categories. In reading the parables, the reader
receives the gift of a new possible way of dealing with cosmic time. The
poetic event of reading the parables is nothing less than the event of
grace. The time of the parables thus appears to be the time of grace –
time in which God has time for us and gives us a new temporality,

a new way of living in the world. But we must take a few more steps to reach Ricoeur's notion of biblical time.

In order fully to grasp the temporality presented by the Bible, therefore, we need to interpret its different literary forms. Ricoeur speaks of the Bible's "intertextuality," that is, the textual interplay by which one text affects and is affected by another. Ricoeur applies this principle first of all to the parables. He insists that the parables "make sense together."[25] The parables constitute a symbolic network that together refer to the Kingdom of God: "there is now more in the Parables taken together than in any conceptual system about God and his action among us."[26] Secondly, Ricoeur asks "whether the *insertion* of the parables within the larger framework of the Gospel contributes to its *meaning* as a parable."[27] According to Ricoeur, the parables are the paradigmatic form of intertextuality. Thanks to this constellation of stories, the Kingdom of God has come to speech. In the same way as the parables as narratives only make sense together, so too the stories about Jesus only make sense when read in light of the parables. Intertextuality is not limited to the parables, but characterizes what Ricoeur labels the "biblical imagination."

The principle of intertextuality is central not only for an understanding of biblical time, but for Ricoeur's whole notion of biblical theology. The theologian's task is not to spin propositional paraphrases of the Bible or to reduce the richness of the biblical narrative to the clarity and austerity of the concept. Rather, the theologian is to read the Bible imaginatively, continuing to travel along the "itineraries of meaning" suggested by the biblical text and seeking to recontextualize the texts for the contemporary situation. Here then, are the third and fourth levels of intertextuality: intertextuality pertains to all the immanent relations in the Bible (i.e., the law to the prophets, the OT to the NT), and it pertains to the relation between the Bible and the text that is my life's story. It is on this fourth level of intertextuality, where the Bible intersects the "autobiographical text" or life of the reader, that biblical narrative figures and transfigures the reader's own historicity.[28]

How does intertextuality actually work? Ricoeur illustrates the process from the Gospel of Mark. Intertextuality results from embedding one narrative within another. Ricoeur considers two parables in the Gospel of Mark, one embedded at the beginning ("the sower") and the other at the end ("the wicked husbandmen"). The parable of the sower operates with the metaphor of the "sown word," a reference to the various effects that Jesus' preaching works upon his hearers. The parable is the story of progressive abundance: on good soil, the seed multiplies a hundredfold. The dynamic of the later parable, on the other hand, is one of progressive defeat. The body of the landlord's servant is beaten and the body of the landlord's son is put to death. Jesus is here referring to his own person. Intertextuality means for Ricoeur thinking these two parables together: ''May we not say then that if the word is to increase, the body must decrease? This would be the great metaphor encompassing these two parables.''[29]

But intertextuality involves more than this. The two parables, in turn, can be thought together with the narrative that encompasses them: the story of Jesus and his passion. The deeds of Jesus are just as ''textual'' as the sayings of Jesus. Indeed, to follow Ricoeur's reading, we could say that both Jesus' deeds and his sayings express the same kind of limit-experience: just as the parables speak of gracious Events, so Jesus' deeds, especially his miracles, represent a kind of gift or surprise that disrupts the course of ordinary life. The parables draw attention to the ''miraculous'' dimension of time while the miracles become ''parables'' thanks to Jesus' preaching about the Kingdom of God.[30] The Gospel genre is the locus of this intertextuality between the deeds and the words of Jesus. The speaker who tells the parable is also the hero of the inclusive narrative. The Gospel includes the story about Jesus and the stories of Jesus, and encourages us to think of each in terms of the other. Thanks to intertextuality there is symbolic interplay between the parables and the narrative of Jesus' passion. This textual interplay of the parables and the narratives about Jesus is of the utmost theological importance for Ricoeur. The ''hero'' of the Gospel narratives is both the speaker of the parables and their indirect reference. Jesus proclaims God in parables, but the Gospel proclaims Jesus as the parable of God.[31]

It is significant that Ricoeur views intertextuality as a species of the genus metaphor. Just as metaphor puts the creative imagination to work by associating two semantic fields (i.e., the parable of the sower is built on the extended metaphor of the ''sown word,'' thus combining the semantic fields of sowing and speaking), so intertextuality associates two narrative fields (i.e., parables and passion). In short, Ricoeur sees intertextuality as an extension of his theory of metaphor. To be more precise, intertextuality is for Ricoeur the form of creative imagination at work in the Bible. Intertextuality is first a work of the text itself, and secondly a work of the reader:

The text interprets before having been interpreted. This is how it is itself a work of productive imagination before giving rise to an interpretive dynamism in the reader which is analogous to its own.[32]

The attempt to discover the meaning of the biblical stories is thus a work of the intertextual imagination. Indeed, Ricoeur seems to indicate that theology should be a hermeneutic of biblical intertextuality. The theologian should interpret the parables in light of the Gospels (and vice versa), the Gospels in light of the rest of the NT (and vice versa), the NT in light of the OT (and vice versa). This last criss-crossing, as well as that between the Bible taken as a whole and the "texts" of modernity, has long exercised the imaginations of even the ablest of theologians. In short, Ricoeur's principle of intertextuality gives new meaning to the methodological principle of *sola scriptura*, as well as to the theological method of correlation. On the one hand, the intertextuality which is explicit in the parables is at work in the Bible in general, and the task of the theologian is to interpret the mutual interplay between Scripture's diverse literary forms. On the other hand, the Bible is revelation insofar as its texts illumine and intersect the "text" of our lives.[33] By associating it in this manner with intertextuality, Ricoeur gives a literary and imaginative twist to the method of correlation.

Such is the course Ricoeur himself pursues in order fully to understand "biblical time." This is also why Ricoeur eschews a naive "narrative theology" that considers narratives apart from the other biblical literary genres. This was Cullmann's mistake in his *Christ and Time*, which pitted Greek cyclical time versus biblical linear time. It is Ricoeur's contention that

the biblical narratives, whether the story of the Exodus or the story of Jesus, are always in a dialectical relation with other literary compositions which, even when they are entirely non-narrative, like the Wisdom writings and the Psalms, carry a specific temporal dimension.[34]

As far as the reader is concerned, the meaning of these events has been detached from the original *Sitz im Leben* and now exists in what Ricoeur terms a *Sitz im Wort*. This is consistent with Ricoeur's literary as opposed to historical-critical approach to the Bible. The actions, events and persons in Scripture have a textual existence that permits the reader to make connections between them as if they were contemporaneous.

The first evidence of intertextuality that Ricoeur considers in his essay on biblical time is that between law and narrative. It is of the utmost theological significance that the law is embedded in a narrative framework. The giving of the law is part of a narrative about Yahweh's deliverance of Israel from Egypt. Ricoeur notes that the Sinaitic law is prefaced by an allusion to the encompassing narrative: "I am the Lord your God who brought you out of Egypt, out of the land of slavery"

(Exod. 20:2). This intersection of law and narrative affects both: the law is part of covenant history, and covenant history is a history under the sign of obedience or disobedience to the law. In Ricoeur's words: ''From this union results at one and the same time a narrativization of ethics and an ethicization of narration.''[35] What results from such a union is a Deuteronomistic history – a vast narrative stretching from Deuteronomy itself through 2 Kings that receives its ''configurative'' dimension or principle of coherence from the people's response to covenant law.

But what does such a pairing of narrative and law contribute to an understanding of biblical time? Ricoeur acknowledges that narrative is the ''base'' genre for an inquiry into biblical time, but it does not stand alone. The law is not atemporal. It is given in a particular place at a particular time, yet it is not intended to pass away. In Deut. 4 – 6 the repeated emphasis on not forgetting the law signals that the law is to endure. Here, then, is a distinct temporality. In Ricoeur's view, the enduring temporality of the law carries with it the dimension of God's faithfulness. Yahweh keeps his word. This is what the whole course of the Deuteronomistic history shows: obedience results in blessing, disobedience in downfall. The later events of Israel's history are not simply added to the originating events, but augment their meaning. The combination of law and narrative, in other words, results in a cumulative history of the faithfulness of God. This conjunction of law and narrative is thus of theological significance: not just any theology or form of life results from such a combination. This intertextuality of law and narrative decisively shaped Israel's historical existence, her traditions and her very identity.

If the conjunction of law and narrative orients human time towards memory, the conjunction of narrative with the prophets orients human time towards hope. Ricoeur rightly points out that no reader can fail to perceive the clash between the prophetic writings and the founding narratives. First, the prophets *interrupt* and *disrupt* the cumulative history of the narratives. The narratives confidently assume the continuation of Israel's covenant history. But it is precisely this confident assurance in the continuity of covenant history that the prophets throw into question, and even denounce. Israel's security, thunders the prophet, is only an illusion. Typically, the prophet challenged Israel's present and announced the end of covenant history. The temporal dimension of prophecy is not so much the prediction of the future as the disruption of the present. The prophetic writings represent a powerful temporal dislocation and disorientation. The history that the law and narratives implied was permanent unravels under threats of doom.

Even in prophecies of doom, however, are glimmers of hope. There is a promise of new life after judgment. This future is anticipated as something new, but at the same time the new "is not anticipated as radically other, but as a sort of creative repetition of the old."[36] There will be a new covenant, written not on stone but on human hearts of flesh. The renewal will be a "return": there will be a new Exodus and a new Zion.[37] In other words, the prophetic writings extract from the traditional narratives "an unexpected potential of hope."[38] It is only thanks to prophecy that the promises contained in the narratives reveal a surplus of meaning: "Under the pressure of prophecy, the promise appears essentially unfulfilled. Narrative touched by prophetic eschatology frees a potential for hope ..."[39] Read in light of the prophets, therefore, the past is not simply exhausted but discloses a treasure trove of inexhaustible possibilities. Prophecy thus orients the time of narrative to the future and opens up a time for hope.

The third biblical genre which Ricoeur links to narrative is the wisdom literature, habitually the most difficult form to integrate in a biblical theology. Ricoeur acknowledges that wisdom literature is far removed from the concerns of history, but this does not mean it is indifferent to time. In Proverbs Ricoeur sees a unique coupling of the everyday and the immemorial. Proverbs deals with everyday time rather than with great events. There is nothing much to "tell"; rather, the intent of Proverbs is to gain wisdom about the cosmos and its general principles. And it is precisely through contemplating the everyday that wisdom penetrates to the universal, to the immemorial – that which is beyond the reach of memory, record or narration. Proverbs 8, for instance, displays an eternal Wisdom that governs all of creation. But the wisdom literature also includes the book of Job, where instead of offering advice for successful living (i.e., in harmony with creation) we find instead unavoidable questions about the goodness of creation when wisdom does not work. In Job, the adage gives way to the enigma. Here the immemorial is the human condition confronted by limit-situations such as failure, pain and death. These are universals of human existence, and "wisdom addresses itself to the human condition in its universal character."[40] Wisdom is thus far removed from history, but not necessarily from time and narrative. The immemorial time of wisdom rejoins the mythic time of the creation stories. Ricoeur speculates that the stories of the creation and fall are narrativized fragments of wisdom. In any case, wisdom literature displays a temporality that is as far removed from the linearity of historical narrative as possible.

Lastly, Ricoeur considers the contribution of hymnic literature to our understanding of biblical time. Ricoeur follows Mowinkel's suggestion about the cultic function of the Psalms: "It is the privilege of the cult to reactualize salvation, to reiterate creation, to commemorate the Exodus and the conquest, to renew the proclamation of the law, to repeat the promises."[41] The Psalms celebrate the temporality of the other literary genres in the present. The time of the Psalms is the time of today and of all times. It is the time of prayer and recitation, when the individual or the whole community recapitulates the specific temporalities of the narratives, the law and the prophets. Hymnic literature marks the appropriation of these various temporalities by confessing individuals or communities. The "I" and "we" of hymnic literature invite the reader to make the Psalms his own songs. Hymnic literature thus leads us to the last threshold of intertextuality, where the biblical texts seek to refigure the "text" of the reader's world.

In reading biblical narrative in light of the other literary forms of Scripture, Ricoeur has thus uncovered temporal dimensions to the biblical narrative that involve far more than mere chronology. It is the sum total of these literary forms that constitutes the Bible's answer to the dilemma of the human condition, namely, how to live meaningfully in a world that has no time for humanity. It is Ricoeur's wager that biblical narrative, qualified and illuminated by the other biblical genres, articulates what would otherwise be a mute limit-experience, thereby allowing us to discover a surplus of meaning in the everyday. What remains to be studied is the distinctive contribution the Gospels as "tales about time" make toward this most important project.[42]

End-time and eternity: the historicity of Jesus

The passion for the possible is choked by the myth that the way we are now is the way we always will be. It is the imagination more than anything else that restores our passion by projecting "figures" of human existence that allow us to look at the present in a different light and see what might be and what we might become. What do the Gospels add to an individual's sense of being temporal that the other biblical genres did not? According to Ricoeur, the most striking trait of the Gospels is the conjunction of narrative and kerygma.[43] The Gospels are narratives which announce the good news about the person and history of Jesus. The Gospels, as a literary amalgam of narrative and kerygma, thus preserve the unity and indissolubility of the Jesus of history and the Christ of faith. Indeed, the birth of the Gospel genre which links narrative and kerygma "seems to have its *rationale* in the proclaimed identity between the Christ of faith and the Jesus of history."[44]

Jesus' life is a life of testimony taken to the limit: in the case of Jesus, his testimony about the Kingdom of God leads to his death. The double meaning of *martus* – witness and martyr – is singularly appropriate in Jesus' case.[45] In the same way, we could say that Jesus' passion for this theme of God's free forgiveness led to his passion. Jesus' testimony to the Kingdom and to God's forgiveness of sinners was taken to its limit – death on the cross. Martyrdom, dying for the truth, is thus a form of limit-testimony. The passion narratives recount the story of Jesus who testified to the death about God's forgiveness of sinners. One might say that Jesus was a martyr to divine grace.

This connection between Jesus and Christ raises a number of fascinating questions about time and the temporality of the Gospels, but thus far Ricoeur has addressed only a few of them. For Ricoeur, the Gospels' decisive contribution to the notion of biblical time stems from their announcement of a new epoch. "Now" is the time of salvation. However, this new thing is a creative reinterpretation of a pattern found already in the OT – a "type." The link between a type or figure and its fulfillment is neither causal nor chronological, but a link of meaning and significance. According to Ricoeur, typology fuses temporalities.[46]

Another temporal tension characterizes the sense of time peculiar to the Gospels: that between the "already" and the "not yet." What did Jesus mean when he proclaimed the "nearness" of the Kingdom in the parables and how did he reconcile this theme of nearness with his eschatological teaching about "the last days" – the days of "end-time"? Ricoeur, following Norman Perrin's study of the teaching of Jesus, attempts to think the parables and Jesus' eschatological teaching together. Perrin argues that Jesus interpreted his own ministry as the decisive anticipation of the Kingdom. By forbidding all speculation as to the time remaining until the end, says Perrin, Jesus gave "nearness" a non-chronological meaning. The "last days" are not to be understood in linear terms as the concluding points of a sequence, but rather in qualitative terms. The "end" is not the terminus of a linear progression, but a decisive invasion of the present. To put it yet another way, "end-time" is *immanent* rather than *imminent*. The Kingdom is "near" when hearers are ready to receive it: "the Kingdom is always and unendingly approaching whenever human experience is challenged by the teaching that announces it."[47]

To the extent that Jesus' own story is the indirect reference of the parables, Ricoeur is able to conclude that Jesus' own life is part of the coming of the Kingdom. Thinking the parables and Jesus' eschatological teaching together therefore draws the person of Jesus and "end-time" together as well. The parables point to Jesus' existence and self-understanding (that is, his historicity) and identify them with the coming Kingdom. If Jesus' own person and history is so identified with the coming Kingdom, then any attempt to fix a calendar date of the "last days" becomes idle. Jesus' eschatological teaching, seen in light of his parables, is not about calendar time. This "authentic" teaching of Jesus becomes in Perrin's hands an instrument for critically evaluating the early Church's apocalyptic interpretation of Jesus' message.[48]

End-time is immanent rather than imminent. This is the message of Jesus' parables as well as the story of his life. Both the story about Jesus and the stories of Jesus attest to something new, to an end-time that is encroaching on the present. Jesus' miracles and parables alike testify to the extraordinary in the ordinary associated with his ministry. What remains to be thought is how the Gospels are "tales about time." I suggest that applying Ricoeur's narrative theory to the Gospels leads us to a view which focuses on the temporal aspect of the "extraordinary in the ordinary" in the parables of Jesus as well as the story of Jesus itself. The extraordinary feature about the stories of Jesus is their testimony to the "eternal" in Jesus' temporality. William Thompson correctly perceives this: "the world which the NT narratives open up before us is the world of a human, temporal existence permeated by a divine presence."[49] More precisely, each Gospel presents a different way in which God is involved in Jesus' temporality and, by implication, in the temporality of those who find their own lives illuminated and transformed by the story of Jesus.

Another way of describing the element of the extraordinary in the midst of ordinary time would be to appeal to the notion of *kairos*. *Kairos* is the term that pertains to the qualitative rather than quantitative dimension of time. *Kairos* signifies the "right time" as opposed to "anytime." *Kairos* refers to a time that is ripe with opportunity. John Smith states that *kairos* points to the idea "that there are constellations of events pregnant with a possibility or possibilities not to be met with at other times and under different circumstances."[50] *Kairos* marks that time which calls for historical decision and action, a time that calls for a human response.[51] In nature things happen by chance or by law, whereas in history events happen because of prior decisions and actions. It was Paul Tillich who asserted that *kairos* is the foundation of historical consciousness, that is, of human awareness of the "right" or opportune time to do something. In the Gospels and in the parables of Jesus, *kairos* is taken to its limit. The impending and immanent Kingdom of God creates new opportunities and possibilities and an unprecedented "time to do" something. So even if Ricoeur does not use the word *kairos* to explain the temporality of the Gospels, his thought is not far from the idea. Because of the eternal in the ordinary, we need not feel that our time is meaningless or lost.

The Gospels are "tales about time" because they display Jesus' temporal "limit-experience." Thanks to the story of Jesus, the religious dimension of our lives is refigured. It would therefore appear that Jesus' mode of being-in-time functions in Ricoeur's thought as a "figure" for authentic humanity. That is, Jesus' mode of being-in-time represents a way of dealing with time and death that shows forth faith, hope and love in the trustworthiness of creation and Creator. In the words of David Tracy: "Religious language in general re-presents that basic confidence and trust in existence which *is* our fundamental faith, our basic authentic mode of being in the world."[52] The story of Jesus therefore gives us another possibility of understanding our own lives and our own being-in-time. The Gospels present us with Jesus' way of being-in-time, a way of trust and love, an "agapic" mode of being in the world. Both the parables and the passion narratives show us a mode of being in the world that can consent to the world and to time in love and hope.[53] The question this raises is to what extent Ricoeur reads the passion narratives as referring to "general human experience" as he does the parables. If the passion narratives refigure what it is to be truly human in limited time, and if they refer to universal human experience, to what kind of christology does Ricoeur's narrative interpretation give rise?

In one of the rare articles where Ricoeur discusses the theology of the passion narratives, he insists that the narrative form of the Gospels itself produces a theological interpretation of Jesus' history. Ricoeur applauds Robert Alter's thesis that literary art and theological aims are discerned together in biblical narrative.[54] Alter's literary study of OT narrative led him to a theological conclusion: the narratives convey both the conviction of an inevitable divine plan for history as well as the reality of human opposition to this plan. Ricoeur finds a similar ambivalence in the Gospel of Mark, especially in its passion narrative. In the passion narrative too we see the inevitability of a divine plan and the contingency of human action. Ricoeur is quick to point out that this is a matter of two contrasting temporalities: the time of determinism where the future is closed and the time of indeterminism where the future remains open.

These two temporalities converge at the climax of the passion narrative: the inevitability of "it was necessary that the Son of Man be delivered into the hands of sinners" meets the contingency of "and Judas approached." The verb "deliver" carries a double meaning: just who is doing the delivering? Ricoeur notes that the unity between the temporal and the supratemporal is accomplished not by philosophical speculation but by a narrative mediation.

But what of Jesus' own temporality? Ricoeur states that the "hour" of Jesus' being delivered is both chronological and eschatological. This was the "hour" that Jesus prayed would pass (Mark 14:35). According to the chronological hour, we have to do with the Jesus of history delivered by Judas. According to the eschatological hour, we are dealing with the suffering Son of Man delivered by God. The Gospel narratives present the identity of the Christ of faith and the Jesus of history. But the Gospels are not tragic. The time of the man Jesus is not simply extinguished by an indifferent cosmos. It is true that there is no resurrection account in the Gospel of Mark, but there is an indication that the tomb was empty. Ricoeur believes that Mark's plot of the suffering Son of Man prohibited him from including the resurrection in his account, but the Gospel is certainly told from the perspective of one who confesses the Jesus of history as the Christ of faith.

What kind of possibilities for being-in-time does the story of Jesus have to offer us? Though Ricoeur does not directly address this question, I believe that the necessary ingredients for such an answer are already in place. The passion narrative shows us another kind of existentiell response to our mortality, to our finite time. Despite the evil, corruption and suffering of his life, Jesus is able to live for and affirm his time, his "hour." Indeed, in the Gospels Jesus "resolutely anticipates" (to use Heidegger's language) the hour of his death, but he does so in a way that attests his underlying faith in the goodness of God. Even the end-time of death loses its sting. Jesus is able to affirm the goodness of creation "in spite of" evil.

How is Jesus able to affirm and love the world that crushes him? Ricoeur answers that it is because of Jesus' understanding of end-time as immanent rather than imminent and of eternity in terms of qualitative depth instead of everlasting duration. Jesus' life-time is testimony to his experience of the eternal, that is, to the presence of the divine in the temporal. Jesus was a "God-intoxicated" man long before Karl Barth. The thrust of Ricoeur's work on time and narrative would seem to lead us to a variation of Schleiermacher's thesis: the life of Jesus manifests a being-towards-God that is marked by an elevated God-consciousness.

Was this not the lesson of the parables, that the extraordinary (eternal) is to be found in the ordinary? Could we perhaps say that, on Ricoeur's reading, end-time or eternity is whenever one perceives the presence of God in ordinary time? But what of evil? How can God be present in a time which is rife with evil? Of course, Jesus had to face this question too. This is the point of the twofold meaning of Jesus' "delivery". Jesus faced this question in Gethsemane, but it did not shake his fundamental trust in God. Ricoeur never attempts a speculative answer to the problem of evil, and neither does the Gospel. However, Jesus does respond to evil on the level of feeling. He makes no complaint for himself concerning his delivery into the hands of sinners; his heart is elsewhere. Jesus is living for God and for others. Consequently, Jesus manifests what Ricoeur calls elsewhere grief transformed by "wisdom," a belief in God "in spite of." The "Yes" of Jesus towards Creation is stronger than his "No." Meaning is more fundamental than absurdity.

Christology as schemata of eternity

The passion narratives thus create in the reader a passion for the possibility of "eternal" life. Obviously Ricoeur, a good Kantian, does not believe that we can have knowledge of the divine eternity – this is well beyond the limits of reason, but not beyond the creative imagination. The Gospels are first of all schemata of hope because they create a figure of human time stretched to its limit towards eternity, that is, a figure of human life basking in the presence of the divine. But in creating a figure for human life lived at the limit – before God – the Gospels are also schemata of eternity. The story of Jesus is about the eternal entering into human time. Such an idea, such an impossible possibility, is not susceptible to conceptual comprehension. The relation of time to eternity remains an intractable philosophical problem. Ricoeur believes that narratives offer a poetic rather than conceptual response to the relation of time and eternity. Narrative tales about time can imaginatively "approximate" eternity thanks to their configurative dimension that aims at a time "deeper" than chronology. Indeed, it is precisely in the "depths" that "eternity" is to be found. Narratives do not schematize eternity by recounting an infinitely long story; rather, narratives schematize eternity by creating a sense of the "depths" of time. It is a certain *quality* of human experience that configures eternity, not the quantity. Depth, of course, is Tillich's metaphor for the "limit" aspect of human experience.

Thirdly, the Gospels are schemata of God. It is the naming of God by the Gospels that makes the story of Jesus a religious tale about time. God is named indirectly according to Ricoeur, first in the parables with the naming of the Kingdom and secondly in the story about Jesus' passion and resurrection. The Gospels are on the one hand very realistic: passion plays performed in medieval York caught the wood and iron realism of the story by assigning to the guild of nailmakers the part of the soldiers who crucified Jesus. On the one hand, the narrative is stark, but on the other, there is the aspect of the extravagant and the extraordinary: after passion, resurrection. Ricoeur claims that God is named by the thing that happens in the story. Ricoeur insists that the NT narratives intend to name God: "Hence a christology without God seems to me as unthinkable as Israel without Jahweh."[55] Moreover, Ricoeur argues that "Jesus' humanity is not thinkable as different from his union with God."[56] The story of Jesus is consequently a way of "figuring" God's presence in the world, the way in which the extraordinary-eternal is in the ordinary-temporal.

Ricoeur believes that each of the biblical genres "names" God in a different way. Each of the biblical genres, as we have seen, also "figures" time in a particular manner. To put it another way, each of the literary forms of the Bible represents a schema of the Name, a procedure for producing figures of the divine. The various biblical genres – narrative, prophecy, wisdom, hymn, etc. – produce figures of God's Name. Biblical narrative produces figures for the way God is involved in the world and with humanity. The naming of God and the naming of Jesus Christ intersect in the stories of the passion and resurrection, producing a figure of power through weakness, life through death, hope "in spite of."

To what kind of christology does Ricoeur's narrative theory give rise? The problematic of time and eternity with regard to christology is certainly not unique to Ricoeur. I believe we may gain a clearer idea of Ricoeur's theological affinities if we compare and contrast his view with three other theological approaches to this problem: those of Wolfhart Pannenberg, Karl Barth and process theology. Each of these theological positions represents a possible way of conceiving the relation between human temporality and end-time or "eternity."

For Pannenberg, the history of Jesus does more than alter one's self-understanding. It anticipates, apparently in an ontological manner, end-time or the future of God.[57] Though Pannenberg does not specify the nature of this ontological connection between God's future and Jesus' life, it seems to be somewhat sacramental, involving a "real presence," however hard it is to define. But he does insist that the resurrection is a historical act of the God of the future, over against Bultmann's existential theology which dissolves history into the historicity of existence. The story of Jesus as Pannenberg tells it is the story of the end entering into the middle. There is a clash of temporalities, an anticipation of the future. But Pannenberg, unlike Ricoeur, relates this end-time to the very being of God. The Gospels depict not how to live in the divine presence, but how the divine future has entered human history in order to reveal its ultimate meaning and significance. Pannenberg interprets the life of Jesus as the historical particular in whom the end, and thus the determination, of history is anticipated.[58] Pannenberg believes that it is above all in Jesus' resurrection that end-time or the future breaks into the process of history itself. This eschatological framework for interpreting the life of Jesus is the framework that Jesus and the NT authors employed to explain the universal significance of Jesus' particular fate. Pannenberg insists that Jesus' life does not simply illustrate end-time, but that end-time actually breaks into the present. In other words, there are metaphysical conclusions in Pannenberg's reading of the Gospels as tales about end-time that Ricoeur would be reluctant to draw. For Ricoeur, the Gospels refer to a mode of being-in-time which perceives the eternal in the limit-nature of the moment. The referent is more to human being than to God's being.

Jesus' life-time, passion and resurrection so reveal God that Pannenberg is able to conclude that there is a substantial or essential unity between Jesus and God as well.[59] Pannenberg speaks about the relation of time and eternity as follows: "All Christology must keep in view that the two aspects distinguished here, the eternity of Sonship and the earthly, human mode of Jesus' existence, are a part of a single, concrete life."[60] That the eternal is part of a human life is a "paradox" in its etymological sense – something contrary to literal appearance. But for Pannenberg the Incarnation is an actual reality. Accordingly, the stories of Jesus are not mere "figures" of eternity, but refer to actual facts:

What is true in God's eternity is decided with retroactive validity only from the perspective of what occurs temporally with the importance of the ultimate. Thus, Jesus' unity with God – and thus the truth of the Incarnation – is also decided only retroactively from the perspective of Jesus' resurrection for the whole of Jesus' human existence on the one hand ... and thus also for God's eternity, on the other.[61]

But if the future is "really present" in history, if the resurrection is the definitive anticipation of the end of history, then is history "closed" according to Pannenberg? No, because the reality of God can only be anticipated by models of the end, and these models are subject to subsequent confirmation or refutation by subsequent experience.[62] In Pannenberg's theology, the "whole" is disclosed not by a classic work of art (as for David Tracy), but by a historical anticipation of the end. It is the historical Christ event that "configures" the whole of history. In Pannenberg's christology, it is Jesus' *history* – particularly the historical actuality of the resurrection – rather than his *historicity* or way of being-in-time that is decisive for our understanding of the end.

A thorough comparison of Barth and Ricoeur on the relation of time and eternity is beyond the scope of this chapter, but a few points of comparison are nevertheless of interest.[63] In his *Church Dogmatics* Barth corrects his earlier emphasis on the "infinite qualitative difference" between time and eternity with a doctrine of *analogy* between the temporal and eternal orders. God's eternity is not timeless but temporal. In Barth's words, God's eternity "is authentic temporality, and therefore the source of all time. But in His eternity ... present, past and future, yesterday, today and tomorrow, are not successive, but simultaneous."[64] That is, eternity for Barth involves both total simultaneity *and* irreversible sequence. But if the notion of total simultaneity seems to verge towards timelessness, that of irreversible sequence sends us back to narrative. The question is: to what extent does Ricoeur's narrative theory enable us better to think Barth's definition of eternity?

Of course, Barth's definition of eternity follows from his distinctive method, namely, making God's revelation in Jesus Christ the sole criterion for his theological statements. In Volume I of the *Church Dogmatics*, Barth derives a doctrine of the Trinity from God's revelation in Christ. It is Barth's belief that God reveals his essential nature in the person and history of Jesus Christ. Since the history of Jesus Christ is temporal, Barth reasons, so too must be the life of the Triune God. Accordingly, the history of Jesus is a revelation of God's eternal being. The way God is in the history of Jesus is the way God is in eternity. Specifically, we see that the Triune God is a God who loves in freedom and gives himself to that which is other than himself.

Ricoeur's narrative theory is able to render Barth's understanding of eternity more intelligible. Thanks to the configurative dimension of narrative, temporality need not be limited to chronology. The configurative dimension makes a whole out of a beginning, middle and end; as in Barth's understanding of eternity, there is both simultaneity and ordered succession. To use Ricoeur's terminology, we can say that

Barth understands the history of Jesus as "configuring" God's eternal nature. God is eternally the one who gives himself for others. Accordingly, God's being cannot be explained, but must be *told*. So the Gospels do function for Barth as schemata of eternity, though his understanding of eternity is again too "metaphysical" to please Ricoeur. Barth, pursuing a christology from above, adamantly insists that the Gospels render the identity of Jesus, and thus, the "humanity" of God. Ricoeur is not comfortable with such a final naming of God. As we have seen, Ricoeur continues to view the reference of the Gospels as being universal human experience. God is an aspect of this experience. In Barth's theology from above, the situation is reversed: humanity is a predicate of God's experience.

Perhaps the closest theological approximation to Ricoeur's understanding of the relation between the Gospel narratives, time and eternity and the project of christology is that of process theology. Where Pannenberg focuses too much on the historical Jesus and Barth on Jesus as the Word of God, process theology correlates the becoming of God and man in a way that does more justice to the indirect reference to each that Ricoeur sees as operative in the Gospel narratives. In his theory of metaphor and narrative alike, we have seen Ricoeur claim that, while these forms of creative language cannot be reduced to speculative language, they do call for speculative reflection. In his metaphor book, Ricoeur attempted such a reflection, and concluded that the reference of metaphorical discourse was Being as actuality and possibility, Being as Event. David Pellauer, a former graduate assistant and frequent translator of Ricoeur's works, suggests that Ricoeur's hermeneutic philosophy is well suited to the tradition of process metaphysics.[65] If metaphorical reference calls for process categories, one would expect narrative discourse to do so all the more.[66]

The problem for Ricoeur is to preserve hope without closing history. If history were wide open and entirely indeterminate, would we not have as much, if not more, reason to despair as to hope? In order to fuel our passion for the possible and keep hope alive, we must be able to discern possibilities that are desirable and actually within our reach. Just what is the relation between end-time and our present? Is there anything guiding history towards an ending, anything at all that shows some purpose to humanity's stumbling march toward the future? In Ricoeur's philosophy, knowledge of the end is beyond our grasp. Absolute knowledge is the great temptation of the philosopher, but Ricoeur maintains that we must flee this temptation, even if it means entering into the great conflict of interpretations. These are the only options: either absolute knowledge (the sin of pride) or hermeneutics. Don Ihde shrewdly summarizes the problem for Ricoeur:

> For Ricoeur the burden of proof to be demonstrated in his promised Poetics must be one which at one and the same time preserves the openness of history while making the case for hope.[67]

Process theology solves this problem by viewing God as the power of creative possibility immanent to the world process. While God is not the all-determining reality (*pace* Pannenberg), God does seek to influence history through loving persuasion in one direction rather than another.

    While it is an exaggeration to say that Ricoeur has adopted a process metaphysics, there is a limited amount of "circumstantial" evidence that process philosophy may indeed be the form of speculative discourse that most approximates Ricoeur's thinking about the reference of biblical narrative.[68] For example, in his discussion of why the kerygma developed into a Gospel narrative, Ricoeur mentions that a reconstruction of the history of Jesus uncovers three "occasions" for narration (Jesus' announcement of the Kingdom, controversies about his teaching, Jesus' suffering). Curiously, Ricoeur states that he is borrowing the terminology of "occasion" from Whitehead. Moreover, he cites a number of pages from Whitehead's *Process and Reality*, as well as a secondary source about Whitehead's process thought, in a footnote.[69] The puzzled reader, turning to a standard introduction to process theology, may be surprised to learn that an "occasion" is a definitive event that alters the structures of human existence.[70] Process theology studies and tries to account for those occasions which open up another stage in the history of human subjectivity. David Tracy, who is Ricoeurrian in his hermeneutics, suggests that process thought provides metaphysical categories that are particularly appropriate for a study of human experience that is not restricted to empirical sense experience and for the self-understanding that follows from it.[71] Process philosophy deals not only with perceptual experience, but also with the self's experience of feeling, acting, deciding and so on – the very dimensions that Ricoeur has spent a good deal of his philosophical career trying to decipher. Perhaps Ricoeur's casual reference to the "occasions" underlying the Gospel narrative was no accident.

    Process philosophy supports Ricoeur's hermeneutics with its focus on "becoming" and "possibility." The reader gains a new self by appropriating the world projected by poetic texts. Poetic texts are themselves "occasions" for the reader to transform his self-understanding. Russell Pregeant claims that interpretation in the framework of process theology *uses* the text to lure the feelings of the reader towards certain possibilities.[72] What counts is the *image* of Jesus Christ that lures human feelings towards a certain human possibility. The NT witness to Christ provides a "bifocal" lure: it points to a particular mode of human self-understanding as well as to an apprehension of God as the ground of this possibility. In other words, the figure of Christ is a lure for human feeling but it is also based on the way God is present in the world. We may therefore hope, but we must also act. History is open, but God is luring humanity towards a certain end. For Pregeant, "christology" is simply a way of referring to a quality of human existence before "God."[73] What we have here is a reduction not of theology to anthropology (as with Bultmann), but of christology to anthropology.

According to Pregeant, the text in process hermeneutics appears "as an invitation to its readers to re-examine their lives in light of the symbol it conveys."[74] The real thrust of Jesus' question "Who do you say that I am?" lies in its posing a fundamental question and challenge to the reader: "Is this the way life is?" If the reader appropriates the story of Jesus' passion and finds that its cruciform way of being-in-the-world illumines the reader's world, then the reader encounters the Gospel as revelation. This is, I believe, a fairly close approximation of Ricoeur's theory of interpretation, where poetic possibilities similarly lure poetic feelings. The world of the text is addressed to the reader's imagination. In *Process and Reality* Whitehead states that the primary function of propositions is to be lures for feelings.[75] Interestingly enough, Whitehead discusses Hamlet's speeches and Jesus' sayings in the Gospels together. The reader, he claims, judges these texts more for their value for feeling than for their factuality.[76] David Kelsey gives a helpful summary of Whitehead's thought on this point:

A "proposition" is a "concrete possibility"; it is abstracted from some objective event in the actual world; it is proposed as a possibility that an entity may want to consider for itself in a future moment in its process of self-creation; it is apprehended by the entity in "feeling" and so is preconceptual ...[77]

All biblical texts, even if they appear to be "realistic," are to be construed as proposing real possibilities for the reader's imaginative feeling. Ricoeur and process thinkers alike regard intepretation as the means by which a reader encounters a way of understanding proposed by the text. Insofar as readers follow the lure and appropriate the meaning of the text, they gain new forms of subjectivity.[78] The Jesus that seems to matter most for Ricoeur is neither Pannenberg's Jesus of history, nor Barth's Jesus the revelation of God, but rather the Jesus whose historicity the Gospels invite the reader to share. To put it another way, *the Gospels are tales about human historicity.*

In chapter 6 we saw that Ricoeur, with Bultmann, sees the ultimate referent of religious language as a form of self-understanding. In chapter 7 we saw that Ricoeur is unwilling to consider poetic narrative "realistic." And in this chapter I suggested that Ricoeur reads the Gospels as tales about time, or more accurately, human historicity. We are now in a position to suggest that the closest literary analogue to the way Ricoeur reads the Gospel narratives is the modern stream of consciousness novel. Just as Frei relied on the category "realistic narrative," so I believe that the kind of literary interpretation that seems best to correspond to Ricoeur's reading of the Gospels as tales about time is that which arises from reading modern stream of consciousness novels represented by such authors as Virginia Woolf, Thomas Mann and Marcel Proust – the very authors Ricoeur treats in his discussion of fictive experience of time. These stream of consciousness novelists view the relation of their texts to reality in the same way that Ricoeur views the relation of poetic and biblical narrative to the real. What I hope to show is that these stream of consciousness novels may serve as veritable metaphors for Ricoeur's whole hermeneutic philosophy.

We should first note how the point of view in stream of consciousness novels is radically different from earlier narrative forms. Traditionally, the narrative is told in the third person, and the narrator enjoys an omniscient point of view. The narrator knows what everyone is thinking, and the story is apparently recounted as it actually occurred. No personal judgments of the narrator intrude upon the objectivity of the narrative. Such an omniscient narrator well symbolizes an epistemology such as Descartes' that views the knowing subject as an objective observer who can arrive at Absolute Knowledge. On the other hand, with stream of consciousness novels there is no such epistemic confidence in the narrator, no absolute knowledge, but rather hermeneutics. Stream of consciousness novels display an implicit awareness of the hermeneutical nature of all knowledge. For instance, there are often several different narrators, each representing his own point of view. Moreover, far from attempting a grandiose representation of long chronological sequence, stream of consciousness writers modestly limit themselves to describing one's thoughts over a few days or even hours. Erich Auerbach says that literature reflecting multiple consciousness was inevitable in the period following the First World War:

The widening of man's horizon, and the increase of his experiences, knowledge, ideas, and possible forms of existence, which began in the sixteenth century, continued through the nineteenth at an ever faster tempo – with such a tremendous acceleration since the beginning of the twentieth that synthetic and objective attempts at interpretation are produced and demolished every instant.[79]

But these are the same reasons that forced Ricoeur to hermeneutics rather than absolute knowledge. What modern novelists express in stream of consciousness novels, Ricoeur develops into a philosophical hermeneutics.

Secondly, in both Ricoeur's hermeneutics and stream of consciousness novels the emphasis is squarely on human historicity. Auerbach notes that in Woolf's mature works there seems to be no external or mind-independent reality apart from what is reflected in the thinking of her characters. All the reader knows is the drama of the character's consciousness. However, this does not mean there is no attempt to describe the real. Auerbach admits that Woolf may be trying to describe the reality of human consciousness – the "real" Mrs. Dalloway. However, this is not the traditional form of realistic narrative, where the "reality" of a character is rendered by its actions rather than its stream of consciousness. The streamlike nature of consciousness in Woolf's novels, in other words, renders what Ricoeur calls human historicity.

Thirdly, stream of consciousness novels are particularly able to experiment with temporality, with the ways humans orient themselves in and to time. The ease with which Woolf can experiment with her narrative's temporal organization distinguishes it from earlier realistic narratives. Auerbach notes the sharp contrast in Woolf's novels "between the brief span of time occupied by the exterior event and the dreamlike wealth of a process of consciousness which traverses a whole subjective universe."[80] This contrast is the same *distentio* which is at the heart of all human experience of time according to Ricoeur. The disproportion between cosmic and lived time that is so fundamental to Ricoeur's theory of narrative is wonderfully expressed in Woolf's novels. Auerbach says that the exterior "events" in Woolf's novels, the events that make up the plot in realistic narrative, serve here only "to release and interpret inner events ..."[81] Seemingly insignificant exterior events that last only a few seconds can possess a dreamlike wealth in consciousness. The "falling drop" is a physical event that lasts only an instant, but for Mrs. Dalloway it gives rise to a heightened, even sublime consciousness that joyfully affirms the beauty of life. Might we not say that stream of consciousness novels "bracket out" the literal or realistic level in favor of the level of historicity or way of being-in-the-world? If so, then here is a form that does for literature what phenomenology does for philosophy, namely, allow the meaning of lived experience to be explored without raising the issue of factuality. Action is subservient to feeling. The changes in subjectivity are more important than the ripples outside the soul. In Auerbach's words:

The important point is that an insignificant exterior occurrence releases ideas and chains of ideas which cut loose from the present of the exterior occurrence and range freely throughout the depths of time.[82]

The ordinary becomes extraordinary when elevated or received into consciousness. Auerbach observes that the exterior objective reality in Woolf's novels is only the "occasions" for ideas rising in consciousness.[83]

Mention of the "depths" of time leads us back to Ricoeur's understanding of eternity as a limit-experience. Eternity for Ricoeur refers not to a quantitative aspect of time but to a qualitative one. Similarly, stream of consciousness novels are not so much about chronology as temporality. The Gospels are significant because of the kind of temporality they display, a limit-temporality that approximates eternity. Stream of consciousness narrators share a literary technique that Auerbach describes as "a disintegration and dissolution of external realities for a richer and more essential interpretation of them."[84] *Ricoeur's hermeneutic philosophy of narrative has no better literary approximation than that.* But why has narrative technique changed in this way? Auerbach attributes the shift of emphasis from exterior to interior in early-twentieth-century literature to a "transfer of confidence": for these writers, the "great events" of history are less able to yield decisive information about the human subject than the random moment. However, through a poetic representation of the random moment, nothing less than the wealth of reality and depth of life in every moment appears. The chance moment, configured in narrative, expresses and occasions an experience of the depths of time, and so approximates eternity. In this way twentieth-century literature has applied Aristotle's dictum to narrative: poetry is more "philosophical" than history because it better captures the essential.

Ricoeur's theory about fictive experiences of time has its proper home in the poetics of stream of consciousness narrative. Has Ricoeur, like Frei, foisted a poetics of the modern novel onto biblical narrative? It would seem so. Ostensibly, the Gospel narratives represent external actions and events. Ricoeur, of course, recognizes this. However, in speaking of the "occasions" of biblical narrative, it would appear that Ricoeur believes that what we have in the Gospels are certain "impressions" about the relation of time and eternity that have been configured and expressed in a story. Of course, the stream of consciousness that counts is that of the reader. The Gospel narratives themselves become the "occasions" for the reader to undergo a change in consciousness, thanks to a fictive experience of time that reorients human time toward eternity.

Notes

1 Donald M. MacKinnon, *Explorations in Theology* (London, SCM, 1979), 90.
2 Barth, *CD* II, 1, 611.
3 Paul Tillich notes that the Greeks had two words for time: *chronos* is "clock time" which can be measured, and *kairos*, the qualitative time of the occasion, the right time: "While chronos designates the continuous flux of time, kairos points out a significant moment of time ... Kairos points to unique moments in the temporal process, moments in which something unique can happen or be accomplished" ("Kairos," in Marvin Halverson and Arthur Cohen (eds.), *A Handbook of Christian Theology* [New York, Meridian, 1958], 194).
4 *HT*, 94.
5 *TN* I, 87.
6 "History," 214.
7 Colin Gunton contends that "whereas ancient thought tended to abstract Jesus Christ from history by eternalizing him ... modern thought tends to abstract him from eternity by making his temporality absolute" (*Yesterday and Today: A Study of Continuities in Christology* [London, Darton, Longman and Todd, 1983], 53).
8 "Myth," 23.
9 In "Le temps raconté," Ricoeur explains that refiguration involves the power narratives have to reveal and transform real human action by virtue of their configurative dimension (437).
10 "Temps," 447.
11 The other two novels that Ricoeur discusses are Thomas Mann's *The Magic Mountain* and Marcel Proust's *A la recherche du temps perdu* (see his *TN* II, 112–52).
12 Woolf, *Mrs. Dalloway* (London, Granada, 1976), 6.
13 *TN* II, 110.
14 This tendency to "aestheticize" time is even more apparent in Proust's work, where the tale about recovering time is a tale about Marcel becoming an artist. It is in the work of art that time is regained, redeemed, and made human.

15 *TN* III, 130.

16 Ibid., 141.

17 Ibid., 136.

18 Ernst Fuchs, *Studies of the Historical Jesus* (London, SCM, 1964). For instance, Fuchs interprets the parable of the seed that grows by itself (Mark 4:26–9) as illustrating the principle that everything has its own time and that Christians should wait, care-free. While the present is the time of preoccupation, the Christian is to live out of the future, the time of God's coming. This was Jesus' understanding of time according to Fuchs.

19 "BibHerm," 103.

20 Ricoeur here relies on John Dominick Crossan's *In Parables: The Challenge of the Historical Jesus* (New York, Harper & Row, 1973). Crossan, in turn, draws upon Heidegger's *Being and Time*. For Crossan, "Event" or *Ereignis* is the event of the advent of Being: "Human time and human history arise from the response to Being which comes always out of the unexpected and unforeseen, which destroys one's planned projections of a *future* by asserting in its place the *advent* of Being" (31). For Crossan, the parables express the temporality of Jesus' experience of God. Jesus experiences the unexpected advent of God into his own time. Consequently, "Jesus' parables are radically constitutive of his own distinctive historicity" (33).

21 *PPR*, 241.

22 Heidegger, "The Origin of the Work of Art," *Basic Writings*, 184.

23 Cf. Eberhard Jüngel who says the kingdom of God comes to speech *as* parables, see *God as the Mystery of the World* (Edinburgh, T. & T. Clark, 1983), 289–96.

24 *PPR*, 245 (order slightly altered).

25 Ibid., 242.

26 Ibid.

27 "BibHerm," 103.

28 In his "Preface to Bultmann," Ricoeur locates this tendency from text to life within the NT. Paul invites his readers to read their lives in light of the passion and resurrection: "This idea is that the interpretation of the Book and the interpretation of life correspond and are mutually adjusted" (*CI*, 384). Later in the same article, Ricoeur writes: "Hermeneutics is the very deciphering of life in the mirror of the text" (*CI*, 385).

29 "BibImag," 65.

30 "BibHerm," 103. Ricoeur notes that it is no accident that the author of the Fourth Gospel calls miracles "signs."

31 See "BibHerm," 105. This is also Ricoeur's answer to Bultmann's query concerning how the proclaimer became the proclaimed.

32 "BibImag," 67.

33 Ricoeur believes that human action is a kind of text. See his "Meaningful Action as a Text" in *HHS*.

34 "TempsBib," 26.

35 Ibid., 28.

36 Ibid., 31.

37 Ricoeur suggests that the typological interpretation of the early Church, which viewed the events of the NT in light of OT events, was itself anticipated by OT prophets who also interpreted the new in terms of the old ("TempsBib," 31).

38 "TempsBib," 31.

39 Ibid.

40 Ibid., 33.

41 Ibid., 34.

42 For some reason, Ricoeur did not include a discussion of the Gospels in his article "Temps biblique."

43 "Récit," 19.

44 Ibid., 21.

45 See Ricoeur's analysis of ordinary and religious testimony in his "The Hermeneutics of Testimony" in *EBI*, 119–54.

46 A point made in his fourth Sarum lecture, "The Confrontation between 'Old' and 'New' in the Gospels" at Oxford University, 1980.

47 "Proclamation," 505.

48 According to Perrin, the Church grafted this apocalyptic perspective onto the words and teachings of Jesus. In other words, the Church mistook Jesus' eschatological teaching as dealing with chronology rather than another mode of temporality altogether (see *Rediscovering the Teaching of Jesus*, ch. 4 "Jesus and the Future").

49 Thompson, *Jesus*, 127.

50 John E. Smith, "Time and Qualitative Time," *The Review of Metaphysics* 40 (1986), 5.

51 Ibid., 13.

52 Tracy, *Blessed Rage for Order*, 134.

53 Note that Ricoeur responds both to Freud and to Heidegger: as opposed to these two masters of suspicion (meaningless necessity) Ricoeur responds with the joy/affirmation of possibility and creation (*FP*, 528, 544, 551).

54 Ricoeur discusses Alter's *The Art of Biblical Narrative* in "Récit," 17–18.

55 "Naming," 224.

56 Ibid.

57 See Pannenberg's discussion of the future "as a mode of God's being," in "The God of Hope," *Basic Questions in Theology*, vol. II (London, SCM, 1971), 242–8. Pannenberg has not developed a full-fledged ontology of end-time or God's eschatological being. Philip D. Clayton, in a review of Pannenberg's *Grundfragen systematischer Theologie*, Band 2 (Göttingen, Vandenhoeck & Ruprecht, 1980) makes this point convincingly ("The God of History and the Presence of the Future," *JR* 65 (1985), 98–108).

58 See the fourth of Pannenberg's "Dogmatic Theses on the Doctrine of Revelation" in Pannenberg (ed.), *Revelation as History* (New York,

Macmillan, 1968), 139–45: "The universal revelation of the deity of God is not yet realized in the history of Israel, but first in the fate of Jesus of Nazareth, insofar as the end of all events is anticipated in his fate."

59 "Jesus' unity with God, insofar as it belongs to God's eternal essence, precedes, however, the time of Jesus' earthly life" (*Jesus – God and Man*, 150).

60 Pannenberg, *Jesus – God and Man*, 155.

61 Ibid., 321.

62 Pannenberg, *Theology and the Philosophy of Science* (London, Darton, Longmann & Todd, 1976), 310.

63 Barth devotes several hundred pages of the *CD* to a consideration of the time of God, man and Jesus Christ. See especially I, 2, section 14 "The Time of Revelation," II, 1, section 31 "The Perfections of the Divine Freedom," and III, 2, section 47 "Man in his Time." See also Richard H. Roberts, "Barth's Doctrine of Time: Its Nature and Implications," in Stephen W. Sykes (ed.), *Karl Barth: Studies of his Theological Method* (Oxford, Clarendon, 1979), 88–146. Ricoeur and Barth have not only an interest in time in common, but also narrative. Hans Frei contends that Barth's theological method pursues a realistic reading of the Gospel narratives (see above, chapter 7). Similarly, David Ford makes a convincing case for the literary critical nature of Barth's use of Scripture in the *Church Dogmatics*. Many of Barth's theological arguments consist mainly of close readings of the final form of Scripture. Ford goes so far as to construe Barth's theology as a "monism" of the Gospel story. See Ford's "Barth's Interpretation of the Bible," in *Karl Barth: Studies of his Theological Method*, 55–87.

64 *CD* III, 2, 435.

65 David Pellauer, "A Response to Gary Madison's 'Reflections on Paul Ricoeur's Philosophy of Metaphor'," *Philosophy Today* 21 supp. to 4/4 (1977), 444.

66 This is not to say that Ricoeur believes we can simply translate poetic language about poetic Events into the conceptual scheme of process thought. Ricoeur's position is rather that poetic and speculative language exist in a relationship of tension (cf. *RM*, ch. 8).

67 Don Ihde, "Introduction" to *CI*, xxiv.

68 Another piece of circumstantial evidence is that David Tracy, whom we have suggested is the theological performance of Ricoeur's hermeneutic philosophy, is drawn toward process thought.

69 See "Proclamation," 504 n. 4.

70 John B. Cobb and David Ray Griffin, *Process Theology: An Introductory Exposition* (Philadelphia, Westminster, 1976), 86–7.

71 Tracy, *Blessed Rage for Order*, 172–5.

72 Russell Pregeant, *Christology Beyond Dogma: Matthew's Christ in Process Hermeneutic* (Philadelphia, Fortress, 1987).

73 Ibid., 127.

74 Ibid., 165.
75 Alfred North Whitehead, *Process and Reality* (New York, Macmillan, 1929), 281.
76 Ibid.
77 David Kelsey, "The Theological Use of Scripture in Process Hermeneutics," *Process Studies* 13 (1983), 183. Kelsey believes that if there is a distinctive feature of "process" hermeneutics, it is its central doctrine of "propositions" (184). On process thought and biblical studies, see *JAAR* 47 (1979) "NT Interpretation from a Process Perspective," eds. William A. Beardslee and David J. Lull.
78 Note that process theologians are sympathetic to Bultmann's existential interpretation. John Cobb points out that Whitehead and Heidegger analyzed human existence in remarkably similar ways (*Process Theology*, 80). We could say that process theologians, like Ricoeur, are seeking better foundations for a kind of interpretation that remains existential. See, for instance, David J. Lull, "What is 'Process Hermeneutics'?" in *Process Studies* 13 (1983), 189–201, esp. 192.
79 Erich Auerbach, *Mimesis: The Representation of Reality in Western Literature* (Princeton University Press, 1953), 549. Interestingly enough, Auerbach is the literary critic on whom Frei most relies in his treatment of realistic narrative.
80 Auerbach, *Mimesis*, 538.
81 Ibid.
82 Ibid., 540.
83 Ibid., 541. I doubt, however, that Auerbach intends even an indirect reference to Whitehead by this choice of wording.
84 Ibid., 545.

9

Passion of Jesus, power of Christ: the possibility of human freedom

For freedom Christ has set us free   (Gal. 5:1)

Now the Lord is the Spirit, and where the Spirit of the Lord is, there is freedom
(2 Cor. 3:17)

According to Ricoeur, the most striking feature about the Gospels is the connection between their narrative form and kerygmatic content, that is, the link between the story of Jesus and the announcement of Good News.[1] What exactly is the nature of the connection between the account of Jesus' life and death and the proclamation of this Good News, the news that freedom or "new life" is a possibility, and thus an object of hope? Is the story of Jesus in some way a condition for the possibility of human freedom? If so, just how does Jesus' passion make human freedom possible?

Throughout this work I have maintained that it is misleading to view Ricoeur's hermeneutics apart from his earlier work in philosophical anthropology. Ricoeur is interested in texts, including the Christian texts, because of his prior and primary interest in human existence. To adopt Ricoeur's hermeneutics is to assume, at least partially, a philosophical anthropology that is preoccupied with the problem of freedom. What does Christianity have to offer a philosophical anthropology that is concerned with human freedom? What do the Gospel narratives and the unsubstitutable *history* of Jesus contribute to the human condition and its passion for the possible? Ricoeur's answer is twofold: as we have already seen, the Gospels project a possible world, a possibility for human living, that is oriented towards eternity. The Gospels are true in that they *manifest* authentic human possibilities. But Ricoeur also sees the Gospels' truth as involving the *transformation* of the reader. Accordingly, the present chapter deals with the imagination not in its projecting but rather its appropriating capacity. Can the possibility of new life offered in the Gospels become mine, and, if so, how?

The tie between the Gospel narratives and the actualization of human freedom is, I suggest, the "omega point" of Ricoeur's philosophical project. Hermeneutics here fulfills the ambitions of practical philosophy. We shall continue to ask whether or not Ricoeur ever moves beyond philosophical anthropology to theology. Is there a properly *theological* moment in Ricoeur's explanation of how the Gospels actually transform human life? Perhaps the most appropriate conversation partner we can pair with Ricoeur at this point is Paul Tillich. For Tillich too, as we shall see, the Gospels function not only to express New Being but also to occasion it. However, some have found a structural inconsistency in Tillich at this point similar to the one that plagues Bultmann's thought. Does a focus on transformation rather than manifestation allow Ricoeur to assign universal significance to the history of Jesus and so escape the inconsistency that hounds existentially oriented theologies?[2]

To repeat our fundamental problem: we are embarked on an inquiry to determine whether and to what extent Ricoeur's hermeneutics may be appropriated by Christian theologians. We have wondered several times if Ricoeur's theory of narrative is compatible with a theological realism that assigns universal significance to the actual, historical life and death of Jesus. We have seen that Ricoeur thinks the Gospels project a world in which we are invited to (and should) live. But how can we appropriate this projection? For Ricoeur, a possibility cannot be appropriated or made one's own unless it is first imagined. Though Ricoeur focuses on the question, what makes an imagination of hope possible, I am interested in the conditions for the realization of hope's object – freedom. What are the conditions for the possibility of New Being? Is it enough to change one's imagination?

It is not Ricoeur's intent to be a "Don Juan" of myth, forever flirting with the different worlds that solicit our imaginative interest. I agree with Ricoeur that we need to be "called" again. I also believe, again with Ricoeur, that language and literature can indeed shape human existence, at least within certain limits. But why should one hearken to the Gospels rather than to some other text? Is it because the Gospel is the best story, the most compelling presentation of a vision of the world as Creation that allows us to consent to life not resignedly but joyfully? If so, does Ricoeur wish us to understand the nature of the Gospel's transforming power on the basis of this poetic paradigm alone? What power to effect human liberation do the Gospels have that works of fiction such as *Huckleberry Finn* lack? Is the resurrection of Christ a conjuring trick, as it were, with words rather than bones? Was the apostle Paul the inventor of Christianity, a Palestinian Prospero who created a beatific vision of the risen Christ? These are not idle queries: Ricoeur is aware that language and literature, because they are so powerful, can also be used to enslave as well as free. Projecting a possibility for life that is unattainable is a prescription for frustration rather than freedom. Paul himself acknowledges that the preaching of resurrection without the reality of resurrection (whatever that may mean) is vain.

The word is Ricoeur's "kingdom," for the word can transform one's imagination, and hence one's whole existence. But is this not what Karl Mannheim terms "liberal utopianism"? Must we conclude, as Habermas has of Ernst Bloch, that Ricoeur is a Romantic, one who believes that symbols and ideas alone can "save" us by restoring values to forgetful imaginations?[3] Does Christianity simply help us to interpret the world differently rather than change it, as Marx feared? The question of appropriating possibilities presented in texts becomes important in this regard, for Ricoeur considers such appropriation to be a form of "existential verification."[4] As we shall see, Ricoeur claims that a reinterpreted life *is* a transformed life.

The theological realist might argue, against Ricoeur, that we have had access to the "right ideas" for some two thousand years. Perhaps the basic problem is not simply a forgetful imagination, but a lack of power to put these ideas into practice. The theological realist believes that the self-understanding of faith itself recognizes its need for a historical deliverance, and not simply a change in understanding. This is particularly so given the reality of evil. Moreover, announcing such a historical deliverance seems to be the point of the Gospels. Stated more vigorously, the theological realist claims that some such reference to historical events is necessary if the story is ultimately to make sense.[5] Unless something in the history of Jesus happened which in some way altered the human condition, the Christian theologian will be doomed to continual frustration in the attempt to demonstrate the intrinsic connection between the fate of the particular man Jesus and the universal possibility represented by Christ.

With these concerns in mind, I propose in this chapter to examine more closely Ricoeur's claim that the Gospels are true. But what does "true" mean for a position that encourages us to approach the Scripture with the attitude of a "second naiveté"? We have already seen in the two previous chapters that Ricoeur treats the truth of the Gospels (and poetic language in general) as disclosive: these texts manifest essential possibilities and values for human beings. The Gospels therefore enjoy the status of symbolic truth. Ricoeur is not, however, content to leave the matter there. True disclosures about what is humanly possible enable us to see life in a new way, and thus to change it. The Gospels have the power to transform because they have the power to reveal. What remains to be seen is the place accorded the actual life and fate of the particular man Jesus in Ricoeur's poetic schema. I shall suggest that Ricoeur's hermeneutics of the biblical narrative requires an important supplementation: as the Reformers saw long before, Word and Spirit together are the necessary and sufficient conditions for new life, for the possibility of true freedom. A theological analysis of Ricoeur's biblical hermeneutics will therefore inquire into the role played by the Spirit in effecting Christian transformation, as well as into the conditions for the possibility of the coming of the Spirit in the first place. Consequently, I propose to "graft" Ricoeur's philosophical hermeneutics concerning the efficacy of the Word onto an under-standing of Jesus' history as providing the necessary condition for the efficacy of the Spirit. In the case of the Christian kerygma, we must say that the Word is genuinely creative of new possibilities only because of the prior "creative" action and "passion" of the living Word. The passion for the possible recognizes a double parentage; Christian hope is born of word and deed.

Setting the captives free

The Spirit of the Lord is upon me, because he has anointed me to preach good news to the poor. He has sent me to proclaim release to the captives and recovering of sight to the blind, to set at liberty those who are oppressed, to proclaim the acceptable year of the Lord.[6]

Since the Enlightenment, the primary task of christology has been to demonstrate the universal significance of the historically particular life and fate of Jesus. Various conceptual frameworks have been used to articulate the universal significance of this story. Christians confess their belief in the universal relevance of Jesus by confessing him as Christ. But what makes Jesus the Christ? Philosophers and theologians have suggested several frameworks within which the universal significance of Jesus can be discerned. The christological question – who do you say I am – concerns the nature of the relation of the man Jesus to the Christian possibility. Edward Schillebeeckx puts the issue succinctly:

if the Christian affirmation of Jesus' universal significance is not ideological but is an assent to reality ... [then] in the historical man Jesus there must be present some ground or reason for our being able to acknowledge him in that way.[7]

However, many of the proposed conceptual frameworks swallow up the historical actuality and contingency of Jesus' history. In the words of Pannenberg:

Jesus again and again has become merely the example of a Gnostic or a philosophical idea whose truth is ultimately independent of the history of Jesus.[8]

The price one pays for achieving universality on this scheme is high: the Gospel is dehistoricized and the figure of Jesus of Nazareth is rendered dispensable. One cannot help but feel that such readings are a betrayal of the logic of the story itself. Ricoeur holds up Hegel as an example of one who has exchanged biblical for philosophical language, the rational untidiness of history for the crisp cleanness of concepts. Hegel's conceptualization of the Gospel story is, as Ricoeur has often admitted, a beguiling temptation for the philosopher of religion. To what extent does Ricoeur successfully resist this same temptation to render Jesus universally relevant by appropriating him under some conceptual scheme?

My working hypothesis is that many theologians construe Jesus as the Christ because of his relation to the "Christian possibility" – a possibility that has been variously construed as new life, New Being, authentic existence, or an agapic mode of being-in-the-world. At present, there is a fairly broad consensus which understands the Christian possibility in terms of human freedom, a notion that follows Kantian trajectories and one that already enjoys preeminence in Ricoeur's philosophy. It is precisely Ricoeur's interest in the possibility of human freedom that draws his philosophy toward the biblical narratives. Bultmann's christology well illustrates the difficulty of ascribing universal significance to the particular history of Jesus without reducing theology to philosophy. Even Bultmann acknowledged that the real question concerns not the manifestation of the Christian possibility of faith or freedom but its actualization. Heidegger may have "discovered" authentic existence apart from the NT, but Bultmann asks, "Is it enough simply to show man what he ought to be? Can he achieve his authentic Being by a mere act of reflection?"[9] Bultmann, consistently or not, answers his question negatively, and accordingly accuses the existentialist philosopher of confusing a theoretical possibility with an actual one.

As "fallen" beings, humans have lost the actual (ontic) possibility of faith. Humanity is in bondage to the fleshly project of securing one's own existence by one's works. Faith – the acknowledgement that one's existence is a gift – is a surrender of one's false self-understanding and therefore a liberation: ''The new self-understanding which is bestowed with 'faith' is that of *freedom*, in which the believer gains life and thereby his own self.''[10] Bultmann affirms the Pauline order: no faith without a prior hearing of the kerygmatic word. Is faith therefore a possibility that is always – already available? No, for Bultmann believes that the Christian possibility of faith and freedom is *made possible* by God. It is through the preaching of the cross, the word of judgment on all worldly attempts to make one's existence secure, that the possibility of a new, more authentic, existence is both projected and appropriated. In short, it is Christian preaching that sets our captive self-understanding free: ''The real Easter faith is faith in the word of preaching which brings illumination.''[11] Bultmann at least makes an effort to resist the reduction of theology to philosophical anthropology. However, the actual life and fate of Jesus still lacks universal significance: the sole contingent event that seems to be necessary for Bultmann is the ''event'' of preaching, the proclamation of the word.

With his theory of narrative Ricoeur attempts to demonstrate as intelligible what Bultmann could only fideistically affirm, namely, that only in the preaching of Jesus' passion was authentic existence made possible.[12] Ricoeur has effectively shown that creative literature manifests new worlds and ways of being in the world. But what is the exact relation of the cruciform world of the biblical text and the cruciform way of life of the reader that the text is supposed to open up? Does Jesus merely illustrate the possibility of freedom or actually inaugurate it? Does he manifest a possibility that is always-already there or does he make something new possible?

According to Kant, the Gospels present the Idea and ideal of moral perfection, held out to us as an exemplar to be dutifully embraced. This Idea of human goodness and human freedom does not, of course, actually correspond to what is. It is not literally true. However, the Idea has *practical validity* according to Kant, that is, it serves to encourage us to behave rationally and morally. Kant is quite clear that faith in Christ means faith in the practical validity of the Idea. For Kant, the Idea of Christ is valuable, not factual. The Idea is a product of our practical reason, not of history. The Idea does not extend our knowledge about the world, but is rather at the service of practical reason (i.e., freedom). What prevents Ricoeur from adopting Kant's conclusion that it is the Christ symbol rather than the factual history of Jesus that is important to the project of human freedom?[13] Why not follow Strauss and Feuerbach and the whole tradition that sees orthodoxy as a metaphorical vehicle for humanistic values? As James Barr observes, many stories may have a powerful effect on readers even if the events they narrate never happened.[14]

At times Ricoeur seems to say, like Kant, that Christ is a symbol that changes our self-understanding. The story of Jesus is of universal value because it helps us to envision the world not as an impersonal system of nature that is indifferent to human freedom, but rather as a Creation that is ultimately conducive to human freedom. To this vision of the world, we can freely consent. Faith is precisely this vision of the world as Creation. This vision changes everthing: the way we see ourselves and our being-in-the-world. Ricoeur intimates that the story of Jesus does not answer questions about ultimate reality but about human freedom, and religion for Ricoeur is about the gift of freedom. The tension between philosophy and religion is not fatal "if it is traced to its origin, that is to say, to the distinction between the primordial problems of salvation and speculation."[15] For Ricoeur, as well as for Kant before him, the story of Jesus may indeed be considered by the philosopher – not for the sake of theoretical but of practical reason. The story of Jesus serves the project of human freedom rather than that of metaphysics.

Biblical revelation and the power of the possible

The world of the Gospel narratives is for Ricoeur an imaginative, revealed and possible world. Imaginative, because the world is the reference of poetic narrative. Revealed, because the biblical world illumines and opens up human existence:

I believe that the fundamental theme of Revelation is this awakening and this call, into the heart of existence, of the imagination of the possible. The possibilities are opened before man which fundamentally constitute what is revealed. The revealed as such is an opening to existence, a possibility of existence.[16]

Possible, because this existential possibility can be appropriated by the reader: "The proposed world that in biblical language is called a new creation, a new Covenant, the Kingdom of God, is the 'issue' of the biblical text unfolded in front of this text."[17] The Gospel narratives provide the symbols of that freedom or new life for which humanity hopes. These symbols are dangled before the reader's imagination, both inviting and demanding imaginative appropriation. It is thanks to the reader's appropriation of the text's world that the reader's life can be changed.

What sets the captives free? For Ricoeur it is the reader's appropriation of the biblical world. But how exactly can the possible mode of being pictured in the Gospels be made mine? Before we examine Ricoeur's answer to this query, I propose to examine Paul Tillich's solution. Why Tillich? First and most importantly, because Tillich's philosophical theology focuses on this very problematic, that is, on the way that symbols both manifest and occasion the New Being which the Gospels proclaim. Second, because Ricoeur's philosophy of religion shares more affinities with Tillich's theology, in particular the parallel between the methods of approximation and correlation, than has previously been acknowledged. That Ricoeur was Tillich's successor as John Nuveen Professor of Philosophical Theology at the University of Chicago is only an interesting footnote. More puzzling is Ricoeur's almost total silence about Tillich's achievement, in spite of the many similarities between them. Lastly, a dialog with Tillich will better help us to place Ricoeur among the theologians. We may recall Kelsey's remark that Ricoeur, like Tillich, attends to the Bible for its religious symbols.[18]

Like Ricoeur, Tillich views the story of Jesus Christ as a verbal picture. For Tillich, the revelatory event is the event by which one receives the power of new Being. The picture of Jesus Christ not only expresses the original revelatory event, but occasions subsequent revelatory events. Thus for Tillich, as for Ricoeur, the Gospel narratives manifest and transform. The Gospels are for Tillich less like histories and more like expressionist paintings. That is, they are not realistic representations of what actually happened so much as deliberate distortions and exaggerations of what actually happened for the sake of expressing a deeper reality.[19] Though the Gospels may not give a historically accurate picture of Jesus, they adequately convey what is of universal significance about Jesus, that is, his mediation of the power of New Being.

When it comes to Tillich's discussion of the Gospels as occasions for new revelatory events, however, Kelsey discovers a structural inconsistency. While the narrative structure of the Gospels is necessary for their expressive purpose, Kelsey claims that Tillich ignores the narrative features of the passion picture when he discusses how the symbol occasions new revelatory events. To show how religious symbols actually communicate the power of New Being, Tillich relies not on the Gospel narratives but on his philosophical anthropology. The picture of Jesus Christ functions only as an instance of how the power of New Being is mediated. In other words, there is no intrinsic reason why the picture of Jesus Christ, as opposed to some other picture, mediates the power of New Being. It just so happens that it does. According to Kelsey, Tillich's failure to show any connection between the picture of Jesus Christ as expressive and the picture of Jesus as occasioning New Being "leaves an important structural flaw in his systematic theology."[20] Tillich nowhere explains how the picture's mediating power is linked to its literary structure.[21] Why is this an important omission? Because, in Kelsey's judgment,

If there is no connection between what is said ... about making human life whole today and what is said ... about the person of Jesus, then Christology would seem to have become logically dispensable for contemporary Christian theology.[22]

To rephrase Kelsey's question so as to bring it to bear on Ricoeur, we may ask whether there is anything more than an arbitrary connection between the narrative of Jesus and the possibility of Christian existence or New Being. If the power of the Christian possibility has nothing to do with the narrative of the Passion, then what can it have to do with Jesus?

Is Kelsey right in grouping Ricoeur with theologians who construe Scripture as having the authority of non-informative expressive power? I believe that Kelsey errs in moving too quickly from Tillich's idea of the Gospels as a "verbal picture" of Jesus to the conclusion that the Gospels necessarily have the force only of non-informative expression. This is not so much a theological as a literary mistake. According to Kelsey, "If Scripture is to be interpreted on the model of a picture, then, like any important aesthetic object, it must be understood not to make any claims."[23] But it is precisely this prejudice about the imagination and creative literature that Ricoeur seeks to combat. Ricoeur mediates this dichotomy between narrative structure (story/history of Jesus) and existential event (freedom) thanks to his notion of the metaphorical process of reference to a possible world at work in the Gospels. While Tillich may lack the hermeneutical resources to relate the picture of Jesus (formalistic expression) to the power of Christ (occasion of New Being), Ricoeur's hermeneutics addresses this problem head-on. Indeed, this connection between literary structure and existential event is what Ricoeur's hermeneutical "arch" is all about. The process of understanding moves from the explication of the textual work to the appropriation of a textual world.

Whereas Tillich may not have been able to show the relation between the picture of Jesus and the power of Christ, such a relation between a text's sense and reference is at the very heart of Ricoeur's whole hermeneutic enterprise. The thrust of Ricoeur's entire hermeneutics is toward showing that a literary structure is not closed in upon itself but reaches out, touches, and transforms the world of the reader. Obviously, Tillich felt this to be the case, but as Bultmann before him, Tillich lacked the hermeneutical resources to make this relation intelligible. It is just this dichotomy between the narrative structure (the story/history of Jesus) and the existential event (New Being/freedom) that Ricoeur mediates with his hermeneutical arch and the idea of the metaphorical process at work in the Gospels: "Our general hermeneutics invites us to say that the necessary stage between structural explanation and self-understanding is the unfolding of the world of the text."[24] The world of the text spans the ugly ditch that has for so long separated the Jesus of history from the Christ of faith.

What then sets the captives free? Interpretation! For Ricoeur, hermeneutics involves not only explaining the sense of the text but appropriating its reference. It is through interpretation that the text is able to manifest new possibilities and so transform the reader's world. In short, the reader grasps the possibility displayed in the Gospels through interpretative appropriation. Ricoeur overcomes the structural inconsistency that plagued Tillich by making the transformation of the reader (the power of the possible) part of the interpretation process itself. Faith for Ricoeur is essentially the imaginative appropriation of the world of the text. The New Being that is the issue or referent of the Gospels is presented first to the reader's imagination. Believers do not manufacture faith, for faith is the imaginative response to the world first encountered "in front of" the Gospel narratives. Faith, the Christian form of self-understanding, is the imaginative appropriation of a metaphorical world.

What is the Good News that Ricoeur preaches to the captives? "Is not the Good News the instigation of the *possibility* of man by a creative word?"[25] One must read Ricoeur as seeing the captives' plight not so much in terms of a bound will but rather a forgetful imagination. Imagination is the power of allowing oneself to be seized by new possibilities. "For what are the poem of the Exodus and the poem of the resurrection ... addressed to if not to our imagination rather than obedience?"[26] This emphasis on the imagination fits in nicely with Ricoeur's view of religion as concerning the completion of our desire to be whole and reconciled with the Whole rather than the adherence to a strict moral code (*pace* Kant). The possibility of being whole, which is the message of the Gospels, is for Ricoeur a message directed to our imagination rather than our wills. It is a message intended to transform our self-understanding.

How then do the Gospels change us? The Gospels first of all make hope itself possible. Jesus' passion and resurrection narratives create hope, for they speak of New Being that is stronger and freer than the constraints and limitations of our old way of being-in-the-world. Of course, the Gospels are not the only texts that have this capacity to create expectations. Second, the Gospels make freedom possible, because the possibility of freedom is appropriated by the imagination. Ricoeur is able to call the imagination the "power of the possible" because of its appropriating capacity. It is the imagination that grasps new existential possibilities and so changes our self-understanding.[27] Ricoeur goes so far as to say that we are "prophets of our own existence" because we can imagine future possibilities. But may one not conclude, if the imagination is indeed the power of the possible, that other poetic texts solicit the imagination's interest and serve as occasions for similar transformations? If so, it is not yet clear whether the Gospels have any unique status with regard to the passion for the possible.

What exactly do the Gospels have to contribute that is distinctive with regard to the scope of what is humanly possible? For Bultmann, Tillich and Ricoeur, the question of the range of possibilities of a thing or person is the primary ontological question. The correlation of ontology and biblical hermeneutics is particularly clear in Tillich's thought. For Tillich, ontology poses the fundamental questions of human being – questions about human possibilities – and Scripture provides the answers.[28] Ricoeur shares with Tillich this interest in "correlating" contemporary human experience in general with the biblical description – or better, redescription – of human experience.[29] In pursuing ontological questions we are concerned not with logical possibilities, but with the structural or constitutional possibilities of human being. While there is nothing logically contradictory about the idea of human freedom, the ontological status of freedom is another matter. Are freedom, salvation and New Being permanent fixtures in the stock of what is humanly possible? In what way do the passion narratives function with regard to human possibilities differently from other "poems" of existence? Is the purpose of the Gospel to remind us of general possibilities that have been there all along?

Ricoeur sometimes uses the metaphor of "awakening" when discussing the relation of poetic texts to the possible. Poetic language "awakens possibilities,"[30] and revelation "is this awakening and this call, into the heart of existence, of the imagination of the possible."[31]

It is not as though poetic language alters the fundamental structures of human existence, making something possible which before was impossible by altering our very constitution; rather, the change is on the ontic level, the level of our concrete existence. We need to be reminded, in the midst of concrete existence, of certain important possibilities that have, for whatever reason, been forgotten or obscured. On this view, the passion narrative truly is a ''poem of existence,'' whose purpose is to recall and awaken us to a vital, though forgotten, human possibility. Ricoeur's reading of the passion narrative would have to be classified with what Gustaf Aulén calls the ''subjective'' or ''humanistic'' type of atonement theology, which sees the significance of the cross in terms of its effect on man rather than God.[32] Specifically, the passion narrative serves to redescribe human experience in terms of the root metaphor of the Kingdom of God. One's vision of life and oneself will henceforth be shaped by a cruciform narrative and oriented to a resurrection hope. This enables us to go on ''in spite of.''

Here again we must wonder to what extent David Tracy represents the complete theological performance of Ricoeur's philosophical anthropology and hermeneutics. In Tracy too we find the twin themes of the disclosive and transformative power of the story of Jesus. The story of Jesus affords hearers ''a redescription of life's possibilities and a transformative reorientation of life's activities.''[33] Theology is to reflect on the ''transformative existential possibilities'' of the story of Jesus.[34] Fiction is relevant because it speaks of possibilities that an analysis of the present actualities cannot provide.

What of the ''fact'' that Jesus is the Christ and its relation to the Christian possibility? Tracy makes an important distinction between a fact as an actualization of a possibility and a fact as a re-presentation of a possibility. In Greek philosophy, says Tracy, ''factual'' meant ''actual.'' Reality is a matter of what is, and what is can be spoken of descriptively. On the other hand, Tracy wants us to consider that symbolic re-presentations of certain possibilities are also facts. The possibilities expressed in symbols are not ''mere'' possibilities, but ''deep'' possibilities that articulate what was, what could be and what might be. These ''universal'' possibilities are factual not in the sense that one can point to their actual instantiations, but in virtue of their universality and permanence. This is the kind of factuality enjoyed by religious language in general, and the story of Jesus in particular.[35]

Accordingly, the ''fact'' that Jesus is the Christ has less to do with historical events than with the essential human possibilities that the Gospels project. Tracy draws a comparison between the possibility that a Hemingway character represents, such as "grace under pressure," and the possibility that the figure of Jesus represents, which we might term "being-towards-God." Tracy's point is that fictions, if they represent possibilities of universal human experience, may also be termed factual. For Tracy, the "classics" of art and religion are so defined because of their power to disclose a universal human possibility. Their universality is precisely what makes the classics relevant and challenging to each new generation. Exposure to the classics allows the hearer or beholder to transcend his finite situation and live in a new world. For Tracy this is a liberating experience, for in encountering the classics "lies the one finite hope of liberation to the essential."[36] All this seems to be to be a faithful application of Ricoeur's hermeneutical principles to the biblical texts.

For Tracy and Ricoeur alike, the ultimate referent not only of Jesus' parables but of the passion narrative itself is common human experience. The point of the story of Jesus is to enable the reader to look at life in a new way. Tracy expects readers to find in the Gospels the expression of their deepest faith and hopes. The Gospels, by displaying the possibility of meaning in spite of meaninglessness, enable us to trust and to affirm life, thereby reconciling human freedom and nature. The reconciliation Jesus effects is poetic: thanks to the story of the passion and resurrection, we can see that life may be affirmed in spite of death. However, it is not as though Jesus actually changes something in the structure of the world or human nature; rather, through the story of Jesus we are able to look at the world differently. One might say that Jesus came not to abrogate our structural possibilities but to fulfill them.

In short, the passion story discloses an existential possibility that is always-already there. Jesus did not inaugurate a new way of being-in-the-world, but rather illustrated a universal possibility. Interestingly enough, Tracy links his understanding of "fact" as re-represented possibility with the notion of sacrament. The story of Jesus is a means of grace, a verbal channel of salvific possibility. Both Ricoeur and Tracy view the truth of the Gospels not as correspondence to past actuality but in terms of manifesting a universal possibility.

Ricoeur calls for a mediation between a theology of sacred symbols and a theology of the word. After all, he notes, the Church has always had preaching and sacraments. Nevertheless, I believe that Ricoeur's own mediation of sacrament and word is slanted in favor of sacrament, insofar as the salvific function Ricoeur assigns to the kerygma is essentially sacramental in nature – a verbal mediation of a gracious transformation. This preference on Ricoeur's part is partly due, I think, to his perception that denizens of the twentieth century feel lost in the cosmos. The sound of the sacred cannot easily be heard over the hum of technology. But Ricoeur also believes that we are on the verge of a renaissance of the sacred.[37] By this he means that people will return not to idols and totems to gain access to the sacred, but to poetic language – we wish to be called again. Ricoeur hopes that language itself will mediate the sacred. Ricoeur's achievement is to have given theologies of manifestation a verbal and literary twist.[38]

The theological significance of Ricoeur's move to a manifestation-oriented understanding of language and literature should not be underestimated. First, explaining the truth of religious discourse in terms of manifestation fulfills one of Ricoeur's great ambitions: to restore to us that sense of participation in and belonging-to the world. Poetic language allows us to envision the world as always-already graced and loved by God, as Creation. Second, the idea that the Gospels' truth is a function of their manifesting essential human possibilities allows Ricoeur to account for the universal aspect of the Gospel narratives and so satisfies the exigencies of the philosopher of religion. But it is just here that Ricoeur's mediation appears to break down, for in stressing the always-already availability of the Christian possibility, the particularity and contingency of the story of Jesus is overshadowed. The concrete actuality of Jesus, what Frei calls his unsubstitutable history and identity, is in danger of being lost. Moreover, if the actual course of the events of Jesus' life is unimportant, I wonder in what sense we may speak of the Gospels as announcing something radically new. Is not the "new" possibility of which Ricoeur and Tracy speak one that has "always-already" been there? And if it is indeed a universal possibility, as Tracy explicitly states, then of what significance is the particular life and fate of the man Jesus? What does the story of Jesus accomplish that the narratives of John the Baptist or the apostle Paul could not? Jesus is not the only biblical figure to show "grace under pressure," or agape, or even "being-towards-God."

That Ricoeur of all thinkers proffers a sacramental interpretation of proclamation is both startling and ironic: is not Ricoeur the philosopher who desires to be called again? Does he not invoke the name of Barth and the centrality alloted to the Word in Barth's theology to account for his own fascination with the word? A further irony lies in the fact that Barth offers what is perhaps as effective a critique as any against the manifestation model. Barth, zealous to preserve the freedom of God in his revelation, attacks any notion that revelation – much less salvation – is always-already available in nature. For Barth, the biblical concept of revelation is an historical event, that is, one that takes place at a specific time and place. Barth states that when the Bible gives an account of revelation

> it means to narrate history, i.e., not to tell of a relation between God and man that exists generally in every time and place ... but to tell of an event that takes place there and only there, then and only then, between God and certain very specific men.[39]

Ricoeur's view of the biblical narrative better fits Barth's description of myth: "Myth uses narrative form to expound what purports to be always and everywhere true."[40] Myth speaks of general possibilities. The assumption, says Barth, is that man stands in a potentially present relation to God at every time and in every place. Natural or philosophical theology embraces this assumption, thus compromising the free initiative of God to reveal himself. Furthermore, Barth claims that myths do not deal with new or unique events: they do not recount changes but express what is permanently the case. Barth's verdict, with its evocation of the spectre of Hegel, should give the would-be Ricoeurrian pause: "Myth is the preparatory form of speculation and speculation is the revealed essence of myth."[41]

Barth's comments raise the question of whether, and to what extent, Ricoeur has dehistoricized the concepts of revelation and redemption and appropriated them as general categories for his philosophical hermeneutics. Does Ricoeur, in seeking to overcome the ruinous dichotomy between history and fiction, do equal justice both to the Gospels' historical intent as well as their story form? Ricoeur speaks frequently of the "revelatory power" of a text.[42] It is the symbol or text that "gives." Language need not wait to be taken captive by God, as Barth maintains, for the capacity to display a new world and transform the reader's existence is a prerogative of poetic texts. Revelation need not rely on a special divine initiative – nor, apparently, need salvation. In the constellation of Ricoeur's thought, fiction orbits closer to revelation than does history, for fiction is concerned with, and best able to express, the essential.

Ricoeur's weighted emphasis on fiction over history is best understood when we recall the broader context of his philosophical anthropology. Together, history and fiction constitute a "schematism" of human action and show us what is humanly possible. But Ricoeur seems unnecessarily to limit what is worth remembering about the past to values:

> For to recognise the values of the past in their *differences* with respect to our values is already to open up the real towards the possible. The "true" histories of the past uncover the buried potentialities of the present.[43]

But is it not possible that certain actions are worth remembering for what they *accomplished* rather than for what they exemplify? To mine the past only for values is to overlook the possibility that something radically new might be brought about through human (or divine) action. History is unique in that it deals with the actualization of certain possibilities and not only their imaginative projection. Be that as it may, Ricoeur often treats the biblical narratives more like imaginative literature than history.[44]

There are several reasons for Ricoeur's *de facto* preference of fiction over history. First, the language of fiction is not "bound by the facts, empirical objects, and logical constraints of our established ways of thinking."[45] Ricoeur, as I have shown, objects to a language and a vision that is bound to actuality. But this is precisely the constraint that sets history off from fiction. Second, Ricoeur seems to hold to Aristotle's maxim that poetry is more philosophical than history since it aims at the essential rather than the contingent. Only poetic language restores to us that sense, so sought after by the Romantics, of belonging-to the world. Third, as we saw in the previous chapter, fiction has the capacity to display new modes of temporality, and at the limit provides schemata for eternity itself.[46] Lastly, Ricoeur's recent preoccupation with metaphors rather than symbols indicates his fascination for the secret workings of language itself. Whereas symbols are linked to the cosmos, metaphor is "a free invention of discourse," a purely linguistic phenomenon.[47] The question that remains is whether a creative word alone can set the captives free.

Evil, resurrection and the "logic" of hope

Ricoeur's philosophy exudes a confidence in the humanizing and liberating power of creative language. As we have seen, the central problem of the human condition concerns not a bondage of the will so much as an atrophied imagination. That Ricoeur believes in the healing power of creative language and the "redemption" of the imagination should come as no surprise, for we have argued that the whole structure of his thought points to this very correlation between human being and textual interpretation. Hence the significance of the Gospel narratives: "It is in *imagination* that the new being is first formed in me."[48] Imagination is thus the power of the humanly possible.

But does the matter of redemption remain on this level? Can one appropriate the Christian possibility of freedom by imaginative fiat? Given the stubborn fact of radical human evil, is one's imagination of freedom anything more than the freedom of the imagination? Ricoeur, as Kant before him, refuses to shirk this difficult question: "evil makes of freedom an impossible possibility ... not only our knowledge but our power has limits."[49] According to Ricoeur, Kant serves as a positive contribution to "a critique of hope within the limits of reason alone."[50] Given radical evil, can we genuinely hope for human freedom? Is it true that imagining a possible way of being-in-the-world is a sufficient condition for actualizing that possibility? Are we not sometimes false prophets of our own existence? This question must be voiced in an age shaped by the masters of suspicion, an age marked by ideologies and ideology-critique, if we are to avoid deceiving ourselves. What is the difference between an imaginative way of being-in-the-world that is a genuine individual or social possibility and a utopian dream derived from the pathology of hope?

Our concern is with the status of the possibilities for human existence that are projected by texts. How can we be sure that a given text is projecting a world that is a genuine possibility for individual and social practice? One might argue that humans have unlimited potential; thus no possibility can be ruled out. Of course, this position is harder and harder seriously to maintain at a time when the limitations of humanity, and of the earth itself, starkly confront us. Though Ricoeur sometimes says, with the existentialists, that "man is possibility," it is clear that Ricoeur recognizes that man is actually a "possibility within limits."[51] But what are these limits? What is the range of possibilities open to humanity? Must we include among our inventory of genuine possibilities, as does John Wesley, the idea of Christian perfection? Ricoeur is surely correct in insisting on the vital role played by language and literature in expanding our consciousness of the possibilities open to us, but is imagination really the power or "ground" of the possible? Are there not a great many ideas that have been expressed in texts that have never been expressed in concrete human history? Specifically, can the imagination free us from the bondage indicated by the symbols of evil and the doctrine of sin?

Ricoeur recognizes that there are limits to human power and possibilities. In *Freedom and Nature*, for instance, he portrays human freedom limited by one's body and character. We do not choose these but find ourselves already tied to them. Heidegger's term for human being captures both aspects: *Da* situates me in a particular place and time – I am "there" and not somewhere else. *Sein* opens my existence to the future; I can choose between various possibilities. Open and closed, infinite and finite, possible and necessary; these are the twin poles that constitute the mystery of incarnate existence according to Ricoeur. It is most important to note, however, that Ricoeur refuses to identify this fundamental human polarity with evil. Finitude per se must not be confused with evil. That is why a philosophy concerned merely to describe the fundamental structures of human being does not reach evil. All Ricoeur can reach in *Freedom and Nature* is the concept of an "only human," that is finite, freedom. The most a philosophical description of essential human being can reach are the concepts of finitude and fallibility, but not evil.

The question for Ricoeur then becomes how to incorporate radical evil into one's thinking while at the same time preserving the case for hope. Ricoeur's strategy, as we have seen, was to shift from phenomenology to hermeneutics, that is, to a form of thinking about evil not in terms of essential human possibilities but in terms of concrete existence as expressed in language and literature. This shift was necessary according to Ricoeur, for we cannot deduce either radical evil or hope from a conceptual system. However, stories of original innocence and eventual deliverance allow us to understand and consent to existence as we now have it. Indeed, it is this freedom of consent, this ability to affirm life, that most matters to Ricoeur. Consent "is the ultimate reconciliation of freedom and nature which both theoretically and practically appear to us torn apart."[52] It is the imaginative vision of a possible world that permits us to consent to life with joy rather than stoic resignation.[53]

This clarification of what Ricoeur means by freedom is important. We need to distinguish the freedom of consent from the freedom of movement, that is, the change from possibility to actuality. I shall argue that the kind of freedom that Ricoeur believes to be the correlate of the Christian kerygma is not the freedom of Christian perfection, nor is it the freedom to act rationally or morally, as Kant believed. In articulating his concept of freedom, Ricoeur appeals to Descartes' three precepts in his *Discourse on Method*: (1) use your mind to know what to do (virtue of decision) (2) execute all that reason counsels (virtue of effort) (3) do not desire what is outside your power (virtue of consent).[54] Whereas Kant understood freedom primarily in terms of the first and second precepts, Ricoeur sees freedom in light of the third precept. I hope to show that this difference in focus leads Ricoeur to espouse an entirely different view of the world and the meaning of the story of Jesus from that of Kant.

Among the several possible visions of the world, Ricoeur prefers the one that is the correlate of biblical literature, the world that exists at the intersection of the stories of Adam, Job and Jesus. This does not mean that Ricoeur finds the other stories about the beginning and evil uninteresting or irrelevant, or even false. However, Ricoeur claims that we can best hear what all the other stories mean to say from the vantage point of the biblical narratives. Of course, this is a wager, as Ricoeur admits. But Ricoeur's wager is no blind leap of faith, for symbols, myths and stories can be put to the test: ''In understanding himself better, the philosopher verifies, up to a certain point, the wager of his faith.''[55]

One of the leading rivals to the Christian vision of the world is the tragic vision, best expressed by Sartre's description of human freedom as a ''useless passion'' and by Heidegger's construal of authentic human existence in terms of being-towards-death. What characterizes this tragic view of the world is the identity between finitude and evil. The tragic vision inscribes evil and guilt into the fundamental structure of human being. This identity, for Ricoeur, is effectively to eradicate any possibility for hope. The story of Adam, however, is anti-tragic in its intent. Ricoeur interprets the figure of the serpent as indicating that, though evil is committed by man, it is somehow already there.

Ricoeur's interpretation of the story of Adam provides an essential backdrop for his interpretation of the story of Jesus. Ricoeur takes great pains to refute a particular reading of the Adam narrative that has proven influential in Christian theology, a reading that leads to the moral or ethical vision of the world. According to the ethical vision of the world, God is both Lawgiver and Judge who rewards and punishes, and History is a vast tribunal. The moral vision of the world seeks to explain evil in terms of the misuse of freedom. This is the purpose of Augustine's concept of original sin, which according to Ricoeur tries to conceptualize radical evil and rationalize divine reprobation.[56] Ricoeur claims that Kant too interprets biblical narrative according to an ethical vision of the world. In Kant, the reduction of religion to ethics is explicit. Why is this ethical vision of the world so misleading? Ricoeur avoids it for several reasons: first, in the ethical vision of the world the human subject is autonomous. On this view, the human subject constitutes itself, for better or for worse. Second, God appears more as a lawkeeper than as a God of love. Third, hope is strangled in a system where grace or God's favor has to be won through moral obedience rather than received in spite of disobedience.

It is the literal reading of the Adam story that leads to the ethical vision of the world. The literal reading treats the fall as an actual historical event that introduced suffering, evil and divine retribution into the world. Interpreted literally, the story of Adam means that God deals with persons on the basis of what they do. Ricoeur believes that the OT itself discourages this literal reading. OT wisdom literature calls the ethical vision of the world into question when it meditates on the suffering of the innocent. Unjust suffering is an insuperable problem for the ethical vision of the world insofar as it holds that God deals justly with persons according to their works. Ricoeur sees Job's friends as apologists for the ethical vision of the world: they conclude that Job must have done evil to merit his troubles. For Ricoeur, the whole point of the story of Job is to falsify the ethical vision of the world. Job penetrates beyond the God of morality to a new dimension of faith that is unverifiable. God's speech to Job out of the whirlwind does not explain unjust suffering, but God asks Job to contemplate the fact that Creation has overcome chaos. Contemplating God's inscrutable order of creation provides a way ''between agnosticism and the penal view of history and life – the way of unverifiable faith.''[57] God's speech provides no conceptual resolution of the problem of evil, but it does change Job's essential vision of the world. How? By conjuring up the world as ''Creation'' in a series of rhetorical questions. Job is subsequently able to affirm and consent freely to life.

A third biblical figure completes the case against the ethical view of the world. Whereas the story of Adam stands for evil committed and the story of Job for evil suffered, the story of the Suffering Servant transcends the dichotomy by making suffering ''an *action* capable of redeeming the evil that is committed.''[58] Ricoeur suggests that the figure of the Suffering Servant ''reveals an entirely new possibility – that suffering gives itself a meaning, by voluntary consent, in the meaninglessness of scandal.''[59] Far from contributing to an ethical vision of the world and its concomitant penal substitutionary view of atonement, the figure of the Suffering Servant displays a way to overcome evil by actively adopting suffering. Taking up human suffering into the divine life both completes and transcends the tragic view of the world and falsifies the ethical vision.

Because the ethical vision of the world is linked to a literal reading of the Adam story, Ricoeur insists that only a symbolic reading of the stories of Adam and Jesus gives rise to an eschatological vision. Ricoeur is explicit in this regard:

I am convinced that the full acceptance of the non-historical character of the myth – non-historical if we take history in the sense it has for the critical method – is the other side of a great discovery: the discovery of the *symbolic* function of the myth.[60]

It is Ricoeur's belief that the Adam story functions to dissociate the actual evil state of humanity from the original state. Our ontic condition of corruption does not adequately reflect our ontological constitution. The narrative of Adam and Eve displays a two-beat rhythm: humanity is destined for good but inclined towards evil. The Creation is a figure that plays the role of a Kantian regulative Idea: the narrative progression from Creation to fall provides Ricoeur's philosophical anthropology with a key concept, namely, the contingency of that radical evil that the penitent confesses as his nature. The story of Adam articulates the paradox of our original destination and our contingent inclination: "I am radically evil but fundamentally good. It is this confrontation of the originally good and the radically evil which is explored by means of a story."[61]

The eschatological vision of the world thus pertains to one's ability to see hopeful, though yet unrealized, possibilities in the midst of an evil present. The promise of a new creation allows us to consent to the actual state of the world with joyful anticipation. Thanks to the eschatological vision of the world as it might be, we are freed from despair and able to entertain a passion for the possible. One might question, however, Ricoeur's explanation of the conditions for the possibility of hope. Does the eschatological vision take account of faith's self-understanding which acknowledges the need for some kind of historical deliverance? The penitent realizes that the heart is wicked and needs to be transformed. The penitent desires a new way of being-in-the-world, not simply a new way of seeing it. In other words, it seems to be part of the very logic of hope to look for some change in the human condition, rather than a change of vision alone. Ricoeur apparently believes that the story of Jesus saves by changing the way we look at ourselves and our world. Marx here receives a hermeneutic refutation: Ricoeur's point, against Marx, is that to interpret the world differently *is* to change it.

Kant acknowledged the confession that "the world lieth in evil" is a complaint as old as history itself. The question that must be squarely faced is simply this: is changing one's self-understanding a sufficient condition for the realization of freedom and new life? Given the reality and predominance of evil in the actual world, does not the logic of hope demand that there be some kind of historical change in the human condition if this hope is to be more than an illusion? Is this not what Paul means by saying that if the resurrection did not actually occur we are to be pitied? If neither the fall nor the resurrection is historical (in some sense), then Creation is inherently flawed and will always remain so. Now while Ricoeur is careful not to confuse Creation and the fall (so as to make evil part of the essential human condition), he is not so careful when it comes to Creation and Salvation. It sometimes seems that Christ saves us simply by showing us that the world is Creation – only then can we achieve the freedom of consent. But this makes fallibility and redemption alike permanent possibilities.

If freedom and fallibility are permanent human possibilities, what does the story of Jesus contribute to the passion for the possible? In Ricoeur's reading of the Gospel narratives, the point of the story of Jesus is to show us that freedom is more fundamental than fallibility. Jesus' resurrection means that death and meaninglessness are not the last words for the believer. "The passion for the possible implies no illusion; it knows that all resurrection is from among the dead, that all new creation is in spite of death."[62] The phrase "in spite of" defines the relation of resurrection to death. Ricoeur believes that the story of Jesus makes possible a "hope in spite of." Furthermore, Ricoeur believes that the story of Jesus shows us that there is more reason to hope than to despair: "Hope means the 'superabundance' of meaning as opposed to the abundance of senselessness, of failure and destruction."[63] Indeed, this understanding of hope leads Ricoeur to define freedom as follows:

For my part I should say that freedom is the capacity to live according to the paradoxical law of superabundance, of denying death and of asserting the excess of sense over non-sense in all desperate situations.[64]

Ricoeur applauds Jürgen Moltmann's emphasis on the resurrection as promise rather than past event.[65] With Moltmann, Ricoeur considers the resurrection in an eschatological perspective: the story of Jesus schematizes (creates a temporal figure of) the God who is coming. The resurrection is theologically significant not as past event, or as present experience (*pace* Bultmann), but rather as promise of a future. Christian freedom therefore becomes a way of being-in-the-world in light of the resurrection promise. In Ricoeur's words, Christian freedom "is to belong existentially to the order of the Resurrection."[66] What does this mean? It means that the believer will hope and consent "in spite of." In spite of the cross, there is resurrection. This is Ricoeur's response to the problem of evil: belief "in spite of." The story of Jesus shows us a way of being-in-the-world that consents to life in spite of unjust suffering by discerning the promise of the God who is coming.

This denial of evil and death is for Ricoeur the inverse of a life-force, of a power of affirmation, that Ricoeur sees expressed in another Pauline phrase – "how much more." Ricoeur notes Paul's strange logic in

Rom. 5:12 – 20. If it is certain that as a result of the one sin of the one man Adam many died, "how much more" is it the case that the many will be saved through Jesus Christ, the second Adam. Of course, Paul is speaking from a resurrection perspective. In the present, evil often appears triumphant. But from an eschatological perspective, grace is greater than justice. Indeed, this is precisely why Ricoeur rejects the ethical vision of the world with its "logic of identity." In the ethical vision the cosmic principle is "an eye for an eye and a tooth for a tooth." But in the eschatological vision embodied in the story of Jesus, we have not a logic of identity but what Ricoeur terms the logic of superabundance – "how much more":

This logic of surplus and excess is as much the folly of the Cross as it is the wisdom of the Resurrection. This wisdom is expressed in an *economy of superabundance*, which we must decipher in daily life, in work and in leisure, in politics and in universal history. To be free is to sense and to know that one belongs to this economy, to be "at home" in this economy. The "in spite of," which holds us ready for disappointment, is only the reverse, the dark side, of the joyous "how much more" by which freedom feels itself, knows itself, wills to conspire with the aspiration of the whole of creation for redemption.[67]

This eschatological vision of the world completes Ricoeur's philosophy of the will by answering the question, "What may I hope?"

The eschatological vision that has informed Ricoeur's philosophy is nourished by the story of Jesus and other poetic texts that express this original and eschatological unity of man and the world. The story of Jesus is for Ricoeur perhaps the most adequate expression of the eschatological vision of the world. The cross symbolizes God's judgment on actual reality. But actual reality – the present – is not the whole story. The resurrection symbolizes the promise and power of the future. The passion and resurrection of Jesus symbolize Ricoeur's belief that human being and reality itself is best understood in terms of possibility rather than actuality. Ricoeur's philosophy is best understood as handmaiden to an eschatological vision of the world, a philosophy that proceeds according to the twofold belief that the unity of man and world is both original and eschatological. Accordingly, Kierkegaard's description of the philosopher as a "poet of the religious" is especially apt in the case of Paul Ricoeur.[68] Religion for Ricoeur is not ethical in the sense of moralism, but "hyper-ethical," concerned with the gift of freedom rather than its lawful regulation.

The Gospel narratives contribute to an eschatological vision, that is, a view of original or primordial goodness that is only temporarily interrupted by actual evil. The Good News of the Gospel is that human beings are destined for goodness and freedom. The victory of Jesus the Christ reminds us that "goodness is more primordial than evil."[69] And Ricoeur believes that this Word "has the power to change our understanding of ourselves."[70] This Word makes it possible for us to consent with joyful anticipation to this world "in spite of" evil, suffering and death. By changing our imagination, the Gospel narratives transform our existence.

Certain questions, however, remain. First, how can we discern which imaginative worlds to appropriate? The Bible is clear in its insistence that the imaginings of the heart may be evil as well. That is, the imagination itself has the potential for perversity. Ricoeur is, of course, aware of the pathological side of the imagination. Idols and ideologies constitute the offspring of vain imaginings. Second, how do we know what kind of world and possibility is displayed in the Gospels? Generations of believers understood the NT to reveal not the possibility of consent to the world, but the possibility of becoming right with God, the possibility of being declared righteous. Ricoeur resists this reading because of its affinity with an ethical vision of the world. If the literal reading of the NT leads to a "bloodless moralism" or a magical conception of grace, how do we move from the sense to the reference or world of the text? Once one abandons the plain sense and the literal referent, the move from sense to reference becomes much more problematic. And, indeed, Ricoeur has seen fit to drop the notion of reference altogether and instead speak of redescription. To what extent does Ricoeur actually derive his eschatological vision from the Gospels? And to what extent does Ricoeur's reading of the Gospels guarantee the universal significance of the particular story of Jesus?

Most importantly, is the regeneration of the will really a matter of refiguring the imagination? As we have seen, reading is redemptive insofar as the narrative presentation of a possible mode of being-in-the-world refigures the self.[71] Ricoeur is adamant in his conviction that we gain self-understanding through appropriating the possibilities displayed in poetic texts:

The self of self-knowledge is the fruit of an examined life, to recall Socrates' phrase in the *Apology*. And an examined life is, in large part, one purged, one clarified by the cathartic effects of the narratives, be they historical or fictional, conveyed by our culture.[72]

Is the freedom to consent to the world in joyful expectation a possibility that is always open to us? Does not the logic of hope compel us to look for a change in the human condition that actually frees us from the bondage of despair, suffering and evil? Can we say ''how much more'' if Christ was not actually raised, however complicated it might be to specify the truth conditions for such an event? Would not the world continue to ''lie in evil'' even if we saw it through resurrection-tinted spectacles?

While I believe that poetic texts can transform our existence within certain limits, is it not the message of the Gospel that the very limits of human existence have somehow been stretched? Surely the New Testament authors believe that the possibility created by the Christ event is *sui generis*: the necessary conditions for its being genuine include historical acts and events. Is this not Paul's meaning when he claimed that the historical actuality of the resurrection is a prerequisite for a faith that would not be vain? Ricoeur agrees that a change is necessary, but identifies it with that which takes place in the reader and pertains to self-understanding. Even in his earlier work, Ricoeur maintained that *ideas* have changed the world.[73] While this is certainly true, the theological issue is whether ideas can vanquish the kind of bondage presupposed by the Gospels and the entire New Testament. Significantly, Ricoeur appears to agree with Kierkegaard that despair – a form of negative thinking rather than some actual historical bondage or problem in the human constitution – is the fundamental sin. It therefore comes as no surprise that Ricoeur associates salvation and freedom with positive thinking and joyful consent.

From passion to Pentecost

I believe in the Holy Spirit ... the Giver of Life.[74]

Throughout this study of Ricoeur I have been at pains to show the extent to which we may rightly deem Ricoeur's philosophy ''Christianly apt.'' We have seen that at several points Ricoeur's philosophy approximates biblical and theological notions such as creation, fall, revelation, faith – even resurrection. In the previous section, however, I have hinted that Ricoeur's approximation of the creation – fall – redemption schema may not be fully adequate. I now wish to explore this potential criticism in greater detail by asking whether Ricoeur has been able to effect a philosophical approximation of the Holy Spirit in his hermeneutic theory. This will involve us in looking at the Gospel narratives in order to discover the connection between Jesus' passion and the actuality of salvation. I believe we shall see that

Ricoeur's hermeneutic philosophy has been informed by a reading of the Gospel narrative that does not fully account for the story's own logic.

As I have shown, the Christian possibility – freedom, existence "in the light of resurrection," the ability joyfully to consent to life "in spite of" – is a possibility displayed in the story of Jesus. Ricoeur believes that this life-transforming possibility may be appropriated by the reader. This is not some kind of poetic Pelagianism, however, for Ricoeur is careful to note that the appropriation of the world of the text is really a "letting-go" of self – not a work, but a surrender. It is important to note that Ricoeur describes the phenomenon of appropriation in religious terms. He is careful not to confuse appropriation with "taking"; rather, it is primarily a "letting-go," a "dispossession" of the self.[75] Specifically, the reader "lets go" of previous self-understandings and "receives" a new form of self-understanding from the reference – the revealed world – of the text.[76]

Now faith for Ricoeur is a matter of imaginative appropriation. This faith does not come by works, for the event of appropriation is not in the control of the reader.[77] On the contrary, appropriation involves a certain dying to self. But Ricoeur does not restrict this self-surrendering to discussions about biblical hermeneutics. The phenomenon of imaginative appropriation characterizes the process of textual interpretation in general. Appropriation thus appears in Ricoeur's writing as a secular, hermeneutic counterpart to what earlier Christians meant by conversion. Again we are faced with a puzzle: should we construe Ricoeur's hermeneutics as a generalization of principles that find their proper home in biblical hermeneutics, or should we view Ricoeur as reading the Bible with the same principles that characterize his general hermeneutics? If other texts can transform human existence, what is unique about the Gospels?[78]

Ricoeur concludes his textbook on general hermeneutics with some thoughts on imaginative appropriation:

I would oppose the self, which proceeds from the understanding of the text, to the ego, which claims to precede it. It is the text, with its universal power of world disclosure, which gives a self to the ego.[79]

This giving a self to the ego is also what Ricoeur means when he speaks of a "second Copernican Revolution." If Kant's first Copernican revolution taught us that subjects partly constitute objects, Ricoeur is keen to press home a further lesson: we human subjects are not autonomous but are ourselves constituted by a power – a word – that founds us. As readers we are not only interpreters but we are interpreted. Ricoeur regards reading itself as potentially redemptive, for the word has the power to transform our existence (viz., our self-understanding):

Faith is the attitude of one who accepts being interpreted at the same time that he interprets the world of the text ... The feeling of absolute dependence would remain a weak and inarticulate sentiment if it were not the response to the proposition of a new being which opens up new possibilities of existence for me. Hope, unconditional trust, would be empty if it did not rely on a constantly renewed interpretation of sign-events reported by the writings, such as the Exodus in the OT and the Resurrection in the NT. These are the events of deliverance which open and disclose the utmost possibilities of my own freedom and thus become for me the Word of God.[80]

Hope, absolute dependence, faith, ultimate concern – the concerns of Kant, Schleiermacher, Bultmann and Tillich alike – are for Ricoeur correlates of a creative word that precedes them.

Imaginative appropriation – dying to self and receiving a new self – is clearly a feature of Ricoeur's general hermeneutics.[81] That is, the "grace" of imaginative appropriation is not limited to biblical texts. Poetic texts in general both reveal and save in conjuring up the world as Creation. How do we pass from sin to salvation, from despair to affirmation, from the possibility to the actuality of freedom? One student of Ricoeur suggests the following:

The answer seems too simple and too easy to be true: the work of the imagination ... Imagination, as the metaphysical power that allows man to symbolize, and thereby create, the new self in accordance with the promise and hope of redemption, is the means by which the soul can, and eventually does, come to *live* the resurrection of Christ in anticipation of its own resurrection.[82]

This faith in the healing power of creative language is also the answer given by a second Ricoeur scholar. David Klemm observes that poetic texts do not merely refigure the self; rather, "the metaphorical mode of being can actually enable and empower the authentic existence it depicts."[83] But how can this be? While it is true that poetic language conjures up possibilities, it is not obvious that poetic language carries with it the power to actualize possibilities.

I believe that it is just here that Ricoeur's hermeneutic philosophy requires modification if it is to approximate the historic Christian faith. It is one thing to conjure up visions, and quite another to embody them – to make the visions visible – in individual and community life. Can the problems of unjust suffering and radical evil be eradicated simply by adopting a new vision of the world? While this may be a romantic notion, I contend that it is less than realistic, because the efficacy of the poetic word is only part of the Christian story. The New Testament, especially Luke-Acts, its largest narrative block, displays the power of the Christian possibility not in the imagination but in the figure of the Holy Spirit. Does Ricoeur's interpretation theory adequately approximate the biblical figure of the Holy Spirit with the notion of imaginative appropriation?

Both Bultmann and Moltmann relate the Spirit to the passion for the possible. For Moltmann, the Spirit is connected with the question, "what may I hope?", and therefore with the question of the possibility of human freedom.[84] Bultmann associates the gift of freedom with the Spirit, conceived of not as a mysterious power, "but as the new possibility of genuine, human life which opens up to him who has surrendered his old understanding of himself."[85] And for Bultmann, "freedom is nothing less than being for the genuine future, letting one's self be determined by the future. So Spirit may be called the power of futurity."[86] In Bultmann, however, we find that theology and pneumatology alike are existentially interpreted. David Lull, a process thinker, attacks Bultmann's reduction of the Spirit to an aspect of human being. Lull states that the Spirit is the "*power* that makes the new structure of human existence possible."[87] Against Bultmann, Lull further claims that "For Paul, the Spirit brings a real *structural change* in the believer's existence, and not merely a change of '*self-under-standing*.'"[88] My query to Ricoeur is whether he does not similarly reduce the figure of the Spirit to an aspect of philosophical anthropology by assigning the power of possibility to the imagination in its appropriating capacity. In what follows, therefore, I will examine the Spirit's role as an historically emergent power and active agent in creating the possibility of freedom.[89]

A reading of Luke-Acts will, I trust, enable us to answer several questions: (1) What is the connection between the Jesus of history and the Christ of faith? (2) Why did the Gospels have to take on a narrative form? (3) How does the resurrection make freedom possible? (4) Does Ricoeur adequately account for or approximate the figure of the Spirit in his biblical hermeneutics and his reading of the Gospels? Our choice of Luke-Acts is felicitous for several reasons. First, Luke-Acts is the longest narrative in the New Testament. Second, the author of Luke-Acts was both theologian and literary artist.[90] Third, Luke-Acts gives a prominent place to the figure of the Spirit, as has widely been recognized. Lastly, Luke-Acts gives us a unique insight into the nature of the connection between Jesus and the Spirit. The tie that binds

passion and Pentecost together is, in my opinion, at the very heart of
the mystery of salvation, for this narrative progression reveals how Jesus
is related to the Church, the body of Christ.

Karl Barth explores christology in his *Church Dogmatics* by reflecting
on two stories: the story of the sending of the son into the far country
(Jesus' humiliation or Incarnation) and the story of the homecoming
of the son (resurrection and exaltation). But in Luke-Acts there is a third
movement in the story of Jesus the Christ, namely, the "deputation"
or sending of the Spirit. Indeed, I believe that the link between passion
and Pentecost is the central feature in Luke's narrative, central not only
because the Ascension-Pentecost episode is placed at the end of Luke
and the beginning of Acts, but also because the theological point of the
narrative of Luke-Acts is to demonstrate the connection between the
power of the Spirit and the passion of Jesus Christ.

Luke's attention in the Third Gospel and Acts to the figure of the
Spirit is well known. The Spirit figures at the beginning of Jesus' public
ministry (Luke 3:21–2, 4:18–20) as well as at the beginning of the
ministry of the church (Acts 1:14, 2:1ff). Jesus' ministry as well as that
of his disciples is shown to be borne along by the power of the Spirit.
But what exactly is the relation of the Spirit to the person and work of
Jesus Christ? In his study of Luke-Acts, Tannehill admits that the
purpose of Jesus' death appears to be an enigma. What accounts for
the element of necessity with regard to Jesus' death that is so predomi-
nant in Luke's Gospel? Why was Jesus' death necessary for salvation?
Tannehill wonders whether Jesus' death was not necessary simply
because Scripture predicted it: "The fact that it is predicted in Scripture
makes it necessary, whether it makes sense or not."[91] In the end,
Tannehill adopts the position that the passion of Jesus was necessary
because suffering is the inevitable lot of the prophet.[92] This matter of
prophetic destiny is important because it should also characterize Jesus'
followers. Jesus' witnesses in Acts will fit the same pattern: "In Acts,
Jesus' call to follow him in suffering is dramatized in narrative."[93]
According to Tannehill, the necessity of suffering "derives from the fact
that God's purpose must be realized in a blind and recalcitrant
world."[94]

Tannehill's reading of the Gospel narrative is similar to Ricoeur's.
For both, the point of the Gospels is to deny the temptation to despair,
the temptation to believe that the good principle – God – has been
defeated. Jesus embodies a sacred narrative pattern of the way God
works in the world. He therefore represents the Christian way of being
to the world. Significantly enough, Tannehill claims that references to

the salvific significance of Jesus' death are virtually absent in Luke-Acts.[95] For Tannehill, the Spirit appears only as a secondary figure in his explanation of the logic of Luke-Acts. For Ricoeur as well as Tannehill, Jesus is significant primarily as a prophet. In Ricoeur's reading of the Gospel of Mark, for instance, the story's logic hinges on the inverse relation of Jesus' body and his word. According to Ricoeur, the Gospel of Mark tells the twofold story of the progression of the word and the diminishing of the body: "the body must decrease so that the word may abound." This emphasis on the word of Jesus and his prophetic office leads inevitably to the question of the necessity of the passion and crucifixion, as well as to Bultmann's query, which contained for him the riddle of the whole NT: why did the proclaimer become the proclaimed?

Such a question will continue to act as a nettle in any NT theology that limits Jesus' significance to his prophetic office. If the teaching is what matters, then why do we have four narratives of Jesus' life and death? Charles Talbert suggests that the narrative form itself of Luke-Acts is a device designed to illustrate the way of life that follows from a certain teaching. He argues that the genre of Luke-Acts is similar to ancient biographies of the philosophers and their disciples. The narrative form functions to show the kind of life – the way of being-in-the-world – that defined a given philosophical school.[96] Luke-Acts shows the life of the founder as well as the lives of his disciples. In Talbert's opinion, this genre performed an indispensable function in an age searching for the source and content of the true tradition about Jesus. Again, the emphasis is on Jesus the practicing preacher-prophet.

At this point I will put forward my own reading of Luke-Acts in order to examine the extent to which Ricoeur's approximation of the Christian story is Christianly apt. Does a reading of the story of Jesus as displaying a certain value or way of being-in-the-world do justice to the intent of the Gospels and to the role of the Spirit as depicted especially by Luke-Acts? I propose to journey along the itinerary of meaning that begins at the juncture that connects the Third Gospel to the book of Acts. My working hypothesis is that the Gospels are testimonies to an event that in some way expanded the limits of what is humanly possible. I take the Christ event as referring to the whole complex of ideas and actions that effect the transition from passion to Pentecost.

At the center of Luke's narrative lies the account of Jesus' going away and the Spirit's coming. Indeed, the account of the ascension (unique to Luke) is given twice: in Luke 24 and in Acts 1. It is both ending and beginning – a fact of literary and theological importance. Talbert calls the parallel accounts of Jesus' ascension a "guarantee device." First, the parallel assures the *continuity* between the Jesus of history and the Christ of faith. The one who suffers and dies is the same as the one who is lifted up and ascends. Talbert explains the necessity behind Jesus' going to Jerusalem in terms of the necessity of his being "received up."[97] In Luke's account of Jesus' transfiguration, Moses and Elijah speak of Jesus' "exodus" which he would accomplish in Jerusalem (Luke 9:31). Talbert takes this exodus to refer to the complex event of passion-resurrection-ascension: "It is almost an impossibility to read Jesus' exodus otherwise in light of its proximity to 9:51 where Jesus goes to Jerusalem to be received up and its location in a context which foreshadows the ascension."[98]

Second, the ascension account in Luke 24 and Acts 1 guarantees the *corporeality* of the Christ of faith. Luke is at pains to stress the visibility of the event of the ascension. The language of Acts 1:9–11 stresses the disciples' visual perception of Jesus' ascent.[99] Luke also emphasizes the corporeality of Jesus in the passion narrative. "They did not find the body" (Luke 24:3) is a remark unique to Luke. Moreover, in the account of Jesus' post-resurrection appearance Luke portrays Jesus as proving that he is not a spirit but flesh and bones. Talbert accounts for this Lucan emphasis on the body of Jesus by proposing that Luke was trying to refute the Docetic tendency to separate the spiritual Christ of faith from the material Jesus of history.[100]

Unfortunately, Talbert neglects a third factor that is guaranteed by the repeat account of the ascension – the *connection* between the "going" of Jesus and the "coming" of the Spirit. The hinge on which the whole of Luke-Acts turns is the constitution of Jesus as life-giving Spirit and the constitution of the Church as empowered by this Spirit. The first coming of the Spirit was at Jesus' baptism, that point at which Jesus was equipped for his special task and publicly presented as God's Son. In Luke 24:49, the risen Christ explains why it was necessary that he first suffer. In this context he tells his disciples that he will send to them what God had promised (Luke 24:49) and equip them with power from on high. This is repeated in Acts 1:4, 8 and fulfilled in Acts 2:33 at the coming of the Spirit. The Spirit is the promised power from on high that enables the disciples to have a ministry like that of Jesus.

The Third Gospel and the book of Acts share more than an arbitrary connection because it is through the life, death, and resurrection of Jesus that the Spirit comes, the Spirit that constitutes and enables the Church to minister and extend its influence to Rome itself. That is why Luke's repetition of the account of the ascension is of such import. *The necessity of Jesus' passion lies in its being the condition for the coming of the Spirit.* This theme is not confined to Luke-Acts, however. In the Fourth Gospel the link is just as explicit. Jesus tells his disciples in the discourse of the upper room that unless he goes away, the Paraclete cannot come (John 14:16–17; 16:7–11). In this discourse, Jesus' "exodus" appears as the condition for a greater blessing. Indeed, Paul's confession of faith, his "how much more," is perhaps best understood in precisely this way. Death may have come through Adam, but something greater than death came through the second Adam, Jesus Christ. Whereas the first man Adam became a living soul, the second Adam has become life-giving spirit (1 Cor. 15:45). In other words, Jesus is the Christ because through his passion, resurrection and ascension he is able to send the Spirit, the power of the Christian possibility.

In Paul as in Luke, the materiality of the resurrection is of paramount importance. If Christ is not raised, Christian preaching is in vain (1 Cor. 15:14). In other words, preaching that proclaims freedom is only a con-juring trick with words unless the resurrection "happened."[101] Deed stands behind efficacious word. The Good News of new life depends on historical as well as poetic conditions for its possibility: something new must have been done for something new to be said. Jesus' passion was a prerequisite for resurrection, as his resurrection and subsequent ascension were prerequisites for the coming of the Spirit.[102]

The Lucan emphasis on the materiality of the passion-resurrection-ascension event as the necessary condition for the coming of the Spirit is precisely what the logic of hope in spite of evil would seem to demand. But everything depends on one's view of the human predicament. As Russell Pregeant points out, if the will is not so completely under the power of sin so as to undercut the possibility of faith, then we do not need to refer our salvation to a single event that would somehow release us.[103] We seem to have only two options: either evil is so radical that only a divine intervention could free us, or faith and the freedom to consent are universal possibilities in spite of present evil. To put it another way, does the Christ event make something entirely new possible, or does it manifest a possibility that has always been there? Our reading of Luke-Acts suggests that Luke did indeed present the Christ event as a complex historical occurrence that alone sets the captives free.[104] The power of the Christian possibility – what the NT calls the Spirit – follows from deed and word, from passion and proclamation. In Luke-Acts, the apostolic preaching focuses on an event that liberates humanity. The passion for the possible is not quelled, but redirected back to its ground in actuality. The Good News of the Gospel is that an event has decisively changed our situation – a change that does not merely pertain to how we look at ourselves and the world. The Gospel narrative seeks to guarantee that, thanks to the Christ event, our *consent* to the world in spite of evil is truly in accord with the way things are, or better, will be. The Spirit is not only the power of this future, but its promissory note.

For Ricoeur, however, the Gospel does not announce a new possibility so much as remind us of a possibility that has always been there. What is ''new'' is only the proclamation of this possibility, the word-event. This construal of the way salvation is related to Jesus follows from his analysis of the human predicament. Ricoeur holds that our fundamental problem is a forgetful imagination rather than a rebellious will. We have lost that understanding of ourselves that allows us to live meaningfully and joyfully in the world. The story of Jesus ''saves'' us by disⱼ.laying a vision of the world that allows us to have both meaning and joy in spite of present evil, meaninglessness and death. Jesus is Savior because his story illumines and transforms our existence. We may recall that for Ricoeur a life that is seen anew *is* a transformed life. The word transforms us insofar as it helps us to new self-understandings. It would appear that for Ricoeur, resurrection power is more a matter of metaphorical than historical reference. It is the metaphor – an event of discourse rather than history – that saves by redirecting our imagination and refiguring our existence.

Ricoeur's reading of the Gospel narratives as having metaphoric reference leads me to believe that his narrative theory labors under a ''weighted focus'' that threatens to throw his whole philosophy off balance. In his earlier work, Ricoeur displayed a convincing balance between human nature and freedom. With regard to human beings, the early Ricoeur was conscious both of possibilities, which he associated with freedom and the imagination, and with actualities, the real situation of man as rooted in nature and history. Indeed, it is possible to read all of Ricoeur's work as variations on his fundamental exploration of how humans are mysterious compounds of freedom and nature. The achievement of Ricoeur's early work was to make this tension productive: thanks to this dialectic he was able to resist both a fatalism that subjected human being to the laws of nature and a utopianism that refused to recognize the historical limitations of human being.

Ricoeur's work on symbols continued this equilibrium. Symbols are ''bound'' to the cosmos. The symbolic sense may transcend the literal sense, but it can only be had by ''living'' in the literal sense, which remains indispensable. Metaphors, on the other hand, are not bound to the cosmos, but are rather free inventions of discourse, pure productions of the play of language. Symbols are therefore compatible with history in ways that metaphors are not. In his earlier work Ricoeur treated the Exile as a symbol "because it is a historical event made to signify human alienation analogically."[105] It is as if the symbol receives its ontological backing in historical actuality. Conversely, the power of metaphor is a function of its *independence* of actuality. Ricoeur appreciates metaphorical discourse precisely because it is not confined to historical actuality but instead refers to the possible, which as we have seen, has equal claim to the status of the "real."[106] To what extent has Ricoeur's recent preoccupation with metaphor, and his reading of biblical narrative as having metaphorical reference, caused him to favor the pole of human freedom over nature? If it is within the scope of our natural possibilities to renew our imaginations and to appropriate the possibility of freedom, then it is not surprising that Ricoeur omits the Spirit from his account of interpretation. It is metaphor rather than the Spirit that opens our eyes and causes us to see new things. Ricoeur's "optimism of metaphor" finds its closest approximation not in Christian theology but in Romanticist humanism. The theological realist might well object that Ricoeur is unable to discern which possibilities are genuinely available to us and which are only imaginary utopias blown by the windmills of metaphor.

The resurrection, testimony and truth

Ricoeur has, of course, anticipated this last objection. He is too good a philosopher not to have some means for distinguishing what is possible from what is impossible. He is neither a Don Juan nor a Don Quixote of myth. While it is true that his hermeneutic philosophy privileges poetry and fiction, Ricoeur attempts to "save the historical" with his category "testimony." Ricoeur's philosophical wager of faith is not blind but relies in part on proofs, namely, the possibility of existential verification. The truth of a certain poetic possibility is determined by its ability to illumine and transform life. "Testimony" refers to this attestation that a given possibility is no empty passion but gives meaning and power to human existence, that is, to our desire and effort to be.

As Ricoeur understands it, testimony "introduces the dimension of historical contingency which is lacking in the concept of the world of the text."[107] The world of the text sheds its ideality only when someone confesses, "This is my world." Thanks to testimony, I am able to "recognize as existing what is only an idea for me."[108] Testimony therefore constitutes evidence that a possibility is not merely illusory or utopian. Ricoeur writes: "Only testimony that is singular in each instance confers the sanction of reality on ideas, ideals, and ways of being that the symbol depicts to us and which we uncover as our ownmost possibilities."[109] Ricoeur claims that a philosophy which allows for "testimony" is willing to contemplate not merely the idea, but also the experience, of the absolute. Far from denigrating historical contingency, a philosophy that takes testimony seriously is one that is willing to consider that a moment of history may be invested with an absolute character:

The term testimony should be applied to words, works, actions, and to lives which attest to an intention, an inspiration, an idea at the heart of experience and history which nonetheless transcend experience and history.[110]

Does "testimony" enable Ricoeur to preserve the balance between freedom and nature, fiction and history, possibility and actuality, invention and discovery, ideal and real? Does testimony, by confessing what was previously an ideal possibility to be actual, allow Ricoeur to discern what humanity may truly hope from what belongs to hope's pathology? These are no idle queries. Lewis Mudge proposes that testimony is the central concept in Ricoeur's hermeneutic philosophy. Moreover, Mudge says that Ricoeur considers the NT to be "'testimony' to the transforming power of the Resurrection."[111] In other words, testimony to actual transformation gives historical substance to the possibilities or ideas displayed in the text which would otherwise remain abstract and mute.

Ricoeur wishes to "make room" in his philosophy for the idea that something of "absolute" significance has entered history. Surely this desire to give ultimate significance to contingent events belies our criticism that he privileges fiction and the imagination over the concrete events of history? Significantly enough, Ricoeur notes that testimony to the absolute cannot take place within Kantian limits. Kant's critical philosophy inclines us "to look only for examples or symbols, not for testimonies, understood as accounts of an experience of the absolute."[112] As Paul Helm points out, Kant considered testimony to be a form of knowledge, not faith.[113] The absolute was for Kant beyond the limits of reason and experience. Here then we find Ricoeur departing from Kant in two important respects: first, Ricoeur believes that the absolute can be experienced. Second, this experience cannot be subsumed under concepts. As we have seen, Ricoeur believes that poetic language may indeed articulate what is beyond the scope of conceptual understanding. The symbol gives rise to, but ultimately eludes, conceptualization.[114]

As we have seen, the resurrection story is testimony to a freedom in the light of hope. But what exactly does Ricoeur mean by testimony? It is not primarily the eyewitness testimony to the "materiality" of the passion-resurrection-ascension narrative of Luke-Acts. Indeed, this sense of testimony suffers from a naive literalism. This testimony to literal events is not what interests Ricoeur; we do not gain true self-understanding by studying objects in the world. Nor do we gain self-understanding by accepting the subject's pretension to be the source of its own meaning and existence.[115] Ricoeur is not interested in prideful self-testimony either. Instead, Ricoeur links the idea of testimony to what he has elsewhere called the second Copernican revolution – the admission that the foundation of human existence and its meaning transcends the self as well as the realm of objects.[116] Testimony is thus the acknowledgement that the ultimate source of one's existence and its meaning has been encountered in signs which the absolute "in its generosity has allowed to appear."[117]

And yet when Ricoeur deals with the biblical texts he makes a special effort to preserve the ordinary sense of testimony together with the notion of historical reference. Testimony has a quasi-empirical meaning: though it is not the perception itself, it is the narration of a perception. Consequently, testimony "transfers things seen to the level of things said."[118] Ricoeur is quick to insist that both the Old and New Testaments preserve this quasi-empirical sense:

Where a "history" of liberation can be related, a prophetic "meaning" can be not only confessed but attested. It is not possible to testify *for* a meaning without testifying *that* something has happened which signifies this meaning.[119]

Indeed, the tension between a narration of things seen and a confession of faith is constitutive of the tension that inheres in biblical testimony, a tension best seen in the accounts of the passion and resurrection: "The confession that Jesus is the Christ constitutes testimony par excellence."[120] Noting that the Fourth Gospel inclines more to the side of confession and Luke to that of perception, Ricoeur observes that it is necessary to preserve the tension: "Testimony-confession cannot be separated from testimony-narration without the risk of turning towards gnosticism."[121]

Not only texts, then, but events also find a place in Ricoeur's hermeneutic philosophy. Self-understanding may be tied to certain events as well as texts. Faith – the Christian's self-understanding – is for Ricoeur bound to certain "foundation" events in the life of Jesus:

> The task of understanding ourselves through them is the task of transforming the accidental into our destiny. The event is our master. Each of our separate existences here are like those communities we belong to – we are absolutely dependent on certain founding events.[122]

Self-understanding is therefore to be found in front of texts as well as certain events: in both instances, text and event, we are constituted by something outside ourselves.

As with the event of speaking, however, so it is with the historical event: the event fades away but the meaning endures. It is because we do not have direct access to the event that we need to examine testimony critically. The conflict of interpretations pertains not only to texts, but also to events. In the case of events, there are two problems: whether an event truly occurred and what it means. Testimony may be misleading on both counts, as Ricoeur is well aware: "We must always decide between the false witness and the truthful one, for there is no manifestation of the absolute without the threat of false testimony."[123] It is therefore no accident for Ricoeur that the theme of trial is one of the major marks of the prophetic testimony in the Old Testament, not to mention the trial scene in the story of Jesus.

How does one go about determining the truth of testimony according to Ricoeur? Not by relying on historical criticism to find out "what actually happened," for no amount of empirical research will discover the transcendent. Ricoeur turns instead to existential verification. Ricoeur speaks of a "criteriology of the divine" that seeks to discover whether a testimony to having experienced the absolute is authentic. The question that apparently demarcates true from false testimony is this: does this testimony not only express but occasion new experiences of the absolute? Confronted with true testimony to the absolute, we too confess, "Yes, here is the source of my being and its meaning." In the face of testimony to the absolute, we relinquish our own paltry attempts to justify or constitute our existence and recognize or discover that our existence is illumined and transformed by the testimony.

The best "proof" of testimony is often the life of the witness. When he dies for the sake of his testimony, the witness becomes a martyr. The "true" witness is more than an exact narrator. The true witness must be capable of suffering and dying for the sake of testimony.[124] Ricoeur finds these ordinary connotations of testimony intensified in the Gospel narratives. The Passion of Jesus becomes for Ricoeur the paradigm for every witness: testifying to the truth entails suffering. To his credit, Ricoeur is able to appropriate even this biblical idea into the very fabric of his hermeneutic philosophy. The biblical theme of dying to self becomes in Ricoeur's philosophy the idea of the subject's abandoning all pretensions to justify and give meaning to his own existence. Ricoeur's hermeneutic philosophy internalizes Jesus' maxim: whoever would save his life must first lose it. With this thought, we approach the very core of Ricoeur's thought about human beings, texts and interpretation. Transposed into a Ricoeurrian framework, Jesus' maxim may be paraphrased as follows: whoever would posit himself as a self-constituting subject will never achieve authentic human existence.[125]

Though Ricoeur speaks of testimony as conferring the sanction of reality on ideas, it is my belief that testimony ultimately belongs more with poetry than with historical prose. What began as an attempt to "save the historical" eventually resembles the phenomena of aesthetic recognition that so dominate the theologies of Paul Tillich and David Tracy. Poetic language creates new worlds, and testimony is the discourse in which the self implicates itself in these new worlds. Ricoeur is clear about this association, for he avers that testimony is the "most appropriate concept for making us understand what a thinking subject formed by and conforming to poetic discourse might be."[126] Accordingly, we see that testimony links the two central foci of Ricoeur's hermeneutic philosophy: the interpretation of texts and self-understanding. Despite Ricoeur's nod to the quasi-empirical sense of testimony, the test of testimony is not empirical but rather that of existential recognition: does testimony challenge the hearer's self-understanding to the point of dispossession? The event that matters to Ricoeur is the event of self-understanding. That is, the decisive event is not the one narrated in the text, but the one occasioned in the reader. It is this event that is historically contingent, dependent on the reader's imaginative appropriation of a poetic word.

By "testimony," then, Ricoeur is referring to the subject's experience of the "absolute" and to the subsequent expression of this experience. Again, the experience is absolute because it results in the subject's abandoning all attempts to master his existence and its meaning. Ricoeur rejects Descartes' suggestion that we posit ourselves: "I think, therefore I am." Ricoeur believes that this mentality creates a division between the knowing subject and known object and ultimately alienates us from the world we live in. As we have seen, it is the dream of the romantic to unite what science has torn asunder. Whereas the scientist seeks to dominate and exploit a hostile or indifferent nature, the poet seeks to let the world show itself to be an hospitable dwelling place. Testimony is a response to just such a poetic vision.

We need to return to Ricoeur's earliest work if we are fully to understand the critical role that testimony plays in his later thought. The figures of Jean Nabert and Gabriel Marcel provided Ricoeur with the initial direction of his hermeneutic philosophy, namely, by showing that philosophy may legitimately examine experiences of hope, love and meaning to discover the nature of human being. These "Christian existentialists" were responding to the atheistic existentialism of Sartre and others who took as their chief clue to human existence experiences such as dread and alienation. Ricoeur's tacit conversation partner in his early works is Sartre, and he is especially keen to refute Sartre's notion of freedom as nothingness and of human being as a "useless passion."

Ricoeur firmly believes that the passion to be is more basic than dread. He made this point against Sartre, and in *Time and Narrative* he makes it against Heidegger. Heidegger privileges the experience of being-towards-death, and through this filter the rest of philosophy assumes a fatalistic hue. Ricoeur, on the other hand, takes the experience and expression of human hope as his touchstone that guides him through the labyrinthine mystery of human being. Testimony to the absolute is nothing other than a recognition of what Ricoeur calls "originary affirmation," "the intense passion for existence which anguish puts into question ..."[127] Whenever human existence is threatened, we discover a more basic or "originary" will to live. What we discover even in the experience of anguish is a more primordial passion to be, to be "in spite of" the sundry threats – suffering, meaninglessness, death – to our existence. Ricoeur believes that this feeling of hope, of hope "in spite of" and "how much more," is the decisive clue to the true nature of human being. This hope, however, is only an idea until it is attested in reality. It is experience of the absolute that enables a person to affirm the sense of existence in spite of the nonsense. Testimony is an expression of this hope in meaningfulness "in spite of." Who and what I fundamentally am can only be seen through my testimony, namely, the words and deeds I leave behind that witness to my vision of the world.[128]

It should now be apparent that what Ricoeur means by testimony is far removed from the testimony with which historians work. Testimony to "the deeds of man in the past" belongs to the first naiveté that looks to the literal sense and to empirical evidence. But Ricoeur is interested in matters involving consciousness and self-understanding, matters that pertain to the second naiveté and involve existential verification. What Ricoeur calls historical testimony perhaps finds its closest correlate in Tracy's notion of the classic. The classics are expressions of an experience with something absolute; as such, they constitute permanent challenges to one's home-made self-understanding. Moreover, one does not verify artistic classics by historical research: we declare an artwork to be true when its vision compels us to acknowledge and affirm that life is indeed "like that." Though Ricoeur claims to invest the historical moment with absolute significance, in fact the "literal" or actual event is not as important to him as its meaning and its effect on consciousness. As in art, so too with biblical narrative the "truth" of the text may be had apart from the events it narrates actually having happened. Testimony speaks not of the literal but the spiritual event of recognition. We recognize essential truths through contingent testimonies. It is not the truths that are contingent, but the testimonies. Accordingly, "testimony" in Ricoeur's thought more properly relates to the reader's historicity (the manner of his being-in-the-world) than to "the deeds of men in the past."

Where does this leave us with regard to Ricoeur's construal of the New Testament as "testimony" to the power of the resurrection? Does Ricoeur follow Bultmann's lead and say that the Easter event is about the birth of the disciples' faith? Is the resurrection testimony of Luke-Acts qualitatively different from other artistic expressions of the absolute? I have already mentioned James Barr's suggestion that biblical authority need not be surrendered even if the accounts are found to be historically inaccurate (guilty of a first naiveté); it is well known that fictional literature can be true to human experience and change people's lives. Does the significance of the story of Jesus' resurrection – dubbed by Ricoeur "that great poem of existence" – similarly derive from its artistic power?

Ricoeur treats the meaning aspect of the resurrection at greater length than its event aspect. On this view, the Gospel narratives are "true" not because they correspond to historical acts, but because they illustrate something essential in the human condition. The story of Jesus itself thus becomes a parable of how genuine human existence is attained. It is difficult to see why the historical events actually having happened should matter to Ricoeur. After all, what does the story's actually having happened add to its essential meaning? History continues to be an important factor in Ricoeur's hermeneutic philosophy primarily because meanings must be concretely experienced and expressed. The actual

life and death of Jesus does not inaugurate something new in the human
condition, but rather illustrates and expresses what is already there,
namely, the possibility of joyfully assenting to the ultimate meaningfulness of human existence, or, in short, the possibility of love.

Like Bultmann, however, Ricoeur is unwilling to part with the story
of Jesus. In some way, these narratives are indispensable – but how?
Ricoeur's answer is consistent with the basic premise of his hermeneutic
philosophy. Human existence – the scope of our possibilities – is
largely shaped by the texts that bear witness to this existence. If there
were no texts to project possible worlds, hope would not be possible.
The Gospels are texts that open our imaginations to the possibility that
God loves the world in spite of evil, and to the possibility that God's
love is ultimately greater than any evil. Without this story, this precious
thought would elude us. While the possibility of God's love may in fact
be universal, we need the contingency and particularity of the poetic
and proclaimed word in order to apprehend it. Without the biblical
narratives, the feeling of absolute dependence on a power greater than
ourselves would never be evoked. The passion for the possible and the
self-understanding of faith rely on a prior poetic word.

Ricoeur accounts for the priority of the word or testimony over self-
understanding by drawing another comparison to Kant's *Critique of
Judgment*. Just as for Kant the creative imagination "presents" certain
Ideas of Reason for which we have no concept, so too historical
testimony is a presentation of an idea, "the idea of a letting go wherein
we affirm an order exempt from that servitude from which finite
existence cannot deliver itself."[129] The relation between the Kantian
Idea and its aesthetic presentation thus parallels the relation between
originary affirmation and its "historical" presentation in testimonies.
In both cases – aesthetic imagination and historical testimony – we
are faced with poetic language whose meaning is inexhaustible, neither
within nor without the limits of reason alone, but on the boundary line.
Ricoeur's own comparison between historical testimony and aesthetic
ideas seems to confirm our hypothesis that what is significant about
testimony is its "spiritual" meaning. The sheer contingency of the
historical event remains a philosophical embarrassment for Ricoeur.

In observing that this is not the testimony of historians I am doing
nothing other than what Ricoeur himself demands: pursuing a transcendental inquiry into the imagination of hope that seeks the conditions
which make hope possible. Ricoeur admits that he is not sure of the
connection between the ontological feeling expressed in the world of
textual testimony and the historical events associated with the testimony

and depicted in the narrative. Ricoeur also acknowledges the problem this poses for christology:

> Have we then to say, about the Resurrection, that something happened, but that we have only the trace of the event in testimonies, which are already interpretations? ... But to give to such elusive events the equally elusive status of the Kantian *Ding an sich* is a price that nobody wants to pay after Fichte's and Hegel's critique of the *Ding an sich*.[130]

As we have seen, however, Ricoeur is unwilling to view the resurrection as a "literal" event in the sense that certain historical happenings serve as its truth conditions, even if we are unable to specify what they are. The elusive quality of an event that is inaccessible both to empirical examination as well as conceptual understanding is, perhaps, the price Ricoeur must pay in order to be "called again."

Though Ricoeur clearly wishes to maintain the "realism" of the event of history over against the "idealism" of the word-event in theology, in practice he reads historical narratives for the sake of the human values they communicate. For Ricoeur, resurrection testimony is not the proclamation of an event that opens up new possibilities but the manifestation, experience and expression of an essential, though forgotten, possibility. The grace of the imagination is conveyed through the sacrament of the word. I have argued that there must be two conditions for the Christian possibility: the historical deed and the poetic word. Something new must have happened for something new to be said. The logic of the biblical narrative points to the resurrection of Jesus Christ as this new epoch-making event, an event which in turn proves to be the necessary condition for the coming of the Spirit. The Spirit, I have claimed, is the third condition for the possibility of new life insofar as the Spirit – not the imagination – is the power that appropriates the kerygma.[131]

I offer these comments as correctives rather than fatal criticisms, not against Ricoeur but rather for him and for the sake of that delicate vision between freedom and nature, fiction and history, possibility and actuality, that is at the heart of his thinking about human being and poetic language. In light of Ricoeur's most recent work on metaphor and narrative, we must conclude that Ricoeur's "graft" of historical contingency into his hermeneutic philosophy ultimately does not take. The contingent event does not fit nicely into a framework where Creation and Eschatology are virtually synonymous, each referring to possibilities that have always-already been there and may be there again. The unsubstitutable life and particular fate of the historical Jesus remains something of a scandal even in a philosophy that recognizes the limits of reason and listens to the word.

Notes

1 "Récit," 19.
2 As Pregeant puts it: is the NT's deepest intention "served or distorted by understanding it as a cipher for a particular vision of the human possibility before God, rather than as an assertion regarding an exclusive and once-for-all act of God on behalf of human salvation" (Pregeant, *Christology Beyond Dogma*, 48).
3 Jürgen Habermas, "Ernst Bloch – a Marxist Romantic," *Salmagundi* 10 (1970), 311–25. Cf. Tracy's discussion of Bloch in his *Blessed Rage for Order*, 246.
4 See *SE*, 306–46.
5 I earlier argued that it was not entirely clear just how Ricoeur moves from sense to reference (chapter 5, 105–8). Once one abandons the literal sense, how can one know just which value or possible way of being-in-the-world is being projected? Hayden White's comment that Ricoeur allegorizes narrative is not, therefore, without some warrant. The line of questioning I am now pursuing pertains to the "ground" of these (allegorical) references to human values and possibilities, and my problem is twofold: first, how can reference to human possibilities be anything but arbitrary if the literal sense provides no check on the creative imagination, and second, if these values and possibilities are creations of the imagination, how can we determine which may genuinely be appropriated in real life?
6 Luke 4:18–19.
7 Edward Schillebeeckx, *Jesus: An Experiment in Christology* (London, Collins, 1979), 611.
8 Wolfhart Pannenberg, *Jesus: God and Man*, 2nd edn (Philadelphia, Westminster, 1977), 83.
9 Bultmann, "NT and Mythology," 27.
10 Bultmann, *NT Theology* I, 331.
11 Bultmann, "NT and Mythology," 42.
12 Process theologians such as Schubert Ogden and John Cobb also go beyond Bultmann in arguing that Jesus made a new structure of existence possible. Drawing upon Whitehead's work, these thinkers argue that Jesus' life and death was the occasion of a change in the human situation, a new form of human subjectivity or spiritual existence (see John B. Cobb, Jr. and David Ray Griffin, *Process Theology: An Introductory Exposition* [Philadelphia, Westminster, 1976], ch. 5 "Human Existence"). At the same time, the way these thinkers relate Jesus to Christ, the power of creative transformation, remains tenuous.

13 We shall try to answer this question later in the chapter when we discuss the phenomenon of human evil.

14 "Why should we not consider the Bible as a literary work of supreme and classic quality, which influences and patterns our lives through the stories it tells and the images it uses, independently of the question whether the entities mentioned in the Bible have any objective existence" (*The Bible in the Modern World* [London, SCM, 1973], 55). Barr also suggests that we understand biblical inspiration along poetic lines: the Bible is inspired not because it relates accurate information of universal significance, but rather because of its sublimity and power.

15 "Jaspers," 640.

16 *PPR*, 237.

17 *EBI*, 103.

18 See chapter 7, p. 151 above.

19 See Kelsey's account of Tillich's expressionist theology in *The Uses of Scripture*, 64–74, esp. 69.

20 David Kelsey, *The Fabric of Paul Tillich's Theology* (New Haven, Yale University Press, 1967), 127–28.

21 "The picture's religiously important content now turns out to be the power which can end men's existential quests. But just how is the fact that the picture can mediate power related to the peculiar structure it has? Tillich does not explain that" (Kelsey, *The Uses of Scripture*, 73).

22 Kelsey, *The Uses of Scripture*, 74.

23 Kelsey, *The Fabric of Paul Tillich's Theology*, 196.

24 "PhilHerm," 26.

25 *PPR*, 238.

26 *EBI*, 104.

27 John Blackwell, in his *The Passion as Story* (Philadelphia, Fortress, 1986) makes a similar point. Speaking of literary patterns in Mark's Gospel, Blackwell suggests that the story captures the imagination: "It speaks to the situation in which we find ourselves. It enables the listener to hear and understand things he or she has not heard before. It enables one to see and understand the human condition in a way that, until the hearing of the story, was not possible. Furthermore, it enables the human being to see and understand ways in which the human condition can be transformed" (92).

28 Cf. Tillich's *Biblical Religion and the Search for Ultimate Reality* (University of Chicago Press, 1955).

29 "It is the task of theology to coordinate the experience articulated by the Biblical text with human experience at large and as a whole" ("BibHerm," 130).

30 *PPR*, 231.

31 Ibid., 237.

32 See Gustaf Aulén, *Christus Victor: An Historical Study of the Three Main Types of the Idea of the Atonement* (New York, Macmillan, 1969), ch. 8 "The Three

Types.'' Along with its anthropocentric emphasis, the subjective type according to Aulén also tends to minimize the aspect of God's justice as well as the reality of sin.

33 David Tracy, *Blessed Rage for Order: The New Pluralism in Theology* (New York, Seabury, 1975), 204.

34 Ibid., 214.

35 Tracy states that ''religious language is basically re-presentative as making present anew, through symbolic expression, a human reality ... which somehow had become threatened or forgotten'' (*Blessed Rage for Order*, 215).

36 Ibid., 119.

37 ''Manifestation,'' 74.

38 Again, the Reformers provide a necessary corrective. Sacraments – even verbal or literary ones – ultimately depend for their efficacy on the working of the Holy Spirit. In Ricoeur's thought, the disclosure and appropriation of salvific possibilities through texts appears to be *ex opere operato*.

39 Barth, *CD* I, 1, 326.

40 Ibid., 327.

41 Ibid., 328. Barth's verdict on modern liberal theology's handling of biblical narrative is equally blunt: ''the philosophy of religion from the Enlightenment, from Lessing by way of Kant and Herder to Fichte and Hegel, with its intolerable distinction between the eternal content and the historical 'vehicle,' can only be described as the nadir of the modern misunderstanding of the Bible'' (*CD* I, 1, 329).

42 See, for instance, *HHS*, 191.

43 *HHS*, 295.

44 This is especially the case with the narrative of the fall. Such a reading of the fall narrative is not innocent, for as I hope to show in the next section, Ricoeur's interpretation of the fall narrative affects in a decisive manner his interpretation of the Gospels.

45 *IT*, 59.

46 See the preceding chapter.

47 For Ricoeur's careful distinctions between symbol and metaphor, see his *IT*, ch. 3.

48 ''PhilHerm,'' 33.

49 ''Hope,'' 68.

50 Ibid.

51 Cf. the whole flow of the argument in *FN*.

52 *FN*, 346. Ricoeur defines consent as the adoption of necessity.

53 Ricoeur contrasts Heidegger's quasi-Stoic consent to existence with Christian consent (cf. *FN*, 471–80; *TN* III, 63–8). These differing types of consent appear to be functions of contrasting myths. Heidegger consents to a vision of the world informed by the myth of the eternal return.

54 See the conclusion of *FN* ''An Only Human Freedom.''

55 *SE*, 306.

56 See Ricoeur's "'Original Sin': A Study in Meaning" in *CI*.
57 *SE*, 321.
58 Ibid., 324.
59 Ibid., 325.
60 Ibid., 235 – 6. Ricoeur is uncharacteristically harsh in his judgment of the literal interpretation of the Adam story: "The harm that has been done to souls, during the centuries of Christianity, first by the literal interpretation of the story of Adam, and then by the confusion of this myth, treated as history, with later speculations, principally Augustinian, about original sin, will never adequately be told" (239).
61 *CI*, 236.
62 "Hope," 58.
63 Ibid.
64 Ibid., 59.
65 Ricoeur's admiration for Moltmann's *Theology of Hope* is particularly evident in his "Freedom in the Light of Hope" (*CI*, 402 – 24).
66 *CI*, 409.
67 Ibid., 410.
68 Ibid., 448.
69 *SE*, 156.
70 *CI*, 454.
71 "The self characterized by self-sameness may then be said to be refigured by the reflective application of such narrative configurations" (*TN* III, 246).
72 *TN* III, 247.
73 *HT*, 4.
74 Nicene Creed.
75 *HHS*, 191.
76 "The link between appropriation and revelation is, in my view, the cornerstone of a hermeneutics which seeks both to overcome the failure of historicism and to remain faithful to the original intention of Schleiermacher's hermeneutics. To understand an author better than he understood himself is to unfold the revelatory power implicit in his discourse, beyond the limited horizon of his own existential situation" (*HHS*, 191).
77 Ricoeur discusses the objection that appropriation puts the meaning under the power of the interpreting subject in *IT*, 94.
78 Tracy contrasts his "inclusivist" christology with the "exclusivism" of fundamentalist theologies as well as the theology of Karl Barth. For the exclusivist, only God's revelation in Jesus Christ yields a proper human self-understanding. For the inclusivist, on the other hand, the Christian revelation is disclosive and transformative of self-understanding, but so are the revelations of other religious traditions (*Blessed Rage for Order*, 206). In his later work, *The Analogical Imagination*, Tracy goes further and suggests that all "classics," religious and secular, disclose authentic human possibilities.
79 *IT*, 94 – 5.

80 "PhilRel," 84–5.

81 Van den Hengel agrees that the subject's coming to authentic self-understanding is not a "work" but a gift given to the interpreting subject by the poetic word. Van den Hengel then goes on to suggest that Ricoeur may rightly be called a philosopher of justification by faith (*The Home of Meaning*, 256–9).

82 Mary Rose Barral, "Ricoeur: The Resurrection as Hope and Freedom," *Philosophy Today* 29 (1985).

83 Klemm, *The Hermeneutical Theory of Paul Ricoeur*, 128.

84 See his *Theology of Hope*, 212.

85 Bultmann, *Theology of the NT* I, 336.

86 Ibid., 335.

87 David Lull, *The Spirit in Galatia: Paul's Interpretation of PNEUMA as Divine Power* (Chico, CA, Scholars Press, 1980), 12.

88 Ibid., 197.

89 I shall not, however, adopt the underlying process metaphysics that shapes Lull's work.

90 B. H. Streeter calls Luke "a consummate literary artist" in his *The Four Gospels* (London, Macmillan, 1924), 548. The literary features of Luke-Acts are the object of special study in Charles H. Talbert, *Literary Patterns, Theological Themes, and the Genre of Luke-Acts* (Missoula, Montana, SBL and Scholars Press, 1974) and Robert C. Tannehill, *The Narrative Unity of Luke-Acts: A Literary Interpretation* (Philadelphia, Fortress, 1986). See also Robert J. Karris, *Luke: Artist and Theologian; Luke's Passion Account as Literature* (New York, Paulist, 1985).

91 Tannehill, *Narrative Unity*, 286.

92 Tannehill here follows the suggestion of Richard J. Dillon, *From Eye-Witnesses to Ministers of the Word: Tradition and Composition in Luke 24* (Rome, Biblical Institute Press, 1982), 139.

93 Tannehill, *Narrative Unity*, 287.

94 Ibid., 288.

95 Ibid., 285 n. 15.

96 Talbert, *Literary Patterns*, ch. 8. Interestingly enough, Talbert acknowledges an important discontinuity between Luke-Acts and the ancient biographies of philosophers, namely, "the strong Lucan accent on the gift and guidance of the Holy Spirit" (132). Talbert is strangely silent, however, when it comes to discussing the role of the Spirit in the narrative of Luke-Acts.

97 Talbert observes (114–15) that Jesus' going to Jerusalem to be "received up" (Luke 9:51) is at the same time the first stage of his going to heaven (Acts 1:10–11).

98 Ibid., 115.

99 See Talbert, *Literary Patterns*, 113.

100 "Since no one argues a case where there is no challenge, the strong emphasis on the materiality of the passion-resurrection-ascension and the

attempt to guarantee such by the presence of eyewitnesses must surely point
to a problem which the Evangelist was facing'' (114). For more on Luke's
purpose, see Charles H. Talbert, *Luke and the Gnostics* (Nashville, Abingdon,
1966).

101 This is not to say that it is possible exactly to describe just what happened
in Jesus' resurrection. But it is to say that, though we may be able to speak
of the resurrection only metaphorically (i.e., coming to life again), we can
still refer to something that happened. Reference to the past need not always
be couched in descriptive language.

102 Luke-Acts, because of its concern to show the universal benefit of Jesus'
work, also helps us respond to the scandal of historical particularity. Luke
inscribes the story of Jesus into the larger history of the nation Israel and,
if I may say so, universal history: Jesus fulfills the divine promise to
Abraham to make his seed a blessing to all nations. The risen Christ gives
a commission to his disciples to preach the forgiveness of sins to all nations
in the power of the Spirit (Luke 24:46-9; Acts 1:8). Indeed, the universal
benefit of Jesus' passion-resurrection-ascension is perhaps the central theme
of Acts, detailing as it does the enlargement of the boundaries of the
covenant as Gentiles too receive the Spirit. Perhaps this is also the reason
for another characteristic feature of Luke's Gospel, namely, his special
concern with the underprivileged of his day – the poor, the outcast,
women.

103 Russell Pregeant, *Christology Beyond Dogma: Matthew's Christ in Process
Hermeneutic* (Philadelphia, Fortress, 1987), 127.

104 A full exploration of the meaning of Christian freedom is not possible in
this context. Is it the freedom from the curse of the law and the penalty
of sin that comes with justification by faith? Is it freedom from the power
and dominion of sin in one's life? For our purposes, we will remain within
the limits of Ricoeur's understanding of freedom: the freedom to consent
to life, to resist despair, to hope. My argument is that some kind of historical
event is necessary in order to make even this freedom a genuine possibility.

105 *SE*, 18.

106 See chapter 4, 67-73 above.

107 *EBI*, 109.

108 Ibid., 151.

109 Ibid., 11.

110 Ibid., 119-20.

111 Mudge, ''Introduction'' to Ricoeur's *EBI*, 2.

112 Ibid., 111.

113 Helm correctly observes that, for Kant, religious belief cannot include
assent to testimony, for testimony implies that *someone* experienced what
testimony refers to, namely, the absolute. Testimony thus depends on
knowledge rather than practical reason. Helm writes: ''It is the argument
that underlies Kant's distinction between historical-ecclesiastical faith and

pure religious faith in *Religion Within the Limits of Reason Alone*. So religious faith is not a species of belief on testimony, for testimony is distinguishable from knowledge only by contingent factors. It could be knowledge. But faith could not be knowledge. Hence faith cannot be, or include, belief as assent to testimony'' (*The Varieties of Belief* [London, George Allen & Unwin, 1973], 120).

114 As I have tried to demonstrate, the kind of ontology that Ricoeur feels best approximates poetic language is that of Heidegger. Unlike Heidegger, however, Ricoeur preserves the distinction between poetic and philosophical or speculative discourse.

115 This false confidence in the subject's ability to constitute itself is for Ricoeur "the most formidable obstacle to the idea of revelation" (*EBI*, 109).

116 "Recourse to testimony occurs in a philosophy of reflection at the moment when such a philosophy renounces the pretensions of consciousness to constitute itself" (*EBI*, 110).

117 *EBI*, 111.

118 Ibid., 123.

119 Ibid., 133.

120 Ibid., 134.

121 Ibid., 139.

122 Ibid., 114.

123 Ibid., 112.

124 Of course, sincerity in belief is not a hard and fast criterion of truth. Terrorists, fanatics and lunatics are often totally engaged in their beliefs and values as well.

125 Testimony is essential for Ricoeur, for there is no other way that the subject can give up its attempts to constitute its own existence and meaning: "reflection cannot produce this renouncing of the sovereign consciousness out of itself. It may only do so by confessing its total dependence on the historical manifestations of the divine" (*EBI*, 115).

126 Ibid., 105.

127 *HT*, 288.

128 We may recall that for Ricoeur, "ethics" is not the science of morality but rather the process of our desire and effort to be. Our only access to the meaning of human existence is through the signs (deeds and words) that attest to it. Ethics thus deals with discovering the meaning of our desire and effort to be through an interpretation of what we say and do.

129 *EBI*, 116.

130 Ibid., 45.

131 "He saved us through the washing of rebirth and renewal by the Holy Spirit, whom he poured out on us generously through Jesus Christ our Savior, so that, having been justified by his grace, we might become heirs having the hope of eternal life" (Tit. 3:5 – 7).

CONCLUSION

Poetry is more philosophical than history ...

Aristotle, *Poetics*

10

The Bible and one philosopher

What may we conclude about the prospects for a theology and christology informed by Ricoeur's thought? To what extent does his narrative theory, struggling to overcome the old distinction between history and fiction, yield new resources for dealing with the ruinous dichotomy between the Jesus of history and the Christ of faith? The question about the meaning of the Gospel narratives is indeed a crucial one, but it is important to note that Ricoeur's ties to the Bible are much more profound. While it is true that many followers of Ricoeur limit themselves to applying various aspects of his interpretation theory to biblical texts, Ricoeur's significance for theology is much broader than his having supplied exegetes with methods for interpreting symbols, metaphors and narratives. For the Christian theologian, Ricoeur's most intriguing mediation, even more than his treatment of the history – fiction question, may well be the larger one between philosophy and the Bible.

Ricoeur's is an essentially "believing" philosophy, that is, a philosophy that depends on and trusts in words that precede it. Ricoeur's dictum that philosophy does not begin empty-handed is more than a philosophical recognition of Kantian limits. Indeed, the image of the philosopher with cupped hands – or better, open ears – is especially appropriate for describing the humble spirit of Ricoeur's philosophy that only begins with a revelation from poetic texts. With his namesake the apostle Paul, Ricoeur asks the would-be philosopher, what do you have that you did not receive? One's very selfhood is not an autonomous construction but rather a gift of language and literature. The task of the philosopher is to think what has already been given in speech. The meaning of human being, the scope of what is humanly possible, has already been expressed in a pre-reflective manner. Such are the contours of Ricoeur's second Copernican revolution, a revolution that seeks to disenfranchise the autonomous knowing subject and to commend to the philosopher an attitude of second naiveté.

Conceived in this light, Ricoeur's hermeneutic philosophy is uniquely poised to justify, and profit from, biblical exegesis. By insisting that self-understanding is always a correlate of textual exegesis, Ricoeur has made space once more for biblical exegesis.[1] Thanks to Ricoeur's recovery of the poetic dimension of texts and especially narratives, we may indeed be called, challenged and constituted by the Gospel – and this in spite of historical criticism's suspicion of the naive or literal sense of the text. By recovering the meaning and power of poetic texts in this way, Ricoeur has not only preserved an indispensable role for the Gospels but also woven the biblical idea of revelation into the very fabric of his hermeneutic philosophy. Accordingly, his entire hermeneutic philosophy is a secular variation on a biblical theme – that faith comes by hearing the word.

It is just at this point, however, that I find Ricoeur's work somewhat puzzling. Like Wittgenstein's figure of the duck-rabbit, so Ricoeur's thought appears to vacillate: is his hermeneutic philosophy a faithful re-presentation of a view of the self, world and interpretation that is fundamentally Christian, or does his thought make of Christianity simply a particular, albeit powerful, illustration of more general principles, thus betraying its kerygmatic intent? Is Ricoeur a philosophical theologian or a theological philosopher, and in so relating philosophy and theology, does he guarantee the autonomy and integrity of each? To decide these questions it is not enough merely to apply Ricoeur's interpretation theory to the biblical texts. This has been the failing of several recent studies of Ricoeur. I have argued that fully to understand Ricoeur's hermeneutics involves relating it to his earlier (and continuing) project of philosophical anthropology.

My thesis in Part I is that Ricoeur's more recent theory of narrative interpretation is the culmination of a larger project which continues the work of Kant and Heidegger by seeking to answer the question, "what is human being?" From Heidegger, Ricoeur accepts the idea that human being is temporal in a way that other beings are not because humans are concerned and oriented towards their futures. Only human beings understand themselves in light of the possibilities that have been chosen in the past, are being contemplated at present and projected for the future (chapter 2). From Kant, Ricoeur borrows the notion of the creative imagination in order to explain how thinking can continue beyond the reach of present experience or concepts (chapter 3). That human being is temporal and capable of creatively imagining various possibilities leads Ricoeur to bring his philosophical anthropology into convergence with a hermeneutics that interprets man's expressions of the various modes of being or living in the world. Ricoeur turns to metaphor as the paradigm kind of speech that refers to the real in terms of possibilities. Because metaphor asks us to contemplate the world and ourselves in a manner that differs from present actuality, Ricoeur links metaphor's power to "refigure" the world and ourselves in the world to our being able to hope (chapter 4). Stories and histories, the two major modes of narrative discourse, share the power of metaphor to "refigure" the world by displaying different ways of being in the world and in time. By "configuring" human action into various modes of human being-in-time, stories and histories together attest to what is humanly possible (chapter 5).

Part II, which treats Ricoeur's interpretation of biblical narrative, presupposes our conclusion in Part I, namely, that Ricoeur's narrative theory is best understood in light of his fusion of the projects of Kant and Heidegger. One cannot have Ricoeur's narrative theory without the philosophical baggage that precedes and accompanies it. To what extent then does Ricoeur's narrative theory serve the theologian who seeks to be called again by the Christian kerygma? I argued that Ricoeur's narrative theory may be viewed both as foundation and corrective to Bultmann's existentialist interpretation of the NT. With Bultmann, Ricoeur interprets the Gospels' religious significance in terms of their ability to illumine and transform one's self-understanding by refiguring human existence in the light of its authentic possibility, namely, faith. But, against Bultmann, Ricoeur is not willing simply to abandon the original narrative form of the Gospel. The existential possibility by its very nature is bound to the story itself (chapter 6). The Yale school, led by Hans Frei, accuses Ricoeur of ultimately betraying the biblical narrative, or at least its "literal" sense, by making the Gospels mere instances of a revelatory phenomenon that pervades Ricoeur's general hermeneutics. The Yale theologians charge that Ricoeur, in abandoning talk of reference for refiguration, has effectively made the story of Jesus an existential allegory: the story of Jesus, like the parables, is more about common human experience than the particular figure Jesus Christ. Ricoeur's remarks about his Barthian affinities are thus seen to be somewhat misleading (chapter 7).

As narratives concerned with the meaning and "end" of history, the Gospels provide Ricoeur with a way of orienting human temporality to eternity. The time – eternity relation, usually considered to lie at the heart of christological inquiry, becomes for Ricoeur an avenue for responding to Heidegger's elegiac view of human being. The Gospels allow Ricoeur to pit a passion for the possible over against Heidegger's pathos for the possible – being-towards-death. In other words, the Gospels are important stories for Ricoeur because they display a way of being-in-time that satisfies our desire for the infinite in spite of our finitude. Our examination of Ricoeur's interpretation of the Gospels as "tales about time" confirmed our belief that Ricoeur's hermeneutic philosophy is best seen as providing a surer linguistic and literary foundation for existential theology (chapter 8). I then argued that, while Ricoeur is remarkably successful in providing a philosophical approximation for many biblical ideas (e.g., revelation, resurrection, creation, the fall, justification by faith), his hermeneutic philosophy lacks an adequate approximation for the Christian teaching about the Holy Spirit. To suggest that the work of the Holy Spirit has its approximation in the phenomenon of imaginative appropriation is, in my opinion, to miss the whole point of the Gospels, namely, that it is only thanks to a divine initiative of deed and word that the power of the possibility of resurrection freedom becomes ours (chapter 9).

If I have confronted Ricoeur's work with so many philosophers and theologians, it is only because this is always how his thought has progressed: through conflict, imaginative mediation and appropriation. Along the way, I have suggested that theologians should not be overly hasty in adopting Ricoeur's insights. I have especially tried to examine one central feature in Ricoeur's work – the passion for the possible. While granting that the story of Jesus is indeed a source – even criterion – of hope, I have argued that Ricoeur needs to be more explicit concerning the conditions for this possibility if he wishes to distinguish it from fantasies, utopias and illusions. Ricoeur's growing appreciation of the creative imagination in his work on metaphor and narrative leads him, I believe, to lose his balance while mediating some important oppositions: freedom and nature, fiction and history, invention and discovery, ideal and real, possible and actual. In his later work there is a weighted focus on the first member of these pairs. Though he strives to overcome several false dichotomies between fiction and history, in the end the Gospels achieve their theological importance in Ricoeur as works of the creative imagination. Ricoeur never denies the factuality of the Gospel accounts outright, but it is primarily the meaning of the accounts rather than their factuality that is of greatest human value.

Such a weighted focus does endanger a theological realism which contends that among the fundamental truth conditions of the Christian possibility are "the truth of propositions that might have been otherwise,"[2]

propositions more properly connected to the history rather than the story
of Jesus. I do not believe that this weakness in Ricoeur's hermeneutic
philosophy is a fatal one; indeed, there are indications that Ricoeur's
performance of his mediations does not live up to his prescriptions. It
is clear, for instance, that Ricoeur is unwilling to do away with the
realism of the resurrection event. And yet, it is also evident that his
hermeneutic philosophy as a whole is slanted in favor of "the idealism
of the word event"[3] where new forms of self-understanding arise in
front of poetic metaphors and narratives.

The poet, the historian and the believer

To measure the scope of Ricoeur's achievement, we need both to place
his hermeneutics in the context of his philosophy, and then to go on and
try and place the whole in the context of modern theology. It is important
to see Ricoeur's work in light of the challenges to which it responds.
It is consistent with the humility of Ricoeur's philosophy that he
addresses particular problems and situations rather than trying to
formulate an abstract and universal system. Chief among the problems
that Ricoeur addresses is the loss of meaning in certain texts and of
meaningfulness in the human condition: "We must recognize the fact
that philosophy at the present time is entirely at an impasse concerning
the problem of the origin of values."[4] Two centuries of biblical and
historical criticism have in large part silenced the Scriptures, even in
the Church. Outside the Church, atheist existentialism proclaimed the
loss of meaning in the world. Sartre, while acknowledging the mystery
of human freedom, declared that bereft of any meaningful context
(creation), man was a "useless passion." Ricoeur's hermeneutic
philosophy is aimed at recovering meaning in texts and the meaningfulness of human life, and in showing that the two tasks are at root one.
It is thanks to an abundance of meaning in poetic texts, meaning that
exceeds our actual situation, that we are able to have a passion for the
possible, and to associate the possible with hope rather than despair.

Ricoeur's rediscovery and philosophical rehabilitation of the imagination is no small contribution. I believe that Ricoeur's assessment of
the human predicament in our time is essentially correct. In a
technological age oriented towards material progress and domination
over nature, it is indeed difficult to perceive the "place" of human
beings. Are we objects of nature, subject to the fateful necessity of
natural laws, or are we ourselves testaments to technology, with minds
that used to be understood as "spirit" now seen as brains that are more

like glorified computers? Or are we autonomous, self-made beings that create our own meanings? This crisis in articulating the value of the human is accentuated in a culture that is increasingly illiterate.[5] The major texts that seem to be shaping the social imagination are those devised on Wall Street or in Hollywood.

Ricoeur brings an essentially romanticist response to these pressing questions concerning the nature and value of human being. We belong to a Creation that is larger than ourselves. Though it often appears that we do not fit in the world or that nature is against us, romantic poetry evokes visions of a reconciliation between humanity and nature, thereby revealing the basis of their profound unity. Since Kant, of course, knowledge of Creator and Creation is not open to us. But thanks to poetic language we may continue to think beyond the limits of reason alone. Ricoeur stands in the long line of those who seek to articulate the "Transcendence" or "Sacred" that eludes our concepts as well as our everyday experience. Ricoeur's agenda is a variation of Kant's: "I have taken away knowledge in order to make room for hope." Like another post-Kantian, Schleiermacher, Ricoeur believes that certain human feelings, such as the feeling of absolute dependence on a power that is not myself, are actually ontological clues to the meaning of human being. By attending to these feelings, and to the poetic texts that evoke and express them, Ricoeur is trying to effect a "second Copernican revolution" which would turn philosophy to Transcendence the way Kant turned philosophy to the subject. Ricoeur's goal as a philosopher is nothing less than making room for the Transcendent in the modern world.

Because philosophy begins by reflecting on linguistic and literary expressions of certain key experiences, Ricoeur turns to stories and histories. In Ricoeur's thought, both poet and historian are at the service of the believer. We need both visions and visible testimonies in order to renew our imaginations. The poet creates visions of worlds replete with meaning and possibilities; the historian discovers actual testimonies to the transforming power of these visions. We might amend another Kantian formula to say that *history without poetry is blind, but poetry without history is empty*. That is, life without an orienting vision is meaningless, but visions that have no historical visibility lack the "sanction of reality." The historian plays the role of critic with regard to poetic visions. While the poet may spin out vision after vision and so multiply meanings, the historian looks for signs that a vision or way of being in the world is true. As we have seen, this is the role that Ricoeur assigns to historical testimony. Testimony is the historical attestation that one has found a certain possibility illuminating and life-transforming.

In their respective ways, then, both poetry and history contribute to the stock of the humanly possible. Indeed, Ricoeur insists that the human passion for the possible is constituted by history and poetry together. Just as Freud and Hegel represented the archeology and teleology of the subject, so history and poetry represent the memory and hope which together constitute the unique way of being-in-time or historicity of human being. Only human beings are nourished by memory and hope.[6] Without stories and histories that remind us and encourage us towards possibilities, perhaps hidden or lost to the present, the believer would indeed be empty-handed. It is Ricoeur's contention that only by interpreting texts that project possibilities can we come to self-understanding. Ricoeur goes so far as to define the world as the referent of all the stories that he has read, known and loved. Similarly, our individual identity is a correlate of those stories and histories in which we see ourselves and our world. What we call the self is not an autonomous construction, but a "gift" of poetic language and literature.

Ricoeur's rehabilitation of the imagination is, I think, to be applauded. My world – the scope of my possibilities – indeed opens up and expands in proportion to the number of poetic texts I read. A life that has never read or appropriated the biblical narratives, for instance, is more diminished and impoverished than one which has. However, I have suggested that Ricoeur, in his zeal for the possible, has oriented his philosophy more to poetry than to history, thus overturning a balance that his own philosophy mandates. In the end, Ricoeur agrees with Aristotle that "poetry is more philosophical than history." Philosophical, perhaps – but not necessarily more theological. I have assumed throughout this study that the theologian must be concerned with actual events that have universal significance. Interestingly enough, Ricoeur seems to share this understanding of the role of the theologian. Ricoeur distinguishes philosophy from theology by saying that the theologian deals with witnesses and events rather than desires and visions.[7]

By way of evaluation of Ricoeur's project, I have questioned whether the power of the possible is in fact the poetic word. In his actual practice, Ricoeur seems to favor the poet and fictional narrative, for reasons that I have already discussed. Poetic flights of the imagination need to be tempered by the earthbound sobriety of the historian if they are to keep from degenerating into utopian fantasies.[8] I think Ricoeur would be truer to his own principles if he allowed the historian to testify to certain deeds as well as values that have universal significance for the human condition. Certainly the Gospel, with its testimony to blood and death, qualifies as a "realistic" narrative. The historical intent of the Gospels need not mean that they refer to actuality *tout court*. Ricoeur fears that descriptive language stifles the passion for the possible by confining us within the limits of the present and closes our imagination to the future. But, with Moltmann, for whom Ricoeur has a high regard, could we not regard the resurrection as God's "deed" of promise, in both senses of the word deed? The NT presents the resurrection as God's act, an act of promise. The deed is an actual event that is also the promise of a possible future. We may thus preserve the realism of the event of history as well as the importance of the poetic word that conjures up a vision of what the world may be like in light of this central event. Such a reading comes closer to achieving the balanced mediation after which Ricoeur professes to seek.

My query to Ricoeur is, ironically, the very one Ricoeur himself posed to Karl Jaspers: if all human existence is a "cipher" of transcendence, then what, if anything, is unique about the story/history of Jesus and the subsequent history of the Church? As Ricoeur phrases it so well: "One must choose between the 'encipherment' *of all things, and the Christian Incarnation.*"[9] Is Christianity only a cipher or symbol of a general phenomenon of human existence? It is evident that Ricoeur wishes to avoid this conclusion, but it is not at all obvious how he intends to avoid it by treating the resurrection as a "poem" of human existence. As I have argued, Ricoeur's hermeneutic philosophy seems to lack the capacity for appropriating the significance of contingent events – their meaning, yes, in testimonies, but even testimony cannot preserve the event.

Must we conclude that Ricoeur's project is in the end incoherent, at war with itself? How can he hold onto the indispensability of the particular events that comprise Jesus' story and at the same time find symbols and stories of hope elsewhere? I do not think such a verdict is necessary. Indeed, I have already suggested that Ricoeur's own prescriptions for mediating history and fiction and preserving the realism of the event are a sufficient cure for the occasional lapses in hermeneutic equilibrium. One way to do justice both to the particular passion of Jesus as well as to the general passion for the possible represented by poetic language is to conceive their relation along lines charted by two other thinkers – C. S. Lewis and J. R. R. Tolkien – who, in many respects, anticipated Ricoeur's rehabilitation of the imagination.[10]

I would like to focus on one particular point where I believe Lewis and Tolkien provide an alternative to the dichotomy that Jaspers' thought posed for Ricoeur – either Incarnation or the encipherment of all things. Both Lewis and Tolkien reject, as does Ricoeur, the facile distinction between factual and fictional narrative when it comes to the Gospels. For Lewis and Tolkien, the Gospel is best understood under the rubric of "myth become fact." In other words, Lewis and Tolkien have no trouble holding the mythopoeic power of the Gospels together with its historical intent. Lewis, a professional literary critic, could not regard the Gospels as myths, much less allegories. While the content dealt with matters of great myths, the humble style was far from the grand style of myth: "If ever a myth had become fact, had been incarnated, it would be just like this."[11] That the meaning of the story remains tied to the person it depicts remained for Lewis a stubborn fact: "This is not 'a religion', not 'a philosophy'. It is the summing up and actuality of them all."[12] For Lewis, it is only the fact of Jesus' incarnation-passion-resurrection that justifies and guarantees the joy he experienced through reading other myths.

Tolkien makes much the same point. In his essay "On Fairy-Stories," Tolkien too reflects on the joy that is the correlate of fairy-stories and romance. As an author of mythopoeic literature, Tolkien acknowledges his desire that the world of the text that is the product of his creative imagination be somehow derived from Reality. For Tolkien, the joy that successful fantasy evokes is not an artificial consolation for the sorrow of this world but a satisfaction and answer to the question, "Is it true?" Now for Tolkien, the Gospels contain the essence of fairy-story or romance – the eucatastrophe, a cataclysmic event with a beneficial effect. Although Ricoeur does not employ this term, I believe he employs ideas that are very like it, namely, the ideas of hope "in spite of" and "how much more." The point is that this joy or hope is in accord with reality only if the story is, in some sense of the word, historical, historically true. Tolkien eloquently makes this point:

The Christian joy, the *Gloria*, is ... pre-eminently ... high and joyous. Because this story is supreme; and it is true. Art has been verified ... Legend and History have met and fused.[13]

Word and deed are wed; Art has been verified. Because the Gospels attest to a divine initiative that has actually taken place in history and affected the human condition, all other fairy-stories that speak of a eucatastrophe ring "true." The Gospel has not abrogated but "hallowed" poetic literature. For Lewis and Tolkien, that all things are "ciphers" of transcendence works not against the story of Jesus but *because* of it. Because Jesus' history ends in resurrection, the believer may hearken to the poet's promise that all will be well.

The Bible and the philosopher

In assessing the theological significance of Ricoeur's hermeneutic philosophy, perhaps the most important conclusion we can draw is that Ricoeur is not a theologian. That is, he never crosses the limits of reason to affirm that God has indeed entered, spoken and acted in history to redeem humanity. Though it is evident that Ricoeur views himself in the vanguard of a renaissance of the sacred, he is more concerned with elaborating the condition for the possibility of revelation and redemption rather than with proclaiming their historical achievement. Ricoeur sees himself more naturally paired with the exegete rather than the theologian. Both exegete and hermeneutic philosopher share an interest in listening to the original forms of religious discourse. The theologian in Ricoeur's opinion tries to translate biblical language into another language and conceptuality – a potentially misleading exercise, as Ricoeur believes he has shown in his study of Augustine's doctrine of original sin.

Ricoeur is perhaps best viewed as an apologist for the intelligibility of the Christian kerygma. This is no little task in an age dominated by the hermeneutics of suspicion. Ricoeur's philosophy prepares the way for the reader of the biblical text to be called again, to attain not exactly hermeneutical innocence (after all, Kant expelled us from our interpretive Edens) but a second, chastened, naiveté. I have suggested that what Ricoeur has recovered, however, is the sense rather than the reference of the biblical text. Ricoeur has never been quite at ease with the notion of the reference of biblical discourse: the parables (and possibly the Gospels) are about human experience. Indeed, in his most recent work on narrative, the notion of reference is replaced by the idea of redescription. Ricoeur's philosophical approximations of the Gospel therefore remain on the hither side of theology while simultaneously "making space" for biblical notions such as Creation, justification by faith and resurrection. Ricoeur is more concerned to defend the meaningfulness of the Christian vision of the world than the factuality of the events depicted in the Bible.

Granted that Ricoeur is not himself a theologian, can we at least construe Ricoeur's philosophy as a hermeneutic handmaiden to theology? I have argued that this is indeed Ricoeur's intent, for his interpretation theory fulfills his early promise to serve as a "foundation" to Bultmann. But in so associating himself with existential theology, does Ricoeur suffer from the structural inconsistency that so plagued Bultmann? Does the fundamental "enigma" of demythologizing – the impulse to reduce the story of Jesus to an existential allegory while at the same time preserving the kerygma – appear in Ricoeur as well? For Ricoeur the narrative is indispensable because poetic language cannot receive an exhaustive conceptual paraphrase. More remains in the story than can be thought in any system. It is because the narrative is indispensable that Jesus is not simply a cipher for an existential possibility.

In my opinion, we find in Ricoeur not a structural inconsistency but a structural *ambiguity*, the ambiguity between philosophy and theology. The ambiguity stems from the fact that Ricoeur's philosophy is not autonomous but depends on the word that precedes it. Philosophy is therefore like theology because of this characteristic.[14] Complicating this ambiguity are Ricoeur's philosophical approximations of the Christian kerygma. It is the very success of his approximations that has given rise to our suspicion that Christianity is for Ricoeur only an illustration of philosophical truth. Does one need the Gospel story if the principle "only by dying to self do we live" is inscribed at the very heart of Ricoeur's philosophy? Or, on the other hand, is this idea in Ricoeur's thought because of the story of Jesus' passion and resurrection? Stated simply, what accounts for the approximation between Ricoeur's philosophy and biblical theology? There seem to be only two options: either his philosophy is from the start informed by biblical themes, in which case we would expect the Bible to have a special status in his philosophy, or his philosophy is informed by the belief that poetic language and literature in general are "salvific" in the sense that they render us more fully human, in which case the Bible is only a case in point. Does Ricoeur's philosophy try to capture and express the particular and unique Christian kerygma, or does it use the Christian kerygma to illustrate a general ontology and anthropology that is ultimately independent of Christianity?

Throughout his career as a philosopher, Ricoeur has been intrigued – perhaps even "haunted" – by the spectre of Hegel's philosophy, the exemplar of a philosophy that seeks to be systematic and all-encompassing. Ricoeur's humility, whether Christian or Kantian, keeps him from following Hegel to what could only be a premature, and thus dangerous, synthesis. We have already remarked that Hegel errs in

Ricoeur's eyes when he attempts to translate Christian symbols into philosophical concepts, thus cutting short the play of meaning that allows the Bible to challenge each new generation. But Ricoeur also acknowledges that systematic comprehensiveness is the horizon of all philosophy. He agrees with Kant that such totalization is a "practical" demand of Reason. Hegel thus represents for Ricoeur "the greatest attempt and the greatest temptation" of the philosopher. How does Ricoeur's philosophical approximation of Christianity measure up against Hegel's philosophical reduction of the Gospel?

A mediating philosophy that claims to be neither within nor without the limits of reason but on the boundary line itself is bound to be attacked from both sides. Such has always been the fate of mediators, and Ricoeur is perhaps no exception. What is Ricoeur's ultimate intent? Ironically, opinion may well be divided on this point, just as it was for Hegel. On the one hand, "left-wing" Hegelians argue that for Hegel the truth of Christian faith was merely pictorial and illustrative; the Christian religion is reduced to philosophical idealism. On the other hand, "right-wing" Hegelians took the position that Hegel tried to render Christian truth more acceptable, intelligible and rational, thus preserving the integrity and irreducibility of the Gospel.

Ricoeur would doubtless appreciate the poetic justice of his situation. He who has called our attention to the conflict of interpretations has himself become the subject of such conflict. According to Ricoeur, authorial intent is not the ultimate arbiter of meaning; this role falls to the text. On the strength of most Ricoeurrian texts, I suspect that the "left-wing" interpretation of Ricoeur will predominate. Though there are indications that Ricoeur does not want to lose the realism of the event of history, his hermeneutic philosophy privileges fiction over history in order to correct what Ricoeur perceived to be an imbalance in the discussion. The historical-critical method of reading the Bible had, in Ricoeur's opinion, to be overcome if we were to be called again by the biblical texts.

In the end, the structural ambiguity of Ricoeur's thought remains to tantalize. Left- and right-wing interpretations vacillate like Wittgenstein's duck-rabbit figure. Ricoeur's long-awaited third volume of his *Philosophy of the Will* that was to have dealt with the problem of Transcendence remains a glimmer in his eye. Though I believe the left-wing interpretation will predominate, I tend to take the right-wing view. That is, I believe that Ricoeur's deepest wish is to restore to the text its ability to speak, and to modern man his ability to hear. Can I demonstrate this to be the true view? No – I can only make a wager – and hope. But there is yet another possibility. Perhaps Ricoeur the mediator intends this structural ambiguity after all? We have seen how he appreciates the productive tension which is the essence of metaphor. Perhaps Ricoeur's work, poised dynamically between the shifting figures of theology and philosophy, is itself metaphorical, able to bring near two disciplines that for most of their recent histories have remained far apart. The very ambiguity of Ricoeur's philosophical approximation of the Gospel compels the reader to look at both philosophy and theology in a new light. But this is precisely the essence of metaphor, to project new ways of looking at ourselves and the world. What better legacy could a thinker with a passion for the possible leave behind than a philosophy that itself exercises the reader's imagination? By refiguring the very relation between theology and philosophy as well as the Bible and poetic language, Ricoeur calls us to consider the Scriptures, and ourselves, again. What we have termed the structural ambiguity in Ricoeur's thought is justified insofar as it, like symbols before it, gives rise to thought.

To sum up: Ricoeur's philosophy approximates in style and content the theological virtues of grace, hope and love.

Grace – the whole point of Ricoeur's correlation of philosophical anthropology and hermeneutics is to help us see that the meaning of life is a gift. Our self-understanding is a gift of language – in the beginning was the Word. Ricoeur insists that the subject is not its own maker but receives and recovers itself thanks to the mediation of language. Our being would be diminished to the extent that we did not have access to certain texts. For it is poetic language that opens up before us the scope of what is humanly possible. This is Ricoeur's "second Copernican revolution": we are not self-constituting but are rather constituted from without, from the Word that shapes our imaginations and therefore our existence. What do we have that we have not received? To be sure, I have argued that the theologian will want to complement Ricoeur's work. We are formed by Events as well as words, and it is important to classify the passion and resurrection of Jesus with the former as well as the latter. In both cases, however, existence and its meaning is a gift to the human subject.

Hope – throughout this volume I have concentrated on the privileged position that Ricoeur accords the phenomenon of hope. Ricoeur ministers the word to an age rife with suspicion, anxiety and despair. Without negating the validity of criticism, Ricoeur strives to restore the possibility of hope, which he equates with the passion for the possible. Metaphors, narratives and poetic language in general nourish this

ʾon by displaying visions of possible futures and possible worlds. ᴀᴜᴄᴏᴇur listens especially to stories which convey an eschatological vision of the world which portrays meaningfulness as more abundant than meaninglessness, and the passion to be as stronger than despair.

Love – Ricoeur's hermeneutic philosophy is in the style of "yes" rather than "no." It is essentially affirmative in its intent and practice. It is a philosophy marked by a passion for existence. Here is no stoic resignation to living in a hostile world, but rather a deep sense of belonging to a world that, thanks to poetry, becomes a Creation. Because there is more meaning than absurdity, we can risk loving the world and those who people it. Thanks to poetic language, values and possibilities that are perhaps buried and overshadowed in the present can be remembered, hoped and worked for. The method of Ricoeur's philosophy approximates Christian charity: he is more concerned to affirm and assimilate the work of other philosophers than to refute them. This charitable impulse, this willingness to believe that others may be "in the truth," accounts for Ricoeur's many mediations. This may account for Ricoeur's tremendous appeal: his style of "yes" caters to our longing to belong.

It is only fitting to conclude our study of Ricoeur's thought and its significance for Christian theology with yet another metaphor. The Word is Ricoeur's kingdom, and his hermeneutic philosophy is at the service of this sovereign. Ricoeur marshals all the resources of his philosophical anthropology and hermeneutics to come to the aid of this Word in a critical time. The kingdom of the Word appears weak in a deaf and unbelieving world. It is not the least of Ricoeur's service, then, that he makes space for a new hearing and appreciation of this Word. Such a hearing is vital, for humanity receives its meaning, the scope of possibilities for individual and social being, from this Word. Ricoeur does not serve his own word, but a regenerating Word, a freeing Word. However, Ricoeur is not principally a Proclaimer. His is the more humble task of "making space" for this proclamation and of rendering this proclamation intelligible by providing philosophical approximations. But I repeat, Ricoeur is not himself a Proclaimer – neither preacher nor prophet. A hermeneutic philosophy that stays within the limits of reason cannot announce the Christian possibility. Ricoeur does not proclaim the Gospel. Rather, like John the Baptist, Ricoeur serves the Gospel by baptizing our imaginations, philosophically preparing the way for the Word.

Notes

1 But not theology. In Ricoeur's opinion, theology errs if it seeks to capture the play of biblical metaphors in a conceptual system, and surpasses what the philosopher can say if what counts in the biblical narrative is its reference to God's acts in history.
2 MacKinnon, *Borderlands of Theology*, 88.
3 *EBI*, 80.
4 *CI*, 449.
5 See E. D. Hirsch's *Cultural Literacy: What Every American Needs to Know* (Boston, Houghton Mifflin, 1987) for a fuller exposition of this charge.
6 It is no accident that Ricoeur groups von Rad and Moltmann together as he had earlier grouped Freud and Hegel. Von Rad and Moltmann represent memory (tradition) and hope (promise) respectively. For Ricoeur, the biblical testimony is itself dialectically constituted by memory and hope as well.
7 *CI*, 343.
8 Of course, the historian cannot be the ultimate arbiter of what is humanly possible, for this would remove the possibility of any new way of being-in-the-world.
9 "Jaspers," 624.
10 There are a number of interesting parallels that could profitably be explored between Lewis and Ricoeur. Whereas Ricoeur is a professional philosopher/reader *cum* theologian, Lewis is a professional reader/philosopher *cum* theologian. Whereas Lewis correlates the reading of imaginative literature with the experience of joy, Ricoeur correlates it with hope – the passion for the possible. For Lewis on joy, see especially his autobiography, *Surprised by Joy*. But both thinkers believe that the experience of joy and hope respectively give thought an important clue about the meaning of human being. Like Ricoeur, Lewis puts a premium on imaginative literature, even going so far as to author a number of fantasy stories himself. Lastly, as does Ricoeur, Lewis holds a high view of metaphor's indispensable cognitive value. See especially his essay, "Bluspels and Flalansferes: A Semantic Nightmare," in *Selected Literary Essays* (Cambridge University, 1969), 251–65.
11 Lewis, *Surprised by Joy* (London, Geoffrey Bles, 1955).
12 Ibid.
13 Tolkien, "On Fairy-Stories," in C. S. Lewis (ed.), *Essays Presented to Charles Williams* (Oxford University Press, 1947), 84.
14 For more on the relation of theology and philosophy as well as their specific constitutive principles, see my "Christ and Concept: Doing Theology and the Ministry of Philosophy," in John Woodbridge and Thomas McComiskey (eds.), *Doing Theology In Today's World* (Zondervan, forthcoming).

SELECT BIBLIOGRAPHY

The bibliography is divided into three parts. The first section lists works by Ricoeur quoted in the text. References are made to the editions consulted (usually the English edition if readily available) and listed in alphabetical order. The original publication date, when different, is given in square brackets; the date is preceded by "Fr" if it indicates the original French edition. For an exhaustive bibliography of Ricoeur's writings and their original sources, see the entries under Vansina and Lapointe in the second section which lists works about Ricoeur. For an extensive bibliography of this secondary literature, see Lapointe, "Paul Ricoeur and his Critics." The final section lists other works consulted in this study.

Works by Ricoeur

BOOKS

The Conflict of Interpretations: Essays in Hermeneutics. Ed. Don Ihde. Evanston, Northwestern University Press, 1974 [Fr: 1969].

The Contribution of French Historiography to the Theory of History. The Zaharoff lecture for 1978–9. Oxford, Clarendon Press, 1980.

Essays on Biblical Interpretation. Ed. Lewis Mudge. Philadelphia, Fortress Press, 1980.

Fallible Man. Chicago, Henry Regnery, 1965 [Fr: 1960].

Freedom and Nature: The Voluntary and the Involuntary. Evanston, Northwestern University Press, 1966 [Fr: 1950].

Freud and Philosophy: An Essay on Interpretation. New Haven, Yale University Press, 1970 [Fr: 1965].

Hermeneutics and the Human Sciences: Essays on Language, Action and Interpretation. Ed. John B. Thompson. Cambridge, Cambridge University Press, 1981.

History and Truth. Evanston, Northwestern University Press, 1965 [Fr: 2nd edn, 1964].

Husserl: An Analysis of his Phenomenology. Evanston, Northwestern University Press, 1967.

Interpretation Theory: Discourse and the Surplus of Meaning. Fort Worth, Texas Christian University Press, 1976.

Lectures on Ideology and Utopia. Ed. George H. Taylor. New York, Columbia University Press, 1986.

The Philosophy of Paul Ricoeur: An Anthology of his Work. Ed. Charles E. Reagan and David Stewart. Boston, Beacon Press, 1978.

The Reality of the Historical Past. The Aquinas Lecture, 1984. Milwaukee, Marquette University Press, 1984.

The Rule of Metaphor. London, Routledge & Kegan Paul, 1978 [Fr: 1975].

The Symbolism of Evil. Boston, Beacon Press, 1969 [Fr: 1960].

Time and Narrative. 3 vols. Chicago, University of Chicago Press, 1984–8 [Fr: 1983–5].

ARTICLES

"Beyond Autonomy and Heteronomy" unpublished mss.

"Biblical Hermeneutics," *Semeia* 4 (1975), 29–148.

"The Bible and the Imagination," in Hans Dieter Betz (ed.), *The Bible as a Document of the University.* Chico, CA, Scholars Press, 1981, 49–75.

"Can Fictional Narratives be True?," *Analecta Husserliana* 14 (1983), 3–19.

"The Creativity of Language," in Richard Kearney (ed.), *Dialogues with Contemporary Continental Thinkers.* Manchester, Manchester University Press, 1984, 17–36.

"The Critique of Religion," *Union Seminary Quarterly Review* 28 (1978), 203–12.

"Evénement et sens dans le discours," in Michel Philibert, *Paul Ricoeur ou la liberté selon l'espérance.* Paris, Seghers, 1971, 177–87.

"Foreword," in Don Ihde, *Hermeneutic Phenomenology: The Philosophy of Paul Ricoeur,* xii–xvii.

"The Problem of the Foundation of Moral Philosophy," *Philosophy Today* 22 (1978), 175–92.

"The Function of Fiction in Shaping Reality," *Man and World* 12 (1979), 123–41.

"History as Narrative and Practice," *Philosophy Today* (1985), 213–22.

"History and Hermeneutics," *The Journal of Philosophy* 73 (1976), 683–95.

"Hope and the Structure of Philosophical Systems," *Proceedings of the American Catholic Association* 64 (1970), 55–69.

"Ideology and Ideology Critique," in B. Waldenfels, J. Broekman and A. Pazanin (eds.), *Phenomenology and Marxism.* London, Routledge and Kegan Paul, 1984, 134–64.

"Ideology, Utopia, Faith," *The Center for Hermeneutical Studies in Hellenistic and Modern Culture* (The Graduate Theological Union and the University of California, Berkeley), 17 (1976), 21–8.

"Imagination in Discourse and in Action," in A.-T. Tymieniecka (ed.), *The Human Being in Action.* London, D. Reidel, 1978, 3–22.

"Les incidences théologiques des recherches actuelles concernant le langage." Paris, Institut d'études oecuméniques, 1969 (mimeographed).

"Kierkegaard et le mal," *Revue de théologie et de philosophie* 13 (1963), 292–302.

"Manifestation et proclamation," in Enrico Castelli (ed.), *Le sacré*. Paris, Aubier, 1974, 57–76.

"The Metaphorical Process as Cognition, Imagination and Feeling," *Critical Inquiry* 5 (1978), 143–59.

"Myth as the Bearer of Possible Worlds," in Richard Kearney (ed.), *Dialogues with Contemporary Continental Thinkers*. Manchester, Manchester University Press, 1984, 36–45.

"Naming God," *Union Seminary Quarterly Review* 34 (1979), 215–27 [1977].

"The Narrative Function," *Semeia* 13 (1978), 177–202.

"Narrative and Hermeneutics," in John Fisher (ed.), *Essays on Aesthetics: Perspectives on the Work of Monroe C. Beardsley*. Philadelphia, Temple University Press, 1983, 149–60.

"Narrative Time," *Critical Inquiry* 7 (1980), 169–90.

"Objectivation et aliénation dans l'expérience historique," in Enrico Castelli (ed.), *Temporalité et aliénation*. Paris, Aubier, 1975, 27–38.

"On Interpretation," in Alan Montefiore (ed.), *Philosophy in France Today*. Cambridge, Cambridge University Press, 1983, 175–97.

"Philosopher après Kierkegaard," *Revue de théologie et de philosophie* 13 (1963), 303–16.

"Philosophical Hermeneutics and Theological Hermeneutics," *Studies in Religion* 5 (1975–6), 14–33.

"Philosophy and Religious Language," *Journal of Religion* 54 (1974), 71–85.

"Poétique et symbolique," in *Initiation de la pratique de la théologie I: Introduction*. Paris, Editions du Cerf, 1982, 37–61.

"Poetry and Possibility: An Interview with Paul Ricoeur Conducted by Philip Ried," *The Manhattan Review* 2, 2 (1982), 6–21.

"Pour une théorie du discours narratif," in *La Narrativité*. Paris, CNRS, 1980, 3–68; 251–71.

"The Power of Speech: Science and Poetry," *Philosophy Today* 29 (1985), 59–70.

"Preface: Response to My Friends and Critics," in Reagan (ed.), *Studies in the Philosophy of Paul Ricoeur*, x–xxi.

"From Proclamation to Narrative," *Journal of Religion* 64 (1984), 501–12.

"Le récit interprétatif: Exegèse et Théologie dans les récits de la Passion," *Recherches scientifiques réligieuses* 73 (1985), 17–38.

"The Relation of Jaspers' Philosophy to Religion," in P. A. Schlipp (ed.), *The Philosophy of Karl Jaspers*. New York, Tudor, 1957, 611–42.

"Reply to Lewis S. Mudge," in Ricoeur, *EBI*, 41–5.

"Schleiermacher's Hermeneutics," *The Monist* 60 (1977), 181–97.

"Temps biblique," *Archivio di filosofia* 1 (1985), 22–35.

"Le temps raconté," *Revue de Métaphysique et de Morale* 89 (1984), 436–51.

"The Unity of the Voluntary and the Involuntary as a Limiting Idea," in N. Lawrence and D. O'Connor (eds.), *Readings in Existential Phenomenology*. Englewood Cliffs, New Jersey, Prentice-Hall, 1967, 93–108.

Works about Ricoeur

Albano, Peter Joseph. *Freedom, Truth and Hope: The Relationship of Philosophy and Religion in the Thought of Paul Ricoeur*. Landam, MD, University Press of America, 1987.

Barral, Mary Rose. "Paul Ricoeur: The Resurrection as Hope and Freedom," *Philosophy Today* 29 (1985).

Bourgeois, Patrick L. *Extension of Ricoeur's Hermeneutic*. The Hague, Martinus Nijhoff, 1975.

Dornisch, Loretta. "Symbolic Systems and the Interpretation of Scripture: An Introduction to the Work of Paul Ricoeur," *Semeia* 4 (1975), 1–19.

– "The Book of Job and Ricoeur's Hermeneutics," *Semeia* 19 (1981), 3–21.

Gerhart, Mary. "Paul Ricoeur's Hermeneutical Theory as Resource for Theological Reflection," *Thomist* 39 (1975), 496–527.

– *The Question of Belief in Literary Criticism: An Introduction to the Hermeneutical Theory of Paul Ricoeur*. Stuttgart, Akademischer Verlag Hans-Dieter Heinz, 1979.

– "Imagination and History in Ricoeur's Interpretation Theory," *Philosophy Today* 23 (1979), 51–68.

Ihde, D. *Hermeneutic Phenomenology: The Philosophy of Paul Ricoeur*. Evanston, Northwestern University Press, 1971.

Javet, Pierre. "Imagination et réalité dans la philosophie de Paul Ricoeur," *Revue de théologie et de philosophie* 17 (1967), 145–58.

Klemm, David E. "'This is my Body': Hermeneutics and Eucharistic Language," *Anglican Theological Review* 64 (1982), 293–310.

– *The Hermeneutical Theory of Paul Ricoeur*. London, Associated Universities Press, 1983.

Kohak, Erazim V. "Translator's Introduction," to Ricoeur, *FN*, xi–xxxviii.

Lapointe, Francis. "A Bibliography on Paul Ricoeur," *Philosophy Today* 16 (1972), 28–33.

– "A Bibliography on Paul Ricoeur," *Philosophy Today* 17 (1973), 76–82.

– "Paul Ricoeur and His Critics: A Bibliographic Essay," in Reagan (ed.), *Studies in the Philosophy of Paul Ricoeur*, 164–77.

Lowe, Walter James. *Mystery and the Unconscious: A Study in the Thought of Paul Ricoeur*. ATLA Monograph Series, No. 9. Metuchen, NJ, Scarecrow Press, 1977.

– "The Coherence of Paul Ricoeur," *Journal of Religion* 61 (1981), 384–402.

Mudge, Lewis. "Introduction," to Ricoeur, *EBI*, 1–40.

Pellauer, David. "A Response to Gary Madison's 'Reflections on Paul Ricoeur's Philosophy of Metaphor,'" *Philosophy Today*, 21, supp. to 4/4 (1977).
- "Reading Ricoeur Reading Job," *Semeia* 19 (1981), 73–83.
- "Paul Ricoeur on the Specificity of Religious Language," *Journal of Religion* 61 (1981), 264–84.
- "*Time and Narrative* and Theological Reflection: Some Preliminary Reflections," *Philosophy Today* 31 (1987), 262–86.
Philibert, Michel. *Paul Ricoeur ou la liberté selon l'espérance*. Paris, Seghers, 1971.
Placher, William C. "Paul Ricoeur and Postliberal Theology: A Conflict of Interpretations." Paper read at the American Academy of Religion annual meeting, 1986.
Rasmussen, David M. *Mythic-Symbolic Language and Philosophical Anthropology*. The Hague, Martinus Nijhoff, 1971.
Reagan, Charles E., ed. *Studies in the Philosophy of Paul Ricoeur*. Ohio University Press, 1979.
Schaldenbrand, Mary. "Metaphoric Imagination: Kinship Through Conflict," in Reagan (ed.), *Studies in the Philosophy of Paul Ricoeur*, 57–81.
Schillebeeckx, Edward. "Le philosophe Paul Ricoeur, docteur en théologie," *Christianisme social* 76 (1968), 639–45.
Schwartz, Sanford. "Hermeneutics and the Productive Imagination: Paul Ricoeur in the 1970s," *Journal of Religion* (1983), 290–300.
Stewart, David. "Existential Humanism," in Reagan (ed.), *Studies in the Philosophy of Paul Ricoeur*, 21–32.
- "In Quest of Hope: Paul Ricoeur and Jürgen Moltmann," *Restoration Quarterly* 13 (1970), 31–52.
Sweeny, Robert. "A Survey of Recent Ricoeur Literature 1974–1984," *Philosophy Today* 29 (1985).
Thompson, John B. *Critical Hermeneutics: A Study in the Thought of Paul Ricoeur and Jürgen Habermas*. Cambridge University Press, 1981.
- *Studies in the Theory of Ideology*, ch. 5 "Action, Ideology and the Text," Cambridge, Polity Press, 1984, 173–204.
Van den Hengel, John W. *The Home of Meaning: The Hermeneutics of the Subject of Paul Ricoeur*. Washington, University Press of America, 1982.
- "Faith and Ideology in the Philosophy of Paul Ricoeur," *Eglise et théologie* 14 (1983), 63–89.
Van Leeuwen, T. M. *Surplus of Meaning*. Amsterdam, Rodopi, 1981.
Vansina, Frans D. *Paul Ricoeur: A Primary and Secondary Systematic Bibliography (1935–1984)*. Bibliothèque Philosophique de Louvain 31. Louvain-La-Neuve, Editions Peeters, 1985.
Wallace, Mark I. "Hermeneutics in the Thought of Karl Barth and Paul Ricoeur," *Union Seminary Quarterly Review* 41 (1986), 1–15.
Wells, Harold. "Theology and Christian Philosophy: Their Relation in the Thought of Paul Ricoeur," *Studies in Religion* 5 (1975), 45–56.

Other

The Complete Works of Aristotle, 2 vols. Princeton, Princeton University Press, 1984.

Auerbach, Erich. *Mimesis: The Representation of Reality in Western Literature.* Princeton, Princeton University Press, 1953.

Augustine. *The Confessions.* London, Thomas Nelson, 1938.

Aulén, Gustaf. *Christus Victor: An Historical Study of the Three Main Types of the Idea of the Atonement.* New York, Macmillan, 1969.

Aune, Bruce, "Possibility," in P. Edwards (ed.), *The Encyclopedia of Philosophy*, vol. 6. New York, Macmillan and Free Press, 1967, 419 – 24.

Barr, James. *The Bible in the Modern World.* London, SCM, 1973.

– *Holy Scripture: Canon, Authority, Criticism.* Oxford, Clarendon Press, 1983.

Barth, Karl. *Church Dogmatics*, vols. I – IV. Ed. G. W. Bromiley and T. F. Torrance. Edinburgh, T. & T. Clark, 1936 – 69.

Beardslee, William A. and David J. Lull eds. "NT Interpretation from a Process Perspective," *JAAR* 47 (1979).

Beardsley, Monroe. *Aesthetics.* New York, Harcourt, Brace, and World, 1958.

– "The Metaphorical Twist," *Philosophy and Phenomenological Research* 22 (1962), 293 – 307.

Black, Max. *Models and Metaphors.* Ithaca, Cornell University Press, 1962.

Blackwell, John. *The Passion as Story.* Philadelphia, Fortress, 1986.

Bloch, Ernst. *The Principle of Hope*, 3 vols. Oxford, Basil Blackwell, 1985.

Brentano, Franz. *On the Several Senses of Being in Aristotle.* Berkeley, University of California Press, 1975.

Bultmann, Rudolf, *New Testament Theology*, 2 vols. New York, Charles Scribner's Sons, 1955.

– *History of the Synoptic Traditions.* Oxford, Basil Blackwell, 1963.

– "The New Testament and Mythology," in Hans Werner Bartsch (ed.), *Kerygma and Myth. A Theological Debate*, 2nd edn, vol. 1. London, SPCK, 1964, 1 – 44.

– *Faith and Understanding.* London, SCM, 1969.

Chesterton, G. K. *Orthodoxy.* New York, Dodd, Mead & Co., 1959.

Childs, Brevard. *Introduction to the Old Testament as Scripture.* London, SCM, 1979.

Cobb, John and David Ray Griffin. *Process Theology: An Introductory Exposition.* Philadelphia, Westminster, 1976.

Comstock, Gary. "Truth or Meaning: Ricoeur versus Frei on Biblical Narrative," *JR* 66 (1986), 117 – 40.

Crites, Stephen. "The Narrative Quality of Experience," *JAAR* 39 (1971), 291 – 311.

Crossan, John D. *In Parables: The Challenge of the Historical Jesus.* New York, Harper & Row, 1973.

Despland, Michel, *Kant on History and Religion.* Montreal, McGill-Queen's University Press, 1973.

Dillon, Richard J. *From Eye-Witnesses to Ministers of the Word: Tradition and Composition in Luke 24*. Analecta Biblica 82. Rome, Biblical Institute Press, 1982.

Fackre, Gabriel. "Narrative Theology: an Overview," *Interpretation* 37 (1983), 340–52.

Frege, Gottlob. "On Sense and Reference," *Philosophical Writings of Gottlob Frege*. Tr. Max Black and Peter Geach. Oxford, Basil Blackwell, 1952.

Frei, Hans. *The Eclipse of Biblical Narrative*. New Haven, Yale University Press, 1974.

– *The Identity of Jesus Christ: The Hermeneutical Bases of Dogmatic Theology*. Philadelphia, Fortress, 1974.

– "The 'Literal Reading' of Biblical Narrative in the Christian Tradition: Does It Stretch or Will It Break?," in Frank McConnell (ed.) *The Bible and Narrative Tradition*. Oxford, Oxford University Press, 1986, 36–77.

Frye, Northrop. *Anatomy of Criticism*. Princeton, Princeton University Press, 1957.

Fuchs, Ernst. *Studies of the Historical Jesus*. London, SCM, 1964.

– "The Hermeneutical Problem," in J. M. Robinson (ed.) *The Future of our Religious Past: Essays in Honor of Rudolf Bultmann*. London, SCM, 1971.

Gadamer, Hans-Georg. *Truth and Method*. London, Sheed and Ward, 1975.

Gaillie, W. B. *Philosophy and the Historical Understanding*. London, Chatto and Windus, 1964.

Gelven, Michael. *A Commentary on Heidegger's "Being and Time."* New York, Harper & Row, 1970.

Gerhart, Mary and Allan M. Russell. *Metaphoric Process: The Creation of Scientific and Religious Understanding*. Fort Worth, Texas Christian University Press, 1984.

Goldberg, Michael. *Theology and Narrative*. Nashville, Abingdon, 1982.

Gombrich, E. H. *Art and Illusion: A Study in the Psychology of Pictorial Representation*, 5th edn. London, Phaidon, 1977.

Goulder, Michael, ed. *The Debate Continued: Incarnation and Myth*. London, SCM, 1979.

Green, Garrett, ed. *Scriptural Authority and Narrative Interpretation*. Philadelphia, Fortress, 1987.

Gunton, Colin. *Yesterday and Today: A Study of Continuities in Christology*. London, Darton, Longman, and Todd, 1983.

Habermas, Jürgen. "Ernst Bloch – a Marxist Romantic," *Salmagundi* 10 (1970), 311–25.

Hart, Ray. *Unfinished Man and the Imagination: Toward an Ontology and a Rhetoric of Revelation*. London, Herder & Herder, 1968.

Hays, Richard. *The Faith of Jesus Christ: An Investigation of the Narrative Substructure of Paul's Theology in Galatians 3:1–4:11*. SBL Dissertation Series no. 56. Chico, CA, Scholars Press, 1983.

Hegel, G. W. F. *The Philosophy of Right*. Tr. T. M. Knox. Oxford, Oxford University Press, 1942.

Heidegger, Martin. *Being and Time*. Oxford, Basil Blackwell, 1962 (German 1927).

- *Kant and the Problem of Metaphysics*. Bloomington, Indiana University Press, 1962 (German 1927).

Martin Heidegger: Basic Writings. Ed. David F. Krell. London, Harper & Row, 1977.

Helm, Paul. *The Varieties of Belief*. London, George Allen & Unwin, 1973.

Hempel, Karl. "The Function of General Laws in History," in Patrick Gardiner (ed.), *Theories of History*. New York, Free Press, 1959, 344–56.

Hesse, Mary. *Models and Analogies in Science*. Notre Dame, University of Notre Dame Press, 1966.

Hester, Marcus B. *The Meaning of Poetic Metaphor*. The Hague, Mouton, 1967.

Hintikka, Jaakko. *Time and Necessity: Studies in Aristotle's Theory of Modality*. Oxford, Clarendon Press, 1973.

Hirsch, E. D. *Cultural Literacy: What Every American Needs to Know*. Boston, Houghton Mifflin, 1987.

Hobbes, Thomas. *Leviathan*. New York, Liberal Arts Press, 1958.

Hudson, Wayne. *The Marxist Philosophy of Ernst Bloch*. London, Macmillan, 1982.

Husserl, Edmund. *Cartesian Mediations*. The Hague, Martinus Nijhoff, 1960.

Jeanrond, Werner G. *Text and Interpretation as Categories of Theological Thinking*. New York, Crossroad, 1988.

Johnson, Roger A. *The Origins of Demythologizing: Philosophy and Historiography in the Theology of Rudolf Bultmann*. Leiden, Brill, 1974.

Jüngel, Eberhard and Paul Ricoeur. *Metapher: Zur Hermeneutik religiöser Sprache. Evangelische Theologie* Sonderheft, 1974.

Jüngel, Eberhard. *Unterwegs zur Sache: Theologische Bemerkungen*. Munich, Kaiser, 1972.

- *God as the Mystery of the World: On the Foundation of the Theology of the Crucified One in the Dispute between Theism and Atheism*. Edinburgh, T. & T. Clark, 1983.

Kähler, Martin. *The So-Called Historical Jesus and the Historic, Biblical Christ*. Philadelphia, Fortress, 1964.

Kant, Immanuel. *Critique of Pure Reason*. Tr. Norman Kemp Smith. London, Macmillan, 1933.

- *Critique of Judgment*. Tr. J. H. Bernard. London, Collier Macmillan, 1951.

- *Critique of Practical Reason*. Tr. Lewis White Beck. Indianapolis, Bobbs-Merrill, 1956.

- *Religion Within the Limits of Reason Alone*. Tr. Theodore M. Greene and Hoyt H. Hudson. New York, Harper Torchbooks, 1960.

Karris, Robert J. *Luke: Artist and Theologian; Luke's Passion Account as Literature*. New York, Paulist, 1985.

Kearney, Richard. *Poétique du possible: Phénoménologie de la figuration*. Paris, Beauchesne, 1984.

Kellner, Hans. "Narrativity in History," *History and Theory* 26 (1987), 1–29.

Kelsey, David. *The Fabric of Paul Tillich's Theology.* New Haven, Yale University Press, 1967.
- *The Uses of Scripture in Recent Theology.* Philadelphia, Fortress, 1975.
- "The Theological Use of Scripture in Process Hermeneutics," *Process Studies* 13 (1983), 181–8.
Knapp, Stephen and Walter Benn Michaels. "Against Theory," in W.J.T. Mitchell (ed.), *Against Theory: Literary Studies and the New Pragmatism.* Chicago, University of Chicago Press, 1985.
Kuhn, Thomas. *The Structure of Scientific Revolutions.* Chicago, University of Chicago Press, 1962.
Lash, N. L. A. "Interpretation and Imagination," in Michael Goulder (ed.), *The Debate Continued: Incarnation and Myth.* London, SCM, 1979, 19–26.
Lessing, G. E. "On the Proof of the Spirit and of Power," in Henry Chadwick (ed.), *Lessing's Theological Writings.* London, Black, 1956, 51–6.
Lewis, C. S. *Surprised by Joy.* London, Geoffrey Bles, 1955.
- *Selected Literary Essays.* Cambridge, Cambridge University Press, 1969.
- *Fern-Seed and Elephants, and Other Essays on Christianity.* London, Collins, 1975.
- ed. *Essays Presented to Charles Williams.* Oxford, Oxford University Press, 1947.
Lindbeck, George. *The Nature of Doctrine: Religion and Theology in a Postliberal Age.* Philadelphia, Westminster, 1984.
Lull, David J. *The Spirit in Galatia. Paul's Interpretation of PNEUMA as Divine Power.* SBL Dissertation Series no. 49. Chico, CA, Scholars Press, 1980.
- "What is 'Process Hermeneutics'?," *Process Studies* 13 (1983), 189–201.
McFague, Sallie. *Speaking in Parables.* Philadelphia, Fortress, 1975.
- *Metaphorical Theology: Models of God in Religious Language.* London, SCM, 1983.
MacKinnon, Donald M. *Borderlands of Theology.* London, Lutterworth Press, 1968.
- "Introduction" to *Newman's University Sermons.* London, SPCK, 1970.
- *The Problem of Metaphysics.* Cambridge, Cambridge University Press, 1974.
- *Explorations in Theology.* London, SCM, 1979.
Macquarrie, John. *An Existentialist Theology.* London, SCM, 1960.
- *Studies in Christian Existentialism.* London, SCM, 1966.
- *Twentieth-Century Religious Thought*, 2nd edn. London, SCM, 1981.
Mannheim, Karl. *Ideology and Utopia: An Introduction to the Sociology of Knowledge.* New York, Harcourt & Brace, 1936.
Marcel, Gabriel. *Homo Viator. Introduction to a Metaphysic of Hope.* London, Victor Gollancz, 1951.
Marx, Karl. "Theses on Feuerbach," in David McLellan (ed.) *Karl Marx: Selected Writings.* Oxford, Oxford University Press, 1977.
Mink, Louis O. "The Autonomy of Historical Understanding," *History and Theory* 5 (1966), 24–47.
- "History and Fiction as Modes of Comprehension," *New Literary History* 1 (1970), 541–58.
Moltmann, Jürgen. *The Experiment Hope.* London, SCM, 1975.

O'Donovan, Oliver. *Begotten or Made?* Oxford, Oxford University Press, 1984.

Ogden, Schubert. *Christ Without Myth: A Study Based on the Theology of Rudolf Bultmann.* New York, Harper & Brothers, 1961.

Otto, Rudolf. *The Idea of the Holy.* Oxford, Oxford University Press, 1958.

Pannenberg, Wolfhart. *Jesus: God and Man.* London, SCM, 1968.

– *Basic Questions in Theology*, vol. 2. London, SCM, 1971.

– *Theology and the Philosophy of Science.* London, Darton, Longman & Todd, 1976.

– ed. *Revelation as History.* New York, Macmillan, 1968.

Perrin, Norman. *Rediscovering the Teaching of Jesus.* London, SCM, 1967.

– *Jesus and the Language of the Kingdom.* London, SCM, 1976.

Pregeant, Russell. *Christology Beyond Dogma: Matthew's Christ in Process Hermeneutic.* Philadelphia, Fortress, 1987.

Prickett, Stephen. *Words and the Word: Language, Poetics and Biblical Interpretation.* Cambridge, Cambridge University Press, 1986.

Ramsey, Ian. *Religious Language.* New York, Macmillan, 1957.

Rescher, Nicholas. "The Ontology of the Possible," in Milton K. Munitz (ed.), *Logic and Ontology.* New York, New York University Press, 1973.

– *Conceptual Idealism.* Oxford, Basil Blackwell, 1973.

Richards, I. A. *The Philosophy of Rhetoric.* Oxford, Oxford University Press, 1936.

Roberts, Robert C. *Rudolf Bultmann's Theology. A Critical Interpretation.* Grand Rapids, Eerdmans, 1976.

Rossi, Philip. "Kant as a Christian Philosopher: Hope and the Symbols of Christian Faith," *PT* 25 (1981), 24–33.

Russell, Bertrand. *The Principles of Mathematics.* Cambridge, Cambridge University Press, 1903.

Sartre, Jean-Paul. *L'Imaginaire.* Paris, Gallimard, 1940.

– *L'Etre et le néant.* Paris, Gallimard, 1943.

Schillebeeckx, Edward. *Jesus: An Experiment in Christology.* London, Collins, 1979.

Schleiermacher, Friedrich. *On Religion.* New York, Harper & Brothers, 1958.

Scott, Nathan A. "The Rediscovery of Story in Recent Theology and the Refusal of Story in Recent Literature," in Robert Detweiler (ed.), *Art/Literature/Religion: Life on the Borders.* Chico, CA, Scholars Press, 1983, 139–55.

Sherover, Charles M. *Heidegger, Kant and Time.* Bloomington, Indiana University Press, 1971.

Smith, John E. "Time and Qualitative Time," *The Review of Metaphysics* 40 (1986), 3–16.

Soskice, Janet Martin. *Metaphor and Religious Language.* Oxford, Clarendon, 1985.

Spiegelberg, Herbert. *The Phenomenological Movement*, vol. 2. The Hague, Martinus Nijhoff, 1960.

Steiner, George. *Heidegger.* London, Fontana, 1978.

Sternberg, Meir. *The Poetic of Biblical Narrative: Ideological Literature and the Drama of Reading.* Bloomington, Indiana University Press, 1987.

Stout, Jeffrey. "Hans Frei and Anselmian Theology," paper read at AAR, November 1987.

Streeter, B. H. *The Four Gospels*. London, Macmillan, 1924.

Stroup, George W. "A Bibliographical Critique," *Theology Today* 32 (1975), 133–43.

– *The Promise of Narrative Theology*. Atlanta, John Knox, 1981.

Sutherland, Stewart. *God, Jesus and Belief: The Legacy of Theism*. Oxford, Basil Blackwell, 1984.

Sykes, Stephen W., ed. *Karl Barth: Studies of his Theological Method*. Oxford, Clarendon Press, 1979.

Talbert, Charles H. *Luke and the Gnostics*. Nashville, Abingdon, 1966.

– *Literary Patterns, Theological Themes, and the Genre of Luke-Acts*. Missola, MT, SBL and Scholars Press, 1974.

Tannehill, Robert C. *The Narrative Unity of Luke-Acts: A Literary Interpretation*. Philadelphia, Fortress, 1986.

Taylor, Richard. "Time and Life's Meaning," *Review of Metaphysics* 40 (1987), 675–86.

Thiemann, Ronald F. *Revelation and Theology: The Gospel as Narrated Promise*. Notre Dame, University of Notre Dame Press, 1985.

Thompson, William M. *The Jesus Debate: A Survey and Synthesis*. New York, Paulist, 1985.

Tillich, Paul. *Biblical Religion and the Search for Ultimate Reality*. Chicago, University of Chicago Press, 1955.

Tracy, David. "The Task of Fundamental Theology," *JR* 54 (1974), 13–34.

– *Blessed Rage for Order: The New Pluralism in Theology*. New York, Seabury, 1975.

– *The Analogical Imagination: Christian Theology and the Culture of Pluralism*. London, SCM, 1981.

– "Lindbeck's New Program for Theology: A Reflection," *The Thomist* 49 (1985), 460–72.

– *Plurality and Ambiguity: Hermeneutics, Religion, Hope*. San Francisco, Harper & Row, 1987.

Urmson, J. O. *Philosophical Analysis: Its Development Between the Two World Wars*. Oxford, Oxford University Press, 1956.

Vaihinger, H. *The Philosophy of "As If": A System of the Theoretical, Practical and Religious Fictions of Mankind*, 2nd edn. Tr. C. K. Ogden. New York, Barnes and Noble, 1935.

Via, Dan. *The Parables: Their Literary and Existential Dimension*. Philadelphia, Fortress, 1967.

Von Rad, Gerhard. *Theology of the Old Testament*, 2 vols. New York, Harper & Row, 1962.

Webster, J. B. *Eberhard Jüngel: An Introduction to his Theology*. Cambridge, Cambridge University Press, 1986.

Westburg, Barry. *The Confessional Fictions of Charles Dickens*. DeKalb, Northern Illinois University Press, 1977.

White, Hayden. *Metahistory: The Historical Imagination in Nineteenth Century Europe*. Baltimore, Johns Hopkins University Press, 1973.

– "The Text as Literary Artifact," in Robert H. Canary and H. Kozicki (eds.), *The Writing of History: Literary Form and Historical Understanding*. Madison, University of Wisconsin Press, 1978.

– "The Question of Narrative in Contemporary Historical Theory," *History and Theory* 23 (1984), 1–33.

Whitehead, Alfred North. *Process and Reality*. New York, Macmillan, 1929.

Wiseman, T. P. *Clio's Cosmetics: Three Studies in Greco-Roman Literature*. Leicester, Leicester University Press, 1979.

Wittgenstein, Ludwig. *Philosophical Investigations*. Oxford, Basil Blackwell, 1967.

Woolf, Virginia. *Mrs. Dalloway*. London, Granada, 1976.

INDEX

absolute knowledge, *vs.* hermeneutics
  and hope, 39–42, 213–14
Alter, Robert, 207, 221 n. 54
Anselm, 150, 160, 163, 173, 178
apologetics, 128, 284; and mediating
  theology, 151–3
appropriation, 88–9, 99, 134, 137, 215,
  224–6, 230–4, 247–51, 269 n. 76
approximation, *see* Ricoeur, Paul.
Aquinas, Thomas, 15 n. 24
Aristotle, 8, 9, 24, 33 n. 8, 62, 65, 70–
  1, 83 n. 76, 91–2, 96, 110 n. 30, 111
  n. 33, 115 n. 105, 193, 198, 218, 239,
  281
atheism, *see* religion
Auerbach, Erich, 177, 216–18, 223
  n. 79
Augustine, 32, 79 n. 11, 90–1, 97, 110
  n. 24, 191, 242, 269 n. 60, 284
Aulen, Gustaf, 235, 267 n. 32

Barr, James, 4, 14 n. 7, 230, 263, 267
  n. 14
Barth, Karl, 129, 148–50, 154–6, 157,
  160–2, 164–5, 180–1, 182 n. 17, 183
  n. 22, 185 n. 64, 208, 210, 212–13,
  216, 222 n. 63, 237–8, 252, 268 n. 41,
  269 n. 78
Beardsley, Monroe, 80 n. 29, 80 n. 33
being: as actuality and possibility, 70–3,
  198, 213; manifestation of, 166–7;
  and "God," 122; *see also* human being
belonging-to, 168–9, 237; history, 100;
  and poetic language, 60–2, 169, 237,
  288

Black Max, 64, 80 n. 33
Blackwell, John, 267 n. 27
Bloch, Ernst, 24–5, 34 n. 26, 106–8,
  115 n. 105, 226
Bourgeois, Patrick L., 13 n. 4
Brentano, Franz, 33 n. 8
Brunner, Emil, 153
Bultmann, Rudolf, 25, 35 n. 30, 36
  n. 53, 76, 119–20, 123, 128–37,
  140–1, 141 n. 4, 143 n. 25, 144 n. 52,
  145 n. 70, 145 n. 80, 148–9, 153, 159,
  211, 215, 216, 220 n. 31, 223 n. 78,
  225, 228–9, 233, 234, 245, 251, 253,
  263–4, 266 n. 12, 277, 285
Buri, Fritz, 120, 123

Chesterton, G. K., 12
Childs, Brevard, 4
Chomsky, Noam, 51 n. 41
christology: Barth on, 212–13; *vs.*
  existential philosophy, 130; as schem-
  atization of eternity, 209–13, 218–
  19; task of, 227; time and eternity,
  191, 208–11; Tracy on, 159–60, 269
  n. 78
Clayton, Philip D., 221 n. 57
Cobb, John, 223 n. 78, 266 n. 12
Comstock, Gary, 178
consent, *see* freedom
Copernican revolution, second, *see*
  Ricoeur, Paul
creation, *see* world
Crites, Stephen, 110 n. 22, 188 n. 132
Crossan, John Dominick, 220 n. 20
Cullmann, Oscar, 201

302